Belonging to America

Equal Citizenship and the Constitution

KENNETH L. KARST

Belonging to America

Equal Citizenship and the Constitution

YALE UNIVERSITY PRESS

NEW HAVEN AND LONDON

Published with assistance from the foundation
established in memory of Calvin Chapin of the
Class of 1788, Yale College.

Designed by Jo Aerne. Set in Electra type with
Futura for display and printed in the United States of
America by Vail-Ballou Press, Inc. Binghamton, New
York.

Library of Congress Cataloging-in-Publication Data
Karst, Kenneth L.
Belonging to America : equal citizenship and the con-
stitution / Kenneth L. Karst.
p.   cm.
Bibliography: p.
Includes index.
ISBN 0-300-04322-8 (alk. paper)
1. Citizenship—United States.   2. Equality before
the law—United States.   3. Civil rights—United
States.   I. Title.
KF4700.K37 1989
342.73'083—dc19   88-23438
[347.30283]   CIP

The paper in this book meets the guidelines for permanence and durability of the Committee on Production Guidelines for Book Longevity of the Council on
Library Resources.

10 9 8 7 6 5 4 3 2 1

To Smiley and her heirs,
with pahoehoe and tang

Contents

Preface

" 'Belonging' is a soupy gerund." So said a colleague on hearing of my intended title, and he was right. But the sense of belonging is no trivial matter. We all need it if we are to know ourselves and locate ourselves in the world. That need brings nationhood itself into question in a society of many cultures. Who belongs to America? Successive generations of Americans have answered the question differently, with grave consequences for the people excluded. This book is an extended essay on the past and potential contributions of American law, especially constitutional law, to the definition of our national community. A central theme of the book is equal citizenship, which has long served the nation as a unifying ideal and has emerged in our own time as a principle of American constitutional law.

This is a big country with a complex history and an abundant store of cultural traditions, including all the diverse traditions embodied in our constitutional law. Given the richness of the subject, it would be fatuous to offer a Grand Solution for today's or tomorrow's questions about constitutional equality. Instead, this book offers a perspective, a way of seeing those questions. No doubt the perspective has affected my perceptions of American history and society—but anyone's viewpoint does that. "Small facts speak to large issues . . . because they are made to." [1]

Readers acquainted with the literature of American constitutional law will recognize my debt to a great many writers. To list them all would turn a preface into a directory of scholars. I hope that my references to their work will convey my appreciation. Still, two writers deserve special mention; the othes will understand why.

Charles L. Black, Jr., has led the way for all of us who have sought to explore the meanings of *Brown v. Board of Education*,[2] and in two sets of lectures he has focused specifically on the subject of citizenship.[3] Although this book examines that subject in a different perspective, at every step of the way Charles Black's writings have provided both illumination and a reminder of the urgency of the task of making America whole.[4]

Harry Kalven, Jr., devoted most of his constitutional scholarship to the freedoms of speech and of the press. In one book that has become a modern classic he did address the interaction of those freedoms and the civil rights movement,[5] but my debt to him goes far beyond that work. Harry Kalven loved legal doctrine and knew it was important, and yet he never forgot that doctrine's importance was secondary. For him the social realities came first: the moral and material concerns that led real people to make their claims and that influenced real jurors' and judges' responses to those claims. To Charles Black and to the memory of Harry Kalven, my thanks and my affection.

The subjects of this book are the common property of all Americans, and I have tried to write for an audience that is not limited to lawyers. For that reason, and to maintain the book's essay style, I have abbreviated the notes and relegated them to the end of the book. Where indefinite pronouns are called for, I have alternately used "he" and "she."

A number of the ideas expressed here are distilled from my own previous writings. For further discussion and documentation I refer in the notes to those articles, using italicized abbreviated titles. (Full citations to my articles are given in an appendix. A bibliography fully citing other works cited in the text and notes is followed by a table of cases.) I renew my thanks to the dozens of colleagues who commented on drafts of those earlier writings. I am also grateful for the invitations to present some of these ideas orally: at the Yale Legal Theory Workshop and in lectures at Washington University (St. Louis); Notre Dame University; Wake Forest University; The University of Georgia; Duke University; The University of North Carolina; The Kyoto American Studies Summer Seminar of Doshisha University and Kyoto University; and The College of William and Mary.

Alison Anderson, Julian Eule, William Forbath, Joel Handler, Gerald López, Steven Shiffrin, Margaret Stevenson, Jonathan Varat, and Stephen Yeazell have read this book's manuscript. I thank all of them for their generosity and their thoughtful—and thought-provoking—comments. Lisa Halko Hauser, Lawrence Kupers, and George Brown provided valuable research assistance. Marian Neal Ash of Yale University Press has known how to be patient without seeming indifferent and how to be gracious while being insistent. Carl Rosen, also at the Press, has made editing not only instructive but enjoyable. I am grateful to the UCLA School of Law and Dean Susan Westerberg Prager for the sabbatical leave that allowed me to finish this project and to the staff of our school's law library for their helpful and cheerful responses to my requests for aid. No simple statement can convey my gratitude to my colleagues in the UCLA law faculty and to my students. One aspect of belonging that shapes my own sense of self is my participation in that exceptionally supportive community of scholars.

Above all I am indebted to Catherine Hancock, who has taken this whole project under her wing. In a steady stream of letters and telephone conversations and editorial comments she has brought her enthusiasm, her critical eye, and her imagination to all the work leading to this book from the first tentative outline of chapters to the final manuscript. I am no longer surprised when Catherine understands what I am trying to say better than my own left hemisphere has understood it. Because, in her words, Organization Is All, what has begun as editing often has led in new substantive directions. In every sense but the writing of the words, this is also her book. Beyond all that, she has virtually adopted our entire family. To Catherine—sister and critic, gadfly and fairy godmother—my profound thanks and the fond good wishes of all the Karsts.

The manuscript for the text was completed in the spring of 1987, and I am grateful to Professor James C. N. Wang and his colleagues at the University of Hawaii at Hilo for their kind hospitality during those months. The stay in Hilo also gave this project moral support. Hilo is a multiracial, multicultural town. Like any such society, Hilo has some tensions and resentments across the lines of those social divisions. In particular, many people of Hawaiian ancestry feel keenly (and justifiably) that their land has been invaded and important parts of their culture displaced. Even so, Hilo offers an example that mainland America would do well to ponder: a community that not only respects diversity but values it for its enrichment of everyone's life. Tolerance itself is a unifying ideology, taken for granted because it is part of people's everyday experience.

At a parade in Hilo, among the high school bands and the floats celebrating volcanoes and coconut palms and Hawaiian music, walked a lone man who was handing out small American flags. As he stopped in front of us, a culturally kaleidoscopic group of little children gathered around him, each one reaching upward. Then, flags in hand, they turned around. Before us stood a nation of many peoples, waiting to be realized. That, I grant, is a fairly soupy idea. But it isn't a bad idea.

Belonging to America

Equal Citizenship and the Constitution

one

Equality, Law, and Belonging: An Introduction

The ideal of equality is one of the great themes in the culture of American public life. From the Declaration of Independence to the pledge of allegiance, the rhetoric of equality permeates our symbols of nationhood. Over and over in our history, from the earliest colonial beginnings, equality has been a rallying cry, a promise, an article of national faith. So it is that the ideal of equality touches our emotions. All these aspects of equality—protest, hope, and faith, infused with emotion—came together in an August afternoon over a quarter century ago when Martin Luther King, Jr., spoke to a multitude at the Lincoln Memorial, repeatedly returning to the phrase: "I have a dream."

King's vision of the future centered on the ideal of one nation, indivisible—a nation that would heal its racial divisions by offering justice for all. The metaphor of the dream was his way of making vivid the contrast between the Constitution's promise of equality and the realities of race relations in the America of 1963. But if Martin Luther King was a dreamer, he also knew how to get down to cases, from segregated buses to employment discrimination. The immediate objective of his speech was a change in the nation's law. The huge gathering before him had joined a "march on Washington" to support the bill that became the Civil Rights Act of 1964. He understood that if black people were to think of themselves as belonging to America, the nation must make a reality of the ideal expressed in the motto on the Supreme Court Building: Equal Justice under Law.

Such a faith in the capacity of law is common among Americans. A deep current of egalitarianism has always run through American society, and we have often resorted to law to effectuate our ideals. Yet Martin Luther King, from his awareness of our history and from his own personal experience, also had reason to appreciate Ralf Dahrendorf's mordant epigram: "all men are equal *before* the law but they are no longer equal *after* it."[1] Slavery and racial segregation; discrimination against the foreign-born; religious qualifications

1

for political participation; the virtual exclusion of women from public life—all were reminders that law can be an instrument for the subordination of groups. Equality and citizenship had been explicitly written into the Fourteenth Amendment to the Constitution after the Civil War, and yet our constitutional law had been shaped to accommodate these kinds of legalized subordination.

If the law touching matters of equality looked in two directions, it did no more than reflect prevailing attitudes in American society. Writing during World War II, Gunnar Myrdal called the race-relations aspect of this ambivalence an "American dilemma." Myrdal saw that white Americans were genuinely devoted to the nation's egalitarian and individualistic ideals, yet they also accepted the systematic denial of black people's equality and individuality. Similar paradoxes have attended our society's treatment of other cultural minorities and of women.

How have successive generations of Americans—whites and males and the native born—managed to live with this incongruity between their egalitarian ideals and their behavior? The technique is simple enough: just define the community's public life—or the community itself—in a way that excludes the subordinated groups. The inclination to exclude is not innate; it arises in the acculturation that forms individual self-definition out of attachment to one's own group and separation from other groups. Rodgers and Hammerstein put it best: "You've got to be carefully taught."[2] Culture shapes identity by contrasting "our" beliefs and behavior, which are examples to be followed, with those of the Other,[3] which must be avoided. Our own national experience is replete with examples:

> Americans came early to accept the inevitable presence of outsiders. . . .
> Although every citizen could claim a basic set of legal rights, some of
> these citizens would almost certainly remain outsiders. Actual
> membership was determined by additional tests of religion, perhaps, or
> race or language or behavior, tests that varied considerably among
> segments and over time. Each generation passed to the next an open
> question of who really belonged to American society.[4]

Among full members of the community, the ideal of equality prevails; as to outsiders, the issue of equality seems irrelevant. Equality and belonging are inseparably linked: to define the scope of the ideal of equality in America is to define the boundaries of the national community.

One of this book's main themes is equal citizenship, both as an American ideal and as a principle of constitutional law. I argue that the ideal, as part of the American civic culture, has served a vital unifying function in our nation's past and retains that function today. More specifically, I argue that our courts have a crucial role in expanding the circle of belonging, as they translate the Fourteenth Amendment's guarantee of equal citizenship into substantive reality for people previously relegated to the status of outsiders. These arguments lead to wider inquiries: to understand what equal citizenship means today, we need to know something of the cultural and historical settings in which successive generations of Americans have answered the question, Who belongs?

The principle of equal citizenship, as I use the term, means this: Each individual is presumptively entitled to be treated by the organized society as a respected, responsible, and participating member. Stated negatively, the principle forbids the organized society to treat an individual as a member of an inferior or dependent caste or as a nonparticipant. The principle thus centers on those aspects of equality that are most closely bound to the sense of self and the sense of inclusion in a community. When Rosa Parks refused to move to the back of a bus in Montgomery, she staked her claims as an equal citizen, entitled to respect and to full participation in the community's public life.[5] So did Ford Johnson, Sr., when he would not move to the section of a Richmond courtroom set aside for black people.[6] And so did Mary Hamilton, when she refused to answer questions by an Alabama judge who had addressed her as "Mary," saying she would answer if he called her "Miss Hamilton" as he would have done if she were white.[7] The problem facing Rosa Parks and Ford Johnson and Mary Hamilton was that local law and custom consigned them to a place outside the social boundaries defining membership in the local community. The Constitution, however, recognized them as equal citizens.

In the middle years of the twentieth century the Supreme Court added its own recognition, reviving equal citizenship as a principle of our constitutional law. The Supreme Court constructed its egalitarian doctrine on a political base. Today the constitutional rights of minority groups and of women stand above group politics only in the sense that a temple stands above its foundation. Yet the courts make their own special contribution. In the 1930s, when the leaders of the National Association for Advancement of Colored People (NAACP) began their litigation campaign against Jim Crow education, they knew that the Constitution occupied a place at the symbolic center of the meaning of America. Their constitutional claims focused on the schools but also asserted the right of black people to belong to American society as full members.

The very act of filing a lawsuit implicitly affirms that the plaintiffs and defendants share membership in a community. Any claim of right is an appeal to a community's norms, "a claim grounded in human association."[8] But in the school segregation cases the essence of the black plaintiffs' substantive claim was itself a claim to equal citizenship. In claiming the right to belong, they were exploring the possibility that the white majority shared at least some of their understanding of what it meant to be an American. More recently, other subordinated groups have followed a similar course. Although racial equality is central to the Fourteenth Amendment, neither the amendment's declaration of citizenship nor its equal protection clause is limited to the subject of race. From women's liberation to gay liberation and beyond, people relegated to the role of outsider have believed that one path to effective inclusion in American society is the path of the law. This book reflects the centrality of racial equality but also inquires into that principle's implications for other groups.

Claims to equal citizenship have always carried an emotional charge in America, especially when inequalities have attached to such attributes as race, sex, religion, or ethnicity. These matters touch the heart because they touch the sense of belonging and therefore the sense of self. Belonging is a basic human need. Every person's self is formed within a social matrix; indeed, the very conception of the self is bound up with the idea of a social group. Helen Merrell Lynd captured the idea in one simple but elegant sentence: "Some kind of answer to the question Where do I belong? is necessary for an answer to the question Who am I?"[9] The most heartrending deprivation of all is the inequality of status that excludes people from full membership in the community, degrading them by labeling them as outsiders, denying them their very selves.

The harms of exclusion unquestionably happen to people one by one, but those individual harms result from the subordination of groups. When the instrument for excluding a group is the law, the hurt is magnified, for the law is seen to embody the community's values. For a "degradation ceremony" to succeed, the denouncer "must make the dignity of the supra-personal views of the tribe salient and accessible to view, and his denunciation must be delivered in their name. . . . The denouncer must arrange to be invested with the right to speak in the name of these ultimate values."[10] When a city segregates the races on a public beach, the chief harm to the segregated minority is not that those people are denied access to a few hundred yards of surf. Jim Crow was not just a collection of legal disabilities; it was an officially organized degradation ceremony, repeated day after day in a hundred ways, in the life of every black person within the system's reach.

The main success of the civil rights movement was the formal redefinition of American communities both local and national. Large numbers of Americans, previously excluded from those communities' public life, were formally recognized as equal citizens. It was important to all of us, but especially to black people's sense of self, that the mechanism for inclusion was the Constitution, our national community's most authoritative official embodiment of values. All this Martin Luther King knew when he spoke to us of his dream of one nation, indivisible.

At the same time, no one knew better than he that the formal guarantee of equal civil rights, necessary as it was to achieving the full inclusion of all Americans in the national community, would take us only partway toward that objective. Today it is even more apparent that citizenship implies more than formal equality. Yet throughout the 1980s officers of the government at the highest levels have said that discrimination is behind us, that our collective journey toward equal justice is over, that King's dream has been realized. This is a soothing melody—part recessional, part lullaby—but it is persistently interrupted by dissonant notes. Consider, for example, the following five episodes in our public life during the quarter century since the march on Washington. How could these things happen in a nation committed to the ideal of equal citizenship? What morals can we draw from these cautionary tales?

1. Police chokeholds in Los Angeles.

Adolph Lyons, a young black man, made these allegations in a suit against the Los Angeles police: He was driving at about 2:30 on an October morning in 1976. One of his taillights was out, and he was ordered by two police officers to pull over to the curb. As Lyons got out of the car, he faced the officers' drawn revolvers. The officers told him to face the car, spread his legs, and clasp his hands on top of his head. He complied. After one of the officers had patted him down in a weapons search, he lowered his hands. One of the officers grabbed his hands and slammed them onto his head. Lyons complained of pain caused by a key ring in his hand. "Within five to ten seconds, the officer began to choke Lyons by applying a forearm against his throat. As Lyons struggled for air, the officer handcuffed him, but continued to apply the chokehold until he blacked out. When Lyons regained consciousness, he was lying face down on the ground, choking, gasping for air, and spitting up blood and dirt. He had urinated and defecated. He was issued a traffic citation and released." [11]

Lyons sued the city and the police officers, seeking damages for his injuries and an injunction barring the future use of chokeholds by the Los Angeles police, except when there was a threat of immediate deadly force. [12] Pending trial of the case, the federal district court granted a preliminary injunction, restraining the police from using chokeholds except when death or serious injury was threatened. Reviewing this order in 1983, the Supreme Court held that although Lyons could pursue his claim for damages, he lacked legal standing to sue for an injunction, because he could not show that he, personally, was likely to suffer future injury from a police chokehold. As Justice White put it, when Lyons filed his complaint he had not been choked by the police for five months. To establish his right to an injunction, Lyons would have to show "either, (1) that *all* police officers in Los Angeles *always* choke any citizen with whom they have an encounter, whether for the purpose of arrest, issuing a citation or for questioning or, (2) that the City ordered or authorized police officers to act in such manner."[13]

From 1975 until Lyons's case reached the Supreme Court, sixteen people had died as a result of police chokeholds in Los Angeles, and twelve of them were black males. When the Los Angeles police chief was asked about the high proportion of blacks who had died from chokeholds, he said he had a "hunch" that blacks might be more susceptible to injury from chokeholds than were "normal" people.[14]

2. Welfare in Texas.

In the late 1960s, with substantial financial help from the federal government, Texas operated two large-scale welfare programs: Old Age Assistance and Aid to Families with Dependent Children (AFDC). The state had set the same standard of need for all its welfare programs, but the Texas constitution set a ceiling on aggregate spending for welfare. To bring spending within this limit, the legislature appropriated gross amounts for each welfare category, and welfare officials ordered corresponding percentage reductions of welfare benefits. In this scheme, aid to the aged was funded at 100 percent of need, but AFDC benefits were set at 50 percent of need. After Ruth Jefferson and others filed a lawsuit challenging this disparity, the AFDC percentage was increased to 75 percent. One factor did distinguish the two large-scale programs: 60 percent of the old age assistance beneficiaries were white, but 87 percent of the AFDC beneficiaries were black or Hispanic.[15]

Texas is not alone in its treatment of AFDC benefits. When the program began, most beneficiaries were widows, and white. As the beneficiaries throughout the nation increasingly became black and Latina women who were unmarried, separated, or divorced, the benefit levels declined.[16] The Supreme Court, rejecting Ruth Jefferson's "naked statistical argument," saw no racial discrimination, and upheld the Texas scheme.[17]

3. State jobs in Massachusetts.

On three occasions in the early 1970s Helen Feeney sought advancement in the Massachusetts civil service. She made high scores on the relevant examinations, but the jobs all went to men who had served in the armed forces. Massachusetts law gave veterans a preference in hiring for civil service jobs. Because the armed services had limited women to a quota of 2 percent of the forces and had established more severe enlistment qualifications for women than for men, the state hiring preference effectively excluded women from the best civil service jobs. Until 1971 the law had explicitly exempted from the veterans' preference a number of jobs "especially calling for women." In the better state jobs, however, women did not belong.

When Helen Feeney challenged the constitutionality of this scheme, a majority of the Supreme Court was unable to find any sex discrimination.[18] Although the law had kept her from competing for good state jobs, Feeney had failed to prove that the law was intended as a form of sex discrimination. After all, the Court said, the law also discriminated against men who were not veterans. Perhaps the armed forces had been guilty of sex discrimination, but the military's conduct was "not on trial in this case." A state bureaucrat would easily recognize this response: It's not my department.

4. White Moose in Harrisburg.

The Loyal Order of Moose has a local lodge in Harrisburg, Pennsylvania, licensed by the commonwealth to serve liquor. The lodge is located across the parking lot from the state capitol and is one of the watering places where legislators and others gather to discuss good government. In 1968 a member of the lodge brought a guest, Leroy Irvis, to the lodge's dining room and bar. Irvis was a member of the Pennsylvania House of Representatives. When the two requested service of food and drinks, the lodge's employees refused to serve Irvis, for Irvis was black. Under the lodge's national constitution, its purposes were "to unite in the bonds of fraternity, benevolence, and charity all acceptable white [males] of good character," provided they were "not married to someone of other than the Caucasian or White race."[19] In this vision of fraternity, black people—by virtue of their blackness alone, and irrespective of any personal qualities—were unacceptable either as members or guests.

No doubt Leroy Irvis and his friend could find a place in Harrisburg where they could have a drink and a meal together. But discrimination by "private" clubs on the basis of race, ethnicity, religion, and sex was—and remains—a pervasive practice throughout the nation. Seven years before the Moose Lodge turned Leroy Irvis away, a survey was made of 1152 clubs in forty-six states and the District Columbia, with a combined membership estimated at seven hundred thousand. Of these clubs some 67 percent practiced religious discrimination, mainly against Jews.[20] Many of these clubs are foci for networks of economic power and political influence of scope both local and national.[21] To be excluded from such a club on the ground that you are not a white male Christian is not merely to be told that you don't belong in the club. It is to be told in a more definitive way that you just don't belong.

In Pennsylvania the commonwealth monopolized the retail liquor business and limited the number of licenses for resale by restaurants and clubs. This state-enforced scarcity made a resale license valuable; in Harrisburg itself, the number of licenses already exceeded the established quota. For the Moose Lodge, a license must have been particularly valuable; without a bar, the recruitment of members would depend on the drawing power of fraternal benevolence alone. The commonwealth's Liquor Control Board regulated the conduct of licensees in great detail. Yet, in Irvis's lawsuit against the lodge and the liquor commission, the Supreme Court held that the lodge's exclusion of black guests was only a private act of discrimination, beyond the reach of the Constitution. (Irvis eventually prevailed in the state courts, under Pennsylvania's public accommodations law. At this writing he is Speaker of the state House of Representatives.)

5. City-sponsored Christianity in Pawtucket.

When the city of Pawtucket, Rhode Island, set up an official Christmas display of a Nativity scene, local residents who were non-Christian could be pardoned for thinking that the city had defined them as outsiders. When the Supreme Court added its own benediction to this official celebration of the divine Nativity,[22] non-Christians throughout the country could share the same hurt. The majority Justices showed little concern for this harm to the sense of belonging or for their own role in compounding the harm.[23] Indeed, Chief Justice Warren Burger's majority opinion positively reveled in reciting incidents from our national history in which religious groups have procured governmental endorsement and politicians have reached out for the divine Coattails. The conceded "religious nature of the crèche," said the Chief Justice, did not detract from the display's secular purpose, which was merely to take "note of a significant historical event long celebrated in the Western World." The Court found insufficient evidence that the display was an "effort to express some kind of subtle governmental advocacy of a particular religious message." The Chief Justice's repetition of this extraordinary assertion of secular content in the city's celebration of the divine miracle of the birth of Christ recalls the style of argument of the Bellman in *The Hunting of the Snark*: "What I tell you three times is true."[24] Americans who are not Christian no doubt will agree that the message of the Nativity scene was not subtle. "This is our town" has all the subtlety of a stone wall.

Any of these five pictures of American public life, by itself, would be disquieting; viewed together, the cases suggest that something has gone seriously wrong in the way our courts are addressing issues of constitutional equality. This book offers one perspective on what has gone wrong. I hope to call attention to the importance of citizenship, which begins in the formal recognition of membership in the community but does not end there. Equal citizenship, I argue, is also a principle of substance; the principle goes unfulfilled when substantive inequalities effectively bar people from full membership. I argue further that a nationwide culture of American public life offers the community of meaning that makes possible a national community of equal citizens. Because our constitutional law is a vital part of that civic culture, our judges have a particular responsibility in the community-building process. In assuring that every American is treated by the organized society as one who belongs to America, our courts have much to contribute in making and maintaining a nation.

In setting out these objectives, I recognize that some commentators will think them mistaken, unattainable, or both. First, a large body of constitutional commentary over the last four decades has treated the Fourteenth Amendment's equal protection clause as an abstraction with little substantive content. (Some of these commentators would make an exception for racial equality.)[25] In 1949 an influential article concluded that a court's main task in applying the equal protection clause was to make sure that like cases were treated alike—or, as the authors put it, to determine whether a legislative classification (the differential treatment commanded by a law) was appropriately tailored to the purposes the law was designed to serve.[26] Much of the recent equal protection commentary proceeds in the same abstract mode: parsing equality; adjusting the required "fit" between legislative means and ends; calibrating "levels" of judicial scrutiny of the work product of other officials. Perhaps it was inevitable, given this background, that someone would argue that equality, taken as the principle that like cases should be treated alike, was an empty idea. In 1982 Peter Westen made just this argument, concluding that equality should be discarded as a guide either for moral discourse or

for constitutional decisions. Dramatizing his proposal, he referred to the motto
on the Supreme Court Building, and asked, rhetorically: "Would the phrase
mean less if it said, 'Justice Under Law'?"[27]

Yes, it would. Perhaps, on that desert island where philosophers do their
moral geometry, the motto's form would make little difference. But our Supreme Court and our constitutional law serve our nation, with our history,
our professed ideals, our social structure, our institutions, our sense of a common destiny. In the America where we live, equality matters—not the simple
abstraction that likes should be treated alike, not a philosopher's universal,[28]
but a culturally specific and evolving cluster of substantive values, solidly
based in a particular society's traditions. Equality, in the abstract, may be
value-neutral; the Fourteenth Amendment is not.

From another viewpoint, the project of this book may seem inconsequen-
tial. I mean to reclaim the importance of citizenship and of equality before
the law, two notions that have been pronounced trivial by high authority.
Alexander Bickel dismissed citizenship as "at best a simple idea for a simple
government,"[29] and Max Weber referred slightingly to equality before the law
as merely "formal" equality.[30] I agree that the bare legal status of citizenship
is a constitutional trifle; I agree, too, that equal rules for the strong and the
weak normally will reinforce the advantages of the strong. As we shall see,
however, real membership in the community is more than a legal status, and
real equality before the law can seem trivial only to those who are secure in
their places as equal citizens. In pursuing equal justice under law, Martin
Luther King understood the interdependence of symbol and substance.

The symbols invoked by the civil rights movement were national symbols.
The park stretching between the Washington Monument and the Lincoln
Memorial was an ideal place for the rally that King addressed in 1963. Of
course, he and the other speakers were speaking to the Congress, calling for
new national laws. But they also spoke to the nation. In claiming "inclusion
in the American political imagination,"[31] they appealed to the values of a
national culture. As the civil rights leaders knew, the American civic culture—the culture of our public life—is a major unifying force in our diverse
society. In suggesting that our civic culture defines a national community,
this book proposes an alternative to the view that community can be found
only within smaller, neotribal groups.[32] Validation of a claim of equal citizenship is not merely important to the individual claimant. It also forms part
of the social cement that makes the nation possible.

The line of argument I have sketched necessarily leads backward into our
national history and outward from law to larger social contexts. I ask lawyer-

readers to be patient; in the early chapters, legal doctrine is not in the fore-front of the story. As you read you may wonder, Why all this history? I hope the answer to that question will emerge when we see how our legal doctrines of constitutional equality bear on particular aspects of the question, Who belongs? I also hope that even lawyer-readers will be persuaded that a number of issues they have customarily seen as questions about freedom can also be seen as questions about belonging. To see issues of privacy or religious free-dom in that light is to see them through the eyes of people who have been defined as outsiders, people who are claiming their membership in the Amer-ican community.

Our five illustrative cases show how the current quagmire of constitutional doctrine has claimed real victims. We are not going to find our way out of the bog by heaping up bigger piles of improved abstractions. What we need now is closer attention to matters of substance. We need to understand how inequality hurts, which inequalities hurt most, and how law bears on those hurts, either as cause or as remedy. This book focuses on the hurt of exclu-sion. In the perspective offered here, citizenship means not just rights but responsibility, not just autonomy but belonging.

The five cases mainly portray sins of omission. There is the failure to see that the way we define and operate our social institutions is affected by sys-tems of thought and feeling that serve to justify domination—for example, by racism and sexism. There is the failure to understand how the subordination of a group translates into particular harms to the group's individual members. There is the failure to grasp that the stakes for the plaintiffs in these cases are nothing less than their inclusion as full members of American society. The result is that the judges fail to recognize real harms to real people, and they fail to see those harms as the organized society's responsibility.

The failing here is not that governmental decisions were made by people who were especially callous or unfeeling. Unhappily, the failing is part of a more deep-seated problem that begins in the acquisition of cultural identity and gender identity, a problem that is especially acute in a multicultural society. A child growing up in a middle-class, white, Protestant family is initiated into a culture, a community of meaning. For the child, and for the adult who emerges from that childhood, poor people and black people and non-Protestants are apt to be seen as Others, whose differences define bound-aries between communities—boundaries policed by ignorance and fear. Such a boundary is not inevitably a barrier preventing a legislator or a judge from imagining the experience of people on the other side, but surely the boundary complicates that process.

The problem of understanding the Other is by no means peculiar to law and government, but it emerges regularly there for a reason tinged with irony. The most typical reaction to cultural difference in America has been avoidance: what you don't see won't bother you.[33] Law and government, however, not only provide a public arena that all our diverse cultures necessarily share but also define meanings that hold our society together. The members of different cultures unavoidably confront each other in police-citizen relations on the streets of Los Angeles, in the political dealings in the Texas legislature and the Pawtucket city council, and in courtrooms both high and low. Sometimes intercultural differences become the explicit subjects of conflict in the public arena. More often, those conflicts lie below the surface of discussion. In either case, police officers and legislators and judges, when they make their official decisions, begin with their own acculturated assumptions about the meaning of behavior and come to question the universality of those assumptions only with difficulty.

Consider again our five illustrative cases. What might the judges in those cases have done differently? A preliminary response to that question will provide a preview of the chapters to come. First, the judges might have widened their inquiries to include more in the way of historical and social context. To understand that Adolph Lyons could properly raise the claims of a racial group, the judges would have had to consider why police officers in Los Angeles— and not only in Los Angeles[34]—have been inclined to treat black and white arrestees differently. To understand Leroy Irvis's constitutional claim of access to the Moose Lodge, the judges would need to consider not only the government's role in maintaining the Moose Lodge itself but more generally the crucial role of nongovernmental institutions in segregating American public life, both South and North.

Second, the judges might have had more appreciation for Helen Feeney's and Ruth Jefferson's claims if they had thought a bit about the origins of racial discrimination and sex discrimination in the process of identity formation. As we shall see, that process produces unarticulated assumptions and self-fulfilling expectations about people who are different (women workers, blacks and Latinas, unwed mothers), and those assumptions and expectations can affect the behavior of legislators and judges alike.[35]

Third, the judges in all five cases would have done well to reflect on the special influence of governmental action on our definitions of membership in society. In a constitutional case, in evaluating the acts of legislators or executive officials, the judge ought to consider the effects of those acts in defining people as outsiders. But, as the case of the Nativity scene reminds us, a little judicial self-reflection is also to be desired. We are entitled to hope that judges will consider the effects of their own decisions on the definition of the American community: Will those decisions perpetuate the exclusion of groups from equal citizenship, or will they promote a more inclusive answer to the question, Who belongs?

Such a line of inquiry does not take a judge outside the world of legal principle. Rather, it invites the judge to seek a fuller understanding of the context in which principle bears on the case at hand. In pursuing questions like these, the chapters that follow explore the substantive meanings of equal citizenship.

In one perspective the question, Who belongs to America? raises larger cultural questions: In a nation of many cultures, does it even make sense to speak of an American community of meaning, an American culture? If it does, what are the culture's defining features? In another perspective the question of belonging is a question of social psychology, centered on the interplay between individual beliefs and group membership: Who thinks of himself as a fully participating member of the national community? Or, in a perspective that is more sociological, which people—and peoples—are generally seen by others to be members? Questions like these can be stated separately, but their separateness is only a matter of perspective. The question, Who belongs? turns out to be a question about the meanings of America. To speak of self-definition, of the sense of community, and of the community-defining functions of law is not to identify different parts of a machine but to view a complex social process from several different angles.

And there's the rub. It is artificial to divide an organic process into parts for purposes of analysis, but any attempt to describe the process all at once is doomed. To understand the meanings of the question, Who belongs? and to ask how our constitutional protections of equality come to bear on the answers to that question, we need to make a series of discrete inquiries: into the foundations for community and the varieties of belonging; into the sense of community as the matrix for individual identity; and into the meanings of equal citizenship in the American civic culture, both as an ideal and as a principle of constitutional law.

Despite the need to think about the particulars of our subject one by one, this is a book about connections, and our path will resemble a series of circles. (Ideally, every chapter should be read last, after the reader has read all the others—but that sort of endurance can be asked only of the readers of novels.)[36] We leave to the end (chapters 10–12) the largest questions about the contributions of our Constitution and our courts in defining a national community and in widening the circle of equal citizens. Yet those contributions are a subtext throughout the book. The doctrinal center for our exploration of American constitutional law is the principle of equal citizenship. Chapter 3 looks at that principle's place in the American civic culture, and chapter 4 traces the principle's origins as a legal doctrine in the nation's response to slavery. Law has always been part of our answer to the question, Who belongs to America? Chapters 5 through 9 focus on a series of groups that have been culturally defined as outsiders and excluded from full participation in America's public life: racial, religious, and ethnic minorities; women; the marginalized poor. We shall see how law has been used to effect those groups' exclusion and then see the uses of law in validating their claims to equal citizenship.

Our starting point, in chapter 2, is the 1954 case of *Brown v. Board of Education*. The Supreme Court's decision in that case was a major turning point both for the principle of equal citizenship and for the role of the courts in the American polity. Time and again *Brown* appears in this book as a leitmotiv introducing legal and institutional aspects of the theme of equal citizenship. First, however, the case will serve as a pathway into the central irony of belonging: our impulses to exclude grow out of the very acculturation that initiates us into membership in our communities.

There are no cosmic universals here. This is not a book about equality in the abstract. Some of the questions that lie ahead are, to be sure, big ones: the connections between citizenship and belonging, between individuals and groups, between law and equality, between group politics and constitutional litigation, between constitutional ideals and the realities of our public life. But the underlying assumption is that all these questions are embedded in a particular culture and a particular history. This is a book about American experience, and its meaning for American lives. Our sense of community, our ideals, our constitutional law—none of these abstractions matters at all except as it comes to bear on the lives of flesh-and-blood people.[37]

two

Brown and Belonging

Brown v. Board of Education as a
Problem in Cultural Redefinition

If the students in my constitutional law classes are typical, young adults of today's generation see the Supreme Court's 1954 decision in *Brown v. Board of Education* as not merely right but inevitable. Their perception is one measure of the Court's success in *Brown*, for the decision has legitimized itself, reshaping our civic culture and our sense of a national community. In today's perspective—thanks, in part, to *Brown* itself—a decision upholding official racial segregation of public school children does seem unthinkable. To the actors immediately involved, however, the decision was anything but a foregone conclusion.[1] Only a few months before the decision Robert Leflar and Wylie Davis published an article analyzing eleven different options open to the Court in the five cases before it.[2]

By the time that article appeared in print, a majority of the Justices already had agreed in principle that school segregation was unconstitutional. Yet, throughout the two terms when the cases were pending before the Court, a number of the Justices repeatedly had expressed grave concerns about a decision along those lines. Even after the coalescence of a majority for such a holding, some Justices remained troubled enough to consider dissenting or perhaps writing concurring opinions that would stake out positions independent of the majority's views. Richard Kluger, in his marvelous book, *Simple Justice*, has shown how the troubled Justices, under Chief Justice Earl Warren's sympathetic leadership, overcame their doubts.[3] Considering all the agonizing during the preceding two years of discussion within the Court, the final product was impressive: a unanimous decision, with all nine Justices agreeing on a single opinion.

In leading the Court to consensus the Chief Justice did not work alone. Important assistance came from Justice Felix Frankfurter, who continued to wrestle with his own uncertainties even as he sought to unify the Court. For Frankfurter, as for the equally troubled Justice Robert Jackson, racial segregation was a massive injustice, a betrayal of the basic values underlying the Constitution. How, then, could these Justices regard *Brown* as a problem case? At least for Jackson, concern began in lawyers' questions about the state of the law. Underlying those questions, however, were larger ones about American government and society, issues that ultimately connected with fundamental questions about the sense of self and the sense of belonging to a community. The questions came in layers, each linked to all the others.

The first order of difficulty lay at the surface of the case, in the existing legal doctrine and the institutional setting for an effort to desegregate the schools. A body of Supreme Court precedent upheld the constitutionality of racial segregation, with major precedents supporting school segregation itself.[4] Furthermore, although the intentions of the legislators who adopted the Fourteenth Amendment were debatable, the most plausible view was that neither the amendment's framers in Congress nor its ratifiers in the state legislatures had expected it to forbid school segregation. Frankfurter believed, as he wrote in a memorandum to himself, that the meaning of the equal protection clause could not be reduced to "a fixed formula defined with finality at a particular time," but it must evolve to take account of "changes in men's feelings for what is right and just." Even so, both he and Jackson worried about how the Court would explain a decision that Jim Crow schools were unconstitutional. In a memorandum of his own—probably a draft for a separate opinion— Jackson wrote that "the thoughtful layman, as well as the trained lawyer, must wonder how it is that a supposedly stable organic law of our nation this morning forbids what for three quarters of a century it has allowed."[5]

The question of justification led the two Justices to other questions. Invalidating school segregation might suit a modern reading of the equal protection clause; certainly such a ruling was justified both morally and politically; but what would be the costs to the whole system of constitutional law if the Supreme Court should make a major departure from long-standing doctrine? Even assuming that those costs could be kept within tolerable limits, could the Court frame coherent legal standards to guide desegregation in thousands of school districts? Would a constitutional ruling against Jim Crow schools thrust the federal courts into the rough-and-tumble of partisan politics? Indeed, could the courts accomplish real desegregation? Justice Jackson, pondering those questions at the second oral argument of *Brown*, speculated on the possibility of "a generation of litigation." Later, in his in-chambers memorandum, he mused that whether the "real abolition of segregation will be accelerated or retarded by what many are likely to regard as a ruthless use of federal judicial power" was "a question that I cannot and need not answer."[6]

Underlying these questions was a second order of difficulty: the expectation that much of the white South would greet a ruling against Jim Crow public education with hostility, political resistance, civil disobedience, and even violence. The ruling would inevitably be seen as an attack on a central feature of white southern culture: white supremacy. Justice Black, an Alabaman and the Court's only member from the deep South, strongly supported a ruling against school segregation, but he also warned his brethren that the decision would bring southern liberalism to a standstill. After the first argument of the case in 1952, Chief Justice Vinson, a Kentuckian, had warned that southern legislators might simply abolish the public schools rather than integrate them.[7] The prospect of violence also seemed realistic, given the recent history of southern lynchings of blacks.[8]

These dire predictions rested on a set of assumptions about southern culture, assumptions revealing a third order of difficulty that was the most deepseated of all. Millions of whites in the South remained keenly attached to the racial caste system. The depth of this attachment surely grew out of the ways in which individual cultural identities were formed in a society founded on racial caste. Because race was a supremely important identifying factor, racial identity necessarily carried strong emotional charges, both positive and negative. To identify oneself as white meant, above all, to identify oneself as not black. Furthermore, many southerners clung to the lower rungs of white society, with little to support their sense of self-esteem but the belief that their whiteness made them members of their communities. A reshuffling of the social order that took away those people's supposed superiority to blacks would directly threaten their sense of belonging and thus their sense of personal worth. If violence came, it would run on powerful fuel: fear of the Other and fear of the loss of status. Frankfurter's memorandum hinted at the connections between the questions of constitutional doctrine and the sense of self and belonging: The cases before the Court, he said, presented "a legal issue inextricably bound up with deep feeling on sharply conflicting social and political issues."[9]

The constitutional claims of the black plaintiffs in *Brown* were similarly linked to a particular understanding of American culture and to the plaintiffs' senses of self and belonging. Chief Justice Warren touched on these connections when he opened the Supreme Court's conference following the second argument of *Brown*. He said that the Court's precedents sustaining segregation could rest only on a theory that black people were inferior. Overruling precedents did cause him some concern, but the law could not "in this day and age" set black children apart from whites. He favored approaching the question of remedy in a way that would create "a minimum of emotion and strife," a remark that presaged the Court's ultimate—and, I believe, unfortunate—decision to impose desegregation only gradually.[10] Still, Warren said, if the Court were to follow the teachings of the Civil War amendments to the Constitution, school segregation must be ended.[11]

In a few words the Chief Justice thus made the crucial connection between the governing constitutional doctrine and Jim Crow's separation of blacks from membership in southern society. He recognized the importance of the question, Who belongs? to the sense of self. In anticipating an emotional response from southern whites he showed his awareness that, for many of them, their identities would be on the line if the Court undertook to redefine who belonged to southern society. A similar awareness informed his reference to Jim Crow's foundation on the assumption that blacks were inferior; the stigma of inferiority and the exclusion from belonging were different faces of the same grievous harm.

The Chief Justice's comments also recognized the interrelation of cultural change and changes in constitutional interpretation. By acknowledging the Court's precedents upholding segregation and then saying that in 1953 segregation contravened the Civil War amendments, Warren was not just bowing to the views of Frankfurter and Jackson that a ruling against Jim Crow schools implied a change in legal doctrine. He was also recognizing the strong connection between the meaning of the Constitution and the national community of meaning that is the American civic culture. He saw both meanings as dynamic rather than static: it was today's and tomorrow's civic culture, today's and tomorrow's Constitution, that counted most.

When the Chief Justice wrote the Court's opinion in the *Brown* cases, however, he soft-pedaled the connections linking law and culture and the sense of belonging. On the subject of stigma the opinion was deliberately bland, focusing narrowly on the question of educational harm. Segregation was "usually interpreted as denoting the inferiority" of blacks; the sense of inferiority undermined black children's motivation to learn, reducing their educational opportunities; separate schools were thus "inherently unequal."

The *Brown* opinion was, as Warren described it to his colleagues, "above all, non-accusatory,"[12] saying nothing about Jim Crow as systematic subordination. The Chief Justice did, however, allow the main harm of segregation—the hurt of exclusion—to flash briefly from the shadows. Segregation, he said, generated in black pupils "a feeling of inferiority as to their status in the community that may affect their hearts and minds in a way unlikely ever to be undone." To Edgar Patterson, the black man who had been Earl Warren's driver when he was governor of California, these words echoed the two men's earlier conversations about Patterson's life as a schoolchild in New Orleans. The opinion, said Patterson, "almost quoted the ideas that he and I used to talk about on feelings . . . things that he picked up as he was asking questions about how the black man felt, how the black kid felt." In the hospital, shortly before Warren died, he suggested to Patterson that many other factors had affected the decision.[13] But the opinion itself makes clear that the Chief Justice had absorbed what Patterson had told him. Arrayed against the white segregationists' fear of a future reduction in status was the present and long-standing reality of deep psychic harm to the victims of stigma.

Only a little imagination was needed to enlarge the Chief Justice's comment about the psychological effects of school segregation into a general indictment of the harms to black children and adults alike caused by the system of Jim Crow.[14] In the next few years the Justices proved equal to that task of imagining; they held unconstitutional all manner of state-sponsored racial segregation, with no explanation beyond citations to *Brown.* In those early years, however—no doubt for the purpose of presenting a minimal political target—the Court never explicitly avowed the essential point behind its segregation decisions: the belated recognition of millions of people as belonging to the community of equal citizens.

Brown itself was an exercise in imagination, not only for the Justices who decided the case but for the counsel who argued them and the people who lived in the communities where the cases had commenced. Long before Leflar and Davis suggested their eleven possible outcomes for *Brown,* the NAACP lawyers who filed the cases had imagined a variety of possible results for the litigation—not only effects on legal doctrine and institutions, but effects in other realms: politics, culture, and the individual psyche.[15] The lawyers had to recruit significant numbers of black people to be plaintiffs in lawsuits that had no certainty of succeeding, when being a plaintiff involved the risk of losing your job, or losing your home if you were a tenant farmer, or even being phyically attacked.[16] To make the risks seem worth taking, those people had to imagine a world in which they would be equal citizens in the national and local communities and to imagine further that American courts, in the name of the Constitution, would help them to create that world. Before they ever knew Martin Luther King's name, they had to imagine his dream and have the courage to stake their lives on it. Their willingness to risk so much on going to court demonstrated more than bravery; it showed their faith that the egalitarian ideology of the American civic culture would be extended to include them and would prevail over the South's particularly virulent form of the ideology of white supremacy. Later, when they sang "We shall overcome," they believed that America would deliver on its old promise of equality.

For the plaintiffs in *Brown*, the cases began in the years just after the end of World War II. Southern blacks had begun to stir in response to changes brought by the war: new employment opportunities, new political strength in the national government, new hope that the nation would live up to its wartime rhetoric denouncing Nazi racism.[17] For the plaintiffs' counsel, the process leading to *Brown* had begun in the early 1930s, when the NAACP's leadership decided to embark on a litigation campaign against Jim Crow.[18] Other plausible dates for the beginning of that process might be 1905, when the "Niagara Movement" met for the first time, or 1909, when the NAACP was founded, or even 1891, when black people in Louisiana organized to challenge the state's law requiring segregation of railroad cars.[19] But the identification of grievances and the determination to redress them must be preceded by the experience of hurt,[20] and for black people as a group the hurt of the racial caste system had begun with the pains of slavery. The school segregation litigation was only the most recent form of a perennial struggle to redefine a culture founded on racial subordination—a struggle that seemed to have gone on forever.

The abolition of slavery had not ended the system of racial caste. Under Jim Crow, blacks as a group remained locked into a subordinate status that was inheritable and, for all practical purposes, permanent. As we shall see, the system brought both public and private power to bear on anyone, white or black, who dared to cross the "color line." Jim Crow was not just a set of legal restrictions, but an acculturated set of taboos, regulating belief and behavior by means both formal and informal. The expected southern white resistance to desegregation arrived on schedule, taking all the forms that active political imaginations could devise.[21] There was violence, too, but on a scale well below the predictions of "worst case" prophets. By the late 1960s, and with a push from the federal government, southern governors and law enforcement officials had taken a hard line against racist violence, and southern jurors and judges had begun to convict killers. (It was no coincidence that these attitudes crystallized after the Voting Rights Act of 1965 enabled blacks to vote in significant numbers.)[22] A "generation of litigation" over school desegregation did result and did strain the capacity of the courts. Southern public schools were opened to blacks, but even today "white flight" limits the degree of actual integration in education in both the North and South. As we approach the thirty-fifth anniversary of the *Brown* decision, the effects of the racial caste system are still not behind us. Some of the reasons are to be found in the acculturated fear of outsiders that is part of the process forming individual personalities in every human tribe.

Stigma and Self-Identification

The members of cultural groups often regard themselves as the "true" people and outsiders as inferior. The names many peoples give to their own groups reflect this assumption: "Many tribes call themselves . . . 'we-are-men,' implying that all others are not."[23] Erik Erikson has called this phenomenon *pseudo-speciation*, a false sense of being a member of a separate species. He traces the origins of this attitude to the process in which children are "familiarized by ritualization with a particular version of human existence" and thus instructed in what it takes to be a respected member of the community.[24] A so-called instinctive preference or practice usually emerges from the social history of a group. We have learned it from our predecessors, and we shall teach it to those who follow us.

The child, by this process of socialization, comes to "grasp the symbolic meaning of behavior," which is just another way of saying that the child comes to belong, to be a full participant in a particular culture. The human need for belonging begins in the need to create meanings: ways of organizing our perceptions into patterns we can call reality, ways of interpreting and evaluating other people's behavior and our own.[25] To understand ourselves, to give shape to our lives, we need a community of meaning, a culture.

As we learn who we are, thought and emotion and action are melded in a single process.[26] Meanings cannot sustain themselves when they remain wholly disembodied, abstracted from the human contexts that give them life. An independent and necessary feature of acculturation is behavior itself, behavior that reinforces the individual's attachment to the culture's beliefs by acting them out. Religions the world over—along with nations and other purveyors of faith—use ritual to etch beliefs into the individual psyche. If "ritual is prior to dogma,"[27] no doubt the most important reason lies in ritual's strong emotional content, shared with a group, which reinforces the sense of belonging to a community.

The individual's identification with cultural groups—ethnic, racial, religious, or language groups—plays a major part in the process of self-definition. In defining ourselves, we rely heavily on others' views of us, real or imagined, and on our connections with others. Imagine right now that someone has asked you the question: Who are you? Perhaps the reader is a Walt Whitman who would answer, I am myself, unique in the universe, and I exult in my uniqueness. Most of us, however, would likely respond in words premised on our relations—past, present, or future—to others: I am a mother; I am a student and I am going to be a lawyer; I am black; I am an American; I am an old man; I am a Jew; I am married; I am the child of Korean immigrants.

Although the list of identifying labels is potentially long, every feature you choose to describe yourself will also embrace a group of people who share a history, or a destiny, or a symbolic universe, or perhaps all three. In the raw facts of existence, we are all Whitmans—unique, every single one of us. But as soon as we use generalized language to identify ourselves, the uniqueness of each individual comes down to this: no one of us bears precisely the same list of identifying characteristics as anyone else. And, because the naming of each separate characteristic also identifies a group, it is also correct to speak of the uniqueness of the individual in another way: You are unique in that no one else bears the same labels; no one else belongs to exactly the same combination of groups that you do.

The foregoing may make the reader want to cry out, "God is not a sociologist"—a proposition that seems self-evident. No label makes a person more or less of a person. Yet each of us does go through a process of self-definition, and in this process our primary bonds to family, religion, and ethnic group play a crucial role. These "primordial affinities" not only provide a tie to other people but offer us our very selves. It is no wonder that we develop a bond "to the very tie itself."[28]

Not only do we find our identities through acculturation; each one of us also creates an important part of her identity out of a patchwork of labels. Usually we adopt labels that are offered to us—or imposed on us—by other people, not only when we are children but throughout our lives. Most of us do not resist being labeled; indeed, from childhood on we insist on our labels and on the shared symbols that give meaning to our existence. There are those exceptional moments we all experience when the wonder of sheer existence shines through, and each of us can be a Whitman for a few seconds. But imagine what it would be like to have that feeling all the time. It might be beautiful, but without question it would be terrifying. We need our group identities and symbol spheres in order to go on living our lives. Not only do the labels protect us from being paralyzed by awe, but by designating our places in culture and society they confirm our self-definitions.

But if my group identity tells me where I belong—and *that* I belong—it also tells me that you, who do not wear the same identifying labels, do not belong. We can trust the members of our own cultural group; their stories are our own stories, and so we know the meanings of their behavior and know what to expect of them. Conversely, distrust of the members of a different cultural group flows from fear: not just the fear of the unknown, but the fear that outsiders threaten our own acculturated view of the natural order of society. Thus it was sad, but not surprising, when in 1973 residents of a white neighborhood in Memphis persuaded the city authorities to place physical barriers across a street that previously had been used by the residents of an adjoining black neighborhood to drive to and from downtown. The black citizens expressed their hurt and outrage first in the legislative councils and then in court—ultimately, in the Supreme Court. Justice Thurgood Marshall understood the city's action as a plain case of diverting black people around a white preserve. But Justice Marshall wrote in dissent; the Court's majority, giving the city officials the benefit of a paper-thin layer of doubt, found no violation of the Constitution or of federal laws.[29]

What had moved the white residents in the Memphis case to seek to divert what they called "undesirable traffic" from their neighborhood? To grow up in a culture is to learn that some ways of acting or talking or thinking are right and other ways are wrong. The very sense of one's identity is intimately connected with this learning. A young girl, in order to appreciate the idea of correct behavior, must understand the possibility of behaving incorrectly and recognize that possibility in herself. Each of us thus carries an image of what Erikson calls a *negative identity*, which must be repressed if one is to live up to the expectations of one's cultural group.[30] If we are uncomfortable when we confront the members of other groups, who have other beliefs and other ways of behaving, part of the reason is that our own acculturation has not prepared us to understand their behavior—or, worse, *has* prepared us to expect what we define as misbehavior. (Humans, perceiving, "take whatever scraps they can extract from the stimulus input, and if these conform to expectancy, . . . read the rest from the model in their head.")[31] But ignorance and bewilderment are not enough to account for the dislike, even hatred, that we often fasten on people who are different. It is fear that engages the passions, and the main source of the fear lies not in the other people but in ourselves. The outsiders serve as screens on which we can project the images of our own negative identities.

These projections take on a life of their own; they constantly invite us to turn real people into objects, to see not the person but the abstract image of the Other. The abstraction is powerful partly because it provides a convenient way for us to explain other people's behavior and our own—with the explanations usually serving to rationalize the subordinate position of a group:

"Women are like that"; "That's the only language a Puerto Rican understands." But the idea of the Other draws most of its power from its connection
to our own self-definition. To reassure ourselves that we are worthy and that
we belong, we define the Other as a separate and lesser category of being, to
be "kept in their place."[32] We use that definition to stigmatize whole groups
of people; we try to repress their incorrect, foreign ways; we try to keep them
from living in our neighborhood—or even driving through it; we try to keep
them out of the Moose Lodge.

Much of the most divisive social conflict in American history can be seen
as a series of reenactments on the pattern of this "dramatic template." Men
have repressed women, whites have repressed blacks, Protestants have repressed Catholics—the list goes on and on—not only out of greed or a craving
for power, but also, through domination of others, to provide visible demonstrations of their own worth. Because the domination is first of all a statement
about status, its visibility is crucial. The most serious threat to a dominant
cultural norm is the public demonstration of deviance. The Temperance
movement rarely prevented anyone from drinking liquor, but it did offer public reassurance to Protestants who feared the loss of their dominant status. Jim
Crow could not prevent interracial intimacy, but it did prevent public legitimation of the children produced by interracial unions.[33] Laws that forbid
homosexual conduct are almost never enforced against behavior in private.
In this perspective, the legalization of abortion, which has brought abortion
clinics to every large American city, powerfully threatens a traditional view of
women because "it is a signifier that helps make sex *visible*" and "helps identify and categorize a new sexual subject [i.e., actor], the promiscuous white
teenage girl."[34]

In these examples law is valued not merely as an instrument to be employed by a dominant group but also as a symbol of dominance itself. Further, the examples, by centering on the inclinations of the flesh, remind us
that we often seek to use the law to symbolize the repression of those parts of
ourselves that we have projected onto subordinate groups. The fear of the
Other is, at bottom, a fear of our own inadequacies.[35]

If repression and fear use the law to reinforce each other, an opposite cycle
is also conceivable. Most obviously, law can forbid particular kinds of domination—that is, it can insist on particular kinds of equality. In the end, however, acceptance of people who are different implies some measure of empathy, which means putting aside the mask of the Other. Empathy for one's
own negative identity, after all, is in the most literal sense self-contradictory.
Even tolerating those who are different means tolerating our own ambiva-

lences: love and aggression; strength and weakness; equanimity and anger; autonomy and interdependence; confidence and fear.[36] Fear has always been a special concern of the law. Law can serve the social goal of tolerance by standing as a symbol, a public statement: despite our differences we need not fear each other, for we belong to the same community. Any community shares some important values, and when tolerance itself is a value embodied in law, the law serves its ancient function of reducing fear to levels that are tolerable.

The fear of the Other that lay at the heart of white southern resistance to desegregation had old roots. Nineteenth-century fears of violent slave rebellions were followed by the early twentieth-century myth of the black beast rapist. The orgy of southern lynchings of blacks in the half-century preceding World War II was a natural successor to the previous century's violent repression of any activity that might carry the slightest suggestion (in the eyes of nervous whites) of an insurrection in the making.[37] The syllogism of white fear was not so much spoken as felt: "Of course they are hostile; look at what we have done to them." The Justices who confronted the decision in *Brown v. Board of Education* would understand these fears intuitively, for to live in white America was to be acculturated to similar fears by similar processes of self-identification.

As Charles Lawrence has recently made clear, the rejection of the Other is not the product of reason; once internalized, typically it lies below the level of consciousness.[38] Conscious or not, the rejection carries an emotional charge, for the negative identity of the Other represents a challenge to the sense of self. Not only for threatened, marginal whites in the South but also for comfortable, educated whites all over the nation, black people had come to be the quintessential cultural Other.[39] Throughout America, the overwhelming majority of whites who had reached adulthood by 1950 had been acculturated to deny—to repress—the parts of their own identity that were culturally black.[40] It is just that kind of repression that is the breeding ground for stigma.

The harm of stigma is the harm of a "spoiled identity."[41] The stigmatized person is "reduced in our minds from a whole and usual person to a tainted, discounted one. . . . By definition, . . . we believe that the person with a stigma is not quite human"—or, as the Los Angeles police chief might put it, not quite "normal." Stigma thus represents the breakdown of empathy. It dissolves the human ties we call acceptance; it excludes the stigmatized from belonging to a community. The relationship between stigma and inequality is also clear. Although not all inequalities stigmatize, the essence of any stigma lies in the fact that the affected individual is not "treated as an equal." Inequalities that stigmatize "belie the principle that people are of equal ultimate worth."[42]

The injurious effects of stigmatizing inequalities are both psychological and tangible. It hurts to confront, day after day, the denial of your individual humanity. W. E. B. Du Bois tells us how it feels to be separated from the larger community by the mark of caste:

> It is as though one, looking out from a dark cave . . ., sees the world passing and speaks to it; speaks courteously and persuasively showing them how these entombed souls are hindered in their natural movement, expression, and development; and how their loosening from prison would be a matter not simply of courtesy, sympathy, and help to them, but aid to all the world. One talks on evenly and logically in this way but notices that the passing throng does not even turn its head, or if it does, glances curiously and walks on. It gradually penetrates the minds of the prisoners that the people passing do not hear; that some thick sheet of invisible but horribly tangible plate glass is between them and the world. . . . [T]he people within . . . may scream and hurl themselves against the barriers, hardly realizing in their bewilderment that they are screaming in a vacuum unheard and that their antics may actually seem funny to those outside looking in. They may even, here and there, break through in blood and disfigurement, and find themselves faced by a horrified, implacable, and quite overwhelming mob of people frightened for their own existence.[43]

Any inequality, when it is taken as an index of personal worth, directly wounds self-respect. Although some members of stigmatized groups (some religious minorities, for example) may escape psychic harm or even draw increased self-esteem from seeing themselves as the objects of persecution, most victims of stigma are less hardy and tend to accept at least part of the version of their identities imposed by the stigma. As Chief Justice Warren accurately observed in the *Brown* opinion, the longer term demoralizing effects of a damaged identity may be even more harmful. The victim of stigma may suppress aspirations that look unattainable when seen with the restricted vision imposed by a withered self-concept.

But the harms from stigma are not merely psychological. The society also acts toward the stigmatized person on the basis of the stigma. "We construct a stigma-theory, an ideology to explain his inferiority and account for the danger he represents."[44] If he is treated unequally, he is only getting what he deserves. Thus stigma's victims tend to lose not only self-respect but other goods as well. Jim Crow demeaned its black victims, but it also deprived them of a wide range of goods, from lunch-counter service to legislative representation. Today a whole field of law is founded on the sad fact that jobs and promotions are commonly denied on the basis of stigmatizing characteristics: race, ethnicity, religion, age, sex, physical handicap, homosexuality. Even a victim whose psychic reaction to stigma is heroic resistance or martyrdom will have difficulty avoiding harms of this more tangible kind. Ruth Jefferson could not get the Supreme Court to take seriously the fact that Texas had drastically reduced welfare benefits only in the program that mainly served minority families.

The dismal side of the need to belong, then, is the distancing and objectification of people who are defined as outsiders. The ways in which the need to belong feeds these attitudes is as ironic as it is disheartening. The Justices who saw *Brown* as a problem case understood that the sources of the problem were embedded in the culture of racial caste, with its exclusive definition of the southern community. They understood, too, that a decision portending the redefinition of that culture and that community would be resisted with all the fury released by millions of threatened identities. In their memoranda to themselves and their discussions with each other, however, the Justices referred only fleetingly to the cultural dimensions of their concerns; in their own shared culture, such things went without saying.

The venture that is the United States has always included many cultures, founded on a multitude of races and religions and ethnic identifications. This fact of American life has always complicated the pursuit of American nationhood—the quest for a culture, a community, an identity that will embrace us all. In the last half-century our constitutional guarantees of equality have come to play a major role in this never-ending quest. In making the vital connection between constitutional equality and the reality of stigma, *Brown* was a doctrinal beginning. If today *Brown* seems inevitable, one reason is that the decision tapped one of the oldest streams of the American civic culture.

three

Equality and Inclusion:
Themes in the American Civic Culture

The NAACP lawyers who represented the plaintiffs in the school segregation cases knew well enough that our national history was not a chronicle of Utopia but the story of real people. Americans have always been divided—in considerable measure by our very senses of belonging—into groups that constantly contend. With some frequency the contention breaks into violent conflict. In this more somber perspective, American history was a series of stories in which some groups dominate and others are dependent. Jim Crow was one of those stories. Yet the lawyers believed there was power in the American ideal of equal citizenship. In this chapter we shall see why that belief was not naive. Equality, American style, far from being an empty abstraction, is one of the foundations for American identity and a national community.

Civic Culture and National Identity

What holds America together? Given the impulses toward distrust and domination that result from the process of identity formation, it may seem remarkable that the nation's survival has never been seriously threatened by our cultural diversity. When the United States did break apart in civil war, the rupture did not follow the seams of ethnic or religious division. It was true then and is still true that American nationhood rests on a base that is not just contractual but cultural. When the NAACP lawyers asked the courts to measure the reality of Jim Crow schools against the Constitution's promise of equal protection of the laws, they were appealing to the central substantive values of this national culture and thus to the community of meaning that gives identity to a nation.

The assumption that there is such a thing as the American character has appeared in our literature at least since Independence.[1] The earliest writers on the subject omitted mention of the slave and the American Indian, thus providing early illustration of the intimate relationship between domination and separation. Indians and slaves were implicitly set apart as not belonging to American society—a view that still impresses itself on a great many blacks and Indians.[2] For Americans who did belong, however, there was truth in the idea that they shared a community of meaning, a culture. There is even more truth in that idea today. For all our diversity, undoubtedly our strong sense of national identity rests on a common American culture, widely shared among our people.

To speak of cultural assimilation in America is to recognize the existence of a culture that is national in scope. In the years following World War II, the assimilation process was accelerated by an affluence that dramatically expanded the American middle class and by a national communications system that disseminated the dominant culture to every corner of the country. Yet assimilation cannot completely explain the existence of a national culture. First, contrary to the assumptions of those who sought to Americanize the foreign-born early in this century, assimilation does not imply a thorough conformity with the dominant culture. Rather, assimilation is consistent with a great many "varieties of ethnic experience."[3] What the framers of the Constitution called the problem of faction has always had its cultural dimensions. Second, the dominant culture itself is constantly being changed by the contributions of groups at the cultural frontiers: language and literature; music and art; dress and foods and leisure activities. The mixture resulting from all this diversity and ferment is anything but a recipe for cultural stability. It would be unimaginably difficult to found a nation of continental dimension on a cultural base that was both radically heterogeneous and continually in flux. More is required to account for the common culture that sustains our nationhood.

Americans have tended to see themselves as practical, open to change, future-oriented, optimistic, righteous: innocents in a world full of guile. These characteristics, real or imagined,[4] do reflect features of our culture, but they are hardly the makings of a social bond. Nor can loyalty, or the sense of belonging, be founded on a Constitution that is no more than a contract. Lacking common ancestral origins, religion, ethnic traditions—that is, lacking many of the usual forms of cultural glue— Americans have been required to found a nation on something else.

What is "the nation" that commands our loyalty? For a long time, the answer eluded clear definition. Perhaps for this reason, nineteenth-century America indulged in patriotic rhetoric of an intensity unmatched in our history either before or since. Woodrow Wilson, who was anything but a model of tolerance toward members of racial and ethnic groups that were not his own, implicitly recognized how difficult it was to define the nation. Speaking in 1915 to some newly naturalized citizens, Wilson said: "You have just taken an oath of allegiance to the United States. Of allegiance to whom? Of allegiance to no one unless it be to God. . . . You have taken an oath of allegiance to a great ideal, to a great body of principles, to a great hope of the human race."[5]

New citizens, like officers of government who swear to defend the Constitution, are not merely making a contract. By their rituals they are accepting and reinforcing a set of norms that give meaning to conduct in America's public life.[6] They are, in short, embracing the American civic culture: a mixture of behavior and belief that infuses our law and our institutions, transcending race and religion and ethnicity, professing to offer individual citizens the opportunity to preserve their separate cultural identities and still to identify themselves as Americans.

The essential meaning of American identity is adherence to the ideology of the American civic culture and behavior in accordance with that culture's norms. When Wilson so defined the nation, he merely repeated a view that had prevailed since the founding: "To be or become an American [at the time of Independence], a person did not have to be of any particular national, linguistic, religious, or ethnic background. All he had to do was to commit himself to the political ideology centered on the abstract ideals of liberty, equality, and republicanism."[7]

The sources of our sense of nationhood are older than the nation itself. In the colonies it was widely believed that America had special origins and a special destiny—even a divine mission. This belief grew out of the Puritan ideal of an errand into the wilderness. Protestant traditions of "institutional decentralization and ideological uniformity"[8] also were established well before Independence. But the era of the Revolution left its own legacy of unification. Republicanism not only embedded in the civic culture the central idea of equal citizenship—that "one should consider himself as good a man as another"—but also served as a unifying ideology in its own right. New institutions were established, nudging the states toward union. Although the Constitutional Convention was called to remedy defects in the Confederation, many of the Constitution's framers aimed to do more: they sought a secure base on which to found a nation.

In the early years of the republic, however, strong national loyalty was not to be taken for granted. A local judge, referring to local law, might speak of "the custom in this country." The notion of an American identity, although it had begun to appear in print, was strained by the "triumphant particularism" that characterized both belief and action in a "segmented society."[9] What contributed most to an American identity in the nineteenth century was the flourishing of a national ideology that had emerged at the time of the Revolution—a "large, loose faith"[10] roughly comprehending the central values of today's American civic culture: individualism, egalitarianism, democracy, nationalism, and tolerance of diversity.

The unifying capacities of that ideology were sharply limited, however, for its individualist-democratic-egalitarian impulses extended only to those who were full participants in public life. The national ideology of the nineteenth century also included values that today have lost their acceptability: Protestant domination, white supremacy, and the dependency of women on men. Yet no culture remains static. *Brown v. Board of Education* was not just the culmination of a campaign in the courts but a catalyst for further cultural redefinition. In the last half-century the most important changes in the American civic culture have been the widening of opportunities for women and the expansion of the ideal of tolerance—which previously had been focused on tolerance among Protestant sects—to include racial and religious minorities covering a wide spectrum. Racism and other forms of bigotry still exist, but the "authorized version" of who belongs to America has been radically revised. A culture is a community of meaning; at the very least it implies "a perception of common humanity,"[11] some minimum of sympathy and respect for other members of the community. By claiming their own equal citizenship, and by nudging institutional behavior closer to American ideals, the plaintiffs in the *Brown* cases made their own contribution to the meanings that define American identity.

The connections between culture and identity pose an obvious problem in a society of many cultures, each one shaping a separate identity around its own normative claims. A minimum requirement of nationhood is a set of universal norms. "Apparently, a decent multiethnic society must rest on a unifying ideology, faith, or myth."[12] The American civic culture, as I use the term here, embraces not only citizen allegiances and participation[13] but also a widely shared ideology, a creed that is both manifested in our constitutional doctrine and shaped by it. With more than a touch of moral superiority, Americans have assumed a national mission to be a "city on a hill," an example for the rest of the world to see and emulate. The idea that America is something special was present in the spirit of '76, and came to full flower in the mid-nineteenth century. When we look closely at what is supposed to be special, it turns out to be an ideology, one of "those explicit systems of general beliefs that give large bodies of people a common identity and purpose, a common program of action and a standard of self-criticism."[14] Like many another creed, this one is untidy and sometimes self-contradictory. Americans have tended to place their trust in "a few simple truths."[15] If you are going to do that, you have to take your truths at a high level of abstraction. When you try to apply them in making particular choices, the truths are bound to come into conflict.[16] So, the ideology of the American civic culture stubbornly resists efforts to reduce it to systematic intellectual order. It lends itself as readily to hypocrisy as to genuine observance. Yet if any single feature of our society is central to the definition of an American identity, it is this ideology: "It has been our fate as a nation not to have ideologies but to be one."[17]

The ideological component of the American civic culture performs its unifying function in the way that myth and religion unify, providing the focus for individual self-identification in a system of belief that is founded more on feeling than on logic. The NAACP counsel in the school segregation cases were not just asking the courts for relief; they were asking the American people to live by the ideology that gave them their identity as Americans.

The Egalitarian Tradition in America

Contrary to some of the Warren Court's critics, the decision in *Brown v. Board of Education* was not made up out of whole cloth but was woven from the strands of an old tradition that retains emotional appeal in our time.[18] And, contrary to the suggestion that our constitutional doctrines of equality are empty and should be abandoned, those doctrines retain a vital place in defining the American nation precisely because they draw substantive content from that tradition. The inequality that stirs emotion in America is not a violation of the axiom that likes should be treated alike but the idea of caste, of rigid social hierarchy that traps people in a system that holds them down.

Let me begin by conceding that America's devotion to ideals of equality has always been ambivalent. Thomas Jefferson, who drafted the Declaration of Independence, may have been troubled about owning slaves, but he was not wholly convinced that black people were the equal of whites. Abraham Lincoln, who signed the Emancipation Proclamation and wrote the Gettysburg Address, also found it possible to put in a good word for white supremacy. The first Justice John Marshall Harlan, who said the Constitution was color-blind, thought there was a big difference between legal equality and social equality. Sometimes we choose not to let our emotions be aroused; sometimes we choose not to see people trapped in an inferior status.[19]

Imperfection and evil are, indeed, part of our heritage—not just our heritage as Americans, but the inheritance we share with all humankind. The chapters that follow offer a depressingly generous sampling from the history of group subordination in America. This chapter's objective is different. In accepting Johnny Mercer's invitation to "accentuate the positive," I seek to recall some parts of the American past that offered hope to the civil rights movement and still lend emotional force to the idea of equality. If the long struggle toward constitutional equality be perceived as a contest, what follows is not so much a one-sided picture as a picture of one side.

Four interrelated themes will illustrate the American egalitarian ideal: our traditions of religion, law, and government, and our ideology of social mobility. As you read, please consider your own intuitive response to these old snapshots of our common past. Do they or do they not ring true as part of what many Americans today accept as our national tradition? If your answer turns out to be affirmative, you will be agreeing with the judgment of the lawyers who sought to tap that tradition in representing the black children in the school segregation cases.

1. Religion, Equality, and Belonging.

Many of the earliest English settlers came to America in search of relief from religious persecution. As Calvinists, they believed in one or another version of the doctrine of the priesthood of all believers. There was no room for intermediaries between the individual and God. Calvinists generally, and especially Puritans, carried this idea into their church organization, which was congregational, not hierarchical. Although they plainly did not use the same principle for organizing civil government, their religion did teach them that all persons were equally created in God's image and equally implicated in sin: "In Adam's fall / We sinned all." Every society, they taught, was bound together in a series of covenants, both implicit and explicit. Thus every individual had obligations of varying intensity to other members of spiritual, ecclesiastical, and political communities—and ultimately to all human beings and to God. Today "the brotherhood of man" often seems an advertising slogan; to a conscientious Puritan in seventeenth-century Massachusetts it was a central article of faith.

Ironically but predictably, the Puritans in Massachusetts, who had fled religious intolerance in England, themselves showed little tolerance for dissent. Indeed, the political movement for religious freedom in the United States can be said to have commenced with the banishment of Roger Williams from Massachusetts and the founding of Providence in the 1630s. The literal exclusion of Williams from membership in the Massachusetts community dramatizes the struggle of religious outsiders to belong. Baptists and Presbyterians saw themselves, to use today's language, as oppressed minorities, and they even used the language of slavery to express their unwillingness to pay taxes to support an established church that was not their own. Later, the movement to abolish slavery found early and powerful support among Quakers and other minority churches. In our own time, the southern black clergy provided much of the leadership for local efforts to abolish Jim Crow schools and then for the civil rights movement that developed in the wake of the *Brown* decision.[20] By a happy coincidence, many of those ministers, as Baptists, could see themselves as the spiritual successors of Roger Williams. From the earliest colonial beginnings, the equal citizenship themes of respect, responsibility, and participation have sounded from American pulpits and have been visible in the organization and programs of American churches. In the beginning, "We Shall Overcome" was a hymn.

2. Legal Equality and National Citizenship.

It is not quite a tautology to refer to equal laws. For most of human history it would have been wrong to assume that legal rules applied generally to all members of a given society. In feudal society the law effectively governing an individual's rights and obligations—and, especially, privileges—was very much the product of his personal status. The idea of universally applicable laws is one of the indicators of the arrival of the post-feudal world.

Feudalism's failure to take hold in America, and the failure of the guilds to prosper in colonial towns, now seem perfectly natural developments. The idea of legal privileges attached to personal status was contrary to the animating spirit of most colonial societies. The colonists resented inequalities imposed upon them because of their colonial status. Throughout the later eighteenth century they insisted that they belonged to English society and thus were entitled to the rights of Englishmen. After independence, first the Articles of Confederation and then the Constitution expressly prohibited both the states and the national government from creating titles of nobility. Most of the new state constitutions contained guarantees of equal rights or prohibitions against the granting of special privileges. Slavery, of course, was the glaring, ugly exception.

The very idea of citizenship implies some measure of equality. Daniel Webster, following Blackstone, said, "By the law of the land is most clearly intended the general law. . . . The meaning is, that every citizen shall hold his life, liberty, property, and immunities, under the protection of the general rules which govern society."[21] This connection between citizenship and legal equality derives in part from the social contract idea that was so prominent in the minds of the framers of the Constitution. Almost a century later Justice Joseph Bradley pointed out that, even before the Fourteenth Amendment was adopted, "the citizens of each of the States and the citizens of the United States would be entitled to certain privileges and immunities as citizens, at the hands of their own governments."[22] The original Constitution, in other words, implied some measure of legal equality among citizens, just because they were citizens.

The early nineteenth century accelerated the attack on special legal privilege and the abandonment of legal rights based on a person's status in favor of a universal body of law, equally applicable throughout the society. Changes in the law—the abolition of slavery, the Reconstruction civil rights laws, and the Civil War amendments (see chapter 4)—were specifically aimed at destroying the links between race and legal rights, but they were also part of a larger pattern of breakdown of legal inequalities based on personal status. The white South found a replacement for slavery in Jim Crow (see chapter 5), which founded its systematic denial of real citizenship on the personal characteristic of race. When the NAACP leaders mounted their attack on school segregation, they expected the schools to be only the first step in dismantling the whole system. They could also find hope in the slow decay of status-based legal inequality. *Brown* in turn accelerated this process, serving as the paradigm case for challenges to legal discrimination founded on other kinds of personal status: sex, alienage, birth outside marriage. Who in today's public life says a good word for inequality of legal status?

The idea of one law for all has an appeal not only for the average citizen but also for the leader who seeks to unify a people—from Justinian in sixth century Rome to Napoleon in the France of 1804 to Haile Selassie in the Ethiopia of the 1960s. The motto on the Supreme Court Building, Equal Justice under Law, not only rejects the idea of special legal privilege, but also proclaims our shared membership in a nation.

3. The People and Their Governors.

One of the most important results of the movement sparked by the *Brown* decision was the Voting Rights Act of 1965, which effectively enfranchised black citizens in the South. In its immediate effects this extension of democracy hastened the uprooting of Jim Crow; in a longer perspective it fulfilled an old American ideal. The same Declaration of Independence that proclaimed all men equal also asserted that governments derive "their just powers from the consent of the governed." Today our national political ideology embraces full participation by competent adults in the process of electing government officials. This ideal took an unconscionably long time to be realized. The Nineteenth Amendment, extending the vote to women, was not adopted until 1920. Although racial equality in voting was promised by the Civil War amendments, redemption of that promise had to await the 1965 act. For all that, the democratic ideal did find early expression. Although voting in the American colonies was mostly limited to white male owners of property, one of the important differences between America and Britain was, in the colonists' eyes, the breadth of the franchise. Reading Chief Justice Warren's opinion for the Supreme Court in the 1964 reapportionment case of *Reynolds v. Sims*, one hears echoes of these democratic sentiments. "One person, one vote" is a modern reflection of Americans' long-standing attachment to an ideal that blends equality and community: citizenship is participation; citizenship is belonging.

After independence, some leaders wanted George Washington to be a king. He summarily rejected the suggestion, and surely even if he had been receptive the project would have been impossible. The country was committed to being a republic. Concerned about possible excesses of democracy, John Adams proposed that the First Congress provide for great state ceremonies connected with the presidency to create awe among the people. He suggested that the President should be called "His Most Benign Highness." In the 1970s we had some experience with that sort of thing, but the whole country just laughed those fancy uniforms right off the backs of the guards at the White House. Adams's proposal didn't go anywhere, either, and his defeat by Thomas Jefferson in the presidential election of 1800 represented a definitive "defeat of aristocratic values in American politics."[23] Americans think of government officials as their servants. We may like glamour, but we are not keen on majesty.

The basic meaning of what we now call the rule of law is that the officers of government, as well as the people, must obey the law. The belief that the people's governors should be limited by law is strong in the American constitutional tradition. Twice in the modern era the Supreme Court has invoked that tradition to require a president to obey the law. During the Korean War the Court held that Harry Truman had no "inherent power" to seize the nation's steel mills—and Truman promptly ordered the operation of the mills turned back to the owners.[24] That episode served as both a doctrinal precedent and a political precedent when Richard Nixon, during the Watergate affair, asserted an inherent and uncontrollable power to maintain the confidentiality of taped presidential conversations. Rejecting that claim, the Supreme Court ruled that the president must obey a federal judge's subpoena— and Nixon promptly turned over the tapes.[25] Both Presidents were politically weakened when they compiled with the Court's rulings, but their compliance also reflected awareness of the powerful attraction for the American public of the proposition that "we submit ourselves to rulers only if under rules."[26]

These two strands of American tradition—democracy and the rule of law— came together in the school segregation cases. Effective public schools at once symbolize and promote the democratic ideal, and the courts are seen as a place where ordinary citizens can go when their governors are not obeying the rules. What could be more American than bringing a lawsuit against a school board to vindicate your child's right to equal educational opportunity?

4. The Vision of Equal Opportunity.

The ideal of equal opportunity dates from America's colonial beginnings. Looking at a list of passengers on an English ship bound for Massachusetts in the early seventeenth century, a reader cannot help being struck by the passengers' high degree of social homogeneity. One such list, dated 1635, includes these occupations: minister, clothier, salter, chandler, joiner, weaver, tailor, sawyer, cooper, husbandman, and servant. Most of these people traveled with their families. The environment imposed its own equality on the earliest settlers; they faced considerable hardships just to survive, and there was no room for gentle folk. Even one who came with next to nothing could, in those early days, occupy land and earn a living from it. So a rough sort of equality did characterize those first New England colonies.[27]

From the outset, though, there was something of a social hierarchy, even in New England; it was no accident that the minister's name headed that passenger list. In the natural course of working and trading, too, some were more successful than others. Soon there were social rankings to match differences in wealth and income, and the population grew at an astounding rate. In 1620 there were about twenty-five hundred English settlers in America; within fifty years the number exceeded one hundred thousand. By 1800 there were four and a half million whites and a million black slaves. By then, land in the territory of the original colonies was no longer freely available. Vast portions of it were concentrated in the estates of certain great families, not merely in the plantation economies of the South but in the North as well. As the existence of almshouses and poor laws showed, there was already a significant body of people called poor. By the end of the colonial period, the poor had congregated in the largest cities. Estimates of their numbers run from one-quarter to one-third of the white population of the northern colonies. Indentured servants constituted more than ten percent of the white population well into the eighteenth century. With the exception of the earliest times, when no one seemed poor because everyone was suffering, poverty has been a persistent feature of American society.

For some people, the answer was to head West to such places as Kentucky and Ohio, where land was available and life was hard—much as it had been in the first settlements along the coast. A romantic haze surrounds our collective memory of the frontier, some of it created by historians, but there is nothing mythical about the frontier's offer of social mobility. Frontier society may have been materialistic and narrow-minded, and its professed egalitarianism frequently a cover for envy and the pursuit of private advantage, but opportunity was there for those who would—and could—seize it.

One such person was Andrew Jackson, whose name today denotes a political era. He had risen from modest origins to economic success, political reward, and the status of military hero. Jacksonian Democracy was not a movement of levelers. In 1832, when he issued his famous veto of the bill to recharter the Bank of the United States, Jackson attacked the "artificial distinctions" in government grants of "titles, gratuities, and exclusive privileges, to make the rich richer and the potent more powerful." He agreed that differences among people's natural talents and their efforts would produce social distinctions under "every just government" but argued that "every man is equally entitled to protection by law" in the exercise of his own talents. Jackson's argument has a modern ring; it resonated in Chief Justice Warren's *Brown* opinion. But even in Jackson's day the theme was already venerable: hostility to special privilege and devotion to equal opportunity under equal laws.

Half a century before, James Madison in *The Federalist* had recognized that equal opportunity meant unequal results. To Jeffersonian Republicans, capitalism might seem "a mighty leveller,"[28] but only in the sense that it gave ordinary people a chance to compete with the well-born. Winning and losing are ideas Americans have always understood. What is remarkable is that this country has never been swept up by a political movement devoted to leveling.[29] Labor movements have sought an increased share of control over work, along with some redistribution of profits in the form of shorter hours and higher wages—and have been called communistic for their pains.[30] Yet, successful political reformers, from Jackson to the new Deal and the civil rights movement, have focused on an end to privilege.

Despite our ideal of equal opportunity, both advantage and disadvantage tend to be transmitted from one generation to the next.[31] Still, the large middle ranges of American society have always been characterized by a considerable degree of social mobility. Even today many of those who hold positions of wealth and power have come from more humble beginnings. The currents that produce this mobility are weaker at the very top of the social scale—the naming of Henry Ford II as president of the Ford Motor Company took no one by surprise—and weakest of all at the very bottom. In theory, Americans have accepted wide disparities in wealth and income, so long as the system remains open and people at the bottom of the economic scale are relieved from the kinds of deprivation that stigmatize or exclude them from participation in society. Here the practice at least approximates the theory— with the monstrous exception of the continuation of a marginalized class identified by race (see chapter 8).

The ideal of equal opportunity, well established in the American tradition of constitutional equality, is sometimes contrasted with equality in outcomes.[32] In a great many situations, however, there is no clear distinction between equalizing opportunity and equalizing result. Today, for example, we can see, as Andrew Jackson could not, that education is a case in which a considerable measure of equality in delivered services is necessary to achieve anything like equal opportunity.[33] If we allow major substantive inequalities to persist in such cases, equality of opportunity will serve mainly as a comfort to the comfortable, a slogan assuring them that they have earned their favored positions.[34]

Naturally, proposals for a greater sharing of society's burdens and benefits find the haves more receptive during times of relative abundance than during times of economic contraction. It is more than coincidence that the 1960s, which saw the flowering of the civil rights movement, were also a period of economic expansion.[35] Even in good times, however, the willingness of the haves to share their abundance has been limited. The polity—ever the domain of the haves—has never gone in for massive redistribution of wealth. Yet if anything is certain about the nation's egalitarian tradition, it is that tradition's dynamism, its capacity for evolution. There is nothing visionary in expecting further development of our appreciation of what equality of opportunity implies.

Some observers have looked at America's relatively high social mobility and have mistaken it for equality of condition. Alexis de Tocqueville so characterized American society during the era of Jackson, and a Charlotte newspaper had said almost the same thing during the Revolution: "the people of America, are a people of property; almost every man is a freeholder." Americans have always been attracted to that sort of hyperbole, in spite of the persistence of economic inequality, poverty, even slavery. Yet, behind this yearning to believe a myth lies another sort of equality that has more substance, a widely shared belief in equality of inherent worth that transcends a person's ranking on the economic scale.[36] In 1780 a New Jersey newspaper expressed this vision of post-Revolutionary society: "one should consider himself as good a man as another, and not be brow beaten or intimidated by riches or supposed superiority." In our own time Simone de Beauvoir saw the same ideal and exaggerated it into a fully realized fact: "the rich American has no grandeur; the poor man no [servility]; human relations in daily life are on a footing of equality."[37]

The ideology of equality in our civic culture has always been part of the cultural cement that holds American society together. Ideology alone, however, is not enough to make any value a durable part of the civic culture. A necessary ingredient of that durability is the behavior of large numbers of people, from one generation to the next, in accordance with the culture's norms. Leonard Levy has recently shown how the freedom of the press emerged in America during the revolutionary generation, not primarily through the adoption of the First Amendment but through the day-to-day exercise by newspaper editors of the freedom they were claiming.[38] So it is with any important societal value, any constitutional right: use it or lose it.

Equality, Behavior, and Belonging

Not only does our acculturation tell us what kinds of inequality are tolerable; it is culture, the sharing of meanings, that identifies something as an inequality in the first place. Most of us make little effort to examine the interconnections between our normative beliefs and our behavior; generally we allow those connections to lie below the level of conscious articulation. Indeed, at least for the present, there seems to be an irreducible element of mystery in the precise mechanisms that lead from awareness to individual behavior.[39] Despite these difficulties of analysis at the level of microcosm, it does seem clear that a society can maintain its unifying ideology only when people generally act in accordance with the ideal. With ideology as with myth, "ritual is prior to dogma." It is the ritualization of correct behavior that supplies the symbolic meanings underlying the sense of belonging. This shared behavior not only establishes and reinforces the culture's norms; it also establishes the individual's cultural identity. An American demonstrates that she belongs to America primarily by acting out the civic culture's ideals. In so doing, she adds her own contribution to the shared emotion that is essential to the sense of community.

American society's central myths—even as expressed in our constitutional law—may seem to be in tension with each other and sometimes contradictory, yet the "real substratum of myth is not a substratum of thought but of feeling. . . . [Its] coherence depends much more upon unity of feeling than upon logical rules."[40] That unity, however, will collapse unless the society's system of beliefs is largely validated in most people's minds by their own experience. It is as true for our civic culture and our law as it is for religion: a system of belief finds its utility, not just in satisfying individual needs for security and the sense of identity and moral worth, but also in providing the basis on which action may be planned and carried out. When a belief system no longer explains experience or serves to guide behavior, it gives way to other beliefs that will explain and guide. If the ideals of the American civic culture are to hold a multicultural nation together, they must find reinforcement in American behavior. "Society's forms are culture's substance."[41]

When the framers of the constitution sought to make a nation, they knew that the centralization of governmental power was only a beginning. Nationhood would demand the widespread sharing of a national identity. Yet the framers explicitly rejected two institutional means that had been used to rally emotional support for nationhood in the countries of Europe: a monarchy and an established church. Low levels of immigration from the beginning of the Revolution to the end of the War of 1812 permitted the consolidation of English as the national language. And early, if halting, successes of the national government helped persuade most white Americans that the nation served their interests. The Revolution itself had produced culturally unifying effects. It provided the liberal and egalitarian ideology of republicanism and also put those values into practice by establishing a new order of status equality both for individuals and for cultural (mainly Protestant) groups. An individual's identification with the new nation, in other words, was closely tied to his sense that the nation was making good on its professed individualistic and egalitarian ideals.

From that time to our own, those who have been full participants in American public life have felt a strong congruence between belief and behavior concerning the civic culture's thread of individualism.[42] This congruence has been shaped by the demands of market capitalism and the opportunities of a continent rich in resources. However, not everyone was admitted to the free play of individualistic activity. Women were not full participants; slaves and Indians simply did not belong. To note these huge exceptions is to recognize that there has been nothing like congruence between the historic American profession of egalitarian ideals and our willingness to live up to those ideals. The most important issue about equality in America has always been one of belonging: should Catholics, or freed slaves, or women, or immigrants from Poland or Mexico be treated as respected, responsible participants in American society? The egalitarian strand in our civic culture centers on the idea of equal citizenship, and law has much to contribute in translating ideals into behavior.

The school segregation cases illustrate several of this book's basic propositions. In our society one of the most prominent bridges between ideology and behavior is the law. In particular, constitutional litigation is a process in which ideology can be brought to life in the behavior of litigants and of law professionals, including judges. *Brown v. Board of Education* was just such an occasion. The litigants on both sides expressed their belonging to the national community by appealing to their competing views of the community's norms. When the Justices enforced the Constitution's protections against group domination, their behavior not only strengthened the perception of the worth of a particular racial group but also reinforced the individualism and egalitarianism that were central to the larger group identity of the American nation.

When the ideology of the civic culture is embodied in positive law, it is not just the formulation of the law that serves to unify the society, but the actual enforcement of the law in real people's cases. Surely law is, among other things, ideology, but in America the application of law is a centrally important form of the ritual behavior that allows ideology to "transform sentiment into significance and so make it socially available."[43] When our constitutional law infuses the spirit of tolerance into the decision of cases, those rituals provide regular, day-to-day renewal of the idea that we are one nation.

four

Slavery and Citizenship

Race, Caste, and Citizenship

Much of the history of race relations in our country is a story of pain and inhumanity and guilt. Yet that very history has served as the crucible for the American ideal of equal citizenship. Our dismal starting point is the *Dred Scott* case,[1] surely the most infamous decision in the Supreme Court's history. Scott, a slave, had been taken by his master from Missouri, a slave state, into the Northwest Territory, where slavery had been abolished by Congress. On returning to Missouri, Scott had sued in a state court to obtain his freedom. When the Missouri courts rejected his claim that residing in free territory had made him free, Scott turned to the federal court, invoking its "diversity of citizenship" jurisdiction. (Scott sued as a Missouri citizen against his new master, a New Yorker.) Chief Justice Roger B. Taney's opinion declared that Scott, and black people generally—not just slaves, but all blacks—were incapable of citizenship, because blacks had not been members of "the people of the United States" identified in the preamble to the Constitution.

From the beginning, Taney said, blacks were excluded from membership in the national community because they had been "considered as a subordinate and inferior class of beings, who had been subjugated by the dominant race, and, whether emancipated or not, yet remained subject to their authority." Discriminatory state laws in force when the Constitution was adopted, Taney said, demonstrated "the inferior and subject condition" of blacks. It was not to be supposed that the states

> regarded at that time, as fellow-citizens and members of the sovereignty, a class of beings whom they had thus stigmatized; . . . and upon whom they had impressed such deep and enduring marks of inferiority and degradation; or, that when they met in convention to form the Constitution, they looked upon them as a portion of their constituents, or designed to include them in the provisions so carefully inserted for the security and protection of the liberties and rights of their citizens.

Taney was right about one thing: the existence, from the beginning, of overt racial discrimination in the laws of the United States and in the laws of the states, both North and South. Still, it took sleight-of-hand to convert that history into the denial of access to the federal courts. The infamy of the *Dred Scott* opinion, however, lay elsewhere: in its smug assumptions of racial superiority; in its shameful equation of citizenship with whiteness; in its sweeping exclusion of black people from belonging to America; in its bland acceptance of their relegation to an inferior caste.

Today's law students do not study the *Dred Scott* opinion, for it is not included in their constitutional law casebooks. The omission is understandable; the decision no longer carries weight as a precedent, and both the students and their teachers would be uncomfortable confronting such explicit racism at the highest level of American law and government. Nonetheless the opinion is worth examination for the light it can throw on the meaning of citizenship in America, and particularly the equal citizenship that later came to be guaranteed in the Fourteenth Amendment.

First, Taney made it clear that citizenship mattered. Far from being "a simple idea for a simple government,"[2] citizenship carried important substantive implications that had given significance to a running debate in the first half of the nineteenth century. The debate was cast in formal terms: Did a person's national citizenship depend on his being a citizen of a state, or was state citizenship somehow derivative from his status as a citizen of the United States?[3] Disagreement over this issue did not prevent a widely shared consensus that there was, indeed, such a thing as national citizenship. (The Constitution not only gave Congress the power to tax and regulate individuals directly, but also referred to United States citizenship in defining the qualifications for serving as president or in the Senate or the House of Representatives.) By 1849, just eight years before the *Dred Scott* decision, Taney himself had remarked, without producing a murmur of opposition, "For all great purposes for which the Federal government was formed, we are one people, with one common country. We are all citizens of the United States."[4]

Why was the nature of national citizenship capable of provoking heated controversy? Again the *Dred Scott* opinion is instructive. Taney went out of his way to say that black people had been not merely subjugated but stigmatized with "deep and enduring marks of inferiority and degradation." In emphasizing the permanence of inferior status Taney was asserting that blacks, as a racial group, had been consigned to a lower caste—a position entirely inconsistent with membership in the "people of the United States." Taney understood that a citizen is a member of a moral community who counts for something in the community's processes of decision. America had only one class of citizens, equally entitled to respect and to the protection of their "liberties and rights." Furthermore, said Taney, citizens, as "members of the sovereignty," had constituted the Constitutional Convention. Here he invoked a long-accepted understanding of citizenship. Aristotle, who more than anyone else set the terms of the western world's discussion of such matters, said that a citizen is one with "the power to take part in the deliberative or judicial administration" of the state.[5] A citizen is a participant, one who bears responsibilities to his fellow citizens.

In his *Dred Scott* opinion Taney not only accepted all these connections between equality and citizenship but made them central to his argument. He assumed that he would demonstrate that Scott could not be a citizen if he could show that black people, from the nation's beginning, had been denied the respect, responsibility, and participation that were the substantive indicia of equal citizenship.

A Marylander, Taney knew the assumptions about racial caste that lay at the heart of the southern defense of slavery. The relation between race and status in America had become an issue soon after the introduction of black slaves. The issue was first raised when churchmen in England and America called for the Gospel to be spread to the slaves. Cotton Mather, who today symbolizes rigid, authoritarian Puritanism, did urge both slaves and indentured servants to obey their masters, but he also asserted the equality of slaves in the sight of God, and—to the consternation of most slaveholders—he urged that slaves be converted and baptized. The English Puritan Richard Baxter said this to slaveholders in 1673: "Remember that they are as of good a kind as you; . . . If their sin have enslaved them to you, yet Nature made them your equals. Remember that they have immortal souls, and are equally capable of salvation with yourselves."[6]

That was the issue: Were blacks and whites equals? An affirmative answer, given the existence of slavery, would call into question the ideal of equality that was fundamental to the American national identity, an ideal inscribed in the Declaration of Independence itself. Thus was born the American dilemma—the existence, side by side, of the ideal of equality and the subordination of a racial group. To avoid confronting the dilemma, white Americans increasingly accepted a system of caste, founded on race. Racial differences are readily used as the cultural indicia of caste. They are durable characteristics, typically visible on first meeting, and transmitted from one generation to the next.

Although slavery and white supremacy in the South eventually became two sides of the same coin, the analogy that categorized slaves with beasts never was fully believed. The law governing slavery was continually concerned with the tension between two characterizations of the slave: as property and as a human being.[7] Furthermore, from the time of Nat Turner's insurrection in 1831 until the end of the Civil War, the fear of slave rebellion was never far from the surface of southern white consciousness. Animals might balk, but they do not organize revolutions. The recognition of the slaves' humanity was nowhere more clearly reflected than in the rules aimed at heading off further insurrections. Slaves could not assemble in large numbers without whites present; they could not possess weapons or handle poisons; they could not be taught to read and write. Even free blacks came under increasingly severe restrictions. In the paramilitary institution knows as "the patrol," every white adult male "was a policeman in the face of every black person," with the purpose of preventing insurrection by putting blacks—especially black men—in fear of severe and summary punishment for infractions of the racial caste system.[8]

After Turner's revolt, no southern black could avoid the fear that the patrol might "shoot first and answer questions later." And, although slave revolts were rare, no southern white could feel completely safe from attack. Yet, although whites tacitly recognized the capacity of slaves to organize for violence, they also assured each other that blacks were docile, childlike, and dependent. Most slaves were outwardly submissive, and some even fit the white's stereotype for blacks.[9] More typically, however, the male plantation slave "used his wits to escape from work and punishment, preserved his manhood in the [slave] quarters, feigned humility, identified with masters and worked industriously only when he was treated humanely, simulated deference, was hostilely submissive and occasionally obstinate, ungovernable, and rebellious."[10]

Although a slaveholder's power was far from absolute,[11] ordinarily it was effective in preventing serious breaches of the social order of the slave system. White violence against blacks, after all, was not merely something to be feared; it was something virtually all blacks had either witnessed or suffered.

The southern white view of slaves—which, by the logic of the racial-inferiority defense of slavery, became extended to all black people—thus had it both ways. Blacks were seen to be incapable of independent living in civilized society but an ever-present threat to the safety of whites. The patrol was a living metaphor for acting out white fears through a rigid confinement of black people's activities. The system of racial caste, by creating conditions that gave those fears plausibility, reinforced its own justifications. The law governing black people was, above all, designed to maintain the identities established for them by the norms of a society founded on slavery.[12] For blacks and whites alike, acculturation to those norms included heavy doses of fear and violence.

Without the assumptions underpinning a racial caste system, there would have been no evading slavery's inconsistency with American ideals of equality. If both master and slave had been white, it is hard to believe that slavery could have survived the Great Awakening of religious fervor in the mid-eighteenth century, let alone the republican fervor of the revolutionary and constitutional eras. Stigma feeds on itself through the process of acculturation. The more slaves were debased, the more they were seen by whites as fit candidates for debasement. The more unequal their treatment, the more justifiable it seemed to set them apart as members of a subordinate caste.[13] Years ago, in casual conversation, my friend Vaughn Ball expressed this idea in the memorable language of a home truth: "You can always forgive people for what they do to you, but you can never forgive them for what you do to them."

The most grievous wrong of the white majority has always been the identification of blacks as a separate category of beings—or, in the words of the *Dred Scott* opinion, "a subordinate and inferior class of beings." Ironically, the existence of a racially identified slave caste served to heighten the sense of social equality among whites. Slaves were outside the boundaries of the community, but whites who were within it could take pride in their equal membership status.[14] As to the slaves, however, it would have been ludicrous to speak of the values of equal citizenship. They were denied respect, participation, and most forms of responsibility.

Still, the idea that black and white souls were equal in God's sight retained vigor, and in the eighteenth century it was strengthened by a secular humanitarianism that grew out of the European Enlightenment. In Winthrop Jordan's words, "Empathy was of course a strong element in humanitarianism, and empathy implied equality, if only in a very limited sense."[15] At least some degree of empathy was in the air of New England during the Revolutionary era. Abigail Adams expressed the mood nicely in a 1774 letter to her husband, John: "It always appeared a most iniquitous scheme to me to fight ourselves for what we are daily robbing and plundering from those who have as good a right to freedom as we have."[16] After the Revolution seven northern states formally abolished slavery, and in New Hampshire it was allowed to die a natural death. The Northwest Ordinance of 1787 forbade slavery in the Northwest Territory.

At the Constitutional Convention, however, a bargain was struck in order to get the southern states to join the Union—a bargain that defined the national community by parceling out to the several states the right to decide who belonged to America. The new Constitution said nothing about abolition and postponed for twenty years any legislation to end the slave trade. In deciding how to calculate the populations of slave states for determining their representation in Congress, the Convention hit on a formula: each slave was to count as three-fifths of a person. Speaking of this arrangement in *The Federalist*, James Madison wrote that it was entirely logical, viewing the slaves as state law had viewed them "in the mixt character of persons and of property." The problem of race relations in America has always revolved around the question whether nonwhites are or are not to be treated as complete persons, as the equals of whites.[17]

Roger Taney, when he addressed the question of Dred Scott's status, understood that the problem of slavery had lain just below the surface of the long-running debate over the nature of national citizenship. To be a citizen was to be a respected and responsible participant in the community's public life. Given these substantive implications of citizenship, slaves certainly could not be considered citizens of the United States without opening their slave status to attack. Scott, of course, claimed that he was not a slave but a free man. Yet, if free blacks were citizens of the nation, they could travel freely to slave states, where their very presence as free persons would not only undermine the theory of racial caste but remind slaves that their own status was not ordained in nature but imposed on them.

If Scott's claim to be free had threatened the white South, Taney's opinion rejecting that claim produced an immediate and scornful reaction in the North. Among northern whites, however, the scorn did not reflect interracial fraternity. The main cause of their ire was Taney's conclusion that Congress could not constitutionally forbid the expansion of slavery into the territories—a conclusion directly contradicting the most important plank in the Republican party's platform.[18]

As for Taney's general comments on the status of black people, white northerners who objected could well be called disingenuous. From the time of the founding until the Civil War, the national government had denied even free blacks a number of the indicia of equal citizenship. Blacks were forbidden to carry the mail, to serve in the militia, to become naturalized citizens, even to receive American passports for travel abroad. During the same time, most northern states had subjected free blacks to various forms of official discrimination, including laws forbidding their immigration into some states, restrictions on suffrage in others, and segregated local schools. Furthermore, even when the equal rights of black people were formally recognized, the actual exercise of those rights was strongly discouraged by private behavior that followed the cultural norm of white supremacy. The ideal of equal citizenship remained vivid for northern whites; they simply excluded blacks from belonging to the community of equal citizens: "Although Negroes and whites could legally intermarry in most Northern states, public opinion would not permit it. Where Negroes possessed the right to vote, they often faced vigorous resistance at the polls. They might seek redress in the courts, but only whites served as judges; although they were legally entitled to sit on juries, the public would not allow it. Segregation confronted them in public places, including churches and cemeteries."[19] Taney's racist assumptions hit home because they highlighted what northern whites preferred to forget: their own frequent betrayal of the ideal of equal citizenship. One effect of *Dred Scott* in the North was a revival of the spirit of liberty that had animated the Revolution. Some northern states reaffirmed the citizenship of black people, and Massachusetts even issued state passports to blacks.[20] If the Taney opinion was a slap in the face, it awakened a dormant northern conscience to the tensions between northerners' professed egalitarian ideals and the realities defining who belonged to their communities.

What matters most about Taney's opinion today is not his appalling racist smugness, or even his reading of history; what is important is that his assumptions about racial inferiority and exclusion from citizenship were just what the drafters of the Civil War amendments and the civil rights acts of the Reconstruction era sought to overturn. Henceforth, there was to be no "dominant race" and no "subordinate and inferior class of beings," but only citizens.

The 1866 Civil Rights Act and the Fourteenth Amendment

A standard feature of war is wartime propaganda. We say we are fighting for an ideal, and we come to believe it. Just as the Revolution had been carried on in the name of liberty and equality, so the Civil War produced volumes of egalitarian rhetoric, much of it taken directly from an antislavery movement that had begun in the eighteenth century.[21] After the war, the major issue before the Reconstruction Congress was the translation of the ideal of equality into institutions that would govern human affairs. Not many in that Congress, it appears, really believed that blacks and whites should be treated as social equals. It was a legal equality that they sought to achieve through the adoption of civil rights laws and constitutional amendments.

The wartime Emancipation Proclamation and the immediate postwar ratification of the Thirteenth Amendment had already begun the nation's quest for redemption for the sin of slavery. But constitutional abolition was not enough. The Thirteenth Amendment took effect in December 1865. By mid-March eight southern states had adopted their versions of the Black Codes—laws systematically imposing legal disabilities on blacks. The codes were designed to exclude blacks from real membership in southern society and to keep them in a status of inferiority and dependence closely resembling slavery.[22] The laws forbade blacks to own or transfer property, to inherit, to purchase, or to seek access to the courts. By combining vagrancy laws with a convict-lease system, they even assured that the former slaves would continue to serve as laborers for the planters. To abolish this new variation on the old theme of racial caste, Congress adopted the Civil Rights Act of 1866.

The first section of the Act provided:

> [A]ll persons born in the United States and not subject to any foreign power, excluding Indians not taxed, are hereby declared to be citizens of the United States: and such citizens, of every race and color [including former slaves], shall have the same right, in every State and territory of the United States, to make and enforce contracts, to sue, be parties, and give evidence, to inherit, purchase, lease, sell, hold, and convey real and personal property, and to full and equal benefit of all laws and proceedings for the security of person and property, as is enjoyed by white citizens, and shall be subject to like punishment, pains, and penalties, and to none other, any statute, ordinance, regulation, or custom, to the contrary notwithstanding.

As the emphasized words make clear, these civil rights were written into the law as the equal rights of citizens; the Dred Scott decision was repudiated. The act plainly proceeds on the assumption that certain substantive rights are necessary if the newly declared citizenship for the freed slaves is to be more than a hollow form. Black and white citizens are to have equal benefit of both laws and proceedings—the practical business of enforcement of rights— for securing their persons and property. Not only judges but sheriffs and tax collectors and governmental officers generally are to respect that equality of status by affording black people equal treatment. Access to the courts is guaranteed on an equal basis, too; a black person is to have his or her say in court—to be heard out, treated as a person and not an object, as any other respected citizen would be heard. Blacks are to be afforded participation in the governmental process as parties and as witnesses. More generally, they are offered participation in the community's public life: buying and selling, dealing with property, protecting their rights—all on the same terms as white citizens.

Respect and participation, yes—but responsibility, too. To be a citizen is not merely to be a consumer of rights, but to stand with other citizens in a relation of mutual responsibilities. Indeed, the recognition (by law and otherwise) of members' responsibilities to one another is one of the chief indicators that a community exists. Under the act, black citizens are to be held to their contracts, their leases, their deeds; as for misdeeds, they are to be subject to the same punishments as are white citizens. Most importantly, through working and acquiring property they are to have a real chance to take responsibility for their own and their families' well-being. In fulfilling this responsibility they can provide for their families by making wills, and their spouses and children can inherit—all in their capacities as citizens.

In short, the 1866 Civil Rights Act recognized that the goal of equal citizenship—respected and responsible participation in the public life of the society—could not be achieved through a bare declaration of citizenship as a formal status, but needed substantive underpinnings. Equality and belonging were melded into a single policy, as was entirely natural, given the framers' objectives. President Andrew Johnson had similarly linked the ideas of citizenship and equality in his message vetoing the bill. Congress overrode the veto, and the act became law on April 9, 1866, one year to the day after Lee's surrender at Appomattox.[23]

The proponents of the 1866 act initially assumed that Congress had the power to enact it under the Thirteenth Amendment. Johnson's veto message, however, challenged this assumption about congressional power. The proposed Fourteenth Amendment had been under consideration for two months before the veto; at least from this time forward, one of the chief objectives of the amendment's framers was to secure the 1866 act from constitutional attack. Whether or not one accept Jacobus tenBroek's argument that the equal protection clause was intended as a substantive guarantee of full protection of fundamental or natural rights, it is beyond dispute that the focus of congressional discussion of the proposed Fourteenth Amendment was the eradication of racial discrimination in the enjoyment of the rights of citizens spelled out in the 1866 act.

The full text of the Fourteenth Amendment's first section occupies only two sentences. The first one says:

All persons born or naturalized in the United States, and subject to the jurisdiction thereof, are citizens of the United States and of the State where they reside.

Plainly, this provision aims at constitutionalizing the rejection of the *Dred Scott* opinion by making clear that citizenship does not depend on race. The second sentence sets out three statement of rights:

No State shall make or enforce any law which shall abridge the privileges or immunities of citizens of the United States; nor shall any State deprive any person of life, liberty, or property, without due process of law; nor deny to any person within its jurisdiction the equal protection of the laws.

The text of the amendment's first section thus bears one striking similarity to the 1866 act, and one striking difference. The amendment follows the pattern of the act in declaring citizenship and then setting out a series of rights that can readily be understood as rights of citizens. But where the act proceeds from a declaration of citizenship to a detailed listing of specific rights of citizens, the amendment's three prohibitory clauses are couched in grand generalities, words obviously capable of bearing larger meanings.

The privileges and immunities clause was added to the proposed amendment late in the drafting process. Although it is scarcely a model of crisp definition, the clause does, of course, guarantee something to citizens. In the hands of a receptive judiciary it would have been an apt vessel for a constitutional protection of the citizenship rights set out in the 1866 act. But the congressional debates show that even if this clause had not been added, the framers expected the amendment to serve the purpose of guaranteeing the equal rights of citizens. There was no serious effort to differentiate the functions of the various clauses—privileges and immunities, due process, equal protection—of section 1 of the amendment. With or without the privileges and immunities clause, the section in its entirety was taken to guarantee equality in the enjoyment of the rights of citizenship.

Charles L. Black, Jr., has argued that even if all three of the prohibitions of section 1 had been omitted, most of what has been done in their names might have been accomplished on the basis of the section's first sentence. Black's argument of chief concern to us is that the conferral of citizenship empowers Congress, in enforcing the Fourteenth Amendment, to forbid racial discrimination both public and private. But he also draws from this same sentence in section 1 a wide range of rights of citizens, including those due process rights that the Supreme Court has found to be the essentials of a "scheme of ordered liberty."[24]

The declaration of citizenship was added by the drafters of the Fourteenth Amendment "almost as an afterthought." It was not part of the amendment as the House of Representatives first adopted it but was inserted at the last minute in the Senate, with minimal discussion. In the absence of legislative history, we are left to speculate on the framers' purposes in adding the sentence. Alexander Bickel advanced two possible explanations. First, the senators might have thought it provident to make clear who was a citizen of the United States, given that the privileges and immunities clause seemed to attach significance to that status. Second, by providing "a definition of citizenship in which race played no part," the framers ensured that "*Dred Scott* was effectively, which is to say constitutionally, overruled." Surely Bickel was right, yet the two purposes he suggested do not exhaust all the possible reasons for adding this definition of citizenship to the proposed amendment. For one thing, the addition of the sentence heightens the textual parallel of the amendment to the first section of the 1866 act, thus strengthening the conclusion that the clauses that follow the definition of citizenship are designed to protect the substantive rights of citizens. Second, the overruling of *Dred Scott* is consistent not only with the narrow purpose to confer the legal status of citizenship on persons born in this country but also with a broader purpose to abolish the system of caste recognized in that opinion, by giving a particular substantive content to the amendment.

Some judges and scholars argue that the only proper course for a court in deciding a constitutional issue is to determine the meanings attached to a constitutional text by the people who adopted it and to apply those meanings to the case before them without adding or subtracting anything.[25] These "originalists" agree that the rights guaranteed by the Fourteenth Amendment are linked with the rights of citizens guaranteed by the 1866 Civil Rights Act. They insist, however, on limiting the reach of the amendment's broad language to the specific rights listed in the act. The most zealous originalists see the Supreme Court's decision in *Brown v. Board of Education* as a judicial usurpation of power. Raoul Berger, in particular, has argued that the congressional debates in 1866 show that the framers of the Fourteenth Amendment did not intend it to outlaw school segregation.[26] Although other broader views of the amendment's reach were also expressed in Congress, Berger's view of the framers' intentions—or, rather, nonintentions—about school segregation seems persuasive. Congress, after all, had funded segregated schools in the District of Columbia. The amendment was designed to protect rights of equal citizenship, not what the congressional debates called social equality; in the culture shared by the framers, school segregation fell in the latter category. Whatever the framers may have expected of the judiciary in the way of interpreting the amendment in years to come, surely they did not expect the immediate invalidation of all manner of government-sponsored segregation. In the very galleries of Congress, spectators listening to the debates over the proposed Fourteenth Amendment were segregated by race.

But suppose a later generation should have a larger conception of what it means to belong to America, to be a citizen. Does it then pass the bounds of legitimacy for the courts to interpret the Fourteenth Amendment as a guarantee of citizenship rights defined more generously then the amendment's framers would have defined them? The wording of the amendment deserves another look. The framers did not choose merely to repeat the "laundry list" of specific guarantees in the 1866 act. Instead they expressed the rights of equal citizenship in quite a different style. True enough, they expected their broad words to apply to some forms of inequality and not to others. By providing firm constitutional protection for the substantive rights of the 1866 act, the framers expected that all citizens, including blacks, who were the most obvious stigmatized caste, would share equally the civil rights that seemed most significant at the time. But they deliberately cast the amendment in general terms, declining to use the language of specific rights and particular groups that they had used in the 1866 act. It was this broad wording that gave the guarantee of equal citizenship a textual base for its modern growth into a protection of other groups and other rights.

The indefiniteness of the language of section 1 of the proposed Fourteenth Amendment did not escape the framers' notice. In opposing inclusion of the privileges and immunities clause, for example, Senator Reverdy Johnson—an eminent constitutional lawyer with considerable experience in Supreme Court litigation—said he simply did not understand the clause's effect. Another member of the joint committee that drafted the amendment, referring to the sponsor of the clause, congressman Hiram Bingham, said, "Its euphony and indefiniteness of meaning were a charm to him." Senator Jacob Howard, who led the amendment's sponsors in the Senate debate, began by suggesting that the amendment guaranteed the same privileges and immunities mentioned in Article IV of the original Constitution, and quoted at length from the leading judicial interpretation of Article IV. That interpretation read the first privileges and immunities clause broadly to forbid discriminations by one state against the citizens of another state concerning rights that were "fundamental." He added that such fundamental privileges and immunities "are not and cannot be fully defined in their entire extent and precise nature." The amendment's friends and foes alike understood that its language would require elaboration as it was applied to future cases.

The question remains, Why use language of such breadth when it would have taken only a few more lines to list specific citizenship rights as the same Congress had done in the 1866 act? The record of congressional debates is silent on this point. But it is reasonable to conclude that the framers found it natural to adopt the mode of generality already used elsewhere in the Constitution to express limitations on the states and on the national government. One example familiar to the framers was the contract clause of Article I, Section 10: "No State shall . . . pass any . . . law impairing the obligation of contracts." Prohibitions of this generality do not define themselves. The contract clause had been a subject of active litigation in the nineteenth century. On the basis of its general language John Marshall had interpreted the clause to reach well beyond the specific intentions of its framers—a fact that Marshall himself had acknowledged.[27] By the 1860s, judicial interpretation had translated the spacious words of the contract clause into a richly detailed body of constitutional doctrine.[28]

A similar need for judicial glosses on the Constitution's general language prohibiting bills of attainder and ex post facto laws was in the forefront of public attention in 1866. The test oath cases, concerning the constitutionality of loyalty oaths imposed on people who had supported the Confederacy in the Civil War, were argued in the Supreme Court while the proposed Fourteenth Amendment was working its way through Congress and were decided before the amendment's ratification was complete.[29] The prohibitions of the Bill of Rights, too, had been written in broad terms. The framers of the Fourteenth Amendment were conscious that they were not drafting a code of laws, but were modifying the nation's basic charter of government.[30]

Furthermore, the Fourteenth Amendment, like most important legislation, was the product of political compromise.[31] Terrance Sandalow, who recognizes the need for a judicial search for the larger purposes that underlie constitutional language, has cautioned that the search is susceptible to mistake and even to manipulation. Seen in proper historical context, the specific judgments of a legislative body may turn out to be "not imperfect expressions of a larger purpose but a particular accommodation of competing purposes."[32] The originalists read the Fourteenth Amendment in just this way, as a specific political bargain to write the particular prohibitions of the 1866 act into the Constitution. The strictest adherents to this view argue that *Brown v. Board of Education*, which carried the amendment beyond the boundaries of that bargain, was wrongly decided.

Yet, as all politicians know, one time-honored way to achieve compromise—especially when political debate is multisided—is to enact broad language that is capable of bearing more than one meaning, leaving to the future the application of that language to particular cases. There is no evidence that any individual senator or representative, or any member of a ratifying state legislature, consciously voted for the indeterminate language of the Fourteenth Amendment on this basis. Still, it is not illegitimate for a court, decades after the amendment's adoption, to take this common fact of political life into account in interpreting a text that is broadly written. After all, the one thing we know with certainty about the intentions of the members of Congress who proposed the amendment and the state legislators who ratified it is that every single one of them voted to adopt the text that became law. Surely it lies within the range of reasonableness to believe that a significant number of the adopters of the Fourteenth Amendment understood that they were adopting broad language in the grand style of the Constitution, knowing that similarly broad words had been and would continue to be the starting points for development of important bodies of judge-made constitutional law. When they chose to express the new constitutional rights of equal citizenship in general "language capable for growth,"[33] they left to future generations, and in particular to the judges of the future, responsibility for articulating the meanings of equal citizenship in their times.

What has changed in the century since the adoption of the Fourteenth Amendment is not the principle of equal citizenship, but the idea of what it means to be a fully participating member of our society. Charles Fairman has written: "The conception [of privileges of citizenship] is not static. As the nation experiences change—in its transportation, commerce and industry—in its political practices—in the way in which people live and work and move about—the expectations they entertain about the quality of American life—surely the privilege of membership in this national community must broaden to include what has become essential under prevailing circumstances."[34] Seen in this light, the Supreme Court's decision in *Brown v. Board of Education* fits comfortably into our generation's understanding of the substantive meaning of equal citizenship.

The early fate of the equal citizenship guarantee, however, was inauspicious. Its very existence was suppressed by an unsympathetic judiciary within fifteen years after the Fourteenth Amendment was ratified. Like the hero of a Victorian novel, equal citizenship has returned in our time to reclaim its rightful place among our constitutional principles. But before recounting that doctrinal happy ending, we must look at other chapters, beginning with the one in which the Supreme Court left the infant principle on a cottage doorstep.

Judicial Neglect and the Persistence of Racial Caste

When it first encountered the Fourteenth Amendment in 1873, in the *Slaughter-House Cases*, the Court by a narrow majority rejected the notion that there was substantive content in the amendment's declaration of citizenship or the privileges and immunities clause. The case was an unlikely vehicle for the defense of the citizenship rights that had occupied center stage in the debate over the Fourteenth Amendment. It involved not a claim to racial equality but a claim that a state could not constitutionally create a private monopoly in the slaughtering trade. The independent butchers who challenged the monopoly statute relied mainly on the privileges and immunities clause, and the Court was not blind to the implications of their argument. If section 1 of the Fourteenth Amendment were a general guarantee of the rights of citizens against their states, as the butchers contended, then under the enforcement power granted in section 5 Congress could legislate to govern "the entire domain of civil rights."[35] To embrace this argument would acknowledge that the Fourteenth Amendment had fundamentally changed the relation between the federal government and the states. It was this prospect that alarmed the majority, not the idea that national citizenship had real meaning. So the Court narrowly circumscribed the privileges and immunities clause. It held that the clause guaranteed only the privileges and immunities of national citizenship—most of which, as the majority saw them, were already guaranteed by other provisions of the Constitution. By thus reducing the clause to near redundancy, the Court consigned it to a constitutional limbo where it still abides.

Two dissenting opinions in the *Slaughter-House Cases* argued for an expansive reading of the privileges and immunities clause. Justice Stephen J. Field argued that the clause embraced the full range of fundamental rights which belong to free citizens, but his main concern was the protection of rights in the economic sphere: the ownership of property and the pursuit of one's chosen employment.[36] Justice Joseph P. Bradley's dissent contemplated broader horizons for the scope of the privileges and immunities clause in protecting the rights of citizens. Among the rights so protected against state interference, Bradley saw the whole catalogue of the Bill of Rights. But the antimonopoly context of the case before him caused Bradley to address himself to the issue of equality. It is here that we find the first important judicial expression of the Fourteenth Amendment's repudiation of a system of caste and its adoption of a principle of equality of status among citizens. Bradley wrote in nineteenth century language, but his ideas have a modern sound:

> A citizen of the United States has a perfect constitutional right to go to and reside in any State he chooses, and to claim citizenship therein, and an equality of rights with every other citizen; and the whole power of the nation is pledged to sustain him in that right. He is not bound to cringe to any superior, or to pray for any act of grace, as a means of enjoying all the rights and privileges enjoyed by other citizens. . . . If a man be denied full equality before the law, he is denied one of the essential rights of citizenship as a citizen of the United States.

Enthusiasm for this early articulation of equal citizenship as a Fourteenth Amendment right dwindles when we remember that it was written in defense of equal economic liberties, rather than some other form of equality; "as to social justice, one must not overestimate what it meant to Bradley."[37] A decade later, when Bradley confronted a constitutional claim of racial equality, he had no trouble in rejecting it. Indeed, his opinion for the court in the *Civil Rights Cases* of 1883, concocting the "state action" limitation on the Fourteenth Amendment, sealed the fate of the equal citizenship principle for some seventy years.[38]

The Supreme Court's decision in the *Civil Rights Cases* was the culminating event of the Compromise of 1877. In that political deal, northern Republicans gained the presidency after the disputed election of 1876, in exchange for an agreement that the national government would withdraw federal troops from the South, terminate Reconstruction, and effectively abandon the whole field of southern race relations to state political control—which meant the control of whites.[39] The *Civil Rights Cases* considered a constitutional attack on an 1875 act of Congress—the last civil rights law of the Reconstruction era—prohibiting racial discrimination in "inns, public conveyances on land or water, theatres, and other places of public amusement." When the Supreme Court invalidated the act, interpreting the Civil War amendments narrowly, it fell to the first Justice John Marshall Harlan, writing in lonely dissent, to champion the ideal of equal citizenship.

Under the Thirteenth Amendment, Harlan argued, Congress had power to eradicate the "badges and incidents" of slavery. And because the private

operators of public accommodations exercised "public or quasi-public functions," their exclusion of would-be black patrons on grounds of race was precisely the imposition of a badge of slavery, the mark of an inferior caste.
Harlan's Fourteenth Amendment argument centered on the amendment's
conferral of national citizenship, which embodied "exemption from race discrimination in respect of any civil right belonging to citizens of the white race
in the same State." In enforcing the amendment, Congress could protect this
right of citizenship against private invasion, irrespective of any formal state
involvement.

The *Civil Rights Cases* majority, speaking through Bradley, rejected both
the Harlan arguments. In so doing, they left a doctrinal legacy that severely
restricted the roles of both Congress and the judiciary in enforcing the Civil
War amendments. First, the Court agreed that Congress could enforce the
Thirteenth Amendment against private persons by prohibiting imposition of
the badges and incidents of slavery, but was unwilling to find any such badges
or incidents beyond involuntary servitude itself. Any notion that the amendment was aimed at ending the stigma of inferiority of the freed slaves, or at
treating them as full members of the national community, was simply waved
away. Next the Court concluded that the prohibitions of the Fourteenth
Amendment standing alone, absent an enforcing act of Congress, applied
only to "state action" that denied due process, or equal protection, or the
privileges or immunities of national citizenship. The idea of a private invasion of these rights was not merely dismissed but was treated as a logical
impossibility, like a five-sided square. Blacks might have a right of equal access to public accommodations, but any such right was founded on state law;
the only national interest in such matters was to make sure that a state did
not discriminate on racial grounds in enforcing any rights of access that state
law might provide. If a state legislature should, for example, abolish the common law duty of innkeepers and common carriers to serve all comers—which
a number of southern legislatures did—that was no concern of the nation
unless the legislators were so unsophisticated as to write the law in racially
discriminatory terms.

Finally, the Court held that the power of Congress to enforce the Fourteenth Amendment was limited by the same "state action" doctrine. Congress
could adopt "corrective legislation . . . for counteracting the effect of State
laws, or State action, prohibited by the Fourteenth Amendment," but that
was all. The second and third holdings, establishing the "state action" limitations, were soon extended to the Fifteenth Amendment's prohibition against
denial or abridgement of the right to vote on account of race.

This restrictive view of the Civil War amendments fails to make the connection between the amendments and their history. Frederick Douglass saw the point clearly when he criticized the *Civil Rights Cases* decision in an impassioned speech. The 1875 act, he said, had told all Americans "that they belonged to a common country and were equal citizens."[40] For the newly freed slaves to be citizens—to be respected participants in the society—much more was needed than the abolition of slavery, narrowly defined. To disable Congress from intervening to protect their claims to full citizenship severely hampered their ability to achieve that status. Furthermore, as Justice Harlan saw, civic belonging implies access to all those activities and places in the community's public life—whether or not they are managed directly by government—that are normally open to the public at large.

As Arthur Kinoy has compellingly demonstrated, the right of black people to free and equal membership in the national political community is something special; it "is *not* identical to the general right of all citizens not to be arbitrarily discriminated against." In other words, the Civil War amendments were not a general charter for active judicial supervision of the fairness of all legislative distinctions. Rather they sought to abolish distinctions of caste by establishing a particular substantive right: the right to equality of status in relation to one's fellow citizens. "Citizenship in this country," Justice Harlan wrote in his *Civil Rights Cases* dissent, "necessarily implies at least equality of civil rights among citizens of every race in the same State."

From time to time during the early years of the Fourteenth Amendment's history, the Court did recognize the equal citizenship principle, either implicitly[41] or, as in *Strauder v. West Virginia*, explicitly. In the *Strauder* opinion of 1880, Justice William Strong referred repeatedly to the status of citizenship that had been newly recognized for blacks and concluded that the exclusion of blacks from jury service was inconsistent with this status because it was "practically a brand upon them, . . . an assertion of their inferiority." But such occasions were as scattered showers on a desert, and even *Strauder* shows how limited was the early judicial conception of equal citizenship. The Court took for granted that jury service could be limited to males, for example.

As for racial equality—the one goal of the equal citizenship principle acknowledged by the *Slaughter-House Cases* majority and vindicated in *Strauder*—the Court's decisions can only be characterized as a betrayal. Thirteen years after the *Civil Rights Cases* radically restricted the guarantee of racial equality to "state action," narrowly conceived, the Court subjected even that diminished guarantee to the specious qualification of the "separate but equal" formula. In 1896 *Plessy v. Ferguson* upheld a Louisiana law commanding railroads to segregate their passengers by race. The constitutional challenge to the law centered on its denial of equal citizenship, its use of race as an official label that denied citizens their common enjoyment of a public facility.[42] For the majority, Justice Henry B. Brown dismissed Homer Plessy's Fourteenth Amendment claim in language that will be long remembered in the annals of hypocrisy: "We consider the underlying fallacy of the plaintiff's arguments to consist in the assumption that the enforced separation of the two races stamps the colored race with a badge of inferiority. If this be so, it is not by reason of anything found in the act, but solely because the colored race chooses to put that construction upon it." Given this stamp of approval, the practice that had begun with railroad cars rapidly grew into the systematic segregation of the races throughout Southern public life. Slavery was gone, the Black Codes were gone, but black people remained relegated to a subordinate racial caste.[43]

For the next half-century, decisions of the Supreme Court vindicating the claims of blacks to full and equal membership in the national community were depressingly few and far between. Yet even at the nadir of the Fourteenth Amendment jurisprudence, a current of judicial opinion kept alive the idea that the amendment contained a guarantee of equal citizenship. Dissenting in *Plessy*, the elder Harlan returned to the theme of his *Civil Rights Cases* dissent: "[I]n view of the Constitution, in the eye of the law, there is in this country no superior, dominant, ruling class of citizens. There is no caste here. Our Constitution is color-blind, and neither knows nor tolerates classes among citizens. In respect of civil rights, all citizens are equal before the law." The Warren Court, in other words, did not invent the idea of equal citizenship, but recognized that its time had come.

five

Citizenship, Race, and Culture

Jim Crow was a southern system, deeply embedded in a culture permeated with the influences of slavery. Northern and western whites, focusing on that cultural connection, often have been ready to assume a posture of self-righteousness as they contemplate the white South. Yet, just as Gunnar Myrdal recognized that the main locus of "the Negro problem" has always been the hearts of white people, northerners and westerners need to recognize that the cultural foundations for racial subordination are planted all over the land. The South, to be sure, has provided the nation's most intense experience of racism's destructive effects. But racial segregation in America was born in the North, and when Jim Crow established itself in the South, it did so with the acquiescence—indeed, the connivance—of the rest of the country.

The Civil War amendments of the Constitution promised to redefine the American civic culture to rid it of the ideology of white supremacy. Yet the way in which northern whites came to make that promise suggests that they had only a shallow commitment to racial equality. The abolition of slavery was not the Union's initial objective in the war but had to be taken seriously when slaves by the thousands crossed into Union territory. Once the Union army appreciated the potential contributions of black laborers and soldiers, their continued slave status was out of the question. Later, the army itself became the instrument of freedom as it drove into the South. When Abraham Lincoln issued the Emancipation Proclamation, he did so as commander-in-chief of the armed forces in the name of military necessity.[1] Nonetheless, his proclamation had the symbolic importance of transforming the North's war goals. The political aim of restoring the Union was transmuted into the more idealistic aim of vindicating the ideology of freedom that had long been part of the American civic culture. "What had commenced as a police action had been converted into a crusade."[2] By the time the Thirteenth Amendment permanently abolished slavery in 1865, abolition was no longer controversial in the North.

As a direct result of the momentum generated by emancipation, another old American ideal—equality—was added to the mix of war aims. After the war radical Republicans found allies in a northern business community that feared the possible effects of a Democratic South on the economic order established during the war while the southern states were outside the Union.[3] In the flush of radical Reconstruction, the Fourteenth Amendment was adopted, with its confirmation of citizenship for black people and its generalized promises of equality and the privileges and immunities of citizenship. Those guarantees undoubtedly reflected the egalitarian purposes of some of the amendment's framers.[4] To others, the promises had appeal because they looked like a punishment of the South.[5] However, the Fourteenth Amendment, and the civil rights laws it validated, also promised an egalitarian revolution in northern society. To succeed, the revolution would have to involve "such unpredictable and biased people as hotel clerks, railroad conductors, steamboat stewards, theater ushers, real estate agents, and policemen."[6] For a great many northern whites, the long-standing perception of blacks as the cultural Other was—again—intensified by anxieties about economic concerns. Fears of black competition in the labor market had produced northern race riots during the war, and those fears were not dispelled by the formal declaration of equal citizenship.

The ideal of full racial equality went against the grain of white society and culture in the North as well as the South. Even as the Fourteenth Amendment was being ratified, not many white northerners thought the freed slaves were entitled to immediate access to the vote. When Reconstruction forced black suffrage on the South in 1868, only five states in the North had embraced the same principle. What carried the Fifteenth Amendment through to ratification in 1870 was the worry of Republicans and northern business leaders that the South, once readmitted to the Union, would swamp Congress with Democrats if southern blacks did not vote.[7] By 1877, both Republican political advantage and the northern business advantage appeared to lie in a reconciliation of North and South—that is, the white North and the white South. In the course of that reconciliation, white northerners abandoned both Reconstruction and the freed slaves with little visible sign of regret from either hotel clerks or Supreme Court Justices.

After the war the freed slaves had moved into roles designed by whites: in agriculture; in urban occupations; in state governments; in institutions of northern sponsorship, such as the schools of the Freedmen's Bureau.[8] In short, "blacks in the South during Reconstruction were becoming the most American of Americans."[9] Then, one by one, southern state governments reverted to the control of the white conservatives known as *redeemers*. The Compromise of 1877, in which northern Republicans secured the presidency in exchange for ending military Reconstruction, simply ratified a "redemption" that had already begun. When the Union forces pulled out, blacks began a steady forced disengagement from the public life of white society. By the end of the 1880s, the term *radical* in the South had acquired a new and sinister meaning, referring to a political mentality that was to dominate the South until World War I—a mentality looking forward to a society in which blacks had no place at all.[10]

Even before the rise of the Jim Crow laws, black people had been largely excluded from the institutions and the public life of southern communities. To some blacks, segregation seemed a modest improvement: segregated access looked better than none.[11] Jim Crow legislation began in a small way with railroad cars,[12] but, after the Supreme Court's validation of the separate but equal principle, it quickly burgeoned into a new form of racial caste system that pervaded southern society and culture. Two generations of southern blacks and whites would grow to adulthood before law would be used as an effective instrument to reshape the culture and create a more inclusive community.

The Culture of Subordination

By the time World War I began, southern Jim Crow laws extended from disenfranchisement to prohibitions on interracial marriage. The laws imposed racial segregation in schools, courtrooms, restaurants, hotels, theaters, parks, streetcars—virtually every place where people of both races might interact in the community's public life. Private racial discrimination also played an indispensable part in maintaining the caste system, producing segregation in housing, employment, and public accommodations. The subordination of blacks was not a by-product of some other policy; Jim Crow's essential purpose was the relegation of blacks to a subordinate racial caste.[13]

The private behavior that interlocked with governmental policy was more than a matter of custom or convention; it crystallized into ritual, symbolizing the avoidance of "contamination" of white society by contact with "impurity." The taboo against interracial marriage was written into law, but the concern for social distance between blacks and whites went much further, requiring a series of rituals that had originated in the taboos associated with slavery. Whites must not shake hands with blacks; whites must call blacks by their first names rather than Mr. or Mrs. Whites and blacks could not live in the same houses except when the blacks were domestic servants. Indeed, a middle-class white was supposed to receive a black person only at the back door. Blacks in line at the post office were supposed to stand aside and allow whites to go ahead of them. In the culture of racial subordination, every little movement had a meaning all its own.[14]

These demands were imposed on whites and blacks alike; for a white to recognize a black as a social equal was at least as much of a transgression as for a black to claim equal status. Every middle-class white was expected to police the status boundary and to correct backsliders of both races. Just as the patrol had kept a night watch during the era of slavery, now night riders in hoods imposed their own summary punishment for offenses against the system of subordination. The system survived the return of black war veterans in 1918 and also survived the first great migration of southern blacks to northern cities. It gave no important sign of crumbling until the eve of World War II. The sources of the system's strength lay in the centrality of race in defining personal identity and status. Jim Crow had begun in fear, and it thrived on fear.

At the outset both national politics and economic decline fed southern white fears. The election of 1888 swept Republicans back into national office amid charges of Democratic corruption in southern elections. Bills before Congress proposed federal supervisors to assure the fairness of federal elections. Another bill proposed federal financial aid to local education, including the education of black children. Blacks were still being appointed to federal jobs in southern states. The 1880s and 1890s brought economic recession and then full-scale depression with dire consequences for southern agriculture. Many good farms remained in the possession of black renters, who were now subjected to terrorism designed to force them to give way to whites. Not coincidentally, the populist movement began to attract support in the South.[15] Southern conservatives deflected the advance of populism by making an alliance with the racial radicals under the banner of white supremacy.

This political plan succeeded famously, accomplishing the complete disenfranchisement and thorough subordination of black people[16]—all with the full cooperation of the southern branch of a movement that called itself progressive. The Jim Crow laws swept the South, going to lengths that would be laughable if their cumulative results were not tragic: separate sections in Birmingham's ball park, separate pay windows for textile workers in South Carolina, separate phone booths in Oklahoma, separate Bibles for witnesses in Atlanta courtrooms.[17]

The most chilling feature of the Jim Crow system was its enforcement through violence. The first great wave of lynchings of black men crested in 1889: "In the 1890s in fourteen Southern states, an average of 138 persons was lynched each year and roughly 75 percent of the victims were black."[18] By the turn of the century lynching was complemented by rioting in which white mobs inflicted violence on blacks indiscriminately—usually after a period of radical agitation. Between the late 1880s and the end of World War II nearly four thousand blacks were killed by southern white mobs.[19] Like the northern race riots during the Civil War, the southern violence against blacks resulted primarily from white anxieties. But now the anxieties went deeper than any economic concerns.

The picture of black people as lesser beings, which had provided psychic support for slavery, was given a new focus in the 1890s in the white southern image of "the black beast rapist." As Joel Williamson has shown, the new image was more than a rationalization for white supremacy; it also gave white males a way to reassure themselves of their masculine identity.[20] In the traditional families that prevailed in the white South, men were supposed to be the providers and protectors, women the passive vessels of purity and piety. This idealization of abstract womanhood is entirely compatible with the belief that individual white women are, if not untouchable, at least not especially inclined toward being touched.[21] The possibilities in this situation for guilt or sexual tension or both are thoroughly plumbed in the novels of William Faulkner and need no elaboration here.[22]

The same economic decline that deprived many white men of the satisfactions or providing for their families also produced the politically inspired scapegoating that gave lower-class whites their "permissions-to-hate."[23] Every episode of white terrorism against black farmers provided a new lesson in the legitimacy of violence against blacks. Radicals trumpeted that crime among black men was increasing rapidly. There may have been truth in the charge, given that poor blacks as well as poor whites had been dispossessed by the depression. But the crimes that captured the radical mind were black-white sexual assault and rape: "it was this threat that thrust deeply into the psychic core of the South, searing the white soul, marking the character of the southern mind radically and leaving it crippled and hobbled in matters of race long after the mark itself was lost from sight."[24]

Myths of black sexuality have gripped the European and white American mind since the earliest European explorations of Africa.[25] The gruesome manner in which many a black man, accused of raping a white woman, was killed and mutilated by a lynching party served, of course, to terrorize other blacks. But surely it also served as a primitive ritual celebrating both white male power and the repression of white men's own negative identities as revealed in their "darker" impulses.[26] Even the lynching of an innocent man would serve to keep black men generally "in their place," avoiding any dealings with white women that might suggest a wish to cross the race barrier, even avoiding eye contact with white women.[27] For a black man to behave otherwise was not just a social transgression; it was a threat to many a white man's sense of identity within the culture of subordination.

For black women Jim Crow reinforced patterns of life established in the era of slavery. They were expected to serve as the center of domestic life and also to work to support the family—field work in rural sharecropping families, wage work in the towns. Especially when they worked for whites as domestic servants, they were vulnerable to the sexual harassments and assaults of white men. They coped, as black women in America have always coped, by providing mutual support in networks of kin and friends. But, as Jacqueline Jones has shown in her vivid and moving social history of black women, it was a labor of sorrow as well as a labor of love.[28]

In another perspective Jim Crow was "a categorical barrier on growing up,"[29] with blackness the category's identifying mark. Blacks could earn limited respect from whites, but only so long as they stayed within the confines of the role their blackness defined. The role implied not only a nonreciprocal deference to whites[30] but strict limits on individual advancement and prestige. In other words, the racial caste system was directly antithetical to the individualist tradition of the American civic culture. One reason why whites have feared blacks—and not just in the South—begins in every American's understanding that racial subordination is inconsistent with the nation's deeply held values of individual freedom and equality. Our civic culture is, among other things, a constant stream of messages encouraging individuals to take action to advance their conditions and those of their families. Blacks living inside the Jim Crow system were not insulated from those messages, and yet they were denied the opportunity to act on them. For some, the frustration culminated in violence. The black beast rapist was a myth, but black violence against whites was enough of a reality to give whites something they could reasonably fear. That fear, however, surely was heightened by guilt. Having employed violence to exclude black people from access to the core values of the American civic culture, how could whites not fear retaliation?[31] The cycle was thus completed: white subordination of blacks, enforced by violence; black frustration and anger; black violence against whites; white fears; further violent repression of blacks.

The economic dependency of southern blacks on whites, even after emancipation and after the invalidation of the Black Codes, had been promoted by the agency that was supposed to preside over their liberation, the Freedmen's

Bureau.[32] This dependency was exacerbated by Jim Crow's multifold restrictions, both governmental and nongovernmental. As Chief Justice Warren eventually recognized in his *Brown* opinion, the law had its own demoralizing effects. Justice Louis Brandeis once remarked that government is "the potent, the omnipresent teacher, teaching the whole people by its example."[33] The lesson taught to blacks by the Jim Crow laws was a lesson in self-deprecation and powerlessness, and the Supreme Court's response was to leave the whole system to a local politics reserved for whites.[34]

Migration out of the South offered a relief that was only partial. Not only did the black migrants take their disadvantages with them, but they also encountered racism. The first large-scale black migration from the rural South to the urban North took place between 1910 and 1930. Immigration from Europe and Asia had dwindled to its lowest volume in generations, partly because of World War I and partly because Congress had severely restricted immigration. Accordingly, masses of unskilled blacks arrived in northern cities just as the native white populations perceived that the threat of "inundation" by foreigners was receding. As soon as they arrived, the black migrants encountered discrimination in the labor market.[35] The white North and West retained the same attitudes about racial inferiority that had permitted northerners to bargain away the rights of black people at the Constitutional Convention and in the Compromise of 1877.

In 1891, when Georgia enacted a Jim Crow law governing railroad cars and streetcars, a Chicago newspaper commented, "A state cursed with such a legislative body almost deserves commiseration."[36] But northerners, including Chicagoans, had little reason for self-congratulation. The Illinois constitution of 1848 had included a provision forbidding black immigration into the state. This clause was specifically approved by the voters of Illinois by more than a two-thirds vote. A similar state constitutional provision was adopted in Oregon by a vote of eight to one. The leading decision upholding school segregation before the Civil War had borne the name *Roberts v. Boston*.[37] In California, the school districts of Orange County continued to segregate Mexican American school children until 1947, when a federal court of appeals ruled the practice invalid. The ground for the decision is itself depressing: the court held that the California statute did not authorize the segregation of Chicano children for it required only the segregation of children who were Indian, Chinese, Japanese, and Mongolian. Dick Gregory put a wry smile on the whole dismal story when he said to white northern audiences in the 1960s: "Down South, they don't care how close I get, so long as I don't get too big: up here, you don't care how big I get, so long as I don't get too close."

In response to subordination various reactions are possible. One is to take on the attitudes of the oppressor. Stigma's cruelest harm is seen in the "self-fulfilling prophecy" that translates into lives that are caricatures of the oppressor's negative stereotypes.[38] For one trivial but revealing example, in the years before World War II many blacks, North and South, set a great store by lightness of complexion.[39] Another response to subordination is apathy and withdrawal. Still another is aggression, either covert or overt. Those who feel powerless in many dimensions of their lives may seek other ways to assert that they count for something. In its overt forms, black aggression simply reinforced the psychic foundations of the culture of subordination: one good fear deserves another.

Politics, Law, and Cultural Redefinition

Quite a different response to Jim Crow was the determination of blacks to work toward ending the system. Early in the twentieth century three avenues of black self-help contended for support; each was personified in an individual. "Washington, Du Bois, and Garvey. These are the big three for our century."[40] First came the separate-development approach of Booker T. Washington, emphasizing "bootstraps" programs in education and economic development and deferring until later the pursuit of political power and social equality. Based in the deep South, where lynching was a persistent reality, Washington rejected confrontation for diplomacy.

W. E. B. Du Bois, along with other blacks based in the North, grew increasingly critical of Washington's accommodationist positions.[41] Their Niagara movement eventually joined forces with the NAACP, an interracial group then led by whites. Du Bois became the NAACP's director of research and edited the association's journal, *The Crisis*.[42] Du Bois and the NAACP advocated political action for full equality in all aspects of American society, North and South. Although Du Bois felt a strong affinity with black Africa and believed that blacks should never lose the sense of blackness that made them a community, the NAACP program looked forward to a society in which black people were fully included because race had become irrelevant to citizenship.

In its early days the association also confronted the explicit black nationalism of Marcus Garvey. Garvey, also based in the North, denounced integration and interracial marriage and urged blacks to "return" to Africa. He scorned Du Bois and other black leaders and found his main support among blacks who were the poorest of all.[43] Garvey shared with Du Bois an awareness that black people needed to replace the skepticism, frustration, and resentment produced by domination with a revitalized sense of pride. Yet, as the young Du Bois knew, political separatism for blacks offered not a community of choice but a community of despair.[44] Although a current of separatism has continued to this day, by the 1920s the NAACP's integrationist strategy no longer faced serious challenge among blacks.

Strategy was one thing; execution, another. In the South the Jim Crow laws would have to go, but even that result would only partially fulfill the promise of full membership in the community. To uproot Jim Crow it would be necessary to challenge white assumptions about racial superiority that had become a central part of southern white identity. For many whites that challenge would be deeply disturbing. On the other hand, it would be no easy task to persuade large numbers of southern blacks to take the risks attendant to stirring up those anxieties. People who are badly demoralized do not readily join movements for social change. In the North and West the target was more elusive. Generally, racial discrimination was not written into law but simply was one acculturated form of behavior of countless individuals from employers to teachers to real estate agents to barbers. A major task of the black leadership was the raising of consciousness among both blacks and whites, both North and South. White people would have to learn to understand, and black people would have to learn to believe.

The cycle of fear and hostility is a plague that has often visited human societies, particularly multicultural ones.[45] To allay fear by controlling hostility is the oldest function of law. The middle-class black Americans who sought to end the deadly cycle of the culture of subordination turned their hopes to the law. What could law contribute? How might law be mobilized? Whatever the answers to these questions might be, by around 1915 it was clear that the effort to redefine the law governing race relations would have to be based in the North, where America's black leadership and black political strength now were concentrated, and where at least some decision makers might be sympathetic. The NAACP leadership sought changes in law through both legislative politics and litigation, and they saw the two as interconnected. When they used litigation as a means of political mobilization they followed an example set a century earlier by antislavery lawyers in the North.[46]

An early NAACP political goal, blocked for decades by southerners in Congress, was the enactment of a federal antilynching law.[47] Another was federal legislation to effectuate the Fifteenth Amendment's guarantee against denial of the vote to blacks. Both proposals looked beyond their specific objects to the more general purpose of reintroducing the federal government as a continuing presence in the South. At the same time, the association sponsored litigation aimed at overturning some of Jim Crow's most egregious wrongs in the fields of voting, criminal justice, and housing.[48] The NAACP, in other words, put its faith in the enactment of new laws and in a more generous interpretation of existing statutes and the Constitution. As they knew, each of these efforts at lawmaking would reinforce the other. The political campaign and the litigation campaign were aimed at the hearts and minds of both blacks and whites, where racial equality must ultimately be founded.

In the early 1930s the association began a program of litigation to lay a doctrinal foundation for constitutional rulings that eventually would end official segregation.[49] The choice to focus that campaign on segregated education was just one more demonstration of the black leadership's sharing of values with the rest of the country: specifically, Americans' almost mystical belief in the power of schooling. At least some of the leaders also held the belief—today we must call it a hope still seeking realization—that regular human contact between black and white children would dispel the fears that underlay the culture of subordination and dissolve the distance that served to perpetuate fears.[50] The litigation project bore its first fruits with the Supreme Court's 1938 decision validating Lloyd Gaines's claim to attend the University of Missouri's law school and a lower court decision in 1940 validating Melvin Alston's claim that Virginia's salary differentials for white and black teachers were unconstitutional.[51] Yet neither decision repudiated the separate but equal doctrine.

By the 1940s some southern whites correctly perceived that the foundations of the racial caste system were weakening. For more than half a century Jim Crow had prevailed over the integrating influences of formal citizenship, a common language, and shared religious traditions. Now, however, much more was ranged against the system. The number of educated black people had increased considerably in the South and elsewhere in the country. Even in the South, the number of black voters had edged upward.[52] An economy of nationwide scope was now an accepted fact of life, along with a new concentration of power in the federal government. National radio networks now brought the same news and the same entertainment to the whole country. If a nationwide program like "Amos 'n Andy" reinforced negative racial stereotypes, the next program might bring into southern living rooms—in black homes as well as white ones—the pathbreaking music of Duke Ellington or the news of a New Deal antidiscrimination measure. In 1942, when his treatise on race relations went to press, Gunnar Myrdal wrote, "the main thing happening to the South is that it is becoming *Americanized.*"[53] In North and South alike, the American civic culture's core values of liberty and equality were speaking in a more insistent voice to all Americans, black and white.

World War II accelerated the flow of power to the national government. The war also produced a second great migration; again large numbers of southern blacks moved to the North and West, where they did vote—and voted Democratic. A concomitant of this increased political participation was the national government's new solicitude for racial equality. In 1941 black leaders headed by A. Philip Randolph, chief of the Brotherhood of Sleeping Car Porters, threatened a mass march on Washington unless President Roosevelt took action against racially discriminatory hiring by the federal government and by businesses dealing with the government. In response (and, it appears, with a timely nudge from Eleanor Roosevelt) the president established the government's first fair employment practices committee.[54] The war also produced its share of propaganda: specifically, that we were fighting against the Nazis and their hateful theories of racial superiority. (This particular bit of preachment had a bitter flavor for the people of Japanese ancestry who were uprooted from their West coast homes and "relocated" in camps in the interior.)[55] Shortly after the war, President Truman ordered the integration of the armed forces.

At war's end the time was ripe for the federal government to lead a major national reassessment of race relations. When Congress defaulted, the Supreme Court responded. Between 1945 and 1950 the Court made a number of rulings that would have been impossible to predict in 1935. The Court reinterpreted a Reconstruction statute to make it a federal crime for a local sheriff to beat a black prisoner to death.[56] Without confronting the question whether *Plessy v. Ferguson*[57] should be overruled, it held that racial segregation of passengers on an interstate bus unconstitutionally burdened interstate commerce.[58] It held unconstitutional the judicial enforcement of covenants in deeds restricting residential property to whites.[59] Most portentous of all for the NAACP's campaign against school segregation, it held that various state universities' attempts to satisfy the separate but equal formula in supplying facilities for black graduate students had failed the test of the equal protection clause.[60]

From *Brown v. Board of Education* forward, the Justices of the Warren Court showed their awareness of interactions of the Court's decisions with congressional behavior and with the larger political environment. First, the pace of enforcement of school desegregation was dictated by the Justices' perception of politics, not by the practicalities of the enforcement process. Some measure of delay, already accepted in principle at the time of *Brown I* (1954), was embodied in the "all deliberate speed" remedial formula of *Brown II* (1955). In the late 1960s, when the Justices finally discarded all deliberate speed and insisted on the desegregation of southern schools "at once," the political climate for civil rights had changed markedly.[61] That change was evident in a civil rights movement spurred by *Brown* itself, and in the Congress's adoption of major civil rights laws in 1964 and 1965. Second, the Court protected the freedom of expression of the civil rights movement against a broad-scale attack by southern states and local governments.[62] Third, when Congress did enact civil rights laws, the Court moved with alacrity to sustain them—thus precluding the possibility that lower court judges would impede enforcement by holding that the laws exceeded congressional powers. The 1964 and 1965 acts were both upheld within a matter of months of their enactment.[63]

If, at midcentury, unimaginable rulings had become imaginable, the reason was not the discovery of new doctrinal arguments. The arguments for racial equality in these cases had been addressed to the Court repeatedly from the time the Fourteenth Amendment was adopted. What made the new decisions possible was a change in the climate of northern white opinion, particularly among decision-making elites, concerning race relations. The politicians who signed the "Southern Manifesto" in 1956 were wrong in accusing the Supreme Court of twisting the Constitution to fit the latest sociological theory.[64] Rather, the Justices who decided *Brown v. Board of Education* perceived the Fourteenth Amendment's guarantee of liberty and equality in the way every one of us perceives: through the filters created by the perceiver's acculturating experience. The Justices understood that the whole system of racial segregation was a betrayal of the central values of American civic culture. And political action, from the Niagara movement to the threatened march on Washington, had helped the Justices to understand.

Citizenship, Culture, and "Private" Behavior

If *Brown v. Board of Education* reflected a change in the American civic culture, it also generated further changes. *Brown* was the Supreme Court's most important decision of the twentieth century. Today it stands as much more than a decision about schools, or even a decision about segregation.

Brown is our leading authoritative symbol for the principle that the Constitution forbids a system of caste.

The decision also served as a catalyst for further political action. Rosa Parks wouldn't move to the back of the bus,[65] and the Montgomery bus boycott of 1955–56 was followed by countless sit-ins and freedom rides and voting rights marches, all designed to dramatize the wrongs of Jim Crow and the possibilities for political and social change.[66] Congress responded, first with limited voting rights measures and eventually with the 1964 and 1965 acts. Both of these laws have had far-reaching effects, and it is unlikely that either law could have been enacted in anything like its eventual form if the *Brown* case had been decided the other way. Finally, *Brown* and the civil rights movement called into question the constitutionality and the political legitimacy of a wide range of systems of dominance and dependence, fostering movements for the liberation of other subordinated groups. Here, however, we are focusing on the interplay of legislative politics, direct action, and constitutional litigation in the campaign to transform Jim Crow's culture of subordination into a new and more inclusive community of meaning.

If the law is a teacher, its instructional techniques include both precept and example. The recognition of the equal citizenship of all Americans would only begin in the abolition of formal legal norms commanding racial discrimination. Ultimately, equal citizenship would have to find a foundation in the sense of whites and blacks that they were part of the same community. Behavior and belief go hand in hand. To end the effects of Jim Crow, black people must not only believe in their equal status but claim it by their actions, and whites must not only accept the idea of racial equality but experience it in their lives. Segregation would not end with the elimination of segregation laws; it would end when blacks and whites came to think nothing of sitting side by side at lunch counters, on buses, and in theaters.

Because Jim Crow was not just a set of laws but a culture, its eradication would require federal law to reach deeply into conduct that was "private"— that is, nongovernmental. The owners and managers of hotels and theaters and restaurants and dime store lunch counters—even those who might be inclined to abandon racial discrimination—felt constrained by the norms of their white patrons to continue that policy. Individual acts of violence against blacks often had gone unpunished, and this tendency was now heightened when white prosecutors and jurors contemplated the victims' connections with the civil rights movement. These private actions, in the aggregate, were a critical part of the behavior that defined the boundaries of community and left black people outside the walls. It may be that "communal membership cannot be commanded by force"; even so, the coercive power of the national government would be needed to tear down the walls, to let the parables of community be heard. [67]

Alexander Bickel sharply criticized the Warren Court for its readiness to "detect the hand of the state in private discriminations," "to circumscribe and displace private ordering, to legalize the society" by displacing private conduct within the reach of federal law. He argued that this vision of "[u]nmitigatedly legalitarian government bears the seed of tyranny."[68] In the context of Jim Crow, this criticism simply misses the mark. For southern blacks, tyranny was no seed, but a vine that would go on choking them until Jim Crow was uprooted. What Bickel called private ordering was an organic part of the system. The problem was not so much that the hand of government was guiding private discrimination; it was that pervasive private discrimination, enforced by private violence, had acquired the influence of a pseudogovernment. Not without reason had the Ku Klux Klan called itself "The Invisible Empire."

Given this "resonance of society and politics"[69] in the racial caste system, it is clear that a Supreme Court committed to effectuating the guarantee of equal citizenship would set about dismantling two doctrines invented by the majority Justices in the *Civil Rights Cases:* a restrictive definition of the badges and incidents of slavery, and the "state action" limitation on the Fourteenth and Fifteenth Amendments. In the quarter century between World War II and the close of the Warren era, the Court very nearly accomplished both tasks. In both areas the Justices constantly evidenced their awareness of the connections between politics and their own doctrinal contributions.

The Court's relaxation of the state action limitation had begun, even before the Warren years, at a natural beginning point: the vindication of voting rights. In a series of cases stretching over three decades, the Supreme Court had effectively rejected the claim of the Democratic party that it was a private group, outside the reach of the Fourteenth and Fifteenth Amendments, and thus could exclude blacks from voting in party primary elections.[70] When the "white primary" cases had run their course, for all practical purposes the state action limitation had disappeared in voting cases, and a doctrinal base had been laid for opening electoral politics to black voters in southern states. Louis Pollak argued that the Fifteenth Amendment, with its specific guarantee of racial equality in voting, should be interpreted without any state action limitation, or alternatively that the amendment imposed an affirmative obligation on a state to eliminate racial discrimination in voting.[71] In this analysis, which amounts to a Fifteenth Amendment version of the principle of equal citizenship, effective participation in elections is inescapably public, even when the state permits part of the electoral process to be managed by nongovernmental organizations. By any test, racial discrimination in the electoral system deeply offends the core citizenship values of respect, responsibility, and participation.

The Supreme Court had further weakened the state action barrier when it held unconstitutional Missouri and Michigan state courts' enforcement of racially restrictive covenants in orders forbidding black families to occupy the homes they had bought.[72] The decision seems irresistibly correct, but the Court's opinion made the case seem to turn on the presence of a court order: the covenants standing alone, the Court said, violated no rights. Here, as in the voting cases, the decision would have rested more comfortably on a doctrine recognizing that the state courts had a positive duty to protect against private racial discrimination that seriously restricted participation in the community's public life. The principle of equal citizenship easily encompasses the state's duty to refuse to enforce racial covenants in deeds.

Once the Supreme Court had extended the principle of *Brown v. Board of Education* to other forms of state-sponsored segregation, it was plain that segregation in privately owned places of public accommodation would soon come under challenge. Here the initiative was taken in 1960 by a handful of black college students in Greensboro, North Carolina, who went to the lunch counter of a five-and-ten-cent store, sat down, and waited to be served. The sit-in demonstration as a form of direct action swept over the South, supplemented by nationwide boycotts of chain stores whose southern branches were refusing food service to blacks.[73] The demonstrators encountered not only violent reprisal[74] but arrest and prosecution under one or another form of criminal trespass statue. When they challenged their convictions on the ground that the state courts were lending support to the private practice of racial discrimination, in violation of the Fourteenth Amendment, the state action issue moved to the center of the constitutional stage.

Now the Supreme Court was being pressed to recognize a wider variety of ways in which private behavior helped maintain the system of racial caste. The students who sat at the lunch counters were not primarily seeking sandwiches, or even the company of white patrons. They sought the dignity of being treated as equals in the community's public spaces. The freedom riders knew that the back of the bus would arrive at the station very soon after the front of the bus, but they had a more spiritual destination. The main question in a segregation case never was the right to sit in a particular place in a courtroom, or a particular place on the beach. Assuredly, though, the central issue raised by segregation was one of place—the place of blacks in society.

Did black people belong to the community as equal citizens, or were they to continue to be stigmatized as inferior?

Long before, in his speech lamenting the Supreme Court's *Civil Rights Cases* decision, Frederick Douglass had clearly seen the connections between citizenship and access to hotels and railroads and theaters.[75] To erase segregation in public buildings and public recreation areas would touch only part of the system maintaining white supremacy. Even that much of an exertion of federal judicial power to redefine the membership in local communities was under fierce political attack, yet the Justices understood that it would not be enough to destroy only the governmental foundations for Jim Crow.

The Warren Court's solution to this doctrinal dilemma was to discover "public functions" and "significant state involvement" in various kinds of connections between the states and private racial discrimination—some connections that were obvious and others that were more tenuous.[76] Although the majority Justices were criticized for failing to detail the factors that would bring the Constitution to bear on private activity,[77] the Court did make clear the importance of a contextual view the state action problem: "Only by sifting facts and weighing circumstances can the nonobvious involvement of the state in private conduct be attributed its true significance."[78] Seen whole and seen in context, some private acts had disastrous public consequences, denying citizens full participation in public life. The consistent pattern of decisions carried a message that was clear enough: the Court was going to find significant state involvement when private behavior was part of the systematic exclusion of blacks from the community of equal citizens.

During the last few years of the Warren Court, the erosion of the state action limitation accelerated. Indeed, the Court appeared to be only a few steps away from explicit recognition of the states' responsibility to protect against various forms of private racial discrimination. A number of commentators, hearing only the faintest of heartbeats, stood poised to announce the departure of the judge-made doctrine that had previously been so effective a barrier to the achievement of equal citizenship for Americans who were members of racial minorities.[79] As it happened, however, the moribund doctrine was revived.

It was Congress's vindication of claims to racial equality that made it unnecessary for the Warren Court to finish off the state action limitation to the Fourteenth Amendment. When the 1964 sit-in cases were decided, the Justices knew that the most important civil rights bill since Reconstruction was on the verge of enactment. Part of that bill, which became the Civil Rights

Act of 1964, established a statutory right to equal treatment in virtually all public accommodations that mattered. So the Court could afford to temporize still further, reversing trespass convictions on the basis of slender connections between the states and the privately owned places of public resort. The Court thus managed—again—to avoid the question whether the Fourteenth Amendment, in the absence of congressional legislation, imposed constitutional responsibilities on a state that enforced a restaurant owner's decision to exclude black patrons.

Even the Justices who would have answered that question negatively suggested that Congress could enforce the Fourteenth Amendment by forbidding private racial discrimination. And in 1966 the Court hinted broadly that it was prepared to uphold congressional power to enact virtually any civil rights measure for which a political majority could be mustered—including the power to regulate private racial discrimination under the Fourteenth Amendment.[80] Congress was just beginning to respond to this invitation when the Court discovered an alternative source of this power in the Thirteenth Amendment. The Justices reached back eighty-five years to accept the elder Harlan's view that even private racial discrimination was a "badge of slavery" that Congress could remove.[81]

The commentators who foresaw the imminent demise of the state action limitation on the Fourteenth Amendment did not misread the Warren Court's opinions; rather, they failed to anticipate changes in the composition of the Court. After 1970 a new majority restored the vigor of the doctrine, sharply restricting the effect of Warren Court state action precedents and even overruling one of them. These opinions, not coincidentally, abandoned the Warren Court's contextual view of facts and circumstances in favor of disaggregation: look separately at each argued connection between the state and the challenged private action and reject that argument as insufficient.[82] Yet, with rare exceptions, the decisions restoring the state action limitation to its former inglories have not involved racial discrimination. Leroy Irvis's case against the Moose Lodge[83] was one of those exceptional cases. It is a textbook illustration of the way in which judges who are focused on concerns about the autonomy of private ordering can ignore—or evade—a citizen's claim to inclusion in the community's public life.

The first Justice Harlan, dissenting in the *Civil Rights Cases*, had agreed that the Fourteenth Amendment did not protect social rights, but argued that rights of access to hotels, theaters, and other public accommodations were properly seen as the legal rights of citizens.[84] The majority accepted the distinction between social and legal equality, but placed the cases in the social category. Today, as we contemplate the interaction of law and other culture-shaping activities, it is harder to separate legal equality from its social context. Even when we focus more narrowly on law itself, it is not useful to draw a sharp distinction between issues of state action and issues of equal protection or between the public and private realms. Early in the Warren years, Harold Horowitz criticized the nineteenth century Supreme Court's invention of the state action limitation in terms that have recently found new vogue: the coercive power of government, after all, underlies all legal rights.[85]

Still, as Harlan the elder and Frederick Douglass understood, the idea of citizenship is centered on relationships in the public sphere of our community life and does accommodate a fair measure of individual autonomy. Of course equal citizenship is flatly inconsistent with the exercise of one kind of autonomy. The behavior that separates people from the community's public life—behavior exemplified by the very conduct at issue in the *Civil Rights Cases*—plainly denies equal citizenship. Just as surely, however, equal citizenship leaves room for an individual's freedom to select his close companions. But the Moose Lodge was about as intimate as a local chapter of the Rotarians or the Jaycees.[86]

During the same period when the Supreme Court has been rebuilding the state action barrier, the Court has repeatedly reaffirmed congressional power to forbid private racial discrimination. For the most part, too, the Court has been committed to a generous interpretation of the federal civil rights acts[87]—at least until now.* Throughout the country today, thanks to the 1964 act, the racial integration of places of public accommodation is an accomplished fact. In the South the status of black people as equal citizens is reaffirmed and given new legitimacy every day, not only by the integration of publicly operated buses and airports and courtrooms, but by the daily, routine presence of black patrons in privately owned hotels and restaurants. If *Brown* and its successor decisions and statutes are stitched together as a legitimizing myth, the myth's ultimate enactment is embodied in the behavior of millions of individuals, black and white.

This pattern that emerged in the civil rights era—the circular reinforcement of politics, private attitudes and behavior, and constitutional law—is the

*There is reason to fear that a majority of the Court is now ready to turn away from that commitment. Last spring five Justices invited counsel in a pending case to argue the question whether the precedent of *Runyon v. McCrary* (1976) should be overruled. The *Runyon* decision recognized a right to damages under the 1866 Civil Rights Act for the harms caused by private racial discrimination—in that case, the exclusion of black children from a "segregation academy." If those five Justices should follow through on this threat, then it will, indeed, be appropriate to start speaking of "the Reagan Court."

modern analogue of the "resonance of society and politics" during the heyday of Jim Crow. To recognize this resemblance is merely to acknowledge that any statement about behavioral patterns or beliefs or politics or law is an exercise in abstracting parts out of a cultural whole; one sort of statement differs from the others mainly in its perspective. If *Brown v. Board of Education* was a critical event in our nation's recent cultural redefinition, it was still just part of a larger process.

Yet in the American civic culture there is something special about constitutional law, something that makes it an appropriate object for particularized contemplation, even as we recognize its connections with politics and with private beliefs and behavior. The "something special" is bound up with the ideal of principled decision. Some delay in enforcement was the price of the initial *Brown* decision—not just unanimity, but the decision itself—and it is arguable that the price was not excessive.[88] When we return to the subject of principle, however, I shall argue, with the benefit of hindsight, that "all deliberate speed" was politically inexpedient, mainly because it failed the test of principle.[89] For the better part of two centuries the Supreme Court has been a major contributor of the meanings that define and redefine the American civic culture. An important part of the Court's influence on that process is the public perception that the Court aspires to the ideal of decision according to law.

No doubt race relations in America eventually would have undergone fundamental changes whatever the Supreme Court might have done in the 1950s and 1960s. Still, it is proper to credit the Warren Court's decisions on racial equality for reviving the principle of equal citizenship, and thus formally redefining our national community. When Earl Warren retired from the Chief Justiceship in 1969, a new generation of constitutional issues remained to be addressed, as efforts to remedy the harms of racial subordination were carried beyond the recognition of formal equality. In today's perspective those issues, which I examine in later chapters, seem difficult and divisive. But in 1954 *Brown v. Board of Education* seemed even more difficult, even more divisive. As Martin Luther King, Jr., reminded us shortly before he was martyred, we had to climb a mountain in order to see that other ascents lay ahead.

six

Nativism and the
Paths to Belonging

At any given time we can identify, with rough accuracy, groups in American society that are cast in the roles of outsiders. Yet all such generalizations must be qualified. Apart from sex differences, the boundaries defining social groups are always indistinct and often in flux. The gradual assimilation of ethnic groups in America is an obvious case in point. Millions of Americans today are full participants in the society's public life, although their grandparents' groups once were excluded. Part of this generational change results from conformity, as young people adopt the values and behavior of the prevailing culture. But part of the change also results from cultural politics: the persistent knocking at the door by cultural minorities who resist exclusion from full membership and whose resistance takes the form of political participation. Consider what it meant to be Irish and Catholic in the America of 1860, and then in 1960, the year John F. Kennedy was elected President.[1] If anything is clear about American society, it is that the definition of who belongs to the national community has always been changing, and that outsider groups frequently have had a say in determining their own acceptance into membership.

Some groups nonetheless have suffered long histories of domination in America. Here we consider some of the ways in which differences in ethnicity, language, and religion have been used to justify separating groups of outsiders from the community's public life or relegating them to subordinate status or forcing them to conform to prevailing models of behavior. The techniques are not mutually exclusive. In our national history, subordinated groups typically have been subjected to all three of these variations on the theme of exclusion from equal citizenship.

This chapter centers on the experience of immigrants and their descendants. But racial discrimination in America began with the subordination of the peoples who were already here when the first immigrants from Europe arrived. There are strong parallels between our society's treatment of the Indians and its treatment of other subordinated groups, and the parallels begin with the way whites assigned Indians to the category of the savage Other. If Indians were savages, then white colonists could see themselves as the vanguard of civilization despite the scarcity of evidence in their own lives of the civilization they had left behind. As the frontier moved West, so did racism—carried, as might be expected, on a tide of white insecurities. The fear of "the Indian"[2] encapsulated those insecurities. A white man might fear his own inadequacy to confront the rigors of frontier life, and in those threatening conditions he might also fear an outbreak of the savage he recognized inside himself. From colonial times to our own times, the history of the Indian nations is a chronicle of virtually unrelieved tragedy: disposession, extermination, and government policies wavering between forced assimilation and forced segregation—all rationalized by assumptions of the racial superiority of whites.[3]

I leave the story of our law's contributions to these sad developments to those who are qualified to tell it. The special status of American Indians has produced an intricate and highly specialized body of law.[4] Furthermore, the separation of the Indian nations from the rest of American society now rests on more than white domination and is actively cultivated by a number of Indian leaders who see separation as the only way to preserve their cultures. Among Indians, cultural politics has always faced issues that differ markedly from those faced by immigrant groups. None of our immigrants, from the Irish to the Vietnamese, have faced anything closely comparable to the questions raised by the role of the reservation, the reach of sovereignty of Indian nations, or the pan-Indian movement.[5] Those issues confront Indians, as individuals and as nations, with some hard choices as they seek to preserve their separate cultures and still to participate in the American economy and society. Whatever political forms may emerge from the current ferment, the larger society has an obligation—the obligation of citizens to each other—to see that the Indian peoples have the resources they need if those choices are to be real.

Immigrants, Nativism, and the Limits of Belonging

In the century between 1815 and 1914—between the final exile of Napoleon and World War I—fifty million people left Europe.[6] Thirty-five million of them came to the United States. Most came from peasant villages, where notions of political equality and social mobility were, to say the least, not well developed. They had come to America not to build a "city on a hill" but to escape poverty, degradation, even starvation. Once here, they took jobs in the cities at the bottom of the economic scale or, in the case of Scandinavians and many Germans, moved West into farming and associated businesses. To replace the security the villages had offered their ancestors, they banded together both geographically and socially. So it was for the first generation.

But immigrants, by definition, are people who "get up and go." They might begin by taking jobs that other Americans scorned, but they believed their children would enter the competition at higher levels. So, although the immigrant might be at the bottom of the heap, "he was a capitalist at heart," confident that equality of opportunity lay just down the road.[7] Sadly, the second generation often met resistance. Oscar Handlin described the effects when a young man encountered one of those help-wanted signs that ended with the words No Irish Need Apply: "The hurt would affect him, but also his father. It would disclose to these immigrants . . . the limits of their belonging to America."[8]

Their belonging—that was the objective. And for millions of immigrants' children, belonging to America meant the agonizing decision to reject their parents' language and culture. The wider society saw it that way, too. A social worker might look around an apartment and write: "This family is not Americanized; they are still eating Italian food." The *melting pot* did not become part of the national vocabulary until the production of Israel Zangwill's play of that name in 1908, but the idea was as old as the nation itself. In 1782 an immigrant from Normandy, Hector St. John de Crèvecoeur, published his *Letters from an American Farmer*, a series of commentaries on life in the new nation. On the subject of assimilation he was rhapsodic: "What then is the American, this new man? . . . I could point out to you a family whose grandfather was an Englishman, whose wife was Dutch, whose son married a French woman, and whose present four sons have now four wives of different nations. . . . Here individuals of all nations are melted into a new race of men."

How did one acquire the status of an American? Crèvecoeur's answer makes two points that have found repeated expression in our prevailing national ideology: "He is an American, who, leaving behind him all his ancient prejudices and manners, receives new ones from the new mode of life he has embraced, the new government he obeys, and the new rank he holds. He becomes an American by being received in the broad lap of our great Alma Mater."[9] For Crèvecoeur, there were two cultural requisites for belonging: participation in the nation's political culture, with the "new rank" of citizen, and rejection of Old World ways of thinking and behaving in favor of the culture of the "new race." Even today American identity is closely bound up with participation in the American civic culture. And, although our tolerance for cultural diversity has increased, Crèvecouer's assumption that a cultural outsider can become a member of the American community only by relinquishing his or her native culture has repeatedly surfaced in our public policy when our fears of the outsider have become acute.

1. Nativism as Coerced Conformity.

The metaphor of melting, so popular from the early nineteenth century until around 1930, implied that both the old stock and the more recent immigrants would contribute to a new American character and culture. The term, however, often served as an integrationist cloak for public and private programs aimed at forcing new Americans and their children to conform to the attitudes and behavior of their British-American predecessors.[10] This Anglo conformity came to dominate the idea of assimilation—and thus to redefine the qualifications for being received in Alma Mater's lap. To call a group unassimilable implied that its people were not sufficiently similar to the old stock to adapt themselves to a society defined by the old stock's world view, and thus that they should be excluded from the American community. Congress implemented this policy of exclusion by denying members of various racial or cultural groups entry into the county and by denying the benefits of citizenship both to certain classes of aliens and to Americans who were black or Indian. The irony is that the universalism expressed by Crèvecoeur—that full membership in America would be extended to all who would embrace the nation's ideals—was so easily twisted into racist nativism. It is no wonder that the members of some ethnic groups today bristle at the very word *assimilation*, and take it as an affront.

The campaign for the Americanization of foreigners, which gained intensity during World War I and culminated in the mania of the Red Scare of 1919–20, was the most determined national effort to coerce conformity to the values and behavior of the dominant culture. Government officials joined with private organizations in a zealous effort to press foreign-born Europeans to become citizens, to abandon their native languages for English, to suppress any expression of "anti-American" sympathies, and generally to demonstrate a "conformist loyalty intolerant of any values not functional to it."[11] The message was simple: to belong, you must conform.

Americanization mixed well-intentioned good works with nativist coercion. Many who took an interest in bringing the foreign-born into American society's mainstream offered vital social services, from adult education to housing assistance to protection against fraud. The coercive face of Americanization had its private aspects but also enlisted government officials at all levels. In 1918 Congress doubled the income tax on nonresident aliens. Although it was not clear who would be considered nonresident, thousands of aliens promptly declared their intention to become citizens. Other measures were proposed and even introduced in Congress but failed to pass: deportation of aliens who failed to apply for citizenship or who failed to learn English within a specified period; and, short of deportation, "suppression of the foreign-language press, mass internments, the denial of industrial employment to aliens."[12]

State and local governments joined the Americanization crusade with gusto. Fifteen states banned teaching in foreign languages in public schools; some states required public school teachers to be citizens; and, after a campaign by the Ku Klux Klan against Catholics and immigrants, Oregon required all elementary school children to attend public rather than private schools. A few years later the Supreme Court held both the ban on teaching foreign languages and the ban on private elementary schools unconstitutional. The governor of Iowa, not to be outdone as an Americanizer, issued a proclamation forbidding the use of foreign languages in public and private schools, in church services, and even in conversations in public places or over the telephone. In an action eventually upheld by the Supreme Court, Cincinnati prohibited aliens from operating poolrooms, to prevent foreigners from gathering in places where they would be away from Americanizing influences. Most of these measures and proposals plainly violate today's constitutional norms. In the frenzy of 1915–20, however, if the foreign-born were to have Americanization imposed upon them, the courts were only rarely disposed to intervene.

2. The Specter of Disloyalty.

The fear and suspicion that produced the fervor of the Americanization movement were nothing new. Suspicions of disloyalty had surrounded various minorities since the colonial era: Catholics, who were thought loyal to a foreign pope; Chinese, who were called subversive in California late in the nineteenth century; Germans, who were required to sign a loyalty oath in Pennsylvania in 1729 and who were again suspect because of the war. In a nation of immigrants, it could hardly be otherwise. Most of the foreign-born do retain ties to their home countries; even their descendants often seek to influence the nation's policy toward foreign causes in foreign lands. Americans of the dominant culture have often suspected disloyalty behind cultural outsiders' political dissent.

The American Revolution itself required people to choose sides. Like the old stock of English ancestry, Germans and other ethnic groups were divided in their attitudes toward the Revolution—"a triumph of environment over heredity."[13] Although nativism found some expression at the Constitutional Convention of 1787, the framers set the residence qualifications for election to the Congress at reasonable levels, and in the same spirit the First Congress set the waiting period for naturalization at two years. Soon, however, the climate changed as a direct result of the influx of political refugees. By 1795 the naturalization waiting period had been extended to five years, and three years later, under the threat of war with revolutionary France, a Federalist Congress extended the period to fourteen years in a legislative package that included the infamous Alien and Sedition Acts.

The expressed fear of the Federalists was that aliens were engaging in "treasonable or secret machinations against the government." The Alien Enemies Act gave the president discretion to seize and deport an alien summarily, without accusation or hearing. The war with France failed to materialize, the Alien Friends Act expired in 1800, and the Alien Enemies Act went unenforced. Yet these laws had their intended intimidating effect. In 1798 several boatloads of Frenchmen left the United States. The Sedition Act, which essentially made strong criticism of government officials a crime, was logically connected with the Alien Acts: "those who corrupt our opinions . . . are the most dangerous of all enemies."[14] This law *was* enforced, chiefly against foreign-born critics of the government. When the Republicans acceded to national political power in the 1800 elections, Jefferson pardoned the victims of the Sedition Act. In 1802 the waiting period for naturalization was again set at five years, where it has remained ever since. The Alien and Sedition Acts were soon discredited. The Kentucky and Virginia Resolutions reflected more than a local opinion when they complained that Congress had exceeded its enumerated powers, and that the laws, by giving legislative and judicial powers to the president, had "subverted the general principles of free government." Those laws remain discredited. In the twentieth century, the Supreme Court has made use of this history to support its development of strongly libertarian First Amendment doctrine.

Yet the Alien and Sedition Acts left a lasting legacy when they recognized nativist exclusion as an appropriate response to fear of foreign people and foreign ideas.[15] The Hartford Convention in 1814 called for a constitutional amendment to forbid a naturalized citizen from holding federal office. In the 1850s the Know-Nothing party renewed this demand and called for extending the residence requirement for naturalization to twenty-one years. None of these proposals came to fruit, although Massachusetts, under the influence of the Know-Nothings, did briefly amend its state constitution to prohibit immigrants from voting until two years after their naturalization. More significantly, the exclusion and expulsion of aliens on political grounds has reappeared periodically in the twentieth century, from the "Soviet Ark" in 1919 to the present day.[16]

The assumed connection between alienage and disloyalty appears to be deeply rooted in the role that negative identity plays in self-definition. No one should be surprised when a legislature translates this antipathy to foreigners into laws limiting a wide variety of state jobs to citizens; the legislature, after all, represents voters, not one of whom is an alien. We might have expected better from the Supreme Court, but that body's recent majorities have turned a blind eye to such bursts of nativism as laws forbidding aliens to be public school teachers or probation officers. When the Court upheld these laws using language about preserving our "political community," its words were more than a little reminiscent of the Federalist rhetoric of 1798 about "those who corrupt our opinions." Who knows what heresy may be propagated when a French citizen, teaching his French language class, helps students to pronounce words such as *liberté, éqalité,* and *fraternité?*

Wartime combines fear with patriotic fervor, weakening the restraints that ordinarily inhibit acts of hostility against cultural outsiders—as the French citizens who left New York in 1798 well understood. The wave of anti-Catholic and antiforeign nativism that swept the country in the mid-nineteenth century similarly was exaggerated by anxieties over an internal conflict that eventually would lead to war, anxieties over the state of a union that seemed to be coming apart. In the twentieth century, two world wars have produced two virulent nativist movements: the treatment of Germans and of black and foreign-born radicals associated with World War I, and the assault on Japanese Americans that accompanied World War II. Even blacks who opposed the Vietnam War risked being charged with radicalism, or disloyalty, or both. It bears emphasis that the question of disloyalty typically is posed not for individuals but for group. General John L. DeWitt, who presided over the "relocation" of Japanese Americans in World War II, provided a textbook illustration in his shameful remark, "A Jap's a Jap."[17]

3. Discrimination as Domination.

The forced conformity of the Americanization movement, like other forms of cultural domination, was not just a means of securing power or material advantage for members of the dominant culture. Equally important, coercion of a cultural minority to conform serves to reassure the majority that their own group identities are secure. It was no accident that the liquor prohibition amendment to the Constitution was proposed and ratified at the height of the Americanization furor; the Temperance movement and nativism had always gone hand in hand. For a century the struggle over prohibition had symbolized the question whether Anglo-Protestant morality would maintain its dominance over the cultural norms that Irish and German immigrants, mostly Catholic, had brought with them.[18] The effort of Protestants to enact their norms into law "polarized the opposing forces and accentuated the symbolic import of the movement. Now that the issue had been joined, defeat or victory was a clear-cut statement of public dominance."[19] The old saw, "The wets have their liquor and the drys have their law," spoke not only to hypocrisy but to nativism as well.

Intercultural domination, however, always rests on shaky foundations, for it is always based on fear. On both sides of the prohibition issue, cultural identifications were strengthened, because both sides saw their cherished cultural values to be under attack. Intercultural domination is also a game that two can play. In 1932 the Democratic party captured the presidency and the Congress with the strong support of Irish voters in the cities of the Northeast, and the repeal of the prohibition amendment was accomplished the following year.

Discrimination against ethnic and religious groups typically has not reached the level of intensity that discrimination against blacks reached in the South. Yet the history of intercultural relations in America provides parallels to nearly all the features of Jim Crow. Jews were forbidden to vote in some states until the mid-nineteenth century; not until 1877 did New Hampshire repeal this limitation on the franchise. School segregation affected not only blacks but Asians, Chicanos, and, for a time, Italians, who were directed to all-black schools in some southern communities. Miscegenation laws forbade intermarriage of whites with persons of any other race. In the West, Asians were subjected to special taxes and prohibited from owning land; a California law even prohibited Chinese people from testifying in court against whites.

Private discrimination, too, victimized a great many cultural minorities, notably including Catholics, Jews, the foreign-born, and persons of Irish and Italian descent. Violence against Chinese and Chicano residents in the Southwest was matched by antisemitic violence, including the lynching of Leo Frank in Georgia. In the same year that New Hampshire repealed its restrictions on voting by Jews, New York's bar association rejected an applicant because he was Jewish. Although some labor unions actively courted foreign-born members, the American Federation of Labor excluded Japanese workers. Even in Hawaii Japanese workers faced wage discrimination. The ethnic neighborhood, sometimes seen today through a haze of romantic nostalgia, was founded only partly on affinity. Ethnic discrimination ranged over the whole housing market, and racial segregation remains the pattern in today's urban neighborhoods. Today's white flight had antecedents in the nineteenth century, when middle-class families in eastern cities fled from neighborhoods that were becoming populated with poorer Irish residents.[20] And if overt ethnic-group exclusion by resorts, hotels, and universities is now largely behind us, such discrimination in private schools and businessmen's clubs[21] remains a fact of American urban life.

Behind the colorless term intercultural relations lies the menace of violence. When two cultural groups are contending in the political arena, each seeking to use the power of the state to impose its values on the other, distrust can ripen into hostility and even into the rupture of the social fabric. No doubt it was this perception that led vice-presidential candidate Edmund Muskie, speaking specifically of "people of different races and national origins," to say in 1968, "the great issue in America is whether or not . . . Americans can trust each other."

Distrust and fear of persons with different cultural backgrounds usually finds expression in language emphasizing a conflict of values. In American history, however, the expressed concern for values has often provided the excuse—as well as the emotional fuel—for hostile action aimed at preserving interests that are mainly economic.[22] Typically, people who are themselves on the margin of the society and economy feel most threatened by cultural outsiders and are the most likely to resort to intercultural violence. When Irish mobs committed violence against blacks in the New York draft riots of 1863, the root causes were fear of the competition of black workers and resentment over the use of blacks as strikebreakers. Chinese workers in nineteenth century California received their harshest treatment at the hands of white labor union members. When a cultural group is stigmatized and made into scapegoats, it is well to ask, *Cui bono?*; whose interests are advanced by the scapegoating?

Like Jim Crow, discrimination against the ethnic outsider is a form of exclusion—not only physical exclusion from the country, but exclusion from belonging as a respected and responsible participant in a community's public life. The types of material and spiritual harm thus inflicted on persons who are denied full citizenship are innumerable, and each harm aggravates the others. Jim Crow wasn't just a collection of particular prohibitions on blacks, but a system of exclusion. The sign in the shop window that said No Irish Need Apply bespoke more than job discrimination.

4. The Lessons of Korematsu.

The Supreme Court's 1944 decision in *Korematsu v. United States* is widely regarded today as a disaster, Eugene Rostow's name for it at the time.[23] The decision upheld President Franklin Roosevelt's wartime order excluding about 120,000 persons of Japanese ancestry (some 70,000 of them American citizens) from their West coast homes, for relocation in camps in the interior. The Court said it was deferring to the president and Congress in matters of military judgment, but there was no threat of invasion, and there had been no acts of sabotage or espionage by Japanese Americans. The military judgment of General John L. DeWitt, the army's commander in California, began and ended in his statement, "the Japanese race is an enemy race."[24]

The main pressure for removing Japanese Americans had come from West Coast politicians. The politicians, in turn, had responded to pressure from certain newspapers and labor unions, along with (as Attorney General Francis Biddle later listed them) "the American Legion, the California Joint Immigration Committee, the Native Sons and Daughters of the Golden West, the Western Growers Protective Association, the California Farm Bureau Federation [and] the Chamber of Commerce of Los Angeles."[25] In Hawaii, which had been attacked, no such order had been issued, for persons of Japanese ancestry constituted almost one-third of the territory's population. On the West Coast, however, Japanese Americans amounted to less than one per cent of the population and lacked political power to resist the combined force of war, racism, and greed.

The Supreme Court's *Korematsu* opinion acknowledged that racial classifications are "suspect," and it said that such laws must be subjected to "the most rigid scrutiny." That pronouncement completed, the Court simply abandoned any scrutiny of the justification for the racial discrimination before it.[26] Today it is almost as hard to find a good word for this decision as it is to find someone who will defend the separate but equal decision in *Plessy v. Ferguson*. Can we learn from this experience?

One lesson is not new: nativist scapegoating can always find a market in a multicultural nation. Read any big-city newspapers for a week, and you will find today's analogies, from the violent harassment of Vietnamese fishermen in Gulf Coast waters to the killing of Vincent Chin in Detroit to the terrorism that drives a black family from its home in a white neighborhood in Boston—

and not only in Boston. Another is that some politicians can always be found to join in the hunt, offering the gloved violence of governmental coercion. Well, you say, aren't the courts supposed to protect against that sort of thing? Yes, they are. But our judges did nothing to impede the enforcement of the Sedition Act against alien critics of the government or to resist any but the most inane excesses of the Americanization program or to protect Fred Korematsu. One of the saddest lessons of *Korematsu* is that we do not seem to learn much from the lessons of the past.

Might our federal judges in 1799 have questioned the validity of the Sedition Act if the law had been systematically enforced against native-born editors? When the Supreme Court held those two silly Americanization laws invalid in 1923 and 1925, did it matter that the main beneficiaries of the decisions were American citizens—that is, teachers and parents—who were largely assimilated to the dominant culture? Might the Supreme Court have taken a serious look at the evidence of military necessity if the people interned in 1942 had been largely assimilated Americans of German or Italian ancestry? Another teaching of *Korematsu* points up the connection between empathy and judicial defense of the Constitution. The invasion of constitutional rights is least likely to encounter judicial resistance when the judges, like the politicians, perceive the victims to be markedly different from themselves.[27] Even a Justice can be blinded by the abstract image of the inscrutable Other.

Not all the lessons of *Korematsu* are so dismal. As a judicial precedent, the decision set the stage for two major egalitarian developments that retain vigor today. One is the application of constitutional guarantees of equality against the national government despite the absence of any explicit equal protection clause in the Bill of Rights.[28] The other is the doctrinal edifice built on the idea that racial classifications are "suspect." The disaster of *Korematsu* was not doctrinal. It was the betrayal of justice then and there for Fred Korematsu and for some 120,000 other Americans—and thus for us all.

During peacetime, four years before the exclusion orders, Franklin Roosevelt had reminded the Daughters of the American Revolution "that all of us, and you and I especially, are descended from immigrants and revolutionists."[29] Today Roosevelt's point seems remote when we think of the descendants of immigrants from Europe. The overwhelming majority of those immigrants' great-grandchildren are today part of one national culture, wearing the same clothes, watching the same television programs, eating the same Italian food. Even the children whose parents were taken to the internment camps are marrying Caucasians at a rate that no one could have predicted in

1942. Yet the "varieties of ethnic experience"[30] in America remain numerous beyond counting, and a considerable degree of cultural diversity is entirely compatible with full and equal membership in American society.

Equal citizenship for cultural minorities, however, has not happened quickly. Virtually every cultural minority in America has experienced exclusion, forced conformity, and subordination. All these patterns of nativism are variations on the same theme: those who are different cannot belong. The victims of cultural domination, therefore, face a serious problem: they must necessarily live their lives within the larger society, and in order to define themselves they must satisfy their basic needs for connection. They may choose to turn inward to the solidarity of the excluded group, banding together to confront the larger society. Alternatively, individual members of the cultural minority may, as to some aspects of their lives and in varying degrees, be assimilated into the culture of the larger society. These two paths to belonging start out by heading in different directions, but for most cultural minorities in America eventually they have pointed toward the same destination.

Cultural Politics: From Group Solidarity to Integration

One principal source of cultural identity in America has always been people's perceived need to band together in defense against domination or hostility. Indeed, the outside world plays an important part in the very definition of a group's identity.[31] The peoples brought to this country by force from Africa were culturally diverse. On the plantations of the American South, however, their common bondage in slavery welded them into one people. The immigrants from a single European country typically came from different regions with marked cultural distinctions, but in America the people from a given village or region generally were few in number; naturally, they sought association with others from the same country. There were, of course, natural affinities: a common language, a common relgion, or both. But much of the sense of community felt by the members of an American ethnic group today originates in the ways in which the members' ancestors were labeled—for example, as Italians or as Jews—and, by those labels, set apart as outsiders. Stephen Steinberg exaggerated only mildly when he said, "Ethnic pluralism in America has its origins in conquest, slavery, and exploitation of foreign labor."

Facing hostility or indifference, the members of a cultural minority may conclude that they can defend themselves more effectively when they act as a group, particularly when their aims can be satisfied only by participation in the larger community. The pursuit of political goals by religious and ethnic groups has been a fixture of American politics since the colonial era and must be seen as a permanent feature of the politics of a mutlicultural society.

Cultural politics is a historically validated avenue to recognition and acceptance for members of minority cultures and especially for their leaders. A constant concern of ethnic leadership is group solidarity. Indeed, ethnic groups are, in some sense, "the creation of their leaders": no clear boundaries define the groups, and the openness of American society is a continuing invitation for marginal members to define themselves outside the group. Each success for the group in the politics of the wider community, each material advance, integrates more and more members of the group into the institutions and processes of the dominant culture with the inevitable result that the group declines as a separate political force. (An analogy is the limited success of the women's movement as a unified political force. Women are distributed over the entire spectrum of economic class, among all races and ethnicities, and across all the other lines of division in our society.)

Observers of ethnic politics have been struck by a development that is, at first glance, curious: as ethnic bloc voting has increased, ethnic identification has decreased. In the middle years of the nineteenth century, Edward Beecher assumed a permanent antagonism between Catholicism and American democracy: "The systems are diametrically opposed: one must and will exterminate the other."[32] In 1960 American voters, sensing that Catholics were largely assimilated into American life, elected John F. Kennedy as the nation's first Catholic president. In the century that intervened between those two events, the Irish had been the nation's foremost practitioners of cultural politics.

The Irish had the advantage of large numbers. Smaller cultural groups are less successful in making alliances and less likely to see their members elected to public office. Yet, for any cultural group, active participation in politics is a step along the path to assimilation. Political party activity makes people feel like insiders. The parties themselves both connect different groups and serve as "carriers of certain basic values that large numbers of citizens [can] accept as common American beliefs."[33] Even a highly localized ethnic power produces the belief that "the system works for us," further strengthening national allegiance. Cultural politics thus begins in the defensive solidarity of the cultural group, but it ends in integration.

The lessons for American law are plain. Voting is not just an instrument for achieving power or status and not just an expression of political preferences; it is an assertion of belonging to a political community. We can share

Alexander Bickel's doubt that "the equal right to vote,"[34] translated into thoroughgoing majoritarianism, adds much to the real political effectiveness of those who have previously been ineffective. Judge Learned Hand, as he approached the end of his constitutional valedictory, voiced the same skepticism. But he added a remark that begins to explain why voting is at the heart of the idea of equal citizenship: "Of course I know how illusory would be the belief that my vote determined anything; but nevertheless when I go to the polls I have a satisfaction in the sense that we are all engaged in a common venture." Voting is the preeminent symbol of participation in the society as a respected member, and equality in the voting process is a crucial affirmation of the equal worth of citizens.[35]

At last, legal restrictions on voting by members of cultural minorities are behind us. Religious tests, long waiting periods for citizenship, racial disqualifications, and English literacy tests have been repealed or otherwise rendered invalid.[36] Yet the danger of faction identified by James Madison remains: one group may capture the legislature and use that power to perpetuate its own dominance.[37] The Supreme Court's early reapportionment opinions saw the issue of legislative districting mainly as a problem of the systematic overrepresentation of rural areas and of political parties favored in those areas. Now, three decades later, to speak of urban-rural or urban-suburban rivalry often is a genteel way of speaking about race and ethnicity. Many of the Supreme Court's recent voting rights cases have arisen out of efforts by state legislators to define—and sometimes to dilute—the voting strength of racial and ethnic groups.

The legislators' keen awareness of patterns of ethnic voting, coupled with the central importance of voting to equal citizenship, make a particularly strong case for relaxation of the courts' usual refusal to find racial discrimination in the absence of particularized proof of discriminatory purpose.[38] Any sensible view of the vote dilution problem would focus on the highly visible effects of districting (especially the use of at-large elections that submerge core cities in huge districts including the suburbs) in muffling the political voice of racial and other cultural groups. The Supreme Court, after fumbling the issue once,[39] got it right in a 1982 decision that approved a lower court's finding of intentional racial discrimination based largely on circumstantial evidence of the racially disparate effects of at-large districting.[40] In so ruling, the Justices paid heed to the nation's two centuries of experience with nativist restrictions on participation in elections. Surely during all that time we should have come to appreciate the importance of voting and cultural politics as paths to belonging.

Tolerance and Belonging

1. Participation, Assimilation, and Tolerance.

The assimilation of white immigrants' descendants into the larger culture of American life is an undeniable fact, verified by the immediate experience of all of us. Assimilation is change—specifically, a change in cultural norms. These changes are most visible in behavior such as the adoption of a language or a style of dress,[41] but assimilation also implies change in self-identification, which is not so much a behavior pattern as a state of mind. Some such changes can be seen in first-generation Americans, but the typical adult immigrant is not inclined to undertake the wrenching transformation involved in a wholesale adoption of the ways of a new culture. Indeed, the change we call assimilation does not take place primarily within any individual. Mostly, it is visible as a group phenomenon, a change from one generation to another.

Even from generation to generation there is no linear movement from community to society, from primordial association to contractual association, from ethnic identity to occupational identity. Rather, these types of association and identity exist side by side in the same individual. There is an "interaction . . . of communal and noncommunal ways in the lives of us all."[42] It would seem odd to say that a fourth-generation American is assimilated. Rather, she is what she is. Having grown up in new conditions, she lacks some of the characteristics that once set her immigrant great-grandparents apart from other Americans. For the individual, assimilation (or its absence) is just a label that we attach to the product of myriad decisions made by that individual and by others, including ancestors and acquaintances and government officials. The assimilation of a group is also a complex, ongoing process that never quite ends: "every one of the racial and national groupings that was created in America has stubbornly persisted."[43]

Although an exact definition of assimilation appears to be impossible, there are some measures of assimilation on which observers can agree: language usage, educational integration, occupational dispersal, residential dispersal, intercultural marriage. By these tests, it is plain that a common pattern prevails for nearly all the ethnic groups in American history: eventually they show a marked degree of integration into the larger American culture.

How does assimilation take place? The details of the mechanism are not well documented, but three generalizations seem true, even in the absence of hard evidence. First, the commonly assumed assimilating effects of occupational mobility in an open society illustrate a larger truth. Assimilation is advanced when the members of a cultural minority take part in the institutions and activities of the larger society: speaking English, attending public schools, listening to the national broadcast media, entering the job market, joining a union, moving away from the ethnic neighborhood, voting in public elections.

If assimilation tends to be associated with entry into the middle class, the reason is plain. In a market, resources mean opportunities, including opportunities to interact with widening circles of people in a variety of arenas: neighborhoods, schools, social activities. Middle class status permits a great many choices about participation in the wider society that are unavailable to poor people. The second generalization about assimilation, then, is that its pace is positively correlated with movement up the economic scale. Cause and effect are blurred here; the best guess is that economic advance and assimilation feed each other. Most immigrants, whatever their class, remain largely unassimilated. In succeeding generations, however, middle-class families tend to live in the suburbs and send their children to college. Higher education not only provides access to occupational elites, but it also erodes social barriers to the point that ethnic intermarriage is now common among young people of the middle class. All these developments tend to weaken a cultural group's internal cohesion.

The third engine driving assimilation is the complexity of our modern society, which presses nearly everyone into a fragmentation of roles and thus of norms. It is virtually impossible for an individual to focus either his loyalties or his identity single-mindedly on an ethnic or religious group. One of the most pernicious features of the Jim Crow system was that it perpetuated itself, polarizing Southern society and inhibiting the diversification of identities and attachments. Conversely, to foster that diversified sharing and those multiple loyalties is to nourish the growth of tolerance.

Tolerance and assimilation thus go hand in hand. When the enforced separation of a cultural minority ends, and its members come to participate in the activities and institutions of the wider society, their participation itself promotes assimilation. Correspondingly, as a cultural minority becomes more assimilated, its members find more tolerance among the majority for the cultural differences that may remain. Was Crèvecoeur right, then, in assuming that the price of belonging to America was the abandonment of any cultural inheritance that was distinct from the dominant culture?

The question goes to the heart of the American civic culture, for it explores the zone where our strong sense of nationalism confronts our professions of devotion to individual freedom and tolerance for diversity. A great many Americans continue to find their most important sense of belonging within their cultural groups and, indeed, to reject parts of the majority culture, such as family patterns that seem isolating and uncaring. Although they are in important ways assimilated to the dominant culture, they also retain important parts of their "primordial affinities." At some level, no doubt, people in this position understand that genuine individuality is not to be found by participating in a vast social or political market. Rather, both individuality and community are attainable only within a particular group of people who share cultural traditions. "Most often, when individual men and women insist on 'being themselves,' they are in fact defending a self they share with others."[44] With the stakes so high, no wonder feelings are intense. The emotionally charged quality of American cultural politics, today as in the nineteenth century, arises out of conflicts over status, with one group's anger matched against another group's fear.

Much of our modern constitutional law consists of a series of accommodations in this zone, fashioned by our judges with doctrinal tools ranging from the freedom of speech[45] to the freedom of intimate association.[46] Often the issue before a court has arisen out of cultural politics, where it has acquired an importance transcending the immediate effects of the issue's resolution on people's day-to-day lives. The cultural issues that have recently aroused the most fervor—abortion, immigration, religion in the schools, affirmative action, and bilingualism—all are status issues, touching the emotions because they touch the sense of self.[47]

In emotionally charged situations such as these, tolerance in its cool, intellectual form[48] has its uses. Suppose, for example, that you are a judge, and you are confronting the claim of someone who differs from you in ways that your acculturation has made important. Although you may have little empathy for her, an attitude of tolerance will help you to make a serious inquiry into the justice of her claim. That inquiry is easier to make when it does not require you to imagine life as it is seen and felt on the other side of the cultural boundary. Probably you will believe that she has a right to those different beliefs and even to the behavior that you have found bothersome. Indeed, one product of the cooler form of tolerance can be an influence in the direction of empathy. Respect, like stigma, is not easily confined to one aspect of human interactions; rather, it tends to affect our attitude toward the whole person. Habits of respectful treatment, regularly visible in our public life, in the long run can have large-scale effects, not just in encouraging further displays of respect but in promoting real respect and thus the feelings that real respect engenders. One of those feelings is empathy.

To conclude our exploration of the constitutional problems associated with cultural identity and nativist domination, we look briefly at two modern issues: bilingual education and government sponsorship of religion.

2. The Languages of Belonging.

A recent proposal would amend the Constitution to declare that English is the official language of the United States.[49] The proposed amendment is little more than a nativist symbol. The public's business already is conducted in English,[50] and the proposal offers no more in the way of improved national cohesion than did the Iowa governor's attempt, seven decades ago, to prohibit telephone conversations in foreign languages. The proposed amendment is an insult to the twenty million people in this country whose mother tongue is not English, and a gratuitous insult at that—unless the real political point here, as in the case of the Temperance movement, is to symbolize cultural dominance itself.[51]

The adoption of English as a primary language is one measure of assimilation into the larger American society. Scholars continue to debate the effects of language on an individual's definition of reality, but no one can doubt that language is one of the symbol spheres that define social groups and provide justification for social structures. A distinctive language sets a cultural group off from others,[52] with one consistent unhappy consequence throughout American history: discrimination against members of the cultural minority. Language differences provide a way to rationalize subordination and a ready means for accomplishing it.

There is no mystery in the desire of immigrant parents in America for their children to learn English. The children's opportunities, not just to find satisfying employment but to make effective choices about a wide range of activities affecting their well-being, will be much improved if they are fluent in the dominant language. The strongest retention of the mother tongue has always been associated with people of the most marginal economic and social status. These incentives are powerful; in the past they have led inexorably to the adoption of English and, for the most part, to the exclusive use of English by the third or fourth generation.

Some characteristics of the Spanish-speaking populations in the United States suggest the possibility of a departure from this historic pattern. Many families retain ties in Mexico, Central America, or Puerto Rico, and some of their members move back and forth between their present and former communities. This "revolving door" phenomenon, along with the high probability of a continued flow of immigrants over the southern border, means that large Spanish-speaking communities will continue to exist in the United States for the indefinate future. Probably the pace of assimilation will be slowed somewhat in these communities. But the recent experience of economic advance from one generation to another among the Latino populations and the large proportion of marriages between Latino and non-Latino spouses indicate that for a great many individuals and families, assimilation is following its historically typical course, even as the communities retain their strong Latino identification.

The expectation that large Spanish-speaking communities will persist is one factor contributing to a call for national support for bilingual education of children in those communities' public schools. Bilingual education can take a number of forms and in those varying forms can serve a variety of purposes. In the 1960s bilingual teaching was proposed to facilitate the learning of English and to avoid disadvantaging children whose English was deficient as they studied other subjects. More recently bilingual education has been seen by some of its advocates as a means to maintain the children's native languages and cultures. The issue is important for people with a wide range of political agendas, from separatism at one pole to absorption at the other. Even the professional literature evaluating bilingual education bears the mark of this political polarization. The evaluations to date are inconclusive.[53]

The issue of bilingual education has nonetheless been a common rallying point for leaders in the nation's Latino communities, even though those communities vary in many respects, including race and national origin. The issue's emotional appeal is grounded in concerns about status that are directly traceable to the nation's history of discrimination against people of Latino background. Like the demands for "Black Power" of the 1960s, the demand for Spanish-language maintenance in the schools is an assertion of the worth of a people and a culture. It should be seen as a demand not for separation but for inclusion.

Unquestionably this kind of culture maintenance carries some risk of rejection for individuals when they deal with the larger society. The history of discrimination by culturally dominant Americans against people they see as cultural outsiders provides one cautionary tale after another. Yet there is no inconsistency between the claim of equal citizenship and the claim for room for some separate cultural development. Those who would preserve their ancestral cultures are seeking something important from American public life, but what they seek is neither cultural capitulation nor political separation. As cultural groups, they seek acceptance in the public arena as groups of Americans. As individuals, they seek to belong as citizens.

In the field of bilingual education, cultural politics has produced its own results. Since 1968 Congress has conditioned the grant of school funds on the adoption of bilingual programs for children of "limited English proficiency." Some state legislatures have ordered school districts to make bilingual education available, subject to parental consent. Local school boards have considerable practical control over the content of these programs. Understandably, the heaviest emphasis on maintenance of the Spanish language and Latino culture is to be found in Miami and in other school districts with large proportions of Latino students.

Against this background, some have proposed to remove the whole issue from cultural politics through recognition of a constitutional right to government support for bilingual education or even the maintenance of foreign languages among cultural minorities. Those proposals seem to be misguided, just as the proposed "U.S. English" constitutional amendment is misguided. Undoubtedly the issue of bilingual education touches the sense of belonging and thus the sense of identity and self-esteem of millions of Americans. However, in this multicultural society the paths to belonging are as numerous as the varieties of ethnic experience. It is for parents and local communities to make their choices about the paths they will follow, including how much culture maintenance they want for their children. Cultural politics can translate those choices into community action, as it has done in Congress, in the state legislatures, and in hundreds of local communities. However, given the range of views among parents in the affected communities, and given the present state of understanding about the effects of bilingual education, it would be unwise to lodge a particular outcome for the issue in constitutional concrete.[54] Whatever course our cultural politics and our constitutional doctrine may take concerning bilingual education, our national experience with assimilation and cultural pluralism suggests that the forms in which various Latino cultures survive will depend on the choices of millions of individuals within those cultures, not on any nationally enforced political norm.

3. The Religious Outsider.

Congress has never threatened to establish a national religion. Beyond the explicit prohibition of the First Amendment lies another insurmountable obstacle: the nation has never approached the religious consensus that an establishment would require. On the eve of Independence, Congregationalists predominated in New England, Anglicans in Virginia; in all the other colonies, however, these two sects were in a minority. In most of the colonies, there was no majority religion. "Accordingly, religious liberty became a practical necessity, no matter what the letter of the law proclaimed."[55] Local orthodoxy, however, was the rule rather than the exception. Within colonial towns and villages, the standard was homogeneity, and dissenters generally chose to create new communities of their own. In one sense "the consent of the governed" meant that local communities were permitted to impose their own conformities, including religious conformities, by means both formal and informal. These practices did not end when the colonies became states. In the 1840s, for example, religious strife in New York and Philadelphia focused on the Protestants' use of the public schools for religious indoctrination, complete with the distribution to pupils of the King James version of the Bible.

Today's constitutional doctrine rests on quite a different premise. Our separate peoples have become a nation, and religious liberty is not to be conditioned on the individual's forfeiture of the status of equal citizenship. The Constitution guarantees "the equality of believers and unbelievers, saints and worldlings, the saved and the damned: all are equally citizens."[56] Justice O'Connor recently addressed one aspect of this wider principle when she wrote, "The Establishment Clause prohibits government from making adherence to a religion relevant in any way to a person's standing in the political community." The Constitution not only forbids various kinds of religious discrimination but also protects the status of religious outsiders as equal citizens by forbidding governmental sponsorship of religion.

In the perspective of these concerns about equal citizenship and religious domination, the Supreme Court's decisions on schoolhouse religion are easily understood. The most serious harm of school prayer is not that it is a first step toward a full-scale state religion. The harm that matters most is that, day after day, the prayer inflicts pain on the children who do not share the dominant faiths represented by the prayer. It sets them apart; it labels them as unbelievers or antagonists or both: "[I]t is not only positive values that sacred symbols dramatize, but negative ones as well. They point not only toward the existence of good but also of evil, and toward the conflict between them."[57]

Separation of this kind would hurt anyone; for a school child, the hurt is devastating. Here is the memoir of a Tennessee writer concerning his experience in a Virginia school in the years just before the Supreme Court's 1962 school prayer decision:

> Every morning the principal, after reading announcements over the loudspeaker, said a prayer while students dutifully bowed their heads over their desks. . . . [The prayer ended with the words,] "In the name of Jesus Christ our Lord, Amen.
> I didn't know what to do. As a Jew, I prayed straight to God, not in anyone else's name. To accept the prayer as mine was more of a sin, according to what I had been taught, than not praying at all.
> My sister and I talked it over. She was as upset about the prayers as I was. But we didn't see a solution. We would have jumped in front of our school bus sooner than ask to be excused. . . . During that year neither of us told a single person that we were Jewish.
> I don't think we were cowardly. We were simply children. "Jesus Christ our Lord" coming over the loudspeaker every morning didn't leave room for any other belief being normal. It built a wall, with my sister and me standing on the outside.[58]

The problem is not solved by one of those nondenominational prayers that lend watery and perfunctory support to Judeo-Christian monotheism. (I have in mind the prayer Vern Countryman once suggested with tongue in cheek: "To Whom it may concern: We appreciate it. Amen.") Wholly apart from those prayers' tendency to diminish—even to insult—both Judaism and Christianity, they simply brand a smaller group of children as outsiders.[59]

A quarter century ago Ernest Brown criticized the Supreme Court's disposition of the school prayer and Bible reading cases. He argued that the Court had failed to appreciate the difficulty of the question of standing to sue: whether the plaintiffs were the proper persons to challenge the constitutionality of those practices. In his view, the standing of a child or parent should turn on a showing, to the satisfaction of a jury, that the child had been coerced to join in the religious exercises or to be present while they were going on. The Court, on the other hand, concluded that coercion was irrelevant. In the prayer case the Court did not discuss standing at all; in the Bible reading case the court said only that the plaintiff school children and their parents were "directly affected" by the laws and practices challenged.

The Court was right in concluding that the children and parents had standing, and it was right in refusing to leave the constitutional rights of religious outsiders to local juries. The institution of jury trial has long served the ideal of local orthodoxy. From an early time in America jurors were seen as "dependable neighbors who would uphold the community canons,"[60] and nothing in our recent experience suggests that things have changed. As for the question of standing to sue, much depends on the way the harm is characterized. The Justices who decided the prayer and Bible reading cases obviously understood that, coercion or no coercion, children were being told by public officials that they did not really belong to the community. That is a particularly painful harm, one that deserves explicit constitutional recognition. The remedy for that harm should not be left to ethnic politics, for two reasons. First, the religious outsider's right to equal citizenship is not a matter for negotiation. Second, local ethnic and religious majorities can be expected, especially when they feel threatened, to exercise their political dominance by creating symbolic exclusions designed to reduce cultural outsiders to a subordinate status.[61]

Unhappily, the Supreme Court, in giving its constitutional blessing to the city of Pawtucket's official Christmas display of a Nativity scene,[62] showed little concern for this kind of symbolic exclusion of religious outsiders. One irony is that Justice Sandra Day O'Connor, who concurred in the decision, chose that occasion to declare that one's standing as a member of the political community cannot be conditioned on adherence to a religion—a pronouncement that is hard to reconcile with her vote in the case before her. Shortly after the decision was announced, a law student of Japanese ancestry came to my office, on the other side of the country from Pawtucket, wanting me to explain what had happened. She was strongly assimilated to the dominant culture; she had been raised, however, as a Buddhist. As she talked, the emotion started to flow; she felt that officers at the highest level of governmental authority had told her that she did not belong. I wish Justice O'Connor could have seen her tear-stained face.[63]

The message in Pawtucket's official celebration of the Nativity of Christ was not, as the Court's opinion suggested, just a recognition of an event in Western history. Jesus is not a folk figure on the order of Paul Bunyan but central to the faith of Christians the world over. Pawtucket's message to non-Christians was a message of dominance that my student understood clearly. In today's America, the addressees of such messages number in tens of millions: not only Buddhists but Jews, Moslems, Hindus, oberservers of Native American religions—the list goes on and on, extending to hundreds of religions that are not Christian.

Nonetheless, three days after the Pawtucket case was decided a government lawyer wrote a memorandum to the regional director of the National Capital Parks, opining that the decision permitted the display of a crèche as part of the Christmas Pageant of Peace. The pageant is an annual three-week celebration, held on government land and jointly sponsored by the National Park

Service. The president of the pageant saw what the majority Justices had somehow missed; "Everyone knows what Christmas is. It's the celebration of the birth of Christ. Whether you believe it or not, that's what it is."[64]

The Supreme Court's unwillingness to recognize this particular symbolism of domination is no less perverse than an earlier Court's refusal to recognize that the racial segregation of railroad cars symbolized the subordination of black people. Very likely, too, the same psychological mechanisms produced both these examples of judicial blindness. In each case, the majority Justices failed even to try to see the symbolism through the eyes of its victims. The question before the Court in the Pawtucket case, as in *Plessy v. Ferguson*, was a cultural one: the meaning that should be assigned to official behavior. Imagine how that question might have been discussed in the Supreme Court's conference on the Nativity scene case if just one of the Justices had been Jewish.[65]

It is no trivial matter for the Supreme Court to countenance governmental conduct that tells some Americans that their differences from the dominant religion exclude them from full membership in the community. Often those religious differences are associated with other cultural differences; most Buddhists in America, for example, are of Japanese ancestry. Given the recent increase in immigration to this country from non-Christian countries in Asia and the Middle East, it would not be surprising if government officials were pressed into further public sponsorship of the symbols of Christianity—precisely in order to assert the dominance of today's augmented family of old stock Americans. If you think it can't happen here, recall the nativist movements that greeted the arrival of earlier immigrants deemed to be unassimilable, such as the Irish and the Italians. Today we recall with no little sadness how the Supreme Court, by upholding the constitutionality of segregated railroad cars, gave impetus to the laws and private behavior that became the pervasive, ugly system of Jim Crow. Let us hope that the Court's embrace of an official governmental symbol of the divinity of Christ will not contribute to a new vicious circle of domination and defensive separatism. Cultural politics has its place in the American civil culture; cultural domination has no legitimate place at all.

seven

Sex and Separation

Women, Men, and "Woman"

A few years ago I was appalled to see, in the corridor of the UCLA law school, a sign advertising a classroom showing by a dress shop of clothes suitable for the young woman lawyer. The idea was to avoid looking too feminine and at the same time to avoid looking mannish.

One woman graduate of our school, some years before she became a partner in a prestigious law firm, was at a firm party, talking with a judge. The firm's managing partner—not some throwback to the nineteenth century, but an unusually civilized man—walked up and said, "Leave it to Judge X to be with the prettiest girl at the party."

The good news here is that women are entering the professional world in large numbers, finding their places in the community's public life along pathways long denied to their female ancestors. In less than two decades American law, including constitutional law, has nearly completed the task of guaranteeing formal equality to women. The bad news is that a great many of the features of social life that hurt women are beyond the direct reach of formal equality.

When the Supreme Court remarks on the existence of "archaic and stereotypic notions" about "the roles and abilities of males and females,"[1] the Justices have an earlier generation's notions in mind. One expression is regularly quoted as a perfect example. More than a century ago the Supreme Court rejected Myra Bradwell's claim that Illinois could not constitutionally bar women from the practice of law.[2] Concurring, Justice Joseph Bradley took judicial notice of the nature of "woman":

> Man is, or should be, woman's protector and defender. The natural and proper timidity and delicacy which belongs to the female sex evidently unfits it for many of the occupations of civil life. The constitution of the family organization, which is founded in the divine ordinance, as well as in the nature of things, indicates the domestic sphere as that which properly belongs to the domain and functions of womanhood. The

harmony, not to say identity, of interests and views which belong, or should belong, to the family institution is repugnant to the idea of a woman adopting a distinct and independent career from that of her husband. . . .

. . . The paramount destiny and mission of woman are to fulfill the noble and benign offices of wife and mother. This is the law of the Creator.

In this passage Bradley made several interlocking points. Women are delicate, and they are timid; they are necessarily dependent on men, needing men's protection; they fulfill their destiny by serving others in the domestic sphere, as wives and mothers; and they are unsuited for independent, active lives in public affairs. All these facts are given, in the nature of things, ordained by God's law. Unaware of the law of the Creator, however, Myra Bradwell had pursued an active and successful career as editor and publisher of a Chicago legal newspaper, taking such emergencies as the Chicago fire in her stride. If God intended women to be delicate, evidently something had gone amiss. Very likely Justice Bradley could not even see the incongruity—and is every male reader sure that if he had been alive in 1873 he would have acted differently? To live in a society is to be conditioned to its presuppositions.

To look critically at our own acculturated assumptions is not easy, for most of those assumptions "go without saying," and remain buried below the level of conscious attention. The senior partner would not intentionally slight anyone; he would not dream of walking up to a black associate and saying, "Leave it to Judge X to be with the best basketball player at the party." Surely he had no idea that his message would hurt, but it did. Here she was, struggling as any young lawyer does to be recognized as a valued contributor of professional work, and the partner's first perception on seeing her was "pretty girl." The men who whistle when a woman walks past a construction site probably would be surprised to learn that most women react to the whistling with a mixture of humiliation and rage. In a thousand ways, our society teaches a woman that she is, first and foremost, a reflection of the image of "woman."

That image is not a picture of a person but an abstraction that not only obscures the real woman but presses her to conform with its image. Here is a list of characteristics women are supposed to exhibit if they are to be seen as true women. This list was not generated by scientific study but was written down, in haste and in some agitation, by a friend of mine, a perceptive professional woman. In her words, women are expected to be: "dumb, helpless, deferential, inferior, lacking in credibility, humble, narcissistic, followers never leaders, self-abnegating, child-like." The stereotype hurts in two different ways. First, it persuades men (and a considerable number of women) that it reflects truth, so that in a great many aspects of their lives women are systematically denied respect, responsibility, and effective participation. Second, the stereotype works to rob women of their individuality. Because women do not fit descriptions like these, most women repeatedly face the absurdity of having to decide whether to engage in play-acting or whether they dare disclose their true selves in the company of men.

Such patterns of self-abasement and hypocrisy are characteristic of a political order of dominance and dependence; the slaves, after all, had to learn how to dissemble, how to avoid the appearance of trying to get "above their place." Here both the dissembling and the self-denial respond to a political order that subordinates women to men's uses. In America, as in all modern societies, men's activities have been valued more than women's and men have been more powerful than women.[3] In the earliest human groups, the fact that women bear and nurse infants, combined with the fact that men, on the average, have greater physical strength, must have contributed to a particular division of labor—and thus power—between women and men. In the modern world, though, these biological differences have lost much of their original significance, and yet the structures of male supremacy remain, reinforced by the abstract image of woman.

The social definition of woman has been constructed around the needs of men. I refer not just to men's wanting someone to take responsibility for the domestic sphere of life, but of men's primary need to overcome deep-seated doubts about their own individual worth and even their identities. Not just the stereotype, but women's subordination, too, has important roots in the process by which men identify themselves through the constructs of woman and man.

In our society, as elsewhere, women have had the main responsibility for early child care. Children identify first with their mothers, but very soon they learn that their identities are bound up with gender. For a girl, the formation of her gender identity takes place within the mother-daughter relationship, in which, in Nancy Chodorow's words, "[m]others tend to experience their daughters as more like, and continuous with, themselves,"[4] and girls see themselves as feminine, like their mothers. Identity formation and attachment are combined in a single process. Mothers see their sons as opposite, and boys, in seeking to be masculine, see that they must separate themselves from their mothers. If masculine identification is initially found in separation, it is reinforced in later childhood years by activities in male peer groups outside the home. Being masculine is something a boy must achieve through attaining status and power in the individualistic, competitive, and uncompromisingly hierarchical society of other boys. Margaret Mead summed it up: "The little boy learns that he must act like a boy, do things, prove he is a boy, and prove it over and over again." It is no wonder that men generally emerge from this process with a sense of separate identity more highly developed than that of women, who typically have a definition of self that is more inclusive. If women as a group have a greater sense of empathy than do men as a group, one reason may be this early process of identity formation.

"Masculinity becomes an issue in a way that femininity does not."[5] A boy becomes a man chiefly by differentiating himself from woman. If a man sees woman as Other, and as dangerous, needing to be controlled, the reason is that his sense of self is at stake. He defines femininity by way of establishing the negative identity he must avoid: he must not be delicate, domesticated, passive, dependent. Hence the man needs woman—not individual women, who differ from each other in the same ways that men do, but this abstract construct of the mind called woman—to define himself. In Simone de Beauvoir's terms, the man defines himself as the Subject, and woman as the Other, the object through which he seeks one or another sort of fulfillment. The construct of woman, in other words, leads to the objectification of women.

At the heart of the construct is a traditional definition of femininity. The definition promotes the dependence of women on men, because femininity in its classical form is fundamentally at odds with a woman's recognition as a complete and independent human being. No wonder that feminists, ever since Mary Wollstonecraft in the eighteenth century, have been calling attention to a conflict between femininity, traditionally defined, and humanity itself. Simone de Beauvoir dramatized the point by identifying the standard definition of femininity with "mutilation."[6]

Lists of masculine and feminine traits have appeared in Western literature for hundreds of years. Most people, of course, have qualities on both lists. Given the luxuriant diversity among individuals both male and female, the traits associated with gender—with masculinity and femininity—are multidimensional. They are not to be found in a bipolar distribution with men at one pole and women at the other. Nevertheless, we largely experience the idea of gender as an either/or classification.

The gender classification powerfully affects our attitudes toward every individual we meet. As Sandra Lipsitz Bem has reminded us, gender works its way into our interpretation of all manner of things we see and know, including things "remotely or metaphorically related by sex, such as the angularity or roundedness of an abstract shape and the periodicity of the moon. Indeed, no other dichotomy in human experience appears to have as many entities linked to it as does the distinction between female and male."[7] Furthermore, once this all-important gender code is learned, we expect the world to fit into our presuppositions, and we sort out new information according to gender categories, even though there are a lot of other categories we might use just as well.[8] The gender code, like our expectations about the behavior of people of other races of ethnicity, serves as a template on which new experience is formed into patterns of meaning: "Isn't that just like a woman?"

The two sides of the gender classification have different imports; the word *woman*, unlike *man*, is an epithet: "Every time a woman describes to a man any experience which is specific to her as a woman she confronts his recognition of his own experience as normal."[9] The epithet and sense of abnormality both arise from the construct of woman, filled with the content of our traditional view of femininity. The result is what Dorothy Dinnerstein aptly calls the "under-personification" of women. Like the black who becomes "invisible" to whites who cannot see the individuality hidden behind his blackness,[10] a woman often finds that men cannot see her individual humanity, obscured as it is by the abstraction, woman.

If men define woman in order to achieve masculine identity within a bipolar ideology, then it will not be sufficient to pick out certain traits and categorize particular human beings, who may be biologically either male or female, as feminine. It is anatomy, not gender, that unfailingly accomplishes the separation of man from woman—which is what men have sought. Some men are more timid and shy than others, some women are stronger and more competitive than others, but the one thing we can count on to differentiate the sexes is the difference in sexual and reproductive function. So, the objectification of women by men cannot stop at identifying woman as the Other; it necessarily proceeds into objectification of women's sexuality. Catharine MacKinnon seems to be referring to both kinds of objectification when she says that women are "socially defined as women largely in sexual terms."

Like the stigma of racial inferiority, the stereotypic construct of woman serves to rationalize the domination of a group: men have power, and women are excluded from public life. A central feature of the classical definition of femininity unquestionably is the quality of being pleasing to men. But femininity of the traditional kind means more than that; it also means submissiveness, dependence, and domesticity—qualities that not only provide a contrasting background for masculinity but also acculturate women to a lifetime of serving men.

These features of the construct of woman reinforce a system of control by men over the sexuality and maternity of women. In American society, this control has been achieved through a variety of institutional means, both governmental and private. Prominent among the means historically used to control women's sexuality and maternity has been the law. The range of controls can be called to mind just by reciting a list of legal topics: marriage, marital property, divorce, control over and responsibility for children, illegitimacy, abortion, contraception, prostitution, and rape. Women have also been kept at home, or submissive, or both, by such private sanctions as: ostracism of "fallen" women, that is, women who were sexually aggressive or had left male protection; discrimination in employment, including sexual harassment on the job; and virtual exclusion from some professions. Until the early twentieth century, women were excluded from voting and thus from any direct influence on changing these conditions by legislation.

This sexual division of labor and life not only differentiates women's and men's roles in society; it also creates inequality of social status, wealth, and power. The feminist's slogan, "the personal is political," is true in at least two senses. One is that women's role in society—which is an issue of power and thus of politics—is crucially affected by a definition of woman designed to serve the most intimate needs of men. Men, consciously or not, seeking masculine identity through separation from woman, define the gender categories and then use the categories to justify women's dependence. The other sense is captured in this passage from Catharine MacKinnon: "It means that women's distinctive experience as women occurs within that sphere that has been socially lived as the personal—private, emotional, interiorized, particular, individuated, intimate. . . . To know the politics of woman's situation is to know women's personal lives."[11] In other words, the personal is political not only in the sense that society's assumptions governing woman's place are grounded in the private ways that men see women, but also in the strict sense that the personal and the political are identical.

The facts of male dominance and the stereotype of female dependence combine to produce a social system that reinforces itself in a circular pattern. A vital element of this system is that women themselves are persuaded to cooperate in maintaining it, to fulfill themselves solely in serving others, especially men.[12] The idea of "woman's place" is sold to women as well as men—and often sold to them by other women. At least by the nineteenth century, the selling became overt. Women were told, first by doctors and later by child psychiatrists, that their place was in the home. More recently the message has changed. Women need not stay home, but when they come home after a day's work they are still expected to fulfill woman's traditional responsibilities: management of the household and service as an emotional anchor for the family. The style of the sales pitch has changed, too; nowadays it is less overt. Consider the messages about woman's role that appear day after day, night after night, on television. Both in the programming and in the commercials, television reflects our awareness that woman's status is, above all, "the ideational envelope that contains woman's body."[13]

Even the Supreme Court, which in recent years has mostly accepted the claims of women to formal equality, has had some trouble getting past the ideational envelope. In 1977 the Court upheld an Alabama state prison regulation that forbade hiring a woman as a guard in a maximum security prison for men, when a position would require close proximity to prisoners.[14] The Court agreed that federal law prohibited the use of sex stereotypes in setting employment standards but said that Dianne Rawlinson's ability to maintain order in the prison "could be directly reduced by her womanhood." Male inmates, deprived of a heterosexual environment, might assault a woman guard just because she was a woman. Of course, in any prison, there is legitimate concern for the safety of guards; it may also be true that women guards in a men's prison are at risk in ways that men are not. But prison experts testified that women guards could be employed safely in such an environment, and the record also contained evidence of California's success with women guards in men's prisons. That real-life experience, however, was lost on a majority of the Justices, who were unable to see beyond the abstraction, woman. The Court thus reinforced the stereotypic view of women as vulnerable sex objects by using that view as its own justification.[15]

Sex and Citizenship

It was the claim of equal citizenship that informed the first manifesto to issue from the American women's movement, the Declaration of Sentiments adopted in 1848 by the first women's rights convention, meeting in Seneca Falls, New York. Claiming "the inalienable right to the elective franchise," the declaration explicitly recognized the instrumental importance of the vote for achieving women's legislative goals, such as a revision of laws governing marriage and property, and an attack on employment discrimination.[16] But the convention also claimed the vote as an attribute of citizenship. The denial of the right to vote was an essential part of a package of discriminations that, in combination, operated to "destroy [a woman's] confidence in her own powers, to lessen her self-respect, and to make her willing to lead a dependent and abject life." The Seneca Falls declaration not only reworked the Declaration of Independence ("all men and women are created equal") but also invoked the analogy of slavery. The authors saw their exclusion from the community's public life as a system of caste. As it turned out, much of their legislative program was formally adopted for the freed slaves, in the Reconstruction civil rights acts, before it was extended to women. But the heart of the women's movement in this country was a claim for inclusion.

When political majorities can be mustered behind laws to forbid governmental and nongovernmental sex discrimination, the Supreme Court routinely upholds those laws.[17] And, despite the Alabama prison decision, generally women's claims to formal equality now rest on a solid constitutional base.[18] The Court has readily accepted the argument that the stereotypical construct of woman cannot justify overt governmental discrimination that denies women access to positions or other forms of power in the public sphere. For example, the Court has recognized that the Constitution gives a woman the same right as a man to serve as administrator of a decedent's estate, to manage community property, or to serve on a jury.

In two other kinds of cases, however, the Court has stumbled. First is the case in which the governmental discrimination is not overt, but indirect, as in Helen Feeney's challenge to the Massachusetts hiring preference for veterans.[19] In rejecting that challenge, the Court followed the precedent of its racial discrimination decisions, refusing to find discrimination in the absence of proof of discriminatory purpose.[20] On this view, Feeney had failed to prove intentional discrimination against women—even though 98 percent of the state's veterans were men, and even though the preference law had, until recently, exempted jobs "especially calling for women."

The motivations of men concerning the proper role of women are buried in the recesses of the psyche. When a male-dominated legislature considers an issue that touches the interests of women, it would be extraordinary if the legislators were to think consciously about the origins of their own personal definitions of woman and to find the ability to transcend those definitions during the process of legislative decision. The point is not just that men and women mostly live different lives and see the world differently. It is that a group of men, in deciding issues that define women's roles, cannot help being influenced by the traditional construct of woman implanted at the core of their own sense of masculine identity.[21]

If male legislators have trouble in appreciating the force of women's claims to equal citizenship, one reason is that men in general are largely blind to the realities of women's lives. Not just the lives of women of other racial or ethnic groups, but the daily lives of the women closest to them, are all but invisible to most men. Part of the reason no doubt lies in the difficulty of empathizing with the abstract negative identity that is the Other. Part, too, surely lies in the inconvenience of recognizing that our own paths through the public world have been facilitated by the delay (or, more typically, the complete sacrifice) of similar opportunities for our mothers, our sisters, and our wives—not to mention the women who might have been competing with us but for the restraining hold of the stereotype of femininity. We do not know women's stories in the way that they know ours. Mostly, we prefer not to know, perhaps because we are aware, at the inarticulate edges of consciousness, that the pain in those stories has something to do with us.

This common-sense view of men's inability to see women in pain has recently found confirmation in an important study of the New York court system. In 1984 the state's chief judge appointed a blue ribbon task force to report on the status of women in the courts. It bears emphasizing that the law on the books in New York has largely rid itself of overt discrimination against women. Yet, after a twenty-two-month study, the task force summarized its findings in these words:

> [G]ender bias against women litigants, attorneys, and court employees is a pervasive problem with grave consequences. Women are often denied equal justice, equal treatment, and equal opportunity. Cultural stereotypes of women's role in marriage and in society daily distort courts' application of substantive law. Women uniquely, disproportionately, and with unacceptable frequency must endure a climate of condescension, indifference, and hostility. . . . More was found in this examination of gender bias in the courts than bruised feelings resulting from rude or callous behavior. Real hardships are borne by women. . . . The courts are viewed by a substantial group of our citizenry as a male-dominated institution disposed to discriminate against persons who are not part of its traditional constituency.[22]

What is remarkable about the task force study is not these conclusions but the impressive mountain of evidence on which they are based. The group heard testimony from litigants, lawyers, prosecutors in sex crime units, judges, representatives of women's and fathers' rights organizations and of battered women's shelters, and members of the public in a number of regions of the state. In addition, the task force conducted far-reaching statistical analyses and surveys, including a survey of New York attorneys that produced 1759 responses, nearly two-thirds of them from men. The survey dramatizes what most women already knew: consistently, in one context after another, women see (and suffer from) gender bias when men just do not see it.[23]

The New York task force report, and especially the results of the survey of attorneys, deserve to be read in full. Here we have room for only a tiny sample of quotations from the testimony. (The reader who is male is invited to engage in a small exercise: after each paragraph, pause for a moment to try to imagine how a woman might feel in the circumstances described.)

> Too often . . . it is still believed that women must like being battered or they would leave their abusers. Intake officers, often the first court personnel to see the victim, are not taking this crime seriously unless the physical signs are too obvious to ignore.

> Judges say to a woman when she walks in the courtroom, what did you do to provoke him?

> [W]hen a [rape] victim testifies, her credibility is questioned as she discussed a highly personal and humiliating attack. The community looks at her credibility, her lifestyle, her reputation and her virtue, while the defendant, to a large degree, is spared that scrutiny.

> [Women in child support cases are seen] as litigious, vexatious, harassing, and a little bit crazy, if they continue to pursue something to which they are entitled. It is almost like a little game, a game in which a person with power can put his hand on the head of the person who is angry and let that person flail away, continue to move until he drops from exhaustion, and many do drop from exhaustion. In fact, perhaps the most stable of them do drop from exhaustion or say "the hell with it, let's let him keep his money."

> Battered women [in child custody cases] are penalized by courts for a lifestyle which is a direct result of the physical abuse. Many battered women may have to move frequently in an attempt to escape the batterer. They may try to keep their home addresses or phone numbers unknown, and . . . be accused of limiting access between the father and the children. The courts are likely to view this as evidence of instability.

> [T]he double sexual standard is prevalent [in child custody cases]. A woman with a boyfriend still gets the Scarlet "A" while it is expected of a separated male. A woman who leaves the children with her husband is a monster; the opposite is readily accepted.

[Quoting, from a practice guide for trial lawyers, a passage finally deleted in the 1985 edition:] Women, like children, are prone to exaggeration; they generally have poor memories as to previous fabrications and exaggerations. They are also stubborn. You will have difficulty trying to induce them to qualify their testimony. Rather, it might be easier to induce them to exaggerate and cause their testimony to appear incredible. An intelligent woman will very often be evasive. She will avoid making a direct answer to a damaging question. Keep after her until you get a direct answer—but always be a gentleman.

Judges, counsel and court personnel will act more favorable towards women who fit their perceptions of a "good" woman, good meaning one who acts "appropriately," e.g., feminine, helpless, who defer to the "better judgment" of men.

I find it disconcerting and a distraction when I have prepared as a professional to begin a pre-trial motion, etc., and a reference, however well-intentioned, is made about my looks. Often it's a remark between a male judge and my male adversary.

It is very disappointing and disheartening to be treated with disrespect even if I conduct myself in a professional manner and I am dressed in a conservative, appropriate manner. (Example: "I don't know if you're smart but, you sure have great legs.") You do not have to be "sensitive" to develop this feeling—it is just a "fact of life" in practice.[24]

Remember the advertisement of a classroom fashion show for women law students? The largest letters on the sign in our corridor read, Dress for Success.

These examples of men's inability to look past the construct of woman to see the lives of real women help to explain why the requirement of proof of discriminatory purpose in a case like Helen Feeney's is a formula for upholding laws. Not only male legislators but male judges, too, have trouble in understanding women's experience—especially the parts of that experience that include violence and humiliation—because their version of the reality of men-women relations is different from the reality of women's experience. Part of this difference in perception surely lies in men's need to rationalize their dominance, but an equally important part lies in the image of woman as the Other, the negative identity that men must repress.

The second type of sex discrimination case that has caused difficulty for the Supreme Court is the case of legislation that looks to be protective. In

1981 the Court upheld the constitutionality of an act of Congress authorizing the president to require young men, but not women, to register for a possible military draft.[25] The draft, said Justice William Rehnquist, was designed to produce combat troops; by law and service regulations, women were excluded from serving in combat. For purposes of the draft, then, men and women were "not similarly situated," and this difference between the sexes was justification enough for requiring men only to register. Wendy Williams, looking at the law's legislative history, has shown convincingly that a major motivation for excluding women from registration lay in a view of men as protectors and women as the center of domestic life.[26] A Senate committee report posed the hypothetical case of a mother who was drafted, leaving the father to stay home to tend the children. That, said the senators, would be "unwise and unacceptable to a large majority of our people." Thus do our acculturated sex stereotypes perpetuate themselves, sometimes with the aid of our judges.

In other cases the Justices have been willing to invalidate protective legislation whenever they conclude that it merely expresses "a traditional way of thinking about females." As late as 1948 the Court had upheld a law disqualifying a woman from being a bartender unless she were the wife or daughter of a male owner of the bar.[27] In 1976, however, the Court expressly disapproved of that decision in an opinion invalidating an Oklahoma law that allowed women over the age of eighteen to buy 3.2 beer but forbade sales to men under twenty-one.[28] Later, when the Court struck down a Utah law authorizing state divorce courts to award alimony to wives but not to husbands, it commented that such laws "carry the inherent risk of reinforcing stereotypes about the 'proper place' of women and their need for special protection."[29]

The Court's opinions do not tell us what it is that makes some protective laws invalid as reinforcements of stereotype and other such laws valid because women and men are "not similarly situated." (It is always possible to find that the sexes are not similarly situated when you are looking for a way to justify treating women and men differently; if you need instruction in the technique, just read Chief Justice Rehnquist's opinions.) If we shift our attention from the opinions to the decisions, the difference between the two categories becomes clearer. Striking down Utah's alimony law or Oklahoma's law on 3.2 beer did not threaten the function of the traditional construct of woman in defining masculine identity. The draft case, however, is another matter. Wendy Williams rightly said that that decision, and the contemporary decision upholding California's gender-specific statutory rape law,[30] reflect deeply held assumptions about "man as aggressor in war [and] aggressor in sex."[31] As she says, these assumptions are built into our acculturated understanding of what it takes to be a real man. But the counterpoint theme is always there. The same assumptions depend on an acculturated image of woman as man's negative identity: passive, dependent—and, above all, powerless.

Women have a realistic basis for apprehending that legislation designed to meet the needs of real women's real circumstances may in the long run serve to perpetuate women's subordination. Protective laws do carry the risk of reinforcing the notion that the differences between women and men justify a broad range of distinctions in the way government deals with the two sexes. Feminists have recently focused attention on the general issue of "same treatment" versus "special treatment," both as a matter of principle and as a question of strategy.[32] On all sides of this discussion writers have effectively blended legal analysis with political savvy, infusing their arguments with a healthy measure of attention to the dilemmas in real women's lives. Catharine MacKinnon, however, has argued powerfully that casting the issue as one of sameness versus difference conceals the effects of gender in making male standards into the standards that define both reality and value in our society. In her approach, which emphasizes gender as dominance, "sex discrimination stops being a question of morality and starts being a question of politics."[33]

A politics aimed at head-on confrontation of the social construct of gender is a daunting prospect. Even for the undaunted, it promises a long struggle. In the meanwhile, "life is what happens while you're making other plans."[34] Both individual women and their lawyers will face choices that are, as MacKinnon says, structured by prevailing notions of gender as difference.[35] In law, many of those choices will center on questions of same treatment versus special treatment. In my view Frances Olsen is right in saying that women need not make any far-ranging choice between the two strategies. Sometimes the same treatment makes a mockery of genuine equality, and sometimes the idea of "women's special needs" is a mask for domination: "Men should be neither a model nor a contrast. Women should not have to claim to be just like men to get decent treatment, nor should they have to focus on *their* differences *from men* to justify themselves whenever they demand a policy different from the present treatment afforded to men. Women can be hurt by false paternalism and by false equality."[36]

Our constitutional doctrine also helps explain why the Supreme Court is ready to conclude that overt governmental restrictions on women's access to public positions are based on an outmoded vision of woman's role but seems to wear blinders when the discrimination or the stereotyping is not overt. A citizen's claim to participation fits comfortably into the pattern of claims to equality that came to the Court during the civil rights era. The civil rights movement aimed mainly at achieving access by racial and ethnic minorities to institutions that had long been white preserves. The analogous claims of women for access to male preserves in the community's public life have a familiar look. From the 1940s forward, when our judges and commentators have looked at our constitutional guarantee of equality, mainly what they have seen is formal equality. In this vision the judicial task is to assure that the classifications created by laws are properly attuned to legitimate legislative purposes. Only likes can be compared—which leaves women's claims to equality permanently vulnerable to casual dismissal. Furthermore, a law that does not overtly place men and women in different classes fits awkwardly into this well-worn doctrinal groove—as Helen Feeney now knows. Although a protective law does classify the sexes differently, it does not fit the civil rights model of a classification that directly disadvantages an already-disadvantaged group. Thus the formal equality model of equal protection—economically captured in the phrase, "not similarly situated"—utterly fails to address the problem of group subordination.

Fundamentally, however, the problem of women's constitutional equality is not doctrinal. A sad commonplace of American race relations is that whites are most likely to accept black people as equals when the blacks express the values that predominate among the white middle class. That is, one path to belonging in America, for racial as well as ethnic minorities, is assimilation in the extreme sense of abandonment of one culture in favor of another. But men do not want women to take on the traditional indicia of masculinity— indeed, men tend to be threatened by women who are powerful or aggressive. Women thus find themselves in a double bind: they must be different (that is, feminine), and that very difference is used to justify their subordination.

The Justices who insist on particularized proof of intentional discrimination, as in Helen Feeney's case, or who refuse to see the stereotype of femininity that underlies protective laws, as in the draft registration case, may have difficulty in appreciating the ways in which the traditional construct of woman comes to bear on the issues before them. The mechanisms by which the personal becomes political almost never reach the level of consciousness. Neither little boys nor adult male judges consciously choose to define the idea of woman around their own needs for masculine self-identification. Each of us—male or female, policymaker or not—is born into a family and a culture. Some of us may ultimately come to see the nature of woman as a social construct, but all of us learn it first as a natural truth, much as we learn that a dropped object will fall to the ground.

Sex, Autonomy, and Belonging

When we turn to what the women's movement has called choice—women's control over their own sexuality and maternity—we do not really leave the subject of citizenship behind. From the early days of the women's suffrage campaign in America, women sought the vote partly as an instrument for taking control over their private lives.[37] Citizenship is a form of power, including the power to influence matters that are personal. Just suppose, for example, that men—men as we know them, with their present political dominance and with their attitudes toward personal relationships—were miraculously transformed so that they, rather than women, were the ones who became pregnant and bore children. Can anyone doubt that "abortions on demand"[38] would be the governing rule of law?

The constitutional claim of choice in the personal, private world is even more fundamental for women than their more general claims to equal citizenship. For centuries male power over women's sexuality and maternity has restricted women to a passive role, permitting them to control conception and childbirth only through a strategy of denial. Such a strategy is capable of affecting not only a woman's behavior but her sense of self. It is not surprising that a woman who sees herself as receptive rather than active in this central aspect of her life—who tends to think of herself as "me" rather than "I"—may display a more pervasive lack of confidence in her own abilities and opinions.[39] If consciousness raising is indispensable to the redefinition of woman's place, then one necessary foundation for that process will be the experience of millions of individual women in taking control over their own personal lives. In this most intimate of contexts, autonomy and equality are mutually reinforcing.[40]

In 1920, the year that the Nineteenth Amendment constitutionalized women's right to vote, Margaret Sanger wrote, "Birth control is woman's problem." Sanger was not being insensitive, but realistic; women generally could not count on men to take any responsibility in the matter. About half a century passed between the Nineteenth Amendment and the Supreme Court's recognition of a woman's constitutional right to prevent or terminate a pregnancy. What the right to vote had failed to bring about, technology and medical opinion achieved, aided by an egalitarian wind that had been sweeping over the whole western world for a generation. Since 1965 the Supreme Court has decided cases covering nearly the whole range of legal rules governing women's sexuality and maternity. In the aggregate, these decisions offer women a degree of legal control over the private sphere of their lives that would have seemed fanciful just a generation ago. Still, it is too early for women to celebrate. Three kinds of qualifications must be recognized.

First, the campaign for formal legal autonomy is not over. An example of the distance yet to be traveled is the marital rape exemption, which excludes a husband's forcible intercourse with his wife from the definition of the crime of rape. In one recent study, about 14 percent of the married women surveyed reported that they had been raped by their husbands.[41] Yet in the great majority of our states, the marital rape exemption remains in force—in plain violation of both the constitutional freedom of intimate association and the guarantee of equal protection of the laws.[42]

The second qualification is political: legislatures continue to press the courts to face new issues concerning the constitutional status of the right to abortion. Here the problem of empathy is acute. Male legislators may consider themselves disinterested decisionmakers on an issue setting the interests of women against those of fetuses,[43] but their thinking on that subject is inextricably bound to the stereotype of woman as child-bearer and child-raiser—a stereotype that grows out of the formation of masculine identity and out of the personal relations between women and men. In this context the personal is literally political.[44]

The third qualification is that a woman's formally recognized right to control her own sexuality and maternity is not the same as actual control—a point vividly illustrated in the New York task force's findings on the treatment of battered women and rape victims.[45] What can legal autonomy mean to a woman who has been so often brutalized, and so often ignored by the authorities, that she is no longer willing to report the man who beats her and yet is afraid for herself and her children if she leaves him?

Indeed, for a great many women in this country, the blessings of formal equality and of formal autonomy will seem remote. Among women who are poor, only a small proportion will be able to claim the benefits of equal citizenship. The "freedom of the city"[46] means little when you have been impoverished by divorce,[47] or you are trying to raise a family on a monthly welfare allowance. And for poor women, the slogan "choice" has a hollow ring, even when applied narrowly to the constitutional right to choose to have an abortion. What good is that right if you cannot afford an abortion, and the state stands ready to pay the expenses of childbirth but not of abortion? And what good is the right to practice birth control when motherhood is the only source of identity in sight?[48] Employment discrimination laws do aid working women, but thus far the Constitution's protections of women's equality have mainly served women of the middle class—a cruel state of affairs that the Supreme Court made worse when it upheld Congress's power to exclude even medically necessary abortions from the Medicaid program's funding of medical care for women who were indigent.[49] It is true that any social change must start somewhere, but it is also true that the constitutional developments of the last two decades have yet to make a real difference in the lives of poor women.[50]

Autonomy—even when it is not just formal but real—is by no means a universal solution to the subordination of women. A rediscovery of our time, no less useful for having become a cliché, is the recognition that both autonomy and connection are essential in the formation of the self.[51] Yet the same processes of identity formation and gender-role socialization that tend to influence boys and men toward valuing autonomy tend to have a different influence on girls and women, who appear to be more likely to define themselves within relationships in a network of connection. These differences in the sense of self are associated with different moral perspectives. The differences, of course, are not universals but matters of tendency within the two sexes. All of us, both men and women, have the capacity to share in both of these views of self and of morality.

Exploring these differences, Carol Gilligan has sounded the same theme of gender identification that we find in the literature that examines the construct of woman.[52] For boys in our culture, gender identification means individuation and separation. For girls, it is found in attachment and empathy. Intimacy generally threatens males but reassures females. Boys play games emphasizing competition under elaborate rules and procedures for resolving disputes; girls play in a more cooperative way, suppressing competition and subordinating the game to their personal relationships. Boys' play leads them toward abstracting human relationships; girls' play fosters empathy for particular people. No wonder that "men's social orientation is positional, while women's is personal."[53]

Perhaps these orientations are founded, in part, on biological difference; Gilligan herself leaves the question open. Undoubtedly, however, "the reproduction of mothering"[54] is promoted by the early acculturation of girls to roles that involve cooperation and nurturing and the deferral of the claims of a separate self—not coincidentally, the very roles specified by the traditional construct of femininity.[55]

The notion of autonomy thus presents problems for many women—and as they work out their individual answers to those problems, women provide a living metaphor for our society's more general problems with the excesses of individual autonomy. A woman who is well socialized to the culture's traditional expectations may see success, in its usual form, as a threat to her feminine identity. In particular she may fear that men will see her success as making her unfeminine, thus a neuter, or, alternatively, men will have trouble in looking behind the abstraction of the Other to see her, the real person, as a valued coworker—or, worst of all, both.

Furthermore, many women appear to see a strong form of individualism as threatening not only their security in the web of relationships, but also their sense of self. A woman who sees herself as continuous with the environment, including the human environment, is likely to see "the need for autonomy [as] selfish and bad,"[56] part of her own negative identity that must be repressed. More essentially, she is apt to find the quest for autonomy illusory; what can a highly individuated autonomy mean to a woman who defines herself as part of a relationship? When Gilligan asked four women who were high achievers to describe themselves, not one spoke of her achievements. Instead, all four chose to "describe a relationship, depicting their identity *in* the connection of future mother, present wife, adopted child, or past lover."[57]

The point is not that women lack the need for active and autonomous expression of the self, but that the processes that form their identities and acculturate them to the traditional definition of femininity impose a cost on many women when they express that need directly. One indirect way for a woman to express the need for autonomy is through what some psychotherapists call projective identification.[58] She projects that need on some man who is close to her—a husband, for example—and this projection allows her the luxury of a single-minded chase after connection.

The parallel of men's own projective identification is just about perfect, and it is no mere coincidence. A man can find the separation from others that frees him for an autonomous climb up the ladder of success by projecting onto his partner his need for intimacy (and the vulnerability that intimacy entails). Such a couple manages to satisfy the dual needs of the self for autonomy and connection by a division of psychic labor. The result should be familiar to students of political systems. At the level of behavior and articulated meaning, man is public and woman private; man is independent and woman dependent; man is separate and woman connected. In the interior world, however, the effective unit is the couple:

She who chases (I use this pronoun because it is more commonly the woman) is dependent on him who runs away to express autonomy needs for both of them. Similarly, he who is in flight from emotional connectedness must be assured that someone is still after him—otherwise he might have to accept responsibility for his own feelings of vulnerability, which she expresses for both of them. They have divided the ambivalence—the needs of the self and the needs of the relationship—right down the middle of their emotional attachment.[59]

In such a partnership in frustration, real intimacy is out of the question. Both the woman who fears autonomy and the man who fears intimacy (and no doubt fears women, too) avoid confronting each other as persons for fear of the projected abstraction of the Other. The cumulative result of all these processes of identity formation, gender-role differentiation, and projective identification is not the division of society into separate cultures, male and female,[60] any more than Jim Crow was two cultures, black and white. The result rather is a single social system that presents formidable obstacles to the self-realization of either women or men.

For women, belonging to American society begins in the same concerns that occupy the members of racial or religious or ethnic minorities: freedom from fear, release from a spoiled identity. But belonging, for women, also means something different. The recent "feminization of poverty" notwithstanding, women are already ranged across the whole spectrum of social and economic status. What women as a group need is release from the frustration of an "inability to find ourselves in existing culture as we experience ourselves."[61] In one perspective this release is a form of equality of opportunity, but the opportunities in question are not mainly chances to fill positions in industry or government. The opportunity that matters most is the chance to be oneself, to be recognized for one's own qualities of individuality—to be allowed to be different, not just from men but also from other women.[62] The American civic culture promises tolerance for diversity, and women need to demand the fulfillment of that promise. A particular woman's self-determination may or may not include a heavy measure of autonomy; may or may not emphasize the self-in-connection. What she needs is to be valued, not for conforming to the traditional construct of woman, not for conforming to a male-defined model of achievement, but for being her own self, the self she fashions out of the cultural materials at hand.

Whatever may be the way out of women's predicament of subordination, surely it is not some direct form of assimilation into traditional male roles. Half a century ago, Emma Goldman—of all people—looked at the movement for women's emancipation and found it wanting. True emancipation, she said, "will have to do away with the ridiculous notion that to be loved, to be sweetheart and mother, is synonymous with being slave or subordinate."

For Goldman, woman was "confronted with the necessity of emancipating herself from emancipation, if she really desires to be free."[63] Some feminists today would call Goldman's assertion a romantic prescription for chaining women to the classical definition of femininity. Making allowance for more than fifty years' worth of change in awareness and rhetorical style, however, Goldman seems to have been touching the edges of a great truth. Women do need to free themselves from the kind of autonomy that not only sets them free but cuts them loose. They do need to find ways of participating actively and powerfully in the public world without simply exchanging a place in the network of connection for a step on the ladder of achievement.[64] But to say that women need these things is only the half of it; men need them, too.

For each of us, the accommodation of the needs for autonomy and belonging must take place in a private life, even an interior life. But the accommodation is needed in our public life as well; we need the freedom to act in the world, and we need our community connections. These two spheres are not separate. The personal is, indeed, political: each individual's self-definition comes to affect his or her conception of communities both large and small. But the political is also personal. When we define our place in a larger community, we say something to ourselves about our own personal identities. To perceive that citizenship is connection is to understand something about the meaning of America and about who we are as individual Americans.

eight

Citizenship, Race, and Marginality

A core value of equal citizenship is responsibility. If today's Americans are true to their tradition of equal opportunity, they will see to it that our marginalized poor are afforded a real chance to participate in the community of equal citizens. Those of us who never have to think about whether we belong have a responsibility to insure that no one goes hungry in America; that the children of the marginalized poor receive effective education, not warehousing; that people who want work can find jobs and the training to perform them.

The argument is simple and straightforward. Yet, such arguments typically have hard going in our society. Among a "people of plenty,"[1] the poor are apt to be seen as deviant, as outsiders. Our acculturation to the norms of individualism uses poverty as a negative identity: don't be a loser; work hard so you won't be poor. Believing in America as a land of opportunity, we are ready to view the poor as people who deserve their poverty because they have chosen not to try. "The availability of work for every ablebodied person who really wants a job is one of the enduring myths of American history."[2] For one who is able-bodied, pauperism—the failure to be self-sustaining—is seen as a moral failing. The long association of social welfare programs with the control of deviance,[3] and the visible departure by many poor people from middle-class norms of dress, speech, and day-to-day behavior, reinforce the characterization of the nonworking poor as the Other.[4]

Perceptions of the poor are complicated by associations between poverty and race. Most American blacks are not poor, and at any particular moment a majority of America's poor are white. But white families tend to move in and out of poverty, and their poverty generally does not persist from one generation to the next.[5] The marginalized poor, who stay poor and whose children likely will stay poor, are in an overwhelming majority members of racial or ethnic minorities, women living outside male protection, or both.[6] The picture of the poor as the Other, those who do not really belong, is thus intensified. This view translates into public policy, which in turn plays its own role in separating the poor—especially the female and minority poor—from the rest of us. The separation of paupers, so evident in the different treatment afforded to need-based welfare programs and to middle-class programs like Social Security,[7] is modern America's inheritance from Victorian England's reform of the poor law.

For the English reformers of 1834, one central purpose of requiring paupers to live in the workhouse was to stigmatize them. Their physical separation would mark them as outcasts, people who lived outside the boundaries of a society that was defined by the market.[8] Today the workhouse is behind us,[9] but the stigma and the separation remain. Some people are defined as full members of our community, and some are not. We concentrate the poor physically by locating low-income housing projects in the poorest neighborhoods[10] and excluding them from the suburbs.[11] We call some forms of governmental assistance insurance, and we use other forms of assistance to control the deviance of, say, mothers who are not only poor but unmarried. The Texas legislature's decision to leave aid to the aged intact while radically cutting AFDC benefits[12] calls to mind an older view linking poverty to cultural and moral pathology.[13] In the Texas of the 1960s Ruth Jefferson fell victim to a mentality with roots in mid-nineteenth century London.

Welfare policy aside, some of the separation of the poor from the rest of us results from a simple lack of means. It takes resources to participate in activities that the community regards as validating[14]—to be an effective husband or wife or parent, for example; to hold a job; or to engage in some leisure pursuits that command respect. These resources begin with income and assets, but they may also include "social contacts or knowledge or political influence or prestige or health or personal attractiveness"[15]—a list notable for its inclusion of things money can buy. The crucial question here is whether a family's resources meet the level that a particular community "regards as the minimum necessary for decency."[16] To fall below that minimum is to subject yourself to the community's judgment that you are indecent, outside the community of persons entitled to respect. The essential harm of this severe form of poverty is stigma, a spoiled identity.

In comparison with the countries of Western Europe, the United States provides low levels of public assistance for poor people.[17] One factor that weakens the American public's support for social welfare programs is the perception, widely shared among middle-class whites, that welfare means aid to the members of racial and ethnic minorities. Although a clear majority of public assistance beneficiaries are white, some assistance programs do disproportionately serve minority beneficiaries[18]—a fact that gives negative racial attitudes a plausible target. Poverty is dispiriting for anyone who experiences it involuntarily, yet, here as elsewhere, there is something special about race. Black people are not merely disadvantaged when they are poor, they are also relatively poor because they are black.[19] If we put racial discrimination aside, we find that structural unemployment normally does not transmit its economic effects from one generation to the next. But, when we are talking about economic conditions in black America,* putting discrimination aside is both obtuse and unjust.[20]

Poverty and the Culture of Isolation

In 1983 the median family income for whites in America was $24,603; for blacks, $13,599. In the same year the unemployment rate for whites was 8.4%; for blacks, 19.5%. In 1985, 11.4% of the white population lived below the federal government's officially defined poverty line; for black people, the figure was 31.3%. For children, the disparity was greater: below the poverty level lived 15.9% of white and 43.4% of black children. (In 1984 the figure for black children was 46.5%).[21]

Statistics like these remind us that yesterday's racial caste system continues

---

* In focusing here on the poverty of black people I do not mean to minimize the severity of living conditions for large numbers of people in other minority communities. For references on Indian tribal communities see chapter 6, nn 2–5. Outside the black ghetto, the greatest concentrations of minority poor are found among Chicanos and other Latinos. The experience of Latinos in recent generations has followed the historic pattern set by earlier immigrant groups: economic advance from one generation to the next, accompanied by an increasing rate of intermarriage with non-Latinos (Thernstrom 23–24). Since 1980 conditions have deteriorated in all poor communities, including Latino ones. In 1985 25.5 percent of "Hispanic" families' incomes fell below the federal government's poverty line (as compared with 28.7 percent for black families and 9.1 percent of non-"Hispanic" white families). On doubts among the "Chicano generation" about the likely continuation of the pattern of intergenerational advance, see Alvarez 49. "In 1981, 30 percent of Hispanic 18 and 19-year-olds were not high school graduates," and some early-1980s projections said the number of Latino children would double by the year 2000 (House of Representatives Report [1948] 4040). On the high school dropout problem, see Ortego 165–69. In the large urban barrios these problems may be closely associated with recent immigration. Language barriers obstruct not only employment opportunities but a wide range of other interactions, including dealings with the governmental agencies that are designed to relieve the most severe kinds of want.

In the long run, intergenerational advance seems a fair prediction. But each of us must live in her own generation, and it is only a partial comfort to be told that your grandchildren will have a better life. In the meantime, poverty is taking its toll on a great many lives. A friend of mine, a legal aid lawyer in Los Angeles, sees barrio residents every day who are in desperate need, keenly aware of their obligation to provide for their families, and filled with a sense of failure for their inability to fulfill that responsibility.

to affect today's world, but the gross figures conceal marked differences within the black population. When the Supreme Court in 1982 pronounced the demise of caste legislation in America,[22] it spoke a truth that was important but limited. The formal barriers are down; what was once called the color line is no longer policed by government. Since midcentury blacks have cracked the race barrier in many labor unions and have found employment in significant numbers in clerical and service jobs both governmental and private. The same period has seen considerable increases in the numbers of black officeholders, black professionals, and black students in colleges and universities—in all, a flowering of the black middle class.[23] The developing black middle class not only provides role models for young blacks but also presents the important lesson for whites that the capacities of black and white people cover the same range. The last three decades have seen a moderate but significant decrease in the differential between incomes of employed blacks and employed whites, both for men and for women.[24] As always, opportunity is leading to acculturation. Naturally enough, blacks employed in steady jobs tend to hold the same attitudes toward the value of work as do employed whites,[25] and families of any race with children in college tend to value higher education. Rising incomes enhance the possibilities for family stability. Modest increases in the number of black-white marriages[26] attest to the beginnings of a new stage of cultural assimilation. The uncompromising rigidity that was the hallmark of the racial caste system is gone. Yet roughly one-third of the nation's blacks are impoverished and living at the margins of society.[27]

A vivid early picture of life in the marginalized group is painted in *Tally's Corner*, Elliot Liebow's book detailing the destructive effects of marginality on the black men who formed a street-corner community in Washington, D.C., a generation ago. For the man who frequents Tally's Corner, the available jobs are menial, intermittent, or both. When a job is available, it is a dead end, requiring no particular skills and leading to nothing better. Wages are low and sometimes deliberately set at low levels on the expectation that employees will steal the rest of their meager incomes, an expectation that tends to fulfill itself. These men value marriage both for its own sake and for the respect it engenders, but for them the support of a family is next to impossible, and the search for respect as a provider soon turns to a search for routes of escape. The young men have seen it all before in the experience of their parents and the parents' serial companions. If their activities emphasize satisfactions here and now, one good reason is that the future offers little hope.

Liebow organized his book around a series of roles occupied by the streetcorner man: "breadwinner, father, husband, lover and friend." Failure in the role of breadwinner reproduces itself as failure in the other roles, with predictable harms to the man's sense of personal worth. Tally Jackson wants "to be a person in his own right, to be noticed by the world"; in this respect he is like his compatriots, who all "position themselves to catch the attention of their fellows in much the same way as plants bend or stretch to catch the sunlight"[28]—but it all comes to naught, as it always has.

Liebow's account of Tally Jackson and some twenty other men brings to life the reality buried in statistics about unemployment and income. These men's tragedy is that, for all their assertion of alternative values, they have absorbed the larger society's cultural messages about the values of work and family.[29] Their sense of failure is thus deep, fundamental, deadening to the sense of self. Ironically, the cruelty is heightened now that the formal system of racial caste is dismantled. The losers are regularly told that they live in an era of equal opportunity. The fault, they are now given to understand, lies not in their stars but in themselves.

The process that undermines self-respect for the men on Tally's Corner also affects the ghetto's women. A stable marriage is extremely unlikely without the expectation of a steady income from employment.[30] When marital breakup is the norm, women and men alike come to view the idea of a permanent union with suspicion. For many women, this suspicion ripens into a generalization that "you can't trust men."[31] Although a young ghetto woman feels little pressure to marry, having a baby is something else again. Her motivation is not a welfare check: "Having babies for profit is a lie that only men could make up, and only men could believe."[32] Becoming pregnant, however, is one way of asserting control over an important aspect of her life. Furthermore, having the baby indicates entry into the responsibilities of adulthood—even when the mother is a teenager and effective responsibility for her first baby is borne by its grandmother. Even with this aid, the result of early parenthood generally is a drastic reduction in the young woman's education and future employment prospects—typically with the result that she has more children and becomes less likely to find employment at a living wage.[33]

The overwhelming majority of ghetto children live in single-parent households, and almost always the parent is a woman.[34] If jobs are available to that woman, they will tend to pay poorly, partly because they are "women's work." The better-paying jobs tend to be part-time work that will not support a family. For middle-class professionals, the two-income family provides material conditions for the good life. Among black working people, the two-income family is increasingly a necessity for survival without public assistance.[35] Even if she is employed, the ghetto woman who is a single parent typically will need welfare benefits;[36] she will supplement that income with contributions from household members whose attachment to the household may not last or who are employed only seasonally or uncertainly. Although the charge that the availability of welfare causes people to refuse work or quit their jobs is false,[37] the cycle of welfare dependence, passed on from one generation to another, is no myth.

Raising a family in these circumstances is not just a challenge but a struggle. For an individual household, uncertainty of income is the normal condition. Carol Stack has shown that the women who head these families cope with this uncertainty by forming networks of domestic cooperation with the households of kin and of friends. The system of support includes men, both relatives and steady companions, but it is the women of the ghetto who manage the network. A woman who has the domestic network behind her, or who controls the welfare money, and who is present from day to day has greater authority over her children than do the children's fathers who live in other households. In this sense ghetto families are matrifocal. But, as Stack shows, it is a mistake to speak broadly of disorganization when the network of kin and friends provides a stability that a single household cannot provide on its own.[38]

The operation of the support network may not be a job in the eyes of the larger society, but it is a never-ending responsibility, constantly occupying the network's members in a life of urban hunting and gathering.[39] Women are regularly on the move, not just having to change residences frequently but moving about every day, seeking help from kin, dealing with the bureaucracies that dispense welfare payments and food stamps and Medicare. The exchange of goods and services normally takes the form of gifts and loans made on the basis of one person's present capacity to satisfy another's pressing need. Only in the long run are the exchanges seen as reciprocal. The network is, in effect, a small community with a group identity.[40] A woman finds much of her self-respect in her ability to use the network to provide for her family's needs and in her responsibility to the other members. She is, in short, creating a substitute for the values of equal citizenship. If her teenage daughter sees motherhood as the first step on the path to respected participation in the adult network, no one should be surprised.

Any resources that come into the network are immediately applied to relieve someone's privation. This feature drastically reduces the chances that any individual or couple will be able to save or invest for their own future needs. It is hard enough to come up with the first and last months' rent for an apartment; a down payment on a house seems fanciful.[41] In fact, relatives may deliberately seek to undermine a marriage that threatens to end the husband's and wife's contributions to their respective networks. Stack tells the poignant story of Julia and Elliot, whose union failed to survive Elliot's loss of his seasonal job, his subsequent demoralization, and the jealous intermeddling of Julia's kin who resented the marriage as an interference with Julia's participation in their network.[42] No one can say whether Elliot and Julia would have stayed together if his employment had been lasting. If stable employment were available for ghetto residents generally, however, there would be no need for the survival networks that drain marriages that are already undernourished.

Liebow's study was made in the early 1960s, and Stack's ended in 1973; since those days employment opportunities for ghetto residents have taken a dramatic turn for the worse.[43] Ghetto neighborhoods today have extremely high rates of unemployment and, worse, of people who have stopped looking for work. Both men and women in the ghetto prefer jobs to welfare,[44] but the closing of factories and other structural changes in the economy have largely eliminated the kind of jobs that European immigrants formerly used as the first rung of the employment ladder.[45] New jobs are being created at the lowest levels, but they do not pay a living wage. Of the eight million net new jobs created from 1979 to 1984, more than half paid less than $7000 a year (almost $4000 below the officially defined poverty level for a family of four).[46] William Julius Wilson remarked: "It's as though racism, having put the black underclass in its economic place, stepped aside to watch technological change finish the job."[47]

Paradoxically, the worsening of the situation of impoverished blacks is partly the result of improvements in the situation of other black people. Antidiscrimination law has opened up employment, education, and housing, but these very opportunities have tended to fragment the black community, an eventuality surprising to no one who is familiar with the effects of economic advance on other cultural groups in America. Many employed blacks living in two-parent families have moved out of the poorest parts of the central city (this option was narrowly limited before the civil rights era). The ghettos have lost population since 1970. Consider what else the ghetto residents have lost in this second migration: personal connections into the employment information network; marriage opportunities that might lead to two-parent (and two-income) families; most of their former community leaders; the stabilizing effects of the departed families and of the businesses and churches and other institutions that served them. The ghetto has become the site of a new culture of isolation, not just the isolation of blacks from whites, but the isolation from middle-class blacks of the poorest and most dependent blacks. In these circumstances the values of education and work and family stability are undermined. Why stay in school if your friends have dropped out, the gang is demanding a lot of your time, and schooling itself seems to offer little promise of a rewarding job? Why spend your days searching for work when everyone you know has stopped trying to find it? No wonder so many teenagers seek the sense that they are somebody by getting pregnant, getting high, getting into trouble.[48]

It understates the case to say that the ghetto imposes strong pressures to depart from the values held by middle-class blacks and whites alike. Those pressures are brought to bear most powerfully on young males, a number of whom become involved in gangs and criminal activity. There is a view of this response—a view I do not share—that begins and ends in the remark, "He never had a chance." Understanding may lead us to forgive, but forgiving is not the same as excusing. These young men are responsible for what they do; burglary and robbery are serious crimes, deserving of condemnation and punishment. Yet there are structural interpretations of juvenile crime in the ghetto that also merit consideration by the makers of public policy.

The point is not that unemployment or poverty directly causes any particular young man to turn to crime. Rather, the unemployment of men in the ghetto translates into families headed by single women, and the existence of such families in an area is the strongest predictor for serious crimes by juveniles, black or white.[49] No one can be sure of the precise mechanisms that produce these results, but we do know that areas with high proportions of disrupted families are also areas in which both formal and informal social controls over young people are weakened. Those areas consistently show low levels of community participation, not only in politics but in the PTA, the YMCA, or the other voluntary organizations that are so important in tying young people to the community. Furthermore, reduced numbers of two-parent families mean a weakening of adult guardianship over children and a weakening of defenses against the influence of the gangs.[50]

Behind structural abstractions like "black male unemployment" stand the men on Tally's Corner and their younger brothers. Suppose you are a teenage boy, living in a ghetto housing project. "Black male unemployment" means that your father doesn't live with you, but it also means that your own chances of finding a job at a decent wage are slim. Being unemployed drastically reduces your opportunities to validate your own identity through work and the things wages will buy. What is left? One obvious way to be someone is to join the gang, to show what you are made of precisely by defying the larger society and its values.

In his biting criticism of the 1834 reform of the English poor law, William Cobbett saw the point in the perspective of political philosophy. To throw the poor on their own resources removed them from the community, sent them back to the Hobbesian state of nature. In the war of all against all, why should they respect others' property,[51] or, we might add, others' persons? As violent crime increases in the ghetto, the vacuum left by the departed community leadership is, in uncomfortably large measure, filled by the leaders of the gangs.[52] Such a neighborhood is not a community, for a community needs a sense of generalized mutual obligation and a sense of purpose. A battleground is not the same as a community of battle.

This cycle of dependency and despair is emphatically not the norm for black Americans; it is seen by most blacks as the pathological case.[53] Yet poverty is a reality for almost one out of three of America's black citizens, and the self-reinforcing features of the culture of isolation signal the danger that today's ghetto residents and their offspring will be relegated to virtually permanent membership in a marginalized group defined by race.[54] In describing these developments some writers have pinned the label *underclass* on a disparate collection of people ranging from mothers who receive AFDC benefits to street criminals.[55] This arresting label, like the *culture of poverty* that has fueled a generation-long debate,[56] focuses attention on the persistent divergence of behavior patterns among the marginalized poor from middle-class norms—a matter about which there can hardly be any dispute. What has generated debate, and no little heat, is the suggestion that some cultural deficiency prevents the marginalized poor from taking advantage of opportunities.

Undoubtedly, patterns of behavior have staying power; the culture of isolation has real consequences for the lives of individuals who live in it. But if anything is axiomatic in human societies it is that behavior ultimately responds to circumstances. The danger in the cultural deficiency thesis is that it so easily translates into moralizing about individual failings and thus into rationalizations for separating the marginalized poor from the rest of society. The tendency to see the poor as the Other, to create mental barriers excluding them from the population of equal citizens, is hard to overcome in a society that prizes individualism. When the marginalized poor are also members of racial or ethnic minorities, the tendency toward distancing is heightened. The view of paupers held by the Victorian Whigs is plainly visible in the policies of our own national government toward social welfare programs in the 1980s.[57]

In raising the specter of a permanently marginalized class, I do not assume that marginality is inexorably transmitted from one generation to the next or that the desperately poor are a group "with the character not so much of a class as of a 'tribe' or 'race.' "[58] Rather, the recurrent patterns of behavior among marginalized people seem predictable adaptations to the recurrent patterns of their circumstances—a "survival culture," if you will.[59] Everyone needs respect; if the usual middle-class avenues to respect seem closed, other avenues will be pursued.[60] In the demoralizing circumstances of the culture of isolation, the sociologists' distinction between caste and class loses much of its utility.

Citizenship and Poverty

A quarter century ago, with the modern civil rights movement in full stride, James Q. Wilson published a study of black leaders in Chicago.[61] Wilson drew a distinction between status goals and welfare goals. By welfare goals he meant tangible improvements such as better schools, new public housing, or better access to health services. Status goals were centered on the principle of equality, on the integration of blacks into the general community: school integration, open occupancy in housing, equal treatment of blacks in the allocation of public offices and honors. Both types of goals are, of course, also found among leaders of other ethnic groups. Indeed, with respect to many immediate welfare goals, there is little to distinguish racial or ethnic groups from other interest groups. A black neighborhood has the same interest in getting the city to repair streetlights as any other neighborhood would have. A subordinated racial group's status goals, however, do differ from the goals of many other interest groups that seek to influence government. The group seeks to replace discrimination and domination with acceptance, recognition, and equal citizenship.

Political participation itself contributes to the sense of belonging. For six decades the enfranchisement of southern blacks was one of the NAACP's most important objectives.[62] One poignant scene, recurrent during the civil rights era, was depicted in the news photographs that accompanied stories about blacks voting for the first time in southern elections. Typically, the picture showed newly registered black voters lining up to vote. To understand what it meant to those citizens to be included in the community's decision processes after a lifetime of exclusion, it wasn't necessary to read the accompanying article; a look at the people's faces told the story. Formal equality by itself is not enough to make good on the promise of equal citizenship, but it is an essential beginning.

The status of a minority group is not just a statistical interpretation; it is a matter of intense personal concern for every one of the group's members. A black person wants the freedom to keep her primordial identity as a member of the group and also to be accepted as one who belongs to the larger society. She is aware that her individual standing in society is tied to the status of blacks generally. For her the group's status goal of equal citizenship is not an airy abstraction but a central aspect of her sense of self.

For all its importance, status equality cannot stand by itself. Just as Jim Crow employed a mixture of formal legal disabilities and informal social and economic sanctions, it will take more than the elimination of formal legal inequalities to end the status harm that is the main evil of a system of caste. To speak of equal citizenship as a status goal, then, is to identify an objective that includes a measure of substantive equality along with formal equality before the law. The best evidence of an end to the harms that are black people's legacy from the racial caste system would be for blacks and whites to be ranged along the socioeconomic scale in approximately the same distribution. On the other hand, a series of antidiscrimination measures focused on welfare goals may, in the aggregate, work important changes in the status of a previously dominated group. So, although the distinction between status and welfare goals has its uses in analyzing day-to-day political strategies, eventually these two types of goals converge. In our national experience, cultural minorities have secured full inclusion in the community's public life only when the great preponderance of their members have visibly advanced into the middle class.

In this process politics certainly can help, and the successes achieved under the civil rights laws of the 1960s provide thousands of cases in point. But poor people constitute a distinct minority of our population, and, in a political world increasingly dominated by extensive campaign spending, their influence cannot even match their numbers. In today's America majority rule means government of, by, and for the comfortable.[63] Yet, when the marginalized poor go to court seeking inclusion in the community of equal citizens, they are apt to be told that they are just another interest group whose claims are properly part of "the routine grist of the political mill."[64] The metaphor of grinding nicely captures the political condition of the marginalized poor in the legislature, where their claims have so often been ground into powder, then blown away on winds of oratory about individual initiative.

It is easy to see how most elected decision makers can ignore the marginalizing of the poor or treat it as a just punishment for deviance from majoritarian norms. A further complication arises from the time scale of many antipoverty efforts. It is hard for any elected official to look beyond the next election, which for many legislators is always less than two years away. A job training program, for example, may be cost-efficient, but its present costs are high and the savings it will produce (in public assistance costs, in the costs of other public services, and in the costs of crime and punishment) will emerge only in the longer term.[65] The judiciary, however, is "the one governmental element that is disposed to take the long-run into account."[66] Furthermore, our courts have their own independent responsibility to the principle of equal citizenship.

In the Warren era, the Supreme Court edged toward a doctrinal recognition of the poor as a minority that deserved special judicial protection. A formally neutral law might have the effect of excluding poor people from some important government service—as where the right to appeal from a criminal conviction was conditioned on furnishing a transcript of the trial, and a transcript would be provided only for a fee. In that very case the Court held that the state must supply a free transcript to a would-be appellant who could not afford to buy one.[67] Nor, said the Court, could a state condition an indigent person's right to vote on the payment of a tax or limit welfare benefits to people with a year's residence in the state.[68] These decisions—and others imposing affirmative obligations on government to make up for a lack of the resources to mount an effective defense to criminal prosecution[69]— reflected not just solicitude for the poor but an awareness that serious concern for racial equality implied a concern for the ways in which status and welfare goals were intertwined.

Yet the Court never explicitly mentioned race—indeed, only occasionally suggested that it was protecting the poor. Rather, its opinions emphasized the importance of the particular items that the state must supply. As a result, it was easy for a later majority to characterize the decisions restrictively, not as decisions about race or poverty, but as decisions about such things as the right to vote or the right to counsel.[70] It is true, of course, that the Burger Court's majority was looking for ways to contain the expansion of the earlier precedents. In 1970 the Court turned away from any generalized constitutional obligation to relieve poor people from the consequences of their poverty; the turning point was the case of *Dandridge v. Williams*.[71]

Linda Williams lived in Baltimore with her eight children, who ranged in age from four to sixteen. She and one of the children were in poor health. The children's father was absent and contributed nothing to the household; the family's total lack of financial resources had befallen after the youngest child was born. Williams was receiving benefits under Maryland's AFDC program. The state had established a schedule of financial need for AFDC families with decreasing amounts for each person after the initial beneficiary but with a fixed additional amount for each person over ten persons. For the Williams family the standard of need was $296.15 per month. The state, however, also limited the amount that any one family could receive; in Baltimore this maximum was $250 per month. It was undisputed that this limit did not represent a calculation of economies of scale and had nothing to do with need; it simply resulted from the legislature's failure to appropriate enough money to satisfy the needs the state had defined.

Linda Williams, along with Junius and Jeannete Gary, a couple in similar circumstances,[72] challenged the maximum grant limitation as a violation of the equal protection clause, and a three-judge federal district court agreed with their claim.[73] A 6–3 majority of the Supreme Court, however, concluded otherwise: Maryland's discrimination—between the benefits per child for the Williams and Gary children and the benefits per child for Baltimore children who lived in smaller families—fell within "the area of economics and social welfare" and thus must be upheld if it had any reasonable basis. The Court's opinion acknowledged that the case involved not the usual run of business regulation but "the most basic economic needs of impoverished human beings." Still, said the majority, it was reasonable for the state to give AFDC recipients generally an incentive to seek employment.

It is worth pausing here to reflect on the ways in which comfortable people, including legislators and judges, are inclined to project their own negative identities on the abstract image of the poor, regarding them as people who just haven't been industrious. Linda Williams and the Garys were not employable; indeed, the trial court had found that only one-third of 1 percent of Maryland's AFDC families included any employable members. Yet the plight of the Williams and Gary families remained hidden behind the mask of the Other. The Supreme Court recognized that the real people in the case were not able to work but dismissed that knowledge with a shrug. The equal protection clause, said the Court, did not require the legislature to "choose between attacking every aspect of a problem or not attacking the problem at all."

One rationalization for this change in judicial course was ready at hand in the dissents of the second Justice John Marshall Harlan from the earlier poverty decisions of the Warren Court. Harlan, echoing Jeremy Bentham's century-old critique of egalitarian reform,[74] raised the stopping-place problem: the problem of defining limits on the potentially infinite reach of the equal protection clause. The Court's more recent majorities, making Harlan's lament their theme song, apparently have assumed that their own response to the effects of poverty, unlike a legislative response, is limited to the choice between attacking poverty wholesale or ignoring the problem altogether. The majority Justices seem to see only two options: either complete judicial passivity or a broad-scale judicial commitment to economic leveling. If this mistaken assumption were the only problem, it would be easily solved. But more fundamental difficulties complicate any effort to apply present equal protection doctrine to the needs of the marginalized poor.

From the casebooks that law students study to the opinions of Supreme Court Justices, the prevailing view is that issues of constitutional equality begin as problems in classification. This view, articulated in an influential paper of the 1940s,[75] focuses on a legislature's different treatment of people or transactions and asks whether those classifications, or discriminations, are sufficiently justified. By the end of the Warren era the Supreme Court and its commentators had developed two kinds of cases in which the state carried a heavy burden of justification: the case in which the legislature uses a "suspect" classification—racial discrimination being the archetype—and the case in which the law classifies people in a way that denies some of them an interest that is "fundamental."[76] A classification of either of these two types, the Court still says, violates the equal protection clause unless the state can show that the classification is necessary to achieve some governmental interest of "compelling" importance. Other legislative classifications are upheld on lesser showings of governmental need.

So it is that huge quantities of high-powered legal energy are expended in persuading courts to use higher or lower "levels of scrutiny," that is, to demand greater or lesser degrees of justification in support of legislative classifications. This whole tedious process of argumentation and opinion-writing is an exercise in rationalization. It began as a way of avoiding the charge of judicial legislation by giving a judicial look—categories, rules, and all—to the courts' interventions to correct particularly serious abuses of legislative power.[77] The exercise continues because it provides lawyers and judges on all sides of equality issues with rhetorical paint to decorate the results they are advocating.

The trouble is that no sensible analysis of marginalizing poverty will fit into this scheme.[78] Where is the legislative classification that puts Tally Jackson in his place on the corner? The question touches more than legal doctrine: it reaches poor people at the center of self-identification. Finding no one in particular to share responsibility for his condition of marginality, Tally Jackson blames himself.

One reason why this self-critical evaluation carries so much force is that it cannot be contradicted by the life experience of a single individual. It is impossible to demonstrate that any one person's economic condition is the result of racial discrimination. The difficulty lies in the importance of indeterminate factors—what most of us call luck—in the success or nonsuccess of particular individuals. Lester Thurow put it this way: "Since everyone is subject to a variety of good and bad random shocks, no one can tell whether any individual has been unfairly treated by looking at that person's income." Judgments about systematic discrimination "can only be made at the level of the group."[79] Considered in isolation, Tally Jackson has no supportable complaint against anyone; he is just down and out. But if we aggregate the lives of Tally and Sea Cat and Richard and Leroy[80]—and their myriad counterparts on other corners in America's other inner cities—their common situation can be seen as membership in a marginalized group that has the look of permanence and is associated with race. It is no accident that the race in question is the same one that previously defined a subordinate caste.

Thurow draws a natural conclusion from his analysis of the measurement of racial discrimination: "the inability to identify anything except group discrimination creates an inability to focus remedies on anything other than the group."[81] Thurow uses the term remedies broadly, to encompass legislative remedies. To a lawyer, however, the reference to remedies calls to mind the court orders that culminate lawsuits: the award of damages to a victim of discrimination or an injunction to end discrimination or its effects. Although the cumulative consequences of generations of group subordination are dramatically visible on Tally's corner, the Supreme Court's present view of the law makes it hard to translate those conditions into a successful lawsuit. Under the Court's present doctrine, judicial remedies are available only to individual plaintiffs who can demonstrate that particular harms have been caused by particular acts of misconduct by particular government officials who intended the harms.[82] Tally Jackson is out of court.

To appreciate the constitutional standing of the marginalized poor we need a fresh start—not a new edifice of doctrine but a perspective that lets us see the faces of real people behind the abstraction, poverty. That abstraction seems immense and impenetrable, and it is easy to see how it gives judges pause. How can a court be expected to end poverty? A market—in fact, any activity—inevitably means that some people will succeed more than others.[83] A judge cannot issue an injunction that runs against the whole economy—and even if you would like to have the judge do that, what would you want the order to command? Putting the matter this way, as the present Supreme Court majority evidently does, guarantees the conclusion that there is nothing a court can do.

Imagine, however, that you are in Tally Jackson's shoes. What hurts the most? Not that you have a low income, or even that your furniture and clothes are shabby. What really hurts is that you are denied the self-respect that comes from supporting a family, from being a producing member of the society. You are excluded from the community of respectable people, denied any citizenship that is more than formal. The worst harm of marginalizing poverty is not being poor but being marginalized.[84]

In the near future, no doubt, the Supreme Court will go on giving politics a free hand in "the area of economics and social welfare," even when "the most basic economic needs of impoverished human beings" are at stake. Yet the one certainty about our constitutional law is its capacity to respond when the need is great. The principle of equal citizenship may yet come to play a more important role in the lives of poor people in America, and it is worth our while to see what that role might be.

The idea of equal citizenship focuses on those inequalities that are particularly likely to stigmatize, to demoralize, to impair effective participation in society, or, to put the matter more positively, on "the needs that must be met if we are to stand to one another as *fellow* citizens."[85] Undoubtedly, some kinds of material want impose a stigma that denies the essential humanity of those who are stigmatized. These stigmatizing inequalities are defined culturally: "The fact that an American slum dweller eats better, dresses better, or has more gadgets than a rich Eskimo, a nineteenth century farmer, or a medieval squire does not console him if he lacks the wherewithal for what his own society regards as a fully human existence."[86] Other inequalities, though, do not have the same potential for demoralizing through stigma. There is a difference, in other words, between being poorer than someone else and being part of "the disreputable poor."[87]

In American society money does not merely buy goods; it buys status. "Unless we own a certain number of socially required things, we cannot be socially recognized and effective persons."[88] Yet not all economic inequalities are presumptively violations of the principle of equal citizenship. One of the primary citizenship values is responsibility; indeed, to be held responsible is an essential part of being treated as a person.[89] The Civil Rights Act of 1866 did more than guarantee rights to the newly freed slaves. The act went on to provide that its beneficiaries could "be parties" to lawsuits—defendants as well as plaintiffs—and "be subject to like punishment, pains and penalties" as were imposed on whites.[90] To be a citizen is to be a member of a moral community, to be a responsible person, not a ward of society.

Given our individualistic expectations that people will provide for themselves and their families, welfare dependence tends to undermine self-respect, which is part of the explanation why most welfare recipients would prefer to work. To be responsible in this way—and, in so doing, to contribute to the society's total product—is part of what it means to be a good citizen in our prevailing ideology, part of the process of maintaining a healthy self-regard. The equal citizenship principle is not an invitation for judges to declare capitalism unconstitutional. What it asks of our courts is a more serious judicial inquiry when inequalities undermine the foundations for assuming the responsibilities of citizenship, and the political branches of government turn a blind eye. The more a particular inequality tends to stigmatize its victims, or to prevent them from participating as full members of the society, the more should be demanded in the way of justification.

Judges will be aided in identifying the types of poverty that are degrading and in detecting official neglect if they will look beyond the abstract idea of poverty to the meaning of being poor in the lives of particular people and in the social histories of particular groups. For example, Linda Williams and Ruth Jefferson are black women. When white male legislators project their own negative identities on the abstraction, poverty, they readily equate it with black or Latina welfare mothers.[91] In fact, marginalizing poverty may go unrelieved precisely because of this association—as surely happened in Ruth Jefferson's case, when the Texas legislature drastically cut AFDC benefits. But that same case shows how the abstraction, poverty, can serve to shield judges from looking claimants in the face.

To look at the human context of marginalizing poverty in America is to recognize that it normally attaches to people who are already, in the perspective of legislative decision makers, members of "outsider" groups. Their marginality comes not from poverty alone but from the combination of being poor with being a woman, a black, a Latino, or handicapped in mind or body. As we shall see in chapter 9, only modest adjustments in constitutional doctrine are needed for the courts to do a better job in recognizing invidious discrimination in contexts like these. Ultimately, however, the equal citizenship principle is less concerned with correcting official wrongdoing than it is with including all Americans in the community of equal citizens. In effectuating this principle in the context of poverty, a judge will look not only at indications of legislative hostility or indifference to the Other but also at another aspect of a case. What, exactly, is lost when a poor person cannot afford to pay for the particular good that is at stake in the case? Some material inequalities do and some do not seriously interfere with the inclusion of poor people as respected members of the society.

In 1982, in *Plyler v. Doe*, five Justices showed their willingness to inquire into both kinds of contextual factor. The Texas legislature withdrew state funding for the education of alien children whose parents were undocumented, and it authorized local school districts to turn those children away or to condition their education on the payment of tuition fees. Here, of course, there was an explicit legislative discrimination against an identified class of people. A 5–4 Court held that the law denied the excluded children the equal protection of the laws.

Justice William Brennan's opinion for the Court treated the doctrine concerning the "levels of scrutiny" question in a cavalier fashion, but I leave the faulting of his behavior to those who believe that body of doctrine is worth preserving. On the matter of the factors influencing decision, the majority was forthright. To deprive those children of free public education was to condemn them to long-term exclusion from effective participation in our society, and the legislature's hostility to their parents—outsiders in so many ways—was evident. Maybe education wasn't quite a "fundamental" interest, and maybe a classification that disadvantaged the children of undocumented aliens wasn't quite "suspect," but the effect of this burst of nativism, as the Court said, would be the creation of a new subordinate caste. Perhaps there is irony in the Court's vindication of the principle of equal citizenship in a case involving aliens.[92] If so, it is matched by the irony of an earlier Court's stirring affirmation that racial classifications are suspect in an opinion upholding the wartime relocation of Japanese Americas, aliens and citizens alike, behind barbed wire.[93]

Plyler v. Doe was not decided as a poverty case, for the children's lawyers were far too sophisticated to argue the case in those terms. The decision nonetheless illustrates how a judge should seek understanding of the constitutional import of a particular form of poverty. The most important questions to ask are questions about belonging: Does this form of poverty marginalize its victims, excluding them from effective participation as equal citizens? Is there reason to believe that the government would have filled the need if the decision makers had regarded the claimant not as part of an outsider group but as a full member of the society? Once these questions are answered, the court can turn to the justifications offered for government's failure to fill the need. It would be possible to undertake inquiries like these within the existing language of fundamental interests and suspect classifications. In the recent past, however, those categories have had the effect of obstructing judges' perceptions of real people's real needs. When judges see their options in all-or-nothing terms, they will likely opt for nothing.[94]

In its remedial aspect the *Plyler* case was easy: all the courts had to do was to forbid state officials to carry out the Texas legislature's discrimination against an identified group. The harms of marginalizing poverty in the ghetto are not so neatly packaged for judicial handling. But it would be quite wrong to conclude that the courts have no role to play in vindicating the constitutional claims of the marginalized poor.

The beginning point would be the recognition by the Supreme Court in an appropriate case that the ghetto's chronic unemployment and welfare dependency are intertwined parts of a social system that marginalizes its victims, denying them equal citizenship. I do not claim that poverty can be abolished by judicial decree, and I am not nominating King Canute for the Supreme Court. Beyond any judicial declaration will lie the crucial questions of remedy.[95] Just as the remedies for segregated schools originated with desegregation plans filed by school boards, remedies that address the harms of ghetto unemployment and welfare dependence should find their initial definition in the proposals of elected officials. Any such remedies will be partial. The benefits of job training, for example, will take time to mature, and large numbers of the ghetto poor will likely remain beyond the effective reach of any judicial decree. Again, the analogy to school desegregation is apt.

No one, then, should expect miracles from the judges who seek to protect equal citizenship against the worst ravages of material want. Modest beginnings hold the most promise. In arguing for a constitutional right of livelihood, Charles Black has sensibly suggested[96] that the courts could well begin with hunger, a problem the nation had largely solved by 1980 and then allowed to return.[97] Here there is no need for a judge to canvass all the theoretical possibilities for solving a polycentric problem like poverty.[98] Before 1980 the national government itself not only had recognized our common responsibility to feed the hungry but had adopted programs that did so. In seeking to respond to the government's abdication of responsibility,. a judge could order the government either to restore the programs that previously worked or to adopt other workable alternatives of the government's own devising. Judicial standards for effectuating the principle of equal citizenship in the poverty area almost certainly will be derived from government's own past assessments of basic need.[99]

As *Dandridge v. Williams* and *Plyler v. Doe* illustrate, presently existing government programs can also identify standards of need. Here, too, a court is not left at sea in specifying the particularized demands of the principle of equal citizenship. The complaint is that government is providing people generally with some vital necessity—be it medical care[100] or basic education[101] or food stamps[102]—but has excluded a group of people without offering substantial justification for the exclusion. We have come full circle to the case of Ruth Jefferson.

Troublesome questions remain in bringing the judicial power to bear on the problem of marginalizing poverty. Which kinds of want are dehumanizing, and which kinds are tolerable in a society that leaves most of its resource allocations to marketplace decisions? There is challenge in questions like these, but the challenge is no greater than those presented by other constitutional issues that have a more familiar ring. What kinds of police behavior amount to unreasonable searches and seizures? How much government regulation of the use of property is allowable before the regulation amounts to a "taking"? Constitutional questions normally turn on matters of degree; the challenge in all these questions is the challenge of judgment. No one thinks the courts alone are capable of solving the problem of marginalizing poverty. Yet they do have a role in keeping pressure on government to fulfill the responsibility we all share for affording every citizen the resources necessary to be a participating member of our society.

What, then, of Tally Jackson himself? Even in the life of a single individual it is no easy thing to replace dependence with resolve, to create hope out of despair. When hopelessness touches groups of people, the remedial difficulties increase in complexity by geometric progression. When very large numbers of people feed each others' dependence and desperation, the task of community reclamation looks forbidding.[103] There is no lack of remedial proposals; indeed, one of the main complications is that the proposals point in different directions.[104] Through all the dispute, we find broad agreement on two interrelated needs: the need for jobs, and the need to break the cycle of welfare dependence.[105] The dispute about remedy remains, however, and it is, indeed, polycentric. Shall we address these needs by adopting family assistance plans that erase the old morality-laden boundaries between poor people who are "deserving" and "undeserving," and between programs of insurance (middle-class programs like Social Security) and welfare (needs-based relief)? By drastically reducing welfare benefits to promote self-help?[106] By conditioning welfare payments on job training or efforts to find work? By establishing government employment or public works programs?[107] Enterprise zones? Programs to take young people out of the ghetto?[108]

Whatever may be your preferred answers to these questions, there are distinct limits on the possibility that those answers will be put into operation in programs initiated by the judiciary. Unless the judges are aided by a legislative standard of need, as in *Plyler*, it is realistic to expect them mainly to respond to politics, only rarely to take initiatives themselves. Even in the years following Chief Justice Warren's retirement, the Supreme Court has proved itself a willing partner in egalitarian reform when Congress takes the lead. On the whole the Court has given generous interpretations to the federal civil rights laws.[109] The lower federal courts, too, have been able to build significant new substantive doctrine, once Congress provides the necessary statutory base.[110] Absent legislative guidance or the political support of Congress, however, the courts have been disinclined to act on their own, in the name of the Constitution, to establish affirmative duties to the poor.

One claim that current constitutional doctrine does support is the equalization of public resources available for ghetto schools, health services, and housing.[111] Serious efforts toward even that much equalizing would be a step forward, and *Plyler v. Doe* shows how some marginalizing forms of poverty are the proper concern of constitutional law. Finally, the Supreme Court may validate some claims of poor people in the name of specific constitutional guarantees outside the domain of equal protection doctrine, as it has done in the criminal justice area and more broadly in the area now labeled "access to the courts."[112] Still, it has to be conceded that the nation's Tally Jacksons are not likely to find comprehensive judicial remedies for the multifold harms that are their inheritance from the racial caste system.

Yet the principle of equal citizenship is not just a legal doctrine. Citizens—all of us—have responsibilities to each other beyond the ones that are enforcible in court. In particular we have the responsibility to see that no one gets left out of the public life of the community. No doubt our legislative bodies, from the Congress down to the local zoning board, are arenas where citizens who want to fulfill our common responsibilities to the marginalized poor will have to focus much of their effort. To reclaim real citizenship for the ghetto's marginalized residents will require a combination of political mobilization, legislative support, self-help, and the participation of public and

private institutions covering a broad spectrum. Those efforts need the cooperation of a diverse set of actors, including the residents of the ghettos and
the whites who govern many of the relevant institutions. Most importantly of
all, middle-class blacks will be needed to provide leadership and to do the
work of cultural and political brokers.[113]

Here the judiciary can make its own distinctive contribution to community
reclamation, for this is one context in which the achievement of welfare goals
will depend on the validation of claims to equal status. It is a commonplace
that the black people who are most race-conscious, and who care the most
about equal treatment, are those who have regular contact with whites.[114] If
middle-class black people are to play their indispensable part in reclaiming
citizenship for blacks who are impoverished and marginalized, they will need
assurance that they are not just being used in a pacification program, that the
goal really is an enlarged community of equal citizens. Our courts can help
provide that assurance, but in doing so they will have to reexamine the constitutional doctrines assigning responsibility for racial wrongs. Any effective
judicial response to these harms will begin by recognizing the central importance of remedies that take account of racial groups (see chapter 9).

From the beginning of the civil rights era the Justices of the Supreme
Court have understood that their actions teach lessons, not only to black people but to whites as well.[115] Consider *Brown v. Board of Education* itself:
measured by the actual desegregation of schools, the decision was, at best, a
mixed success. But *Brown* was never just a case about schools; it was, and
still is, our nation's single most authoritative statement that a system of racial
caste is constitutionally and morally impermissible. *Brown*'s most important
contribution to American public life was not its specific judicial orders to
school boards but its declaration that school segregation denied the equal
protection of the laws.

Today, with the benefit of a generation's experience, we can see that status
harms and material harms are not separate; each compounds the other. The
Supreme Court, in other words, has a new lesson to teach: that the eradication of racial caste will require us to do more than discard the laws that
impose formal equality. In the next generation the Court has no task more
urgent than to teach the lessons that connect citizenship with responsibility,
the lessons of a community that will embrace Tally Jackson's grandchildren.

nine

Responsibility and Remedy

The chief target of the equal citizenship principle is the stigma of caste: the systematic, enduring exclusion of a group of people from the community's public life. The twentieth century constitutional attack on racial caste employed the rhetoric of individualism. Thurgood Marshall, arguing orally to the Supreme Court in the Virginia and South Carolina cases decided along with *Brown v. Board of Education*, encapsulated this individualistic attitude in calling for a race-neutral standard: "What we want is the striking down of race. . . . It is no problem to put dumb colored children with dumb white children and smart colored children with smart white children."[1]

Any effective prohibition against racial discrimination weakens a racial caste system. When Mildred Jeter and Richard Loving vindicated their constitutional right to enter an interracial marriage,[2] they provided a poignant illustration of law's potential use in removing obstacles to individual choices leading toward cultural assimilation. The entire body of antidiscrimination law has the same integrating tendency. When equal legal rights are made into a practical reality, opportunities increase for the members of racial and other cultural minorities to participate in the institutions of government and in privately governed markets, including the employment market. This antidiscrimination principle is mainly individualistic in outlook: treat each person as an individual, not on the basis of the status of a group.[3]

Yet, stigma and caste are group experiences. A characteristic like race, unorthodox religion, or ethnicity is identified as deserving of stigma, and the stigma is imposed on the whole group of people who share the characteristic. When we invent a stigma-theory to justify the stigma, we incorporate our assumptions about the whole group rather than picking on the particular characteristics of this or that individual. Ralph Ellison's "invisible" black man is not unseen by whites; he is invisible as an individual, for he is seen primarily as a member of a racial group.

Race, Group Status, and the Sense of Responsibility

Thomas Reed Powell once remarked that if you could think of something inextricably connected to something else, without thinking of the something else, then you had the legal mind. If anything is clear from the history of race relations in America, it is that the position of individual blacks in our society has always been closely bound to the status of blacks as a group. Yet today's constitutional doctrine often ignores the connection. This failure of recognition is not merely the result of lawyers' and judges' ability to shield themselves from uncongenial experience; it is strongly entrenched in the acculturation of white Americans. Our devotion to individualism inclines us to assume that individual destinies are self-made and makes us unready to recognize harms that people suffer because they are members of groups. More deeply, the tendency to identify blackness with the Other affects our interpretation of the meaning of racial disparities of wealth, status, and power, influencing us toward attributing these disparities to some failing of black people generally.

These two sets of attitudes look in opposite directions, simultaneously denying and affirming the relevance of group identification. Yet they point toward the same denial of responsibility. Neither individual whites nor the managers of governmental institutions are inclined to think they have any responsibility to remedy the conditions of their black cocitizens. Our constitutional doctrines reflect the same disinclination, founded on the same attitudes. Before we turn to some of the doctrinal particulars, let us take note of the ways in which those attitudes are intensified by fear.

The facts of life on Tally's Corner affect the status of black people generally. Entry into the middle class does help blacks to find acceptance in environments dominated by whites. Yet, as Leroy Irvis's experience at the Moose Lodge recalls, that acceptance is incomplete. A quarter century after the *Brown* decision, Kenneth Clark lamented "the mocking reality that moving to the suburbs and achieving middle-class status does not realistically free any sensitive black in contemporary America from the psychological burdens of racism."[4] The reasons for this unhappy fact are multiple, but one important factor is the continued existence of a large number of blacks who are impoverished and living at the margins of society—a group that gives whites an up-to-the-minute excuse for prejudice against blacks as a group.

The typical middle-class white male has been raised in a climate dominated by an individualism that is nervous about connection and empathy. Little in his own experience allows him to identify with the frustration felt by black people generally, let alone the despair that hangs over the ghettos. For him, the American civic culture's ideology of opportunity is validated by the lives he knows best: people "make it" individually, and they fail individually.[5] If substantial numbers of blacks do not succeed, the middle-class white is apt to supply his own reason: blacks as a group must be less talented or less ambitious or too attached to cultural norms that he associates with his own negative identity. Racism, in other words, has not just "stepped aside."[6] It continues to do the work of any acculturated expectation: assigning meaning to behavior. The meanings thus assigned affect attitudes toward public policy proposals ranging from affirmative action to welfare reform.

The street crimes committed by ghetto youths are heavily concentrated in the ghetto itself, but they are not confined there, and their effects reach even to the remote suburbs.[7] When the everyday reality of crime—including interracial violence—enters white homes with the morning paper and the evening television news, it touches fears that are deeply rooted. The fear of the alien, incomprehensible Other now has a foothold in reality: the threat of physical harm, or invasion of the home, or both. These fears are intensified in many a white ethnic neighborhood bordering the ghetto—a neighborhood that has provided sanctuary for people who themselves have been the historic victims of discrimination. Here the threat of violence combines with the fear that the ethnic community will be dispersed as the ghetto expands or as old residents leave to avoid the violence they foresee. In seeking to exclude blacks from their neighborhood—even middle-class blacks—these people see themselves as victims; in their own eyes they are defending not just turf but their sense of cultural identity, of connection.[8] From the white ethnic neighborhoods to the suburbs, all these fears are heightened by white guilt—or at least white awareness of the subordination of blacks and of the resentment thus engendered. In the grip of anxiety, empathy comes hard.

Sometimes whites do articulate their ancient fears of the repressed black male; they may even subject those fears to examination. Often, however, the fears remain below the surface of consciousness, affecting white reactions to black people generally. If, as the figures on chokehold deaths suggest, the Los Angeles police tended to use chokeholds far more frequently against young black men than against other people, the pattern would not be surprising. A chokehold was supposed to be used only when an officer perceived a threat of serious harm. In the minds of white officers, race might well affect perception about degrees of danger.[9] And if blacks who kill whites are considerably more likely to be sentenced to death than are whites who kill blacks,[10] we need not ponder long to understand what lurks in shadows of the decision makers' minds. Even referring to "minds" may exaggerate the level of consciousness; the reactions of police officers and prosecutors and jurors in these cases are likely to be of the kind we sometimes call visceral.[11]

At the heart of racial prejudice in America is the fear that led the Supreme Court to go slowly in enforcing the desegregation of southern schools. The fear is not merely the dread of a violent response to generations of subordination. It also includes the apprehension that blacks will displace whites from their position of dominance. In a world of scarcity, competition is threatening; when the fear of competition combines with the fear of the Other, the result is a potent mixture. When a Massachusetts mob burned an Ursuline convent in 1834, the act expressed not only anti-Catholic feeling but also resentment against Irish workers who were taking over jobs as bricklayers.[12] In the 1960s similar fears for loss of social position were translated into murders and bombings and lesser forms of violence directed against civil rights advocates in southern states.[13] Today's "English only" proposals tap the fears of some people that immigrants will "take over" their communities. American history gives repeated and dramatic evidence that dominance itself—preventing outsiders from belonging—frequently is a status goal.[14] When this fear for the loss of personal status combines with the fear of violence—as it did with the terror of slave rebellions and the early twentieth century myth of the black beast rapist—a white person's sense of self can be threatened at its core.

The fear of a change in the system of racial dominance is not just a collection of individual whites' fears of the competition of individual blacks. It is an experience widely shared among whites concerning blacks as a group. Acculturation happens to people one by one, but acculturation is initiation into a community of meaning, and in the case of racism the meanings are projected onto an entire racial group.[15] When Douglas Glasgow says, "The ghetto hurts all Blacks, not just those entrapped in it,"[16] surely he has this projection in mind. What does the middle-class white see in the young black man deeply mired in the cycle of violence and despair? Not an individual human being who lives in the culture of isolation, but an abstraction. The projected fear of the Other represents not a person but blackness itself; it serves as a receptacle for fears that have accumulated over many generations of white acculturation. The status dimensions of these fears extend to the potential competition of blacks with whites at all levels of the economy and society.

Fear is the enemy of community; it corrodes the sense of responsibility. In several striking parables Derrick Bell has brought into bold relief the ways in which white fears of blacks are translated into constitutional doctrine, and the consequences of that process for black people's perception of themselves and their place in American society.[17] Bell's parable of "The Amber Cloud"[18] encapsulates in two pages the sadness and frustration of millions of American blacks in the face of public policies and private behavior that ignore the needs of black people when America takes care of "our own." The nation's experience with other subordinated groups is richly diverse, but that experience does teach one clear lesson: if the "invisible man" is to become visible as a person, as a full member of the American community, the vast majority of American blacks must enter the middle class. The moral for American law is plain: either we use group remedies for past discrimination, or we give up the pretense that a remedy is what we seek.

Recognizing Discrimination

The abolition of formal caste distinctions obviously does not result in the overnight disappearance of the stigma of racial inferiority. Commentators on racial discrimination have often remarked on two different mechanisms by which stigma harms its victims. Harms from direct, intentional stigmatizing acts are complemented by the harms inflicted indirectly and unthinkingly by officials and others who are systematically inattentive to inequities that fall on members of a stigmatized group.[19] When a legislature deliberately stigmatizes a racial group, nowadays such a denial of formal equality is easily seen as a caste mark, a badge of inferiority. *Brown v. Board of Education* was such a case, and only the most sophisticated argument could make it seem otherwise.[20] In one view, the idea of legally recognizable stigmatic harm not only begins in such a case but ends there. This view assumes that only a deliberate legislative choice to impose an inferior status can stigmatize anyone: "even a dog distinguishes between being stumbled over and being kicked."[21] It is true, as the Supreme Court noted fleetingly in the *Brown* opinion, that a stigma embodied in law is especially harmful.[22] In the generation following *Brown*, the question for the Court was whether the idea of racial discrimination should be limited to such a case. As Ruth Jefferson's case[23] illustrates, the Court has generally answered Yes to this question. On the whole, in constitutional cases the Court has refused to recognize official action as racial discrimination on a showing that the action's effects disfavor blacks as a group, even when the officials who engage in the action know of that effect.[24] To raise a constitutional issue of racial discrimination a plaintiff must prove that officials acted deliberately to achieve a racially disparate result. In Helen Feeney's case[25] the Supreme Court extended this burden of proof of discriminatory purpose to claims of sex discrimination.

The problem of proof is not illuminated by the Court's comment in the *Feeney* opinion that discriminatory motive "either is a factor that has influenced the legislative choice or it is not." This view of the psychology of human motivation would be hopelessly inadequate even if we were talking about the intention of an individual rather than, say, the large body of legislators who voted to cut Ruth Jefferson's AFDC benefits. The factors that motivate even the simplest action are myriad in number and complex beyond the capacity of a judge or anyone else to untangle. The subject of motivation has puzzled psychologists for a century.[26] Recent studies have focused on the subject of reinforcement, that is, the influences on behavior of the satisfactions or dissatisfactions expected to result from the behavior. Current research and theory suggest "that motivation and reinforcement may be the same thing."[27] Then what makes a person behave in a particular way? We might turn the question around and ask, Is there anything in the person's entire experience that we can safely exclude from the factors that motivated his conduct? To extend this question to the collective action of a hundred members of a state legislature is not much different from inquiring into the experience of the whole society.

The complications are compounded when the motivation in question is one of discrimination. Much of the evidence in such a case necessarily will be devoted to proving the harmful and racially (or sexually) disproportionate effects of the governmental action. One of the oldest maxims of the common law holds that "[e]very man must be taken to contemplate the probable consequences of the act he does."[28] The Supreme Court agrees that one element of proving what officials intended is to prove what they did. However, even though the proof may center on what the officials actually accomplished, the prevailing constitutional doctrine requires the issue to be phrased in terms of the goodness or evil of their hearts.

Courts have long regarded such inquiries as unseemly. The main concern, though, is not a matter of protocol; it is that judges' reluctance to challenge the purity of other officials' motives may cause them to fail to recognize discrimination even when those motives are challenged. Both racial discrimination and sex discrimination mainly influence behavior in ways that are obscure to the actors themselves. The motivations of whites concerning blacks, or of men concerning women, are in considerable measure unconscious, for they begin in the formation of individual identity through differentiation from the Other.[29] Here, too, the personal is political.

Thus far we have treated the question of motive as a psychological one, focusing on the legislator's (or administrator's) state of mind. When we shift the focus to the judge, our inquiry becomes more sociological. For a generation the sociologists have seen that the social meaning of motive centers on the interpretation assigned to action. In this sense, "Motives are words,"[30] the names that interpreters give to actions for the purpose of defining situations and their consequences. This perspective on motive is oriented toward the future—specifically, the interpreter's future. What shall the interpreter predict? What should the interpreter do? In our context, the interpreter is a judge. The judge's determination of motive is not merely a prelude to the assignment of responsibility; it *is* that assignment. To see motive as the name an interpreter gives to conduct is to see that a great many alternative motives can be assigned to the same act. When a judge selects from among those alternatives, his own acculturation will do what culture always does: assign meaning to behavior. Ruth Jefferson didn't need formal training in sociology to see this process at work.

Because an individual's behavior results from the interaction of a multitude of motives, and because the attitudes of both officials and judges about race and sex are mostly embedded below the level of consciousness, in any given case the official will be able to argue that the action was prompted by considerations in which race and sex played no part. Indeed, even when the judge finds an unconstitutional motivation, the Supreme Court has invited officials to argue that the same decision would have been made, absent discrimination, for reasons that were legitimate.[31] When either of those arguments is made, should we not expect the judge to give the official the benefit of the moral doubt? When the governmental action is the product of a group decision—say, the adoption of a statute—will not that tendency toward generosity be heightened? Think about who most of the judges are,[32] and then ask yourself this question: In which direction is judicial empathy likely to flow in these disputed-motive cases: to those who are claiming discrimination or to the officials whose motives are challenged? If white male legislators have difficulty in recognizing the ways in which their behavior affecting minorities and women reflects their own acculturation, it is unlikely in the extreme that similarly acculturated white male judges—or Justices—will discern discriminatory motivation except in the most blatant cases.

Consider, for example, the way a white judge might be expected to approach a minority applicant's challenge to a test for government employment. Typically the test will have been developed by other white males, based on their own acculturated assumptions about what it takes to do the job. The individualist values of our culture hold a special appeal for the people who do well in society's various enterprises, assuring them that everyone has had a fair chance at the same outcome. When a white applicant performs well on a test, that experience tends to reinforce not only his belief in the test's validity but also any subconscious assumptions he may have about racial superiority. Minority candidates simply don't succeed, and never mind the question, Who defined the terms of success in this enterprise? Furthermore, when a minority applicant challenges a particular test's capacity to predict job performance, the challenge is apt to go against the grain of the judge's own acculturated assumptions about the testing system. The judge, too, has a psychological stake in the validity of the sorting mechanisms that brought him his own position and status—mechanisms that are cultural analogues of the challenged test. The whole system of testing and credentials turns out to be self-perpetuating.

When the discriminatory purpose doctrine is applied rigorously,[33] its practical result is to convert the burden of proof of improper motive into a substantive rule for upholding governmental action. When Memphis diverted black drivers around a white neighborhood, the Supreme Court's majority showed how judges are able to ignore an ugly motivation that just about anyone else can see.[34] One serious objection to a motive-centered doctrine of discrimination, then, is that it places the burden of justification on the wrong side of the dispute, to the severe detriment of the constitutional protection of equality.

Equally serious is an objection that centers not on judicial empathy but on the effects of the doctrine on relations between the parties in dispute. Perhaps any judicial finding of racial discrimination—even a finding based on racially disparate effects that are insufficiently justified by the state—will carry some implication of blame for government officials. But an inquiry centered on motive guarantees that antagonisms will be intensified, for it forces the litigants into name-calling on one side and self-righteousness on the other. The parties, like the judge, are required to treat the facts of a racial group's inequality as though their main importance were the light they might throw on the question of the officials' motivational purity. But the racial group's inequality in education or housing or employment is not just evidence of somebody's misconduct; the inequality itself is the heart of the problem.

It is bad enough that a motive-centered inquiry should distract the lawsuit from focusing on the community's real ills. Worse still is the effect of this inquiry on race relations outside the litigation process. The effective parties to many a racial discrimination case (as distinguished from the named parties) are institutional litigants—for example, the NAACP versus the school board or the city planners. These people are locked into a continuing relationship touching a variety of race-relations issues. They were negotiating with each other before the lawsuit began, and they will be dealing with each other after it ends—if, indeed, school desegregation litigation ever ends. A constitutional doctrine of racial discrimination centered on the motives of officials inevitably will poison the atmosphere for these dealings. Denunciation and defensive indignation will displace efforts to deal with the racial inequality itself. Given the history of race relations in America, negotiations between different racial groups are unavoidably burdened with mutual suspicion, either conscious or unconscious. These dealings are difficult enough when the negotiating parties focus on the actual extent of racial inequalities and on the costs of lessening them. When a search for evidence of bad faith is added to the mix, the resulting negative emotional charge can only hinder the process of building a healthy interracial community.

In adopting the doctrine requiring proof of discriminatory motive, the Supreme Court let us know, in one revealing passage, what was on its collective mind:

> A rule that a statute designed to serve neutral ends is nevertheless invalid, absent compelling justification, if in practice it burdens one race more than another would be far reaching and would raise serious questions about, and perhaps invalidate, a whole range of tax, welfare, public service, regulatory, and licensing statutes that may be more burdensome to the poor and to the average black than to the more affluent white.[35]

The specter of the stopping-place problem is itself hard to confine. The doctrine of discriminatory motive was a way to contain the reach of the equal protection clause—and the role of judges—by saying, "Thus far and no further."[36] When the context is race, however, the problem of the stigma of caste cannot even be understood, let alone resolved, by limiting inquiry to singular cases of purposeful stigmatizing action.

It is a global problem, this inheritance from slavery and segregation.[37] Consider the picture through the eyes of a black who surveys the entire system of racial dependence and domination and decides to attack one feature of the system. First, you learn that a school board cannot be held responsible for such things as neighborhood segregation, for, as Chief Justice Warren Burger tells you, "One vehicle can carry only a limited amount of baggage." Ignoring that provocation to anger, you may look to the village elders who govern land use—but to no avail. If the village's racially neutral zoning laws zone out persons who cannot afford single-family houses, well, it isn't the elders' fault that the great majority of blacks—as fate would have it—happen to be priced out of the village's housing market. Jobs, then: shall you mount your constitutional attack on the racially disproportionate results of application tests for government jobs? That won't work either. The government employer can't be held responsible for the educational differentials that produce those racially disparate results.

This process is a judicial runaround. Racial subordination today is a living system, just as Jim Crow was a system. Now as then, "everything is the cause of everything else."[38] The main difference between the two systems is that today's racism inflicts a greater proportion of its harms unthinkingly. "One who is stumbled over often enough may, understandably, notice that those cumulative impacts bear a certain functional resemblance to kicks."[39]

If we were talking about some new form of discrimination—say, discrimination against persons with red hair—then the discriminatory motive doctrine might make sense, along with its corollary view that stigmatic harm can result only when there is a purpose to cause it. But in America today, where the problem of racism is the problem of eliminating a long-established stigma of inferiority—that is, a day-to-day assumption that some of our citizens are not quite persons—it is as plain as a cattle prod that we are talking about something quite different.[40] A legislature oblivious to this existing stigma of caste will nonetheless reinforce the stigma when it produces racially discriminatory effects through ostensibly neutral legislation.

Now, let us admit that no constitutional principle can erase all the effects of slavery and segregation. Let us even concede that concerns about the stopping-place problem have a legitimate place in our thinking about remedies for racial discrimination. But let us not align ourselves with the hypocrisy of the opinion in *Plessy v. Ferguson*[41] by pretending that the neighborhood school policy and the single-family zoning ordinance and the test for government employment do nothing to reinforce the stigma of caste. If the guarantee of equal protection fails to reach one or more of those governmental practices, the reason should lie in some showing of substantial justification for the practices, not in the debater's trick of defining stigmatic harm to include only its most glaring examples.

The line between racially disparate effects and racially discriminatory purpose has always been blurred; the inference of a bad motive may be strong when the differential effects are plain and the government's justifications are flimsy.[42] In two kinds of cases, however, the Supreme Court itself has deliberately made the line even more indistinct, allowing the proof of group racial disparity to be all but sufficient to prove intentional discrimination. In northern and western school segregation cases, the Court has placed on school boards the burden of proving that the present separation of the races in schools is not the result of demonstrated acts of deliberate segregation in the remote past—a burden that no board can carry.[43] In cases dealing with electoral districting, the Justices have allowed lower courts to find intentional discrimination largely on the basis of circumstantial evidence of the racially disparate effects of districting legislation.[44]

Both the school board members who draw attendance district lines and the politicians who draw the boundaries of electoral districts know the racial makeup of neighborhoods and the implications of those patterns for school composition and party voting. In other cases, however, the Court has regarded that sort of awareness as insufficient to establish racial discrimination. Why the difference in school and voting cases? Probably the school cases are influenced by the symbolic importance for the whole civil rights field of *Brown v. Board of Education*. It does seem unthinkable to restrict *Brown's* application to the South. Equality in the electoral process, on the other hand, is a central feature of equal citizenship. Both categories may be special cases. Yet these decisions are available as precedents if future Justices should recognize the importance of group racial disparities in assigning responsibility for remedying other effects of societal discrimination.

To focus constitutional doctrine on the facts of racial inequality and on the costs of equalization would not disable the courts from dealing with clear-cut cases of improper governmental motive. A judge fully persuaded that an official has purposefully harmed members of a racial minority should hold the official's action unconstitutional.[45] Where the evidence is less clear, but the judge is conscious that an official may have acted for an evil purpose, no constitutional doctrine will erase this consciousness. In such circumstances the judge would not need to make an explicit finding of improper motive, but—assuming the availability of an "effects" analysis—could hold the official's action invalid if it did not significantly promote an important governmental objective.[46]

In a number of decisions under the First Amendment, many of them with racial overtones, the Supreme Court has adopted just such a course. The Court has protected the constitutional interest in associational privacy on behalf of members of the NAACP in circumstances strongly suggesting improper governmental motives, but it has managed to offer the protection without saying, for example, that the Arkansas legislature was trying to expose teachers who were NAACP members so they could be hounded out of their jobs. By avoiding accusations of bad faith, and emphasizing the harmful effects of the governmental action, the Court avoided handing an additional political weapon to southern racial intransigents and encouraged the moderates. Now that the problem of racial inequality is clearly seen as a national problem, should not the Court draw wisdom from its own experience in assisting the birth of the New South?

If the subordination of a group is a constitutional wrong, then it seems entirely appropriate for a court to insist on a showing of justification when the government's behavior intensifies a group's subordination—especially when it is black people who are disadvantaged.[47] On the whole, however, when the Supreme Court considers an individual black person's constitutional claims, the Court has been unwilling to recognize candidly that the experience of blacks as a group is relevant to the individual's case. This reluctance is most visible in the Court's adoption of the discriminatory motive doctrine, which reached its appalling culmination in the Court's recent 5–4 decision refusing to recognize racial discrimination in Georgia's highly disparate imposition of the death penalty on black defendants whose victims were white.[48] The same reluctance to accept the relevance in individual cases of blacks' group experience of discrimination can be seen in the refusal to grant standing in court to an individual black person who asserts discriminatory treatment of blacks as a group.[49] A vivid example is the Court's dismissive treatment of Adolph Lyons's claim for an injunction limiting the use of chokeholds by the Los Angeles police.[50]

In cases like these the usual result is to leave group harms to majoritarian politics as an earlier majority of the Court did with the group wrong of segregation. Yet when majoritarian politics produces an affirmative action program, the inevitable argument against the program's constitutionality is that it abandons a principle of "individual merit" in favor of a group remedy.[51] Women and blacks and other minorities can be pardoned for perceiving this argument—which the Supreme Court has not accepted—as a variation on "Heads, we win; tails, you lose."

Affirmative Action: Group Remedy and Individual Justice

The fundamental purpose of affirmative action programs is to promote the equal citizenship values of respect and participation by remedying the effects of past and continuing discrimination. The consideration of race, ethnicity, and sex in facilitating the admission of women and minorities to state universities or to government employment differs in the most dramatic way from the use of those factors to exclude candidates. The difference, as Justice John Paul Stevens has remarked, is that "the exclusionary decision" reinforces racial isolation and assumptions of inferiority.[52] The white or male applicant who is turned away as a result of an affirmative action program is not degraded or stigmatized[53]; there is no denial of his humanity. Nor does his failure to gain admission signify a denial of participation in the public life of the society; as Paul Brest remarked, typically the white or male applicant is not faced with a wide array of mutually reinforcing discriminations.[54] On the governmental interest side of the constitutional balance, the equal citizenship principle itself weighs in, identifying interests of the highest importance. These programs of affirmative action result when the leaders of institutions accept responsibility for helping to remedy the historic subordination of groups. In the aggregate the programs are aimed at making today's society into one class of citizens by integrating America's community life.[55]

We saw in chapter 8 that affirmative action, along with other efforts to achieve integration, including antidiscrimination law, has entailed one serious cost: in offering talented individuals an escape from the ghetto, integration has contributed in the short term to the deterioration of the ghetto community. Here, as in the historic assimilation of other cultural groups into the larger society, every integration produces a corresponding disintegration. The immediate benefits of affirmative action, like the immediate benefits of laws forbidding discrimination, generally do not run to the Tally Jacksons but to those who have the skills needed to exploit new opportunities.[56] For at least two reasons, these observations do not imply that we should abandon either antidiscrimination laws or affirmative action. First, we should remember that the families that do benefit immediately from these efforts at integration amount to at least two-thirds of the black population. The creation of opportunities for that group is important in its own right. Second, the improvement of conditions for the ghetto's marginalized citizens will require not one magic solution but a combination of public policies. Although the integration of the work force is not sufficient by itself to offer hope to the ghetto residents, both antidiscrimination laws and affirmative action will be necessary ingredients in any package of programs aimed at that goal. The white employer who has never hired a black worker is unlikely to start by offering a job to Tally Jackson.

Many voluntary affirmative action plans (so called because they are not coerced by a court decree or administrative order) are in fact developed in the shadow of potential lawsuits claiming past discrimination—for example, by an employer. Such a plan typically results from negotiations between the

employer and an organization representing women or a racial group, sometimes with the participation of a union. In these circumstances the plan is
more than a way to achieve integration in the future; it also substitutes a
group remedy for a collection of claims that individual employees have been
reluctant to file.

That reluctance is easy to understand. Imagine that you are a black employee and you think your boss has given a white coworker the promotion
you deserve. In the first place you may be disinclined to "make waves" for
fear of being fired. Even if you should retain your job, and even if you should
be awarded the promotion, from the time you complain your boss will think
of you as a threat and the coworker's friends will shun you. Furthermore, to
prove discrimination in a way that will benefit you directly, probably you will
have to prove that the boss had a racially discriminatory purpose in promoting
the other worker.[57] The boss will defend against this charge, not just to defeat
your complaint but because she doesn't want to think of herself as racist.
What will her defense be? That your work hasn't been up to snuff, that you
just don't measure up? If you complain, your whole employment history,
perhaps your whole personality, is open to attack. The reluctance of potential
claimants to complain obviously is not limited to discrimination cases; a lot
of people "lump it" rather than go through the unpleasantness of a lawsuit.[58]
But if you were considering suing the neighbor who feeds pigeons by the
hundreds, probably you would not expect your personal worth to be debated
in public. Finally, filing the discrimination claim will cast you in the social
role of victim, a role you may see as demeaning, the very role that you—and
women and minority workers generally—have been trying to escape.[59]

Any effective solution to this problem necessarily will be a group solution.
An employment discrimination action, perhaps with the aid of an institutional litigator, would likely begin by focusing on the racially disparate effects
of the employer's policies on minority employees as a group. An alternative
group remedy that even the employer may find more attractive is an affirmative action plan.

These plans are nonetheless attacked, both in partisan political arenas and
in court, on the ground that they submerge the principle of individual merit
in favor of the "irrelevant" criterion of race. Used in this way, the idea of
individual merit is misleading in two dimensions. First, it suggests that a
constitutional claim to equality must be an individual claim, and that such a
claim differs fundamentally from a claim made as a member of a group.
Second, it suggests that merit is something quite different from someone's
perception of community needs.

The equal protection clause offers its guarantees to "any person." In 1938 Chief Justice Charles Evans Hughes said that Lloyd Gaines's claim for admission to the University of Missouri's law school "was a personal one. It was as an individual that he was entitled to the equal protection of the laws."[60] But to say that "the constitutional command is equality for individuals"[61] is not to say that each individual comes to court as an abstraction, stripped of the life history that has made him the person he is. Some writers have mistakenly asserted that the white male who challenges an affirmative action plan is making an individual claim in contrast to the group claim of the women or minority applicants who benefit from the process.[62] The mistake is understandable. Nearly every reader of this book will know Alan Bakke's name, and many will know his face and his story. The minority candidates who were admitted to the medical school ahead of Bakke, however, remain faceless abstractions, readily assignable to the category of the Other. Those candidates were, of course, flesh-and-blood people with stories of individual striving and family sacrifice behind them.[63] They sought admission as individuals, and their personal characteristics were shaped in no little measure by the same context that had produced so much of the sacrifice and the striving: their membership in racial and ethnic groups.

The more fundamental mistake, however, is the failure to see that Bakke himself stood for a group of applicants identified by a particular cluster of credentials centered on undergraduate grades and test scores. Every classification of people defines a group.[64] The criteria for classification select some attributes as relevant ones—the "merits." Once this selection is made, an individual is classified either with those who possess the relevant attributes or with those who do not. Consequently, to complain against a classification scheme is not merely to say, "I am wronged," but to say, "We are wronged." Indeed, every claim based on a rule of law is a demand to be treated in the same manner as all other persons similarly situated. Every claim to consideration on the basis of individual attributes is, in this sense, a group claim— a claim to be treated as a member of the group possessed of certain specified attributes—or else the claim is unintelligible.

An appreciation of group relationships has informed the Supreme Court's pronouncements on school desegregation. Since 1968 the Court has recognized a duty on school boards to "terminate dual school systems at once."[65] It is not enough for the state to abandon its formal statutory authorization of segregation; the "dual system" continues to exist until the school board has taken all reasonable action "to achieve the greatest possible degree of actual desegregation."[66] The same considerations of feasibility of remedy define the substantive constitutional right: the continuation of one-race schools, for example, is only presumptive evidence of a continuing policy of segregation.

Group interests, then, both underlie the constitutional claim (to end the dual system) and limit the reach of the constitutional right (by reference to considerations of remedial feasibility).[67] The desegregation claim is thus, from the judicial standpoint, a group claim. A black child, even while the board is maintaining a dual system, may be attending a predominantly white school. Another black child, even after the dual system has been terminated, may continue to attend a predominantly black school. The judge who decides the desegregation case will become acquainted with those two children only as members of statistical groups. The claim to equality is a claim to education in a system that is no longer dual.

Merit, on examination, turns out to be a function of perceived social needs. We give prizes for achievement partly because it seems fair to reward effort. Mainly, however, achievement is recognized because society needs the products of effort. Yet, giving prizes for achievement does not just reward effort; it also rewards native talents, which are distributed capriciously and are in no sense earned. The principle that careers should be open to talents is not a principle of individual justice but a principle designed to serve a particular definition of social needs.

A federal appeals court said in 1973, "The purpose of racial integration is to benefit the community as a whole, not just certain of its members."[68] The white applicant who claims to be disadvantaged by an affirmative action program aimed at the hiring of blacks is asserting an interest shared by all whites with a certain level of experience or other specified qualification for the job, and that claim is countered by a group interest shared by all black applicants. Each hiring of a black person will help, in several ways, to remedy the effects of group subordination: by reducing the gap in incomes and social status between whites and blacks, for example, or by providing role models for black children. The contending groups in an affirmative action case are appealing to different definitions of individual merit, that is, to different attributes that will answer different kinds of social need.

A related solicitude for individual fairness has surfaced in some of the Supreme Court's opinions on affirmative action. A number of the Justices have made clear their concern for diffusing the burden of affirmative action remedies. Justice Lewis Powell expressed this concern when he suggested that a state university's medical school, in selecting applicants for admission, could constitutionally take race into account for the purpose of diversifying the student body. Under such an admissions system, he said, a white "applicant who loses out on the last available seat to another candidate receiving a 'plus' on the basis of ethnic background will not have been foreclosed from all consideration for that seat simply because he was not the right color or had the wrong surname."[69] The resentment of the excluded candidate cannot be focused sharply on race, because the candidate will have lost in the competition on the basis that "his combined qualifications" have not been quite enough for admission. The diffusion of resentment is furthered if the university does not specify with any precision just how much of a "plus" it is giving to race in making its admissions. Similarly, affirmative action programs in government employment are likely to be upheld when their cost is spread over an unspecified group but invalidated when the cost is exacted from identifiable individuals.[70]

This concern for diffusing the costs of remedying the effects of past discrimination typically is articulated in the familiar idiom of individualism and vested rights.[71] No doubt it is easier to share access to a resource that has not yet been allocated than it is to give up something you think you have already earned. Certainly it is easier for the "haves" to make room for the "have-nots" when everyone perceives the pie to be expanding rather than contracting. The civil rights movement was aided by a common perception in the 1950s and 1960s that the American economy was growing.

The politics of affirmative action, however, suggest another possible judicial motive for drawing the line between diffused-cost and focused-cost programs. Perhaps some Justices believe that the diffusion of cost, and the consequent blurring of focus for the losing candidates' resentment, will save affirmative action by making it less threatening to the status positions of whites and males.[72] In this perspective, some of the Supreme Court's rulings on affirmative action recall an earlier Court's decision to minimize white southern resentment by delaying the enforcement of school desegregation. That decision, however, was not taken with individual justice in mind. The constitutional interest of every individual black schoolchild was an immediate interest in attending a school that was not segregated. Each year of delay in desegregation was, for that child, not just a deferral of her rights but a loss that could not be remedied. Many a black child in elementary school in 1954 had finished high school before her district's schools were desegregated.[73] Today's supporters of affirmative action are entitled to wonder whether the Supreme Court's concern for individual justice is selective, responding in one way to perceived political strength (the group concerns of southern whites in the 1950s) and in another way to perceived political weakness (the group concerns of blacks a generation later).

Still another possible explanation for the Justices' recent concerns about "individual justice" in the affirmative action context is even more unsettling to contemplate. It is that white male Justices, reflecting the same acculturated attitudes that inhibit judicial findings of racially discriminatory purpose, may identify more readily with the resentment of the whites or males who may be displaced by affirmative action remedies than with the black or female candidates who will benefit from them. The white male judge's own life experience is apt to persuade him of the fairness of the selection process that has resulted in racial disparity in the university, for example, or in the work force. As a consequence, he is likely to begin his inquiry into the validity of affirmative action without a strong sense of the justice behind the claim that the racial disparity is something that needs to be remedied. The parallel to the selective empathy that contributed to "all deliberate speed" is close enough to give us pause.

The argument for affirmative action can rest comfortably on the need—in the modern language of equal protection, the compelling need—to integrate American society into one class of equal citizens.[74] Apart from a rhetorical difference, the goal of inclusion is the same as the goal of remedying the effects of past group subordination. But the idea of affirmative action as a remedy for past discrimination carries the stronger appeal in America, given the influence of individualism on our history and culture.

This compensatory justification for affirmative action will not work if the courts limit their inquiry to the fate of individual applicants for employment or university admission. Ordinarily it will be extremely difficult to determine that a particular employer's or university's discrimination has directly harmed the particular woman or minority applicant who is today's beneficiary of affirmative action. (Fortunately for the proponents of affirmative action, the Supreme Court has not required any such determination as an underpinning for a public agency's voluntary affirmative action plan.)[75] A second difficulty is that the individual who is identifiably disadvantaged by today's affirmative action goal or quota normally has not caused any past discrimination. Nor, if Thurow[76] is correct, has he profited directly from that discrimination in any way that is individually demonstrable. Yet in a more diffuse sense affirmative action is always remedial: remedying the general effects on subordinated groups of societal discrimination.[77] Those effects—especially harms to the core values of equal citizenship—are continuing and pervasive, extending to all black people, middle class or not. A court's proper concern, in addressing the validity of an affirmative action program, goes beyond the individual claims of those who are benefitted or burdened by the program. The justice of affirmative action is the same as the justice of recognizing that racial discrimination is not limited to cases of illicit motivation: when a group has been systematically deprived of equal citizenship, government has the responsibility for substantial justification, or rectification, or both.

Perhaps considerations like these were in Justice Powell's mind when he devised his diversity approach to affirmative action programs in state university admissions—even though he denied the legal relevance of past societal discrimination.[78] His opinion in the *Bakke* case has been widely used by universities as a how-to-do-it manual. It is possible to see something of the same strategy in some of the opinions in *Wygant v. Jackson Board of Education* (1986). Both Justice Powell's plurality opinion and Justice O'Connor's separate concurrence denied that past societal discrimination could justify a racial preference in protecting employees against layoffs. Rather, they said, the school board could justify its voluntary affirmative action plan only to remedy the effects of its own past discrimination. It is true, as Kathleen Sullivan has written, that after *Wygant* a public employer's adoption of an affirmative action program must be taken to imply an admission of past wrongdoing, and that this implication may deter some agencies from entering into such a program.[79] But, as Justice Powell made clear, the public employer need not explicitly admit any past discrimination. Its only obligation will be to show, if its affirmative action plan should be challenged in court, that it had "a strong basis in evidence for its conclusion that remedial action was necessary. The ultimate burden rests with the [challenging] employees to demonstrate the unconstitutionality of an affirmative action program." So, the proponents of affirmative action need not confront a government employer with the need to admit past discrimination; the negotiations can go forward without pitting the negotiating parties against each other. To make sure that this point could not be mistaken, Justice O'Connor said in *Wygant* that a contemporaneous finding of past wrongdoing should not be required, because such a requirement "would severely undermine public employers' incentive to meet voluntarily their civil rights obligations."

In *Johnson v. Transportation Agency* a majority of the Court not only reaffirmed this position but carried the analysis a step further, at least for cases presenting only statutory (as opposed to constitutional) challenges to a public agency's voluntary affirmative action plan.[80] Such a plan for promotions was justified, the majority said, by a "manifest imbalance" reflecting underrepresentation of women in "traditionally segregated job categories," considering the number of qualified women in the relevant labor pool. Decoded, this formula—which the Court explicitly made applicable to both race and sex cases—looks like a prescription for validating at least some voluntary affirmative action plans for the purpose of remedying past societal discrimination. The how-to-do-it book now has a second chapter. Despite some doctrinal untidiness,[81] both the law and the politics of affirmative action are remarkably stable as Justice Anthony Kennedy joins the Court.[82]

Midway between the Supreme Court's *Bakke* and *Fullilove* decisions,[83] Antonin Scalia, then a law professor (and now a Justice), mounted a forceful attack on affirmative action programs. He rejected any race-based notion of responsibility. In particular he rejected the notion that there were "evils that 'we' whites have done to blacks and that 'we' must now make restoration for." His own father had come from Italy to America as a teenager, a member of one of those "white ethnic groups that came to this country in great numbers relatively late in its history—Italians, Jews, Irish, Poles—who not only took no part in, and derived no profit from, the major historic suppression of the currently acknowledged minority groups, but were, in fact, themselves the object of discrimination by the dominant Anglo-Saxon majority." The responsibility of such recent arrivals, Scalia argued, should not be confused "with that of those who plied the slave trade, and who maintained a formal caste system for many years thereafter."[84]

There is power in Scalia's attack, but his account is folklore, not history. The Irish were neither late arrivals nor wholly innocent of racial animus. Irish violence against black workers came to Philadelphia early (1829, 1834, 1838, 1849), and in the 1863 Draft Riots "Irish mobs ravaged New York City for four days, randomly lynching blacks, razing a black orphanage, and driving blacks out of the city," where they could no longer compete with Irishmen for jobs.[85] Furthermore, from the Civil War to the present, some of the main beneficiaries of racial discrimination in employment have been white ethnics. By the early twentieth century a great many labor unions had come under an "ethnic lock." In New York City, by the time Scalia's father arrived, a partial list of ethnic unions included "a Greek Furriers local, an Italian Dressmakers Union, and . . . locals of the Bricklayers Union [that] were either Irish or Italian, while the Painters Union was largely Jewish."[86] Most union charters explicitly limited membership to white persons, and leaders of the American Federation of Labor (AFL) from Samuel Gompers in the East to Patrick McCarthy in the West argued for maintaining "racial purity" and "Caucasian civilization" by excluding Asians from the country and excluding blacks from organized labor. These campaigns flowed on a tide of inflammatory racist rhetoric.[87]

To speak of union racial discrimination is not to unearth the distant past but to speak of a practice that has been widespread within the lifetime of any adult and certainly is not unknown today: the award of jobs to friends and relations with ethnicity playing a leading role. The documentation of these practices can be found in scores of lower court opinions in employment discrimination cases.[88] Nonetheless, George Meany, the late president of the AFL, had this to say about affirmative action in a 1975 interview:

> MEANY: . . . to say that I've got some responsibility to make up for discrimination that took place 125 years ago is nuts. . . .
>
> REPORTER: Does anybody have a responsibility in contemporary American society . . .?
>
> MEANY: Not that I know of.[89]

Scalia's attack on affirmative action may lack historical accuracy, but it still carries an emotional wallop in its invocation of our individualist traditions: "I owe no man anything, nor he me, because of the blood that flows in our veins." In another perspective, however, when that young man from Italy stepped off the boat into the American dream of equal opportunity, he bought into a going concern. The community he joined already had a responsibility to the people who had borne the burden of generations of subordination, a responsibility shared by all the community's members, including its newest ones. Wide-ranging racial discrimination in America has consistently translated into differential status founded on race. The other side of the discrimination that has inflicted a status harm on every black is the benefit to whites who have been freed by the same discrimination from the competition of blacks in all manner of social and economic marketplaces. In this sense every white, willingly or not, is a status beneficiary of the acts—fully supported by the community's previous interpretations of its Constitution and laws—that reduced black people to slavery and to membership in a subordinate caste. As we think about our own responsibility (and, for that matter, the responsibility of the young immigrant whose son would be a Justice), the appropriate private-law analogy is not the responsibility of one who deliberately wrongs another. Rather it is the responsibility of a partnership for the wrongful acts of partners now dead—acts that were done in the partnership's name and that benefitted those who would later join the firm.

Affirmative Action as Inclusion

The defense of affirmative action as integration has attracted a criticism that amounts to a denial. In the critics' view affirmative action, far from integrating America, will accentuate racial and ethnic divisions, promoting the fragmentation of the nation into a society of groups.[90] The theoretical side of this argument is that legitimizing affirmative action implies adopting a theory of group rights, a form of ethnic corporatism. The argument's factual component is a prediction: that affirmative action in the sense of "allocation among people by race" or ethnicity will stimulate ethnic politics and intercultural conflict, threatening the country's solidarity.[91] These concerns should trouble anyone who cares about the unity of our multicultural nation. Yet what we know about assimilation and cultural pluralism suggests an alternative view of the likely results of affirmative action. In this perspective affirmative action can be seen as a means to promote not separatism but inclusion—and, indeed, as an instrument in the long-term service of individualism.

We can begin by recapitulating four propositions already developed. First, the main cause contributing to cultural separatism in America has been the subordination of minorities. Second, the most important technique of subordination has been the exclusion of cultural groups from jobs and from other forms of participation in the community's public life—that is, the exclusion of individuals on the basis of their membership in racial, ethnic, or religious groups. To speak of caste is to speak of the subordination of a group. Third, if we are to identify the economic effects of systematic racial discrimination, it is necessary to look at the incomes of racial groups—and, when we do, we see that serious disparities remain between the incomes of blacks and whites. Fourth, participation has always meant assimilation. In the racial context, generally we speak of integration rather than assimilation, but the two concepts are not different in substance. Whichever term we may use, the process is fluid enough to permit a range of "varieties of ethnic experience," a range of individual choices about cultural identification and about participation in the life of the wider community. Speaking of black Americans in 1897, W. E. B. Du Bois said that "their destiny is *not* absorption by the white Americans."[92] He was right then, and he is still right.[93]

Any such wider participation, however, ultimately requires the larger society's acceptance of the group that is being integrated. A group that has been subordinated in the past is unlikely to find that acceptance until individual members of the group have moved into the middle class in very large numbers.[94] The new opportunities for black people in white-collar jobs and in the professions have obvious relevance to the expansion of the black middle class.[95] But we should also recognize the long-term importance of affirmative action programs that affect blue-collar jobs.[96] Work is itself an important integrating mechanism. Without affirmative action the existing racial composition of an employer's work force is apt to be self-perpetuating, even in the absence of union discrimination. Social networks are also networks of communication about job opportunities. Given the prevailing patterns of racially segregated social networks, if an employer's work force is almost all white, the first people to learn about new jobs with that employer are also likely to be white.[97] If this variation on the theme of the "old boy network" seems familiar, the reason is that it is a microcosm of the circular reinforcement of the various "impacts" that add up to group subordination.

One cost of affirmative action, we have seen, is the separation of the new black middle class from their former communities. For all but a few people living in the culture of isolation, entry into the middle class is a considerable distance away. First it will be necessary to find avenues into the working class. Jobs are the key to stable families, to educational motivation, to all the conditions that facilitate a family's advance from one generation to the next. If many of today's black professionals are the children of porters and postal workers,[98] perhaps tomorrow's middle-class blacks will be able to thank the affirmative action programs that gave their parents jobs in factories and firehouses. Without jobs, the ghetto's residents will continue to have little choice about the nature and degree of their integration into the wider society.

Complex processes maintain the separation of the races today. Thomas Schelling has suggested that a variety of mechanisms of individual choice may produce racial "sorting and mixing" in residential neighborhoods even though a generation has passed since the end of segregation imposed by law.[99] If we examine the origins of individual preferences for integration or separation, we find that one major contributing factor is the question of economic class, whether the issue be the integration of neighborhoods or of schools. Nor is the problem of caste solved by ending the exclusion of middle-class blacks from middle-class neighborhoods and institutions. The identification of blacks as a subordinate group in America has always attached to race itself. In this perspective it is evident that a racial or ethnic group's economic disadvantage as a group contributes to the continued separation of the group's individual members from the larger society and, inevitably, to continued intercultural conflict. Correspondingly, a subordinate group's economic advancement as a group promotes both the group's integration and the nation's intercultural harmony.

Given the lasting demoralizing effects of the racial caste system, integration in this sense appears impossible to achieve within the lifetime of anyone now living, if we limit ourselves to the remedy of simply lowering formal racial barriers to entry into the wider society's institutions: "An individualistic ethic is acceptable if society has never violated this individualistic ethic in the past, but it is unacceptable if society has not in fact lived up to its individualist ethic in the past. To shift from a system of group discrimination to a system of individual performance is to perpetuate the effects of past discrimination into the present and future."[100] In other words, for a very long time large numbers of blacks and of other subordinated minorities will have no significant chances for individual advancement and no significant individual choices to make about belonging to the larger society—unless we are prepared to employ group remedies now. Or, to put the matter more succinctly, "In order to get beyond racism, we must first take account of race. There is no other way."[101]

One eloquent critic rejoins: "Rather, one gets beyond racism by getting beyond it now: by a complete, resolute, and credible commitment *never* to tolerate in one's own life—or in the life or practices of one's government— the differential treatment of other human beings by race."[102] As a factual proposition, this response focuses on one aspect of the educative force of legal principle. To defend affirmative action as integration is to emphasize a different and equally important aspect of law, namely the educative force of behavior in establishing norms. Just as stigma cannot be contained, but spoils an entire identity, so respect in one sphere tends to spill over into others. This alternative view draws support from our experience with the desegregation of public accommodations under the Civil Rights Act of 1964. Now, two decades after the adoption of the act, the sight of black people in hotels and restaurants in Southern cities is unremarkable—a fact that surely owes more to the normative force of day-to-day behavior and experience than it owes to any continuing aura of the law's enactment. The heart of the problem of racial caste is not the perception of difference but the perception of inferiority.[103]

The quoted criticism, however, expresses more than a factual disagreement about the probable effectiveness of alternative ways to "get beyond racism"; it also expresses the moral conviction that Justice Scalia once expressed: racial distinctions have no legitimate place in our law. This position equates the status goal of equal citizenship with the achievement of equality before the law. In contrast, the view of affirmative action as integration rests on the premise that equal citizenship requires an equality that is more than formal— that systematic racial subordination cannot be uprooted by trimming away those features of the system that have been written into law.

If affirmative action programs were to settle in institutional concrete—for example, by establishing racial quotas in permanent legislation—there might be some reason to worry about a drift into cultural corporatism. Nothing in our recent experience justifies any such anxiety. Justice Powell's diversity approach to affirmative action in higher education, permitting race-conscious admissions to diversify the student body,[104] does not freeze admissions in racial or ethnic quotas; furthermore, it minimizes the occasions for white resentment. Appropriations bills, including the one approved by the Supreme Court, setting aside a portion of certain public works funds for minority contractors, normally have only temporary influence. When courts impose hiring quotas in employment discrimination cases, generally they limit the quotas' duration. With the historically justified exception of the Indian tribal governments, no racial or ethnic group wields governmental power granted by legislation or judicial decree. In the short run the chief results of affirmative action are not corporatist but individualistic, freeing individuals from being locked into subordinate status because of their group membership. As Michael Walzer has remarked, in the here and now these programs offer "opportunities to individuals, not a voice to groups."[105] In the longer term the hope is that affirmative action programs will contribute to the improvement of the status of black people as a group. The specter of cultural corporatism, however, is like other ghosts; it has the capacity to frighten but lacks substance.

Even so, it does seem inevitable that new claimant groups will emerge. At least some members of virtually all cultural groups except British Americans can claim that their predecessors experienced discrimination in this country. Furthermore, it should not surprise anyone if members of today's subordinated minorities think of such programs as "getting our share." The prediction that affirmative action will stimulate ethnic politics is sound; indeed, the prediction seems already borne out by the ethnic revival of the 1970s.[106] What does not seem justified, however, is the assumption that a resurgence of ethnic politics will lead to a new fragmentation of American society. The history of ethnic politics suggests quite the reverse.[107] Even if an ethnic group were disposed to characterize its political objective as a share in "racial spoils," that group must necessarily turn outward to the wider society. As the leaders of today's cultural minorities turn from solidarity politics to broker politics, no doubt they and their constituents, like the Irish in the nineteenth century, will find that participation means integration.

In offering a view of affirmative action as inclusion, I do not want to contribute to the illusion that such programs of "marginal preferment,"[108] by themselves, will integrate American society. Ultimately, integration will depend on factors no one can foresee, including the ability of our economy to produce an abundance in which all can share. Although the new mobility of significant numbers of members of racial and ethnic minorities may not be a sufficient condition for inclusion, it appears to be a necessary condition if inclusion is to be accomplished before the nation celebrates its tricentennial.

Much in our recent history cautions against the easy assumption that the sense of community of middle-class white America can be enlarged overnight. In a longer view, however, our national history can be seen as one enlargement of the national community after another with each new addition embracing a group of people previously seen as permanent outsiders. Our semiofficial national ideology, reflecting this experience, proclaims that America includes all Americans. Most of us, seeking worthy individual identities in our identification with the nation, want to believe in this platitude. For decision makers who want to promote policies that offer inclusion to our marginalized citizens, this widely shared need to believe in the promise of America is a considerable political asset.

ten

Citizenship and Nationhood

At every turn in this discussion we encounter the same irony: the exclusion of groups of Americans from full participation in our public life is strongly connected to the need to belong. For every one of us, the sense of belonging to a community is one of the foundations of self-identification, of individuality. Because the creation of a self is based on both group identification and differentiation, it is easy for people in one group to distance themselves from the members of other groups. Ultimately that distance serves to rationalize the subordination of the Other: whites subordinating nonwhites, the native-born subordinating the foreign-born, men subordinating women. With increasing frequency since the age of European exploration and colonization, national societies have fragmented into diverse groups, with considerable attendant conflict and no little violence.[1]

Modern life also confronts us with a second kind of potential fragmentation, one that is internal to the individual. Our multiple associations lead us to present different faces to different groups of people, and this "pluralization of life-worlds"[2] presses each of us toward a fragmentation of the self.

Yet the yearning for wholeness remains, intensifying our need to belong. The American civic culture contributes to the sense of wholeness in ways that address both kinds of fragmentation. First, it offers at least one common ground on which all our subcultures can meet; second, it offers the individual a community of meaning, and thus an identity, that overarches his assortment of group identifications. More specifically, effectuation of the Fourteenth Amendment's guarantee of equal citizenship reinforces the civic culture's value of nationalism, nourishing both a national identity and the sense of national community.

Group Identifications and the Divided Self

Throughout American history, communities typically have found their distinctive qualities by cultivating a markedly negative "sensitivity to alien characteristics" of people they call outsiders.[3] Americans have always attached importance to the social boundaries dividing us along the lines of race, religion, and ancestral nationality. Yet, also from the beginning, those dividing lines have been eroded by the process of cultural assimilation.[4] Whatever else assimilation may imply, unquestionably it implies a relaxation of the defensive posture on both sides of a line that previously marked a cultural division. When the cultural Others no longer seem so alien, there is little occasion for us to fear them, to make them the vessels for our negative identities, or to threaten them in ways that make them cling to each other for psychological defense against us.

Assimilation is a redefinition of norms, a redrawing of the boundaries of communities of meaning. For the descendants of people on both sides of the old dividing line, the line has become blurred; at least for some purposes, the old "we" and "they" have become a more inclusive "we." Yet, despite the continuation of the process of assimilation, cultural differences and cultural conflicts appear to be constants in American life. The differences are preserved with the help of the Constitution, which offers a variety of protections for the freedom of cultural choice.[5] In any America now foreseeable, different communities will continue to thrive and to offer their different, and sometimes sharply divergent, visions of the civic culture and the legal order.[6]

Nonetheless, for a century and more, the literature of community all over the Western world has been largely a chronicle of decline. The assimilation, in various degrees, of religious and ethnic groups into a larger American culture is part of this pattern. One by one, the traditional communities—the village, the guild, the church, the ethnic group, even the family—have been eroded by a tide of individualism that has been flowing steadily for some three hundred years.[7]

The seventeenth century, "the century of genius," witnessed the shaking of the foundations of the old intellectual order. In science, a mechanistic view of the universe gave independent substance to separate physical bodies. In philosophy, the individual mind, perceiving, was held by some influential writers to be the only secure starting point on the path to reality: "I think, therefore I am." In literature, the novel emerged, telling its story from the perspective of an individual protagonist. In religion, the century saw widespread acceptance not only of Calvin's movement to decentralize church governance but also of Luther's radically individualistic doctrine of the priesthood of all believers. Taken seriously, Luther's doctrine implies the abandonment of a neofeudal, organic, corporate system, with each person occupying a fixed status in a world ordered by God, and the substitution of a system of individual rights. By the end of the seventeenth century, a theory of government focused on rights to life, liberty, and property had come to the ascendant in Britain and America.[8] The English courts of common law had completed the job of converting feudal obligations into money rents and had begun their attack on the privileges of the guilds. All this had already come to pass when the colonial population in North America was barely a quarter of a million.

When England finally determined to exploit the American continent by populating it, individualism was already entrenched in American ideology and behavior. Feudalism had never taken root here; even the guilds had failed to flower. The ideal of individual rights to life, liberty, and property made its way into the Declaration of Independence and then into the Bill of Rights. By the beginning of the nineteenth century, the dominant form of American individualism was the competitive pursuit of wealth and status, founded on a legal base that guaranteed not only the security of property and transactions but the freedom of contract.

The fragmenting tendencies of this form of individualism have been analyzed to death, and they are as familiar to us as the liberating effects of individualism were to an earlier generation. The impersonality of the market, which is essential to its effective functioning, heightens insecurities by emphasizing that the individual stands alone before forces beyond his or her control. With traditional community supports weakened, the individual is induced to seek security through acquisition and to seek esteem through consumption or display. Even when material wants are mostly satisfied, "the craving remains. It is a craving for the satisfactions others appear to obtain, an objectless craving."[9] David Riesman's words, written a generation ago, are easily verified today: just visit an urban shopping mall on a Saturday afternoon.

Industrialization was an early contributor to the fragmentation of Western societies, and our own century has seen the refinements of high technology and the complications of large-scale organizations and concentrated power. The specialization of functions reduces the sense of wholeness that comes from making decisions of consequence. Face-to-face dealings give way to data processing. Spontaneity gives way to bureaucracy. In the marketplace of human interactions it is hard for us not to see ourselves (and value ourselves) in the light of our salability to others. The perceived need to conform to others' expectations inhibits independent judgment and promotes the expression of pseudofeelings.[10] This process undermines not only self-regard but the sense of community: it isn't easy to identify with others when you are trying to manipulate them.

Our tendency to deal with each other in fragmented ways generates its own power, producing more and more groups, more group memberships for each of us, more pressure toward the fragmentation of individual identities. To the question, Who are you?[11] most of us would respond not with a phrase but with a list of labels: family relationships, age, sex, sexual orientation, race, religion, ethnicity, nationality, place of origin, present residence, occupation, political affiliation, attachment to a cause. Beyond occupation and such "primordial affinities" as race and religion and family, the same person can be identified as a Californian, a person of advanced middle years, a music lover, a Dodger fan, an Anglophile, a jogger, a loyal alumnus, a member of the Sierra Club, an American. Each label identifies a loosely defined group of people who share a world of symbols: a vocabulary, a way of translating raw experiences into culturally coded perceptions, a set of values, a specialized communications network.[12] Behind each of these overlapping self-identifications is a different community of meaning, a different subculture.

This multiplication of every individual's group connections may be disorienting as we move from one of our communities to another. But it also has one major advantage: it helps to unify a national society that might otherwise be torn apart by cultural divisions. If the Catholics and Protestants who did bloody battle in mid-nineteenth century Philadelphia[13] had continued to live in two adjoining but separated (and homogeneous) communities, the long-term results might have been bloodier still. But market individualism went about its usual work of multiplying selves with the result that both homogeneity and separateness were destroyed. Each of the groups became stratified by class and otherwise differentiated within itself, making new integrations possible for succeeding generations. Opportunity called individuals and families, both Catholic and Protestant, to join the move West; in their new surroundings they formed communities in which the old divisions just didn't matter so much. Their grandchildren intermarried and produced children of their own. As daily life in Hawaii makes beautifully clear, nothing else integrates quite so effectively as a baby.

The pattern has been familiar to sociologists ever since Georg Simmel: a multiplicity of criss-crossing divisions tends to unify a society by dampening the effects of any one line of division.[14] Individuals who are opposed on one issue will find themselves aligned on another. This kind of social cohesion, however, is bought at some cost, and the price is paid by the individual whose multiple associations and loyalties are the key to the society's unity. Only with difficulty can we avoid presenting separate faces to all our separate communities and associations. Human interactions in these circumstances involve the sharing of interests and concerns but only rarely the sharing of ourselves. So it is that observers in our time write of "the pursuit of loneliness" and the "escape from freedom" and even "the culture of narcissism."[15] The sadness in these expressions bespeaks the futility of any search for individuality that neglects the importance of being connected.

For Americans today, one important source of the sense of connection is the nation itself. The American civic culture—the national community of meaning centered on our public life—tends to unify us around our hallowed abstractions of liberty, equality, and tolerance. The Constitution, too, has contributed to America's nationhood, serving both as a symbol of the nation and as an instrument for centralizing governmental power in the national government.

Constitution and Union

In the United States as in Europe, the weakening of the traditional communities was hastened by governments that were jealous of competing loyalties to groups that stood as intermediaries between government and the individual. The decline in power of families, guilds, and churches invited the further growth of governmental power and the adoption of laws that applied equally to everyone. In the United States, the process was complicated, for the power to govern was divided between the nation and the states. In one perspective—a view the framers of the Constitution would have understood— the several states can be seen as intermediate groups standing between individuals and the national government. Here, too, in the long run the story has been the same: a decline in the influence of local institutions in the face of growing national identification and national political power. Equality and national community, yes—and centralization, too. Law played its part throughout this nationalizing process from the formation of the Union to the Fourteenth Amendment to the Supreme Court's active egalitarianism during the civil rights era.

The contractual nature of the national union, manifest in the bargaining that produced the Constitution, was reflected in the Supreme Court's nationalizing decisions in the first half of the nineteenth century. The central theme of those decisions was the promotion of a commercial economy of nationwide scope matched by an institutional base for a truly national polity. The Court began by giving a generous reading to the legislative powers of the Congress.[16] Although Congress mostly ignored that invitation until late in the century, in the meanwhile the Court had authorized the federal courts to develop a national body of commercial law[17] and had held unconstitutional a number of state statutes because of their potential for inhibiting the growth of a nationwide market.[18] Yet the bargain with slavery held. Until the eve of the Civil War, that bargain found shelter in the doctrine of "dual federalism": separate spheres for state and national sovereignty, with each sovereign supreme in its own sphere and with slavery assigned to the sphere of state "police" powers.[19]

Dual federalism loosened the states' political connections to the national government and thus might seem to offer little to the formation of a sense of national community. Nor do the dealings of buyers and sellers in a nationwide commercial market seem to be the stuff of communitarian sentiment. Yet both developments contributed to the sense of nationhood. Dual federalism fit comfortably into a national ideology that was increasingly democratic.[20] A national economy not only brought new mobility but also fostered the sharing of market values and provided a common vocabulary, the "language of how much, how many, how far."[21] The result was a new cultural amalgamation: not just the assimilation of immigrants and their children, but the gradual incorporation of large numbers of Americans into a shared national culture that coexisted with regional ones. Morality itself was glued to enterprise, to growth, to success. So, "all issues in the mid-nineteenth century were fundamentally moral, and a common culture fused these issues into one or another moral unity."[22] Even when the union broke apart, the national culture remained truly national: "like-minded people across the land turned a common culture on one another and fought savagely for truth, freedom, and opportunity as their culture defined those fundamental terms. In this sense it was indeed a civil war."[23]

The adoption of the Bill of Rights had been part of the contractual dealing that secured the ratification of the Constitution.[24] Yet, for more than a century, rights such as the freedoms of speech and press and religion were seldom the subject of litigation. Their importance lay not so much their constraints on the government as in their very declaration. By symbolizing "a new system of public morality based on the premise that government is but an instrument of man, its sovereignty held in subordination to his rights,"[25] the Bill of Rights helped define the identity of a nation.

As the nineteenth century began, government in America remained in the hands of the gentry. By the 1820s, however, a "democratic surge"[26] was bringing new opportunity to masses of people even as they were spreading over the mountains and into the West. By 1840, geographical and social mobility had combined to produce a revolution in attitudes toward individual rights. Claims to self-determination and personal freedom accompanied the broadening of the franchise and legislative programs that were increasingly populist.[27] This was the individualist democracy that Tocqueville recorded in the 1830s.[28] It was "a society resting on a new premise of equality"[29] that set the stage for an expansion of individual rights.

Apart from a spate of decisions interpreting the contract clause,[30] however, the Supreme Court had little occasion to translate the ideal of individual rights into a body of national constitutional law. Even after the Fourteenth Amendment was adopted, the Court declined to develop constitutional doctrine to match the earlier (1820–1840) legislative democratization of rights. Indeed, by the end of the nineteenth century, when the Court did enter an era of active judicial review, its constitutional base was the natural-rights doctrine of substantive due process and its practical focus was the protection of property and economic liberty.[31] This alliance of the judiciary with industry and enterprise allowed the Court to strengthen its position in the governmental system, a position that had deteriorated even before the "self-inflicted wound"[32] of the *Dred Scott* decision. The Court became a bulwark for the freedoms that mattered most to people at the top of the heap, and those people's friends at the bar and in the press glorified the judiciary and the Constitution. The patriotic rhetoric of the late nineteenth and early twentieth centuries created a "cult of the Constitution" that blended nationalism and constitutionalism in a single faith.[33] A strong form of judicial review became a symbol of American nationhood, and the century that had opened with John Marshall closed with Andrew Carnegie.

The sense of American nationhood had gained much of its early momentum from the Protestant idea of a divine mission for America. The association of nationalism with Protestantism intensified the national ideology by infusing it with two strong Protestant traditions. One was individual responsibility, and the other was congregationalism, the distribution of control over church governance among local institutions. The secular counterpart of congregationalism was the formation of the local voluntary associations that so impressed Tocqueville. Those associations were the behavioral expression of some large ideas that connected individuals in a nation on the move. By the mid-nineteenth century Americans' "very identity inhered in their abstractions," which included an egalitarianism that was individualistic and a nationalism that made room for the dispersal of political power.[34] The idea of an American national community thus fed on the sharing of values that were diffuse and on a shared understanding that people were engaged in a common task. In our own time Dennis Wrong has remarked on the necessary connection between the sense of community and active engagement in working together purposively:

> The achievement of community . . . cannot come from pursuing it directly but only as a by-product of the shared pursuit of more tangible goals and activities. Community may result from the concrete forms of political, economic, familial, and cultural association among men, but it cannot be willed into existence by exhorting people to immerse themselves in group activity and to find greater significance in their social identities.[35]

True enough—but, as the divine-mission idea shows, the ultimate shared goals of the community can be diffuse. For Americans of the early nineteenth century, the common tasks were the exploitation of a continent rich in resources and the creation of the new local institutions that would make that exploitation possible.

One by-product of the pre-Civil War dispute over the nature of the federal union was the question whether citizens of the states were also citizens of the nation—a question eventually resolved by the Fourteenth Amendment's specific affirmation of national citizenship. Even if that pronouncement should somehow be erased, a strong national identification would remain. My point is not that localism has disappeared; obviously, it remains very much alive, not just as rhetoric but as practice. Participatory democracy, for example, is one of the hallmarks of equal citizenship, and many more citizens are directly involved in local affairs than in national ones. The sense of local community may be most evident in the small city or town, but even for a great many of us in metropolitan America the voluntary organizations noted by Tocqueville continue to flourish, and neighbors continue to share the concerns that grow out of their neighborhoods. The PTA's Halloween carnival at the elementary school is, among other things, an expression of community. Yet, local participation has never been inconsistent with a national identity, and it seems no exaggeration to say that today most of us think of ourselves first as Americans and only secondarily as New Yorkers or Californians or Alabamans. Before the small-town basketball game begins, the high school band plays "The Star-Spangled Banner."

The reasons for this heightened national identification are easy to see. We are all part of one economy. Large numbers of us are highly mobile both in capacity and in inclination—and even those who stay put are part of national networks of relatives and friends scattered across the land. A national system of communications hands us the same news and the same entertainment. With some assistance from the modern Supreme Court, political power has flowed from the states to the national government as the nation has attempted to cope with an economy of nationwide scale and a worldwide political economy. The nation's foreign relations not only are highly visible, but are seen to touch our lives immediately as producers and consumers and potentially as victims of violence ranging from terrorism to war. As power and responsibility have flowed to the nation, we have come to look to the national government as the chief arena for the interplay of political forces, and the President has come to be "the chief focus of public hopes and expectations" for the results that government may accomplish.[36] Increasingly, too, we have come to perceive the obligations of citizenship as running not only to our neighbors but to the national polity: military service, for example, or taxation for the relief of victims of disaster or hunger or disease. All this is part of the everyday business of our lives.

Part of the explanation for the heightened sense of American identity is a widely shared belief in equal citizenship as a cluster of values and as a social fact. As a description of American society, that belief is exaggerated, but as a normative belief, it is one of the essentials of our nationhood. We can see ourselves as Americans to the extent that we continue to see ourselves as experiencing things together and doing things together. The moral should be plain: no national need is more urgent than the need to make equal citizenship into a reality for all Americans. If culture is an "acted document,"[37] the behavior that creates an American culture is influenced mightily by the ways in which judges and the rest of us interpret a document that is not metaphoric: the Constitution.

Tolerance and National Community

The principle of equal citizenship embodied in the Fourteenth Amendment embraces two ideas we have already explored: universal laws, applying equally to everyone, and political participation. The impersonality of law, to be sure, offers no more than a formal equality, but the formality itself is significant as a statement about equality of personal status: we are all citizens. Participation, too, has its symbolic side. In this sense, political community and political equality are congruent; equal citizenship means equal membership in the political community. Political equality and formal legal equality are practical necessities if government is to obtain the consent of the governed in today's Western world. But the Fourteenth Amendment's principle of equal citizenship implies more: the existence of a national moral community, whose members bear responsibility to each other.

The nation, unlike a family or a congregation, is not a community of close personal relations. Rather our civic culture defines a community of meaning for the nation's public life. Even so, the idea of a national community invites questions about scale and diversity. The very word community is apt to call to mind a face-to-face group that is largely homogeneous: a village, a congregation, a tribe. Can a multicultural nation of nearly a quarter of a billion people be a community?

A community sociology specialist might pause over the answer, but most Americans would not hesitate. From the beginning we have understood that we share a past and a future. When a speaker invokes the image of the nation, she is drawing on that persistent sense of community to persuade people to believe something, to do something, to commit themselves.[38] The nation bears many of the commonly defined indicia of community[39]: a definable territorial base, a widely shared language[40] and culture, and its own internal legal order. Organized as a state, the nation is expected to pursue its people's common interests. Because those interests and purposes are seen to extend over many generations, the nation becomes, as Edmund Burke put it, "a partnership not only of those who are living, but between those who are living, those who are dead, and those who are to be born."[41]

Interests and organization aside, the nation is founded on a base that is emotional and spiritual, reinforced every day by symbol and ritual in every city and town in the land. To be sure, the politicians and commercial advertisers who wrap themselves in the flag are promoting interests of their own. But the nationalist feelings they seek to tap transcend particular interests, linking most Americans with each other in the realm of the spirit. The message conveyed by our patriotic symbols is that we are all in this together; we belong.

The counterpoint theme is obvious. In every generation, many Americans have found that message to be false. To speak of a community is to identify a group of people who "have access to one another and are ready for each other."[42] Part of the problem of national community in America inheres in our diversity. In a nation of many cultures, by definition, there is an important sense in which we are not all ready for each other. The American nation has always been superimposed over a multitude of cultural groups, each with its own world of symbols and norms. When these differences are translated into group subordination, it is not easy for the people who are subordinated to think of themselves as part of the nation. In America national unity has never been achieved once and for all; every generation has had to address the fears and dislocations that attend the inclusion of new members in the national community.

Throughout this gradual and typically painful widening of the nation's embrace, the already-included Americans have shared a sense of "peoplehood."[43] Because American identity still inheres in the abstractions of the civic culture, citizens who seek a more inclusive definition of our national community can draw on two valuable resources. First, it is consistent to express both a strong ethnic identification and a strong attachment to the nation.[44] Second, tolerance of other groups is itself proclaimed as a national ideal.

Tolerance was not an invention of the Warren Court; it has always been a necessary feature of the American experiment, a value that makes the nation possible. Religious tolerance was already a political necessity when the Constitution was adopted.[45] Indeed, the dispersal of power that had characterized both religion and government in the colonies was, for the framers of the Constitution, not just an institutional habit but an essential defense against tyranny. Diversity was an important tenet of the national ideology that burgeoned in the nineteenth century. "Variety became fundamental to the dominant American idea of unity: E Pluribus Unum."[46]

A century ago the diverse peoples of a "segmented society" tended to avoid conflict by minimizing interaction with each other. As the black citizens of Memphis recently learned,[47] some of those patterns of avoidance remain. Yet today's ideology of tolerance is nourished, as yesterday's was not, in a civic culture fortified by more than three decades of judicial validation of the equal citizenship principle. To take seriously today's ideals of individualism and egalitarianism is to reject domination in favor of tolerance. It is to believe that every person is entitled to respected participation in the community's public life. Nationalism, too, demands tolerance, as an indispensable antithesis to the urge to domination that so often grows out of the process that forms individual identity. "[S]ocieties have a need to find ways of checking their own tendencies. In these polarities there may be something of a clue to social systems"[48]

Tolerance serves more than the need to moderate group conflict. It is an essential ingredient of the American civic culture, serving our need to identify with the national community in order to identify ourselves as Americans. Yet, as the idea of tolerance implies, for any individual the civic culture itself is only one of many communities of meaning. The civic culture leaves room not only for groups to socialize their members[49] but also for groups to contest the meanings of the civic culture itself.[50] *Brown v. Board of Education* was one such contest, with the two sides offering different views of the meaning of tolerance. The school boards focused on the idea of national tolerance for local autonomy, and the NAACP argued for tolerance as acceptance and inclusion. Both sides appealed to their own understanding of the basic values of the national community. As this example illustrates, conflict has always attended the definition of those values. At the same time, the cultural base for American identity has always depended on some sharing of values, some shared vision of what we are as a nation. The *Brown* decision recognized that the only vision of America capable of being shared by us all is a vision in which all of us belong. That vision has emotional power, as anyone knows who has heard the corporal call the squad roll in a 1940s war movie: Anderson, Chen, Giordanno, Goldstein, López, McGovern, . . .

If the nation is a primary object of people's loyalties, one reason is that the nation is "the community which makes the nearest approach to embracing all aspects of their lives."[51] The adoption by immigrants and their children of the beliefs and behavioral norms of the civic culture plainly is assimilationist in tendency, and for the most part this form of assimilation has been avidly sought and easily achieved. We remain conscious of our cultural differences—even conflicts—but our ideology calls for us to be ready for each other, across those lines of difference, in one important way: we should be ready to encounter the members of other groups as respected participants in our public life.

The nation has always been a community of limited reach. Typically our identification with the national community is less than total, coming to the forefront of consciousness intermittently. That limitation, however, does not detract from the nation's status as a genuine community; in today's world of multiple individual identities, every community is limited. But membership in the national community helps to provide a sense of wholeness, not only for the society but also for the citizen's sense of self. No one's whole personality is captured by the label *American*; yet the nation is the one group membership, the one identity, that purports to contain nearly all the others.

National Citizenship and Local Community

In one perspective the Civil War was a conflict over the question whether the United States would be a nation or a collection of separate political communities, and the Fourteenth Amendment was one effort to institutionalize the war's answer to that question. To its framers, the amendment was not merely a charter of the rights of national citizenship but an instrument of centralized political power.[52] After decades of default, when the Warren Court finally took a strong hand in making good on the promise of a national community, the Justices were criticized for exerting a centralizing influence, advancing the influence of national law and the power of the national government. Alexander Bickel, one of the critics, summarized the Court's main themes as "egalitarian, legalitarian, and centralizing."[53] Fair enough—and the same economical phrase would be an apt condensation of three centuries of Western political history.

The ideal of equal citizenship fosters a national consciousness and a national community. Yet equal citizenship as a principle of law is brought to bear on individuals and institutions at the lowest levels of social organization. An instructive example can be found in our experience with racial segregation in places of public accommodation in the South. Once the Supreme Court had decided *Brown v. Board of Education*, it moved quickly to extend that decision to all forms of state-sponsored segregation, including segregation at public beaches, parks, golf courses, and restaurants.[54] In the Civil Rights Act of 1964 Congress extended the same principle to privately owned places of public accommodation. Because the Jim Crow system was designed to subordinate blacks as a group, the most grievous harm of segregation was a harm to dignity, a denial of full membership in the community. The community immediately in view was the local community, but the claim to participate in that community's public life as an equal member was a claim founded on a national ideal and a body of national law.

From the perspective of many southern whites the whole episode was no more than a power play in which outsiders were wielding the power. In this view, egalitarian national legal norms were simply imposed on the local communities. Robert Cover suggested that this "imperial" pattern is characteristic of the civil community, where "norms are universal and *enforced* by institutions. They need not be taught at all, as long as they are effective."[55] Cover contrasted this "world-maintaining" kind of social control—focused on the preservation of unity in a society of separate normative communities—with the "world-creating" functions of a "strong community of common obligations," such as a tightly-knit religious minority. The latter functions, he said, center on the teaching and elaboration of norms—the transmission of culture—through the close personal interaction of community members.

The enforcement of national norms to displace Jim Crow's culture of subordination was not merely world-maintaining in the imperial mode. To say that the civil community lacks "strong forces of normative world building"[56] underestimates the force of the American civic culture. (It also underestimates the sophistication of the civil rights leaders.) Even in the white South at midcentury there was general agreement on the individualist and egalitarian meanings that defined the American community. The disagreement went to the question of belonging: who was included within the boundaries of the community?

Nor is it always true that the imposition of a legal interpretation on people who are resistant implies "a tragic limit to the common meaning that can be achieved."[57] Undeniably, at midcentury our national law's resolution of the question of belonging was forced on the white South. But the result has been inclusionary in more than one way—a result we are just now coming to understand. Not only did the Supreme Court and the Congress and the national executive recognize the right of black people to inclusion in the local and national communities; they also began the process of bringing the white South into the nation after nearly a century's absence. Here, irony piles upon irony. The Compromise of 1877, which effectively ended Reconstruction, was supposed to reunite the nation—that is, to reunite northern and southern whites.[58] Like many other arrangements conceived in sin, the compromise succeeded at first but eventually succumbed to decay. Not only did the ideals of the American civic culture increasingly lead to divergence between northern and southern whites' views on race relations, but the same values weighed on white consciences in the South in a way that heightened their sense of separation from the rest of the nation—even as the South was, in other respects, "becoming Americanized."[59] The *Brown* decision and the other judicial and legislative products of the civil rights movement may have been imposed on southern whites, but they also invited the white South to come home to America. As the civil rights movement was gathering force, William Faulkner told an interviewer that if matters came to fighting, and he were forced to choose between Mississippi and the United States, he would choose Mississippi.[60] Even today that preference may hold appeal for some Mississippians, but the *Brown* decision set that view on a course headed for extinction.

There are political risks in the centralization of power and loyalty, risks outlined in Robert Nisbet's book, *The Quest for Community*.[61] He begins with the well-founded premise that we all need the sense of belonging, and that we will go to some lengths to invent communities in order to satisfy that need. With the decline in functional importance of traditional communities such as the family, village, and guild, the individual yearns for other forms of community to satisfy the need for identity, for belonging, for the definition of values. Nisbet's main thesis is a political one: either we encourage the maintenance of strong intermediate communities, or the individual in an atomized society will seek the sense of community in the embrace of the totalitarian state.

Two ugly images of intolerant community come to mind, one national and one local. The first is the community of the crowds at those Nazi rallies in Nuremburg in the 1930s, so vividly recorded by Adolf Hitler's favorite filmmaker. The second image came to us on the television screen: the community of a white mob screaming curses at black children being led under armed guard into their newly desegregated school in Little Rock in 1957. Is that our choice?

No, it isn't. My point is not that "it can't happen here."[62] It remains possible that this country, given the right level of crisis, might turn to a home-grown version of totalitarianism in a red, white, and blue wrapper with words like *democracy, liberty,* and *equality* written all over it. In saying that we need not choose between the national community of totalitarianism and the local despotism of the frightened village, I mean that there is no inevitable progression from civil rights egalitarianism to the community of the Nuremburg crowd. Indeed, American history strongly indicates that the impulse toward racist domination (or its religious or ethnic counterparts) will be more powerful in a local community than it will be in the nation as a whole. With religious and ethnic division in mind, James Madison remarked that the diversity of "factions" represented in the national government would promote moderation in contrast to the domination of one group by another that was apt to result in local politics.[63] Madison was right, and it was particularly fitting, a century and three-quarters later, that the institutions of the national government should serve the civic culture's value of tolerance.

When the Supreme Court and Congress imposed a uniform national principle of racial nondiscrimination on the South, they did not destroy the functions of local communities. Rather they opened new opportunities for citizen participation in local public life. Localism was not suppressed; it was set free from the stifling effects of a racially exclusive definition of community. The redefinition has been limited to the community's public life. The Congress has not sought to invade the privacy of homes or of intimate associations, even for the purpose of eradicating racial discrimination, nor has the Supreme Court been inclined to pursue any such objective. The one kind of community that has been displaced by federal civil rights law is the community that seeks to operate an all-white preserve in the public arena. That is one intermediate community we can afford to forgo.

The redefinition of citizenship and community in the South is not just a story of national intervention in local affairs; it is also a story of the effects on national affairs of new local political forces. At the time of *Brown v. Board of Education* Justice Black correctly foresaw that southern liberalism would be an early victim of what we later called white backlash. Today, however, things are different. Black mayors are elected in southern cities with the support of white voters, and, more generally, the participation of black voters has brought southern politics into a closer resemblance to politics elsewhere in the nation. The effects of this expansion of local political communities are felt in Washington on issues from social welfare programs to the confirmation of Supreme Court Justices. The experience of the New South should help us understand that the best defense against totalitarianism in this country is to be found not in a new federalism but in three old facts of American life: the expansion of the middle class, the ideology of tolerance, and our social and cultural diversity. Indeed, the persistent political importance of our diversity is one of the keys to understanding this nation's patterns of ideology and political behavior.

American history is the history of many peoples and of one people. That there is an American people has always been a subject for discussion in this country. Surely no other people in human history has felt a greater compulsion to keep on verifying its own existence, year after year. When we look into the mirror, however, what we see is nothing tangible, but an abstraction: a civic culture that provides us with our identity as a people and a nation. Indeed, it is our need for national self-definition that has given the American civic culture such a prominent role in the life of our society. Because American identity *is* the civic culture, it enters into most Americans' lives as an important part of the sense of self.

eleven

Generations of Inclusion

Any community shares a history and imagines a destiny. Both these time dimensions are bound up with the community-defining role of law. In the law of any stable society, as Justice Oliver Wendell Holmes remarked, "historic continuity with the past is not a duty, it is only a necessity."[1] And in assigning meaning to present behavior, law speaks not only to the question, Who are we? but also to the question, Who shall "we" be tomorrow? Throughout America's history our law has reflected the definitions of community inherited from generations past and has served to perpetuate those definitions. Law has also symbolized our aspirations for a more inclusive community and has served to generate inclusion. It makes no sense to speak of *the* role of law in these processes. The various effects of law in retarding or advancing social change are as complex as the society itself and as difficult to grasp. Jorge Luis Borges once described a mythical land in which cartography became so exhaustive that the map of the kingdom was precisely the size of the kingdom itself.[2] Here I follow Mercator's more restrained example, accepting distortions as inevitable but hoping to aid navigation.

Being and Belonging

Community is an idea as protean as equality itself. In one sense the word describes a social group, sometimes but not always associated with a geographical territory: a family, for example, or a neighborhood or a nation.[3] Some communities are face-to-face groups, and some are not. We are taken into some communities at birth, and we join others by acts of will. The idea of a community, in other words, covers a multitude of types of groups. When we speak not of *a community* but more abstractly of *community*, we refer to one aspect of life in human groups. In the abstract, community is a type of bond or attachment between people, founded at least partly on sentiment. The typical family not only is a community, but evidences community.

For all this diversity, there is a central meaning to community in both of these usages. To belong to a community is to be joined with others for the achievement of some common good. There is something purposive about our communities even when we are born into them. The indispensable feature of a community is the sense of community, the sense that "we are all in this together," sharing a tradition and a commitment, a history and a future. What makes a community is not merely birth or place or values or interests but a state of mind and feeling, the common perceptions of a number of individuals that they are linked in ways that give emotional content to the word *we*. A human community does not exist in the raw stuff of nature; it is the joint artifact of a coalition of hearts.[4] Although we can understand the ideal of community as an abstraction, we experience the sense of community only through belonging to real communities.

Membership in a community implies obligation to the other members, not the specific sort of obligation we associate with contract but the more diffuse obligation suggested by words such as loyalty or commitment. Indeed, the sense of community may weaken as the members' obligations to each other become more sharply focused. We know in some detail the duties of one who borrows money from a bank, but what are the duties of a brother to a sister? When husbands and wives are urged to set out detailed promises in marriage contracts, someone ought to remind them that the marriage community is not reducible to a list of duties. Contract and community are not mutually exclusive; both are present in some degree in any social group. But contract and community are, at the very least, in tension.

The heart of community, then, is not so much the cool calculation of interests as the "moral cohesion"[5] of shared values. The sense of community is a feeling or an intuition, not a reasoned conclusion. The symbols of community—from wedding rings to "soul" handshakes to powder blue football jerseys—are not designed to appeal to anyone's rational estimate of self-interest. Even so, the ingredient of common purpose, necessary to any community, begins to suffer when a community begins to lose its functions. We all know how a fraternity of battle tends to disintegrate once the battle ends. Six people trapped in an elevator for half a day may become a community, but once they escape they are not likely to hold annual reunions. The continuity of feelings needs support in the continuity of joint functions and shared experiences. Nothing integrates like integration.

So it is not enough to say that a community is a creature of symbol and feeling and intuition; it rests also on the shared perception that it performs some function beyond serving as a focus for loyalty. The community that thrives is one that appeals to the sharing of interests as well as to the sharing of values. When neighbors get together to build a recreation center, their participation not only promotes their immediate joint purpose but reinforces their attachment to the neighborhood, their mutual trust, and their sense of diffuse responsibility to each other. To take a gloomier example, a great many black Americans, across a wide age spectrum, are disinclined to trust whites and equally disinclined to celebrate the rituals of American patriotism.[6] Loyalty to a community requires not only the sense of respected membership but regular nourishment of the members' sense that there is "something in it for us."

To say of a community that it shares a history and a future is to acknowledge the two ways in which the dimension of time touches the sense of community. The shared experience of the past is the source of any community's values, and faith in the endurance of those values into the future is the basis for trust among the community's members. The sense of community is not a luxury; it is the matrix for the trust in others that we must have if we are to know ourselves or even be ourselves. When a city planner says that a geographical community must be "legible," he is touching the edges of this larger concern. The same planner goes on to say this: "In order to feel at home and to function easily we must be able to read the environment as a system of signs." The need to feel at home in a city is only partly a need for familiar shapes and sounds; more fundamentally it is a need for assurance about the behavior we can expect from other people—their likely conformance to the norms that express a culture, a community of meaning. One of the main values we get from belonging to any community, geographical or not, is this security, this trust. And at least some capacity to see the world from another person's perspective appears to be essential both to community and to trust.[7]

Although we begin the construction of our identities in our primordial communities of family and tribe, community seldom offers itself without exacting a price. To the extent that individual identity is founded on differentiation, a sense of belonging that is close may be threatening. And, when a community imposes its norms on nonconformists, membership can be oppressive. Yet individuality itself—as reflected in self-knowledge, self-respect, or self-expression—is attainable only within a community.

Self-expression is possible in solitude but unlikely outside a cultural matrix. For nearly everyone, the most rewarding self-expression is a sharing of the self with others. The sharing of experience extends to virtually all that we do and see. Although it is true that every person's experience is in some sense unique,[8] it is also true that all experience is in some sense shared. Culture supplies meaning for nearly everything we perceive and for nearly everything we do. Robinson Crusoe, alone on his island, behaved as an Englishman.

Alone, singing in the shower, you share the song with its composer and its other performers.[9]

We not only think in a language but perceive and feel in ways that are culturally specific. Self-knowledge is necessarily a figure against the ground of community. The closer the community, the more it contributes to self-awareness and the sense of an individual's identity. It is a commonplace of social psychology that we largely see ourselves as we think others see us. If we are to know ourselves as whole persons, and not merely as a collection of social roles, we must be willing to show our whole selves to someone. To take the risks of intimacy, we need the kind of trust that is founded on the sense of community. And membership in any community, intimate or not, supplies a part of our self-definition.

Not only self-knowledge, but self-respect, too, depends on trusting others. The idea of self-respect is almost meaningless in the absence of a community. Sociologists, following George Herbert Mead, express this notion by referring to "the generalized other" when they mean the individual conscience.[10] The notion of shame is linked to a breakdown of trust, the realization that expectations have been false.[11] On the other hand, the sense of control over our own destiny, which is crucial to self-respect, requires an ability and a willingness to trust our environment and especially other people. Many features of our law, of course, are designed to provide particular kinds of security that will permit a measure of trust in strangers. The law's most important contributions to trust, however, lie not in these specifics, or even in the Constitution's protections of religious freedom or cultural identification, but in the more general role of law as a foundation for the sense of community. To carry out its functions, a community needs a measure of independence and power, primarily the power to establish norms to govern its members' behavior

The Logic of Law and Community

Law is one of the defining characteristics of community. To be a member of a community is to be subject to a system of rights and obligations. Beyond this logical interconnection, law contributes to social cohesion in two principal ways, long ago analyzed by Emile Durkheim. First, law provides an institutional base for reciprocity and the sharing of interests, for example, providing the economic freedom and the transaction security that underpin the market. Second, by establishing and enforcing norms, law reinforces the sharing of values, for example, by punishing criminals so that the rest of us can reassert our devotion to the moral order.[12]

Although both of these functions can promote the sense of belonging, it is the second one that is indispensable. Law contributes to community primarily by establishing norms that identify a group as people who owe to each other not merely some specific obligations, but a loyalty whose boundaries are only vaguely defined. In this dimension law is, in Thurman Arnold's phrase, "a great reservoir of emotionally important social symbols."[13] Within a community of shared values, law dampens aggression and promotes cooperation only secondarily by establishing particularized rules of behavior; mainly, law serves these communitarian purposes by standing as a totem, a symbol that community exists.[14]

If we have one preeminent symbol of national community in the United States it is the Constitution.[15] In its origins, however, the document was highly contractual in both letter and spirit, and contract is not the stuff of community. The Constitution has come to symbolize our community because it has come to embody substantive values of the most diffuse quality. What began as a negotiated charter evolved into what Karl Mannheim called an institution: a pattern of cooperative behavior that is "the product of unconscious tradition," embodying "symbolic and intuitive values" whose contribution to the sense of community is not a matter of reasoned argument, but an appeal to emotion.[16]

The irony is that this transformation of the Constitution has been largely the work of the courts, whose special place in our system is sometimes justified on the basis of their devotion to reason. John Marshall himself explained judicial review as a logical deduction, and his constitutional opinions marched from premise to conclusion in Euclidian majesty. It is no trick at all to do that; once you have begged the critical questions, you can hand the decision over to a reasoning machine.

Yet it is not enough to say, "reason is the life of the law."[17] Reason isn't the life of anything; it is a mental instrument to be used by live human beings, and it is by no means our only mental instrument. Judges and the rest of us are blessed with at least two complementary ways of knowing. Reason is one of them; it proceeds in linear, segmented, sequential steps. But on the other side of the brain—literally[18]—we find a way of knowing that deals in textures, patterns, analogies, relations that are grasped intuitively and all at once. Courts do engage in reason, but they also use intuition,[19] and a justification for judicial review that rests on reason alone is an incomplete justification.[20]

We have come to expect our judges, and especially the Supreme Court, to discern and articulate substantive values that provide an important part of the "moral cohesion" that is the cement for our national community.[21] This process is aided by reason, but it is intuition that draws an analogy from one pattern to another, or strikes a balance when competing values are weighed. And it is no accident that our most cherished constitutional values—including equality—are diffuse rather than specific.[22] Their very lack of specificity helps them to serve as symbols of community. The part of the brain that houses intuition and whole-pattern ways of knowing is also the home of dreams, and tears, and laughter.[23] For a value to endure, to do its work in building a community, that value must not merely appeal to our interests but touch our emotions. Diffuse loyalty is the essence of community. There are no footnotes on the flag.

If, in one metaphoric vision, law is a reservoir of emotion, in another it is a filter for perceptions and emotions alike. Richard Wasserstrom has remarked that law is conservative in the way language is conservative, structuring not only behavior but perceptions, beliefs, and feeling.[24] By providing social definitions for events and transactions, law helps to identify what we are perceiving and which emotions are proper under the circumstances. Durkheim's term *anomie* describes a state of breakdown of social norms, caused primarily by the insatiability of wants in a society in which the market has eroded traditional restraints. In these circumstances the individual is burdened not only with the freedom to accumulate and consume, but with the freedom to select a private moral code: "One no longer knows what is possible and what is not, what is just and what is unjust; which claims and hopes are legitimate and which are excessive."[25] If it is hard to tell the difference between right and wrong, or between what is enduring and what is not, then it will be hard to be loyal to a community beyond the individual's own immediate circle. Yet the yearning for community remains. We yearn to belong, and we yearn to know what is right, and those two yearnings flow from the same source.

Law not only expresses and creates power but also serves to limit power. In the United States this is a familiar idea, regularly reinforced as courts limit the actions of governmental officials in the name of higher authority, notably the Constitution. But, irrespective of an institution such as judicial review, the very existence of law limits power. Law expresses community norms, and it applies them to particular situations by interpreting the norms in the light of community morality and other community understandings. The essence of a norm is that it constrains behavior, including the behavior of the powerful. One who resists conforming to a norm can try to redefine the norm, which implies redefining the community. If the effort at redefinition should fail, and no hope remains for further efforts, the plausible alternatives are ranged along a continuum from conformance to resignation from the community.[26] Every disobedience, however, implies some weakening of community's bonds.

Underlying both the notion that power is subject to substantive limits and the notion that power rests on the acquiescence of the governed are two fundamental connections between power and community. First, norms—and thus the power to enforce them—cannot emerge in the absence of at least some sharing of the values on which community is founded. Even when a judge imposes a legal norm on one who rejects it, as Robert Cover has made clear, the actual enforcement of the norm necessarily involves action by other power wielders and thus some sharing of responsibility for the enforcement, whatever their level of agreement with the judge's reasons for her order. At least in this limited sense "legal interpretation is a form of bonded interpretation," requiring the concurrence of "many voices" in the result.[27] Second, the people who wield power have their own needs for a sense of community with the people they command. They want to think of themselves not as despots but as decent people who rule legitimately—and legitimacy can come only from the standards of a particular community.

Thus, both the rulers and the ruled—in American society, political majorities and minorities—need to belong and to believe that the rulers can offer justification for the exercises of power.[28] Those two needs amount to much the same thing, and they imply a logical connection between community and equality. Every community involves the sharing of something. Of course many a community is organized in a hierarchy with striking inequalities in the distribution of wealth and power. Medieval Europe provided the classic illustrations in realms both temporal and spiritual. Yet the lord and the serf held common values, shared the sense of belonging to the same earthly community, and knew they were equals in another community that was not of this earth.

Correspondingly, our ideas about equality are not natural categories but arise out of participation in particular cultures, particular communities of meaning. As the slaveholders knew and as Tally Jackson may suspect, an inequality between two people is not even seen as an issue unless both people are perceived as members of the same community.[29] More importantly, our notions of what constitutes an unacceptable inequality are culturally defined, deriving from community standards of human dignity. If a particular inequality is demoralizing, the reason is that there is a view, widely shared in some specific culture, that one cannot participate fully in the life of that community—cannot be a respected member—when one is deprived of the item in question. Here is an example in a social scientist's comment on the harms of inequality in a village in Southern Italy: "What the peasant lacks is not opportunity for recreation, but opportunities for those particular kinds of recreation—having coffee in the bar in the public square, for example—which are *civile* and which would therefore identify them as persons entitled to respect and admiration."[30]

Equality and community, like law and community, are intertwined by definition. The very idea of community implies at least that members are equal in their membership,[31] and our notions of equality are themselves derived form the standards of a community. At some deep level Americans have always understood: equality among citizens is essential to the community of meaning that defines the American nation. The important question has always been: Who belongs? Over the generations, as America's answers to that question have become more inclusive, the law has served sometimes to widen the embrace of the national community and sometimes as a barrier to further inclusion.

Constitution and Reconstitution

Today's American civic culture rejects two values that were taken for granted in 1850: white supremacy and Protestant domination. Racism and religious intolerance are still with us, both as beliefs and as behavior, but they no longer serve as explicit bases for legitimizing choices in the national polity. How can we know that white supremacy and Protestant domination have become discredited? We can read newspapers and magazines; we can listen to the radio and watch television; we can attend public meetings; even judicial opinions are instructive. From all these sources we can see that some attitudes that once seemed respectable are now outside the generally accepted limits of decent expression in our public life.[32]

These developments in rhetorical style reflect redefinitions of the national community. In race relations, the Civil War amendments themselves appeared to assume—indeed, to be—a major redefinition,[33] but in the *Civil Rights Cases* and in *Plessy v. Ferguson* the Supreme Court made its selection among the constitutional traditions and other cultural materials available to it and chose not to give constitutional recognition to any such change.[34] In *Brown v. Board of Education* the Court referred to *Plessy* but also discussed more recent precedents pointing in a different direction and chose the course indicated by those later decisions. Chief Justice Warren, speaking for the Court, explicitly took account of the change in interpretation: "In approaching this problem, we cannot turn the clock back to 1868 when the Amendment was adopted, or even to 1896 when Plessy was written. We must consider public education in the light of its full development and its present place in American life throughout the Nation. . . . Today, education is perhaps the most important function of state and local governments. . . . It is the very foundation of good citizenship."[35] In a rather condescending passage, the same opinion took note of improvements in the status of black people in American society since the adoption of the Fourteenth Amendment.[36] Patronizing or not, that passage had the look of an announcement that blacks had been admitted to full membership in the national community.

Not only in discarding the values of white supremacy and Protestant domination but also in recognizing that women are entitled to be full participants in our public life, the American civic culture has changed in ways that have the look of permanence. If the pattern looks familiar, one reason is that a similar pattern is visible in the assimilation of the descendants of immigrants from Europe and Asia. This process evidences a ratchet effect: when the great majority of a group's members have become included as full participants, the group stays included, with the aid of judges who interpret the Constitution to protect their inclusion.[37] Since 1850 Americans have progressively redefined the membership of the national community, typically by extending its embrace. When Alexander Bickel attacked the Warren Court's egalitarian activism, he chose an ironic title: *The Supreme Court and the Idea of Progress.* But the irony was misplaced. In the life of the American nation, inclusion *is* progress. Indeed, as Michael Walzer says, "[i]nsofar as we can recognize moral progress, it has less to do with the discovery or invention of new principles than with the inclusion under the old principles of previously excluded men and women."[38]

The Supreme Court is by no means the sole arbiter of the question, Who belongs to America? Since midcentury, however, the Court has contributed in important ways to a widened definition of the national community. Those contributions have most obviously affected the newly arrived whose full citizenship has thus been recognized, notably women and the members of racial and ethnic minorities. In the end, though, everyone is affected. By exercising its special influence on the symbolism of American values, the Court has offered all Americans the chance to redefine our identities as Americans. During these recent decades most of us have learned something important about who we are, and we have said something important about who we intend to be.

In developing a body of law, case by case, judges cannot rest wholly on the reasoned elaboration of existing principles. Reason is part of the process, but when the precedents point in opposing directions, reason will not tell the judge how to determine which analogy is more apt for the present case. To make that selection is to create constitutional meaning, and for that creative task the judge needs a contextual insight, a "situation sense" that is founded not on reason but on intuition.[39] (These qualities are not the exclusive property of law professionals. To be embedded in a culture is to understand what the culture accepts as an argument addressed to the question, What is fair?)[40] It is true that the Supreme Court's opinions emphasize the "authorities" and minimize the role of judicial creativity.[41] But in referring to the demands of the equal protection clause, for example, normally a Justice is using a short-hand expression for the text, the adopters' expectations, and the whole body of principle that emerges from the Court's previous decisions. Given nearly two centuries of judicial development of constitutional norms, it is entirely accurate to say that a Justice appointed today is the inheritor of a creative role soundly based on tradition.[42]

So it is that we celebrate our creative judges. In 1901 Justice Holmes said this about our first great creative Justice: "if American law were to be represented by a single figure, sceptic and worshipper alike would agree without dispute that the figure could be one alone, and that one, John Marshall."[43] If the modern era of American law were to be represented by a single figure, my choice would be Earl Warren. Like Marshall, Warren accepted responsibility for constructing a body of constitutional principle. And, like Marshall, he understood that he was not just creating doctrine but building a nation.

Creative activity normally begins with an intuition,[44] and in constitutional law the elaboration of principle often begins in a sense of justice that is intuitive. The Supreme Court made one such beginning in two 1968 decisions that now stand at the intersection of constitutional law and the status of women. Louisiana law allowed a lawsuit on behalf of a child for damages for wrongfully causing the death of a parent, and a similar action by a parent for the wrongful death of a child. When the child was born outside marriage, however, neither a surviving child nor a surviving parent could bring such an action. The Supreme Court, in two opinions by Justice Douglas, held that this scheme denied the equal protection rights of a surviving "illegitimate" child—the adjective deserves an early retirement—and a surviving mother.[45] The opinions gave voice to a moral intuition about the injustice of state laws discriminating against such children or such parents but offered little further explanation.

Eventually the Court did articulate reasons for intensifying judicial scrutiny of such laws, emphasizing the unfairness of disadvantaging a child for a status outside his control and unrelated to his potential contributions to society.[46] Missing from these later opinions, however, was any suggestion that the Justices were in touch with the human contexts—or, for that matter, the institutional contexts—in which the legal status of illegitimacy has its being. One major effect of the modern law of illegitimacy is that a man's wealth and status will attach to a woman and her children only when he chooses to formalize their union or to formalize his recognition of their children as his.[47] Furthermore, in Louisiana, where this constitutional saga began, the legal disabilities associated with illegitimacy grew out of that society's history of race relations.[48] Seen in context, the constitutional problem presented by the law of illegitimacy is intimately connected with the power of men over women and especially of white men over black women. The problem, as Justice Douglas knew intuitively, is a relative of the problem of caste.

Intuition is a way of understanding that looks at patterns and textures, not analytically but contextually. In the early illegitimacy cases the Court's intuition was not only creative but right. There is injustice in fastening a pariah status to the children of unwed parents—or, for that matter, to the parents themselves. More broadly, there is injustice in the state's imposition of a penalty on the decision to have a child without marrying. The effective doctrinal development of a moral intuition, however, depends on asking the right questions. If the Court should ever seek a wider perspective on these issues, the constitutional problem of the illegitimacy laws will come into focus as a problem in reconstituting a more inclusive community.

How shall we explain the Supreme Court's recent willingness to reshape the constitutional doctrine governing discrimination against children born out of wedlock and their parents? These decisions are best understood as one doctrinal reflection of a social movement of major proportions. As technology and law have combined to give women a greater measure of control over their own sexuality and maternity, their new latitude of choice about their own roles has broadened the range of acceptable forms of intimate relationships both casual and enduring. Marriage without motherhood, motherhood without marriage, nonmarital unions—all have become realistic choices in a social climate that has become more tolerant.[49] Our constitutional doctrine, carried forward on the same tide, has come to embrace the freedom of intimate association.[50] When the Supreme Court in 1984 first explicitly recognized this freedom, it properly emphasized the centrality of intimate personal relations in an individual's self-definition.[51] Here, in these associations, a person has his best chance to be seen (and thus to see himself) as a whole person rather than as an aggregate of social roles.[52] For most of us, our intimate associations are powerful influences over the development of our personalities. Our relations with significant others may add up to a "paradox of sociability"—the paradox being that you can't live with them and you can't live without them—but in the formation of our senses of self they are the only game in town.

An intimate association may influence a person's self-definition not only by what it says to him but also by what it says (or what he thinks it says) to others. In the older, traditional domain of the constitutional freedom of association, this idea of association-as-statement is familiar. In the 1980s as in the 1960s and the 1840s, political association serves not only to promote specific policy goals but also as an outlet for expressiveness, for self-identifying assertions. So it is with many intimate associations. Indeed, as the legal consequences of a couple's living together come to approximate those of marriage, and as divorce becomes more readily available, marriage itself takes on a special significance for its expressive content as a statement that the couple wish to identify with each other. Similarly, the decision whether to have a child is a major occasion for self-definition. To become a father or mother is to assume a new status, a new identity in the eyes of oneself and others.

The Supreme Court's recognition of this cluster of freedoms was hastened by two egalitarian trends in the social history of the last four decades. One was the movement toward racial equality, which brought with it new awareness and acceptance of a cultural diversity that goes well beyond differences based on race. The other was the sudden success of the feminist movement in engaging national attention and changing attitudes of large numbers of women and men toward questions of "woman's role." Both these developments have heightened our recognition of diversity in associational patterns. The changes, in other words, are cultural: they are changes in the meanings assigned to behavior.

Even in the first half of this century, when an idealized picture of "housewife marriage" largely defined the range of the acceptable in intimate association, that picture included only part of our social reality. The picture omitted not only associational patterns outside the majoritarian cultural mainstream but also those forms of intimate association that were skeletons in a family's closet. If the closet doors are opening at an accelerated rate, that is one measure of the distance we have come, not so much in our popular consciousness of associational diversity as in people's expectations concerning the likely consequences of disclosure. But the changes in this area of human interaction are not just changes in perception and belief. Mere recital of divorce rates, the number of unmarried couples who live together, or the number of children born to unmarried parents is enough to remind us that behavior, too, has altered significantly in our times.

We have no reason to expect major departures from this line of development in the near term. Urbanization seems permanent. Families are not likely to regain their lost economic functions. The "wife economy" seems unlikely to make a comeback. Increased longevity will continue to place strains on lifetime marriage. American society will not readily revert to yesterday's assumptions about "woman's role." Technology will continue to promote the practice (and thus the acceptability) of sex without procreation, with the likely result—not the day after tomorrow, but eventually—of a still wider range of the acceptable in sexual orientation.[53] And, whatever directions may be taken in minority communities concerning children born outside marriage, no sane social policy can subject millions of children to treatment as outcasts.[54] These projections suggest the likelihood of a long-term trend in the American civic culture: the continued infusion into our individualist and egalitarian values of new meanings for associational behavior. Our constitutional guarantees of liberty and equality have already begun to accommodate some of those new meanings, and the long-term prospect surely is for further accommodation. In the immediate future, though, the prospect in court is not encouraging.

Inclusion Delayed

If a majority of the Warren Court intuitively grasped the constitutional dimensions of Louisiana's treating a child born outside marriage as an outcast of law, more recently five Justices contrived to avoid confronting the social and institutional contexts that gave similar constitutional dimensions to a homosexual man's challenge to Georgia's sodomy law.

The case ended in a cloud of doctrinal abstraction, but it began as a squalid little flexing of local police muscle. Michael Hardwick tells this story[55]: He had worked all night installing a lighting system in a gay discotheque in Atlanta. Around six o'clock in the morning, he got a beer and left to walk home, about two blocks away. As he opened the door he had the beer in his hand. A police officer was driving by, and Hardwick dropped the beer in a trash can by the front door of the discotheque. The officer stopped and gave Hardwick a ticket for drinking in public, an offense punishable by a fine. Hardwick misread the court date on the ticket, thinking he had an extra day to pay the fine. According to Hardwick, an hour and a half after the time for paying the ticket had expired, the same officer appeared at Hardwick's home with a warrant for his arrest. (Hardwick says that in about ten years of service with the police force, the officer had not previously taken the unusual step of personally processing a warrant.) Hardwick was at work, and when he came home and learned the officer had been there, he went to the courthouse, paid the fine, and was given a receipt by the clerk.

About a month later, the same officer returned to Hardwick's house with the warrant, arriving at the door about fifteen minutes after Hardwick had come home with a friend. (As Hardwick put it, "he had given us ample time to get undressed and such.") A houseguest was staying with Hardwick, sleeping on the living room couch. The officer asked where Hardwick was. The houseguest had been asleep when Hardwick came home and did not know Hardwick was in the bedroom with the friend. The guest also did not realize the inquiry was coming from a police officer. The guest told the officer where Hardwick's room was. The officer went into the bedroom and watched Hardwick and his lover for a time. When Hardwick looked up, the officer told him he was under arrest for sodomy. Hardwick said, "What are you doing in my house?" The officer said he had a warrant for Hardwick's arrest. Hardwick told the officer he had paid the ticket and offered to show him a receipt that stated the warrant was no longer valid. The officer then said that it didn't matter, for he was acting in good faith, and Hardwick was still under arrest. Hardwick was taken to the central lock-up, held for twelve hours, and released.

After a preliminary hearing, the district attorney decided not to proceed with the prosecution. Hardwick himself then went to federal court. He asked for an injunction against enforcement of the law, which defined sodomy, a crime punishable by imprisonment up to twenty years, as "any sexual act involving the sex organs of one person and the mouth or anus of another." Hardwick succeeded in the federal court of appeals, but in *Bowers v. Hardwick* (1986) a 5–4 Supreme Court reversed, upholding the constitutionality of the Georgia law in application to circumstances like his.

The refusal to prosecute Hardwick was not unusual. Sodomy laws are on the books in twenty-four states and the District of Columbia, and they are rarely enforced by prosecution. It would not be accurate, however, to say that they are rarely enforced by putting people in jail. Police officers in Georgia do not arrest married couples, or even unmarried heterosexual couples, for violation of the sodomy law, even though the law's terms plainly apply to them. (During oral argument, Georgia's counsel assured the Supreme Court that the state would enforce the law only against homosexual conduct.) Yet the officer did arrest Hardwick, who then served an informally imposed sentence of twelve hours in jail. It is not impossible to imagine that an arresting officer might have something of the sort in mind in going to the trouble of obtaining an arrest warrant.[56] The real offense that eventually led Michael Hardwick to the Supreme Court, it would appear, was the offense of being gay and expressing his sexual orientation openly.

There is little doubt that a state law explicitly making criminal the status of being homosexual would be unconstitutional.[57] Yet the Georgia law, and the other twenty-four sodomy laws, stay on the books because they serve as official statements branding homosexual conduct as wrongful and stigmatizing gays and lesbians. In fact, one common argument against repealing those laws is that the repeal may suggest state approval of homosexual behavior.[58] The parallel to racial discrimination is close: a cultural majority inflicts a status harm on a minority in order to reassure itself—that is, the rest of "us"—that "we" are "normal." The laws not only result from majority-imposed stigma; like the Jim Crow laws, they also reinforce that stigma, giving heterosexuals official "permissions-to-hate"[59] that encourage not only police harassment but all manner of privately inflicted harm from insults to trashing to violence.[60]

The members of any human population are distributed over a wide range of sexual orientation, and many millions of Americans are gay or lesbian. In a conservative estimate, a task force of the National Institute on Mental Health reported that at least 5 percent of American males, and 2 to 3 percent of females, are exclusively homosexual.[61] Of the remaining 95 percent of males, some 15 to 20 percent have engaged in some homosexual activity.[62] Men and women who are exclusively homosexual do not choose their sexual orientation; it chooses them. "For as long as I can remember, I have been gay," wrote a student of mine in a seminar paper. Some gays and lesbians do not recognize their sexual orientation until their teenage years or even early adulthood. The sources of homosexual orientation are not well established, but for one who is exclusively homosexual the orientation is virtually impossible to change.[63] Yet it makes sense to think of sexual orientation as an aspect of self-definition. In the face of widespread social disapproval, even an internalized recognition of your same-sex orientation involves an element of decision about the way you are going to regard yourself. Your disclosure of that orientation to others obviously implies a major decision about self-identification.

In these circumstances homosexual behavior is not simply a form of intimacy or the index of membership in a cultural group.[64] It is also central to the physical expression of love, and thus close to the heart of the individual's sense of self. For the man or woman who is homosexual, this form of intimacy serves the same functions as do the intimacies of marriage for a married couple.[65] Yet about half of our states have made that physical expression, even between adults, into a crime. As a result of the majority-imposed stigma that keeps these laws on the books, gays and lesbians are under constant pressures and anxieties concerning their own identities. Furthermore, like the pupils in that Virginia school in the 1960s who never told anyone they were Jewish,[66] and like the women who must always wonder whether they dare let men know who they really are,[67] gays and lesbians constantly face the question of how, or whether, to make those identities known to their families and friends, let alone their employers and coworkers.

These abstractions come to life in the story of Donald Baker, as told by Judge Jerry Buchmeyer in his opinion in a 1982 case, *Baker v. Wade*. For more than ten years Baker struggled against his same-sex orientation and repeatedly experienced fear and self-loathing. The fear was only partly a dread that his desires would be discovered; more fundamentally it was a fear for his own soul. Like many another victim of stigma, he had been led to accept the culturally dominant characterization of gays as outcasts who did not belong. And, like a great many gays before and after him, he seriously contemplated suicide. Baker was twenty-seven years old when he began to tell some people that he was gay. Within another year he had satisfied himself that he could be homosexual and still be a devout Christian. Soon thereafter he "came out" to his family. His story is the story of millions of individual Americans, some of whom eventually will reach a resolution like Baker's, and some of whom will live out their whole lives in fear, self-hate, or both.[68]

The Supreme Court's decision in Michael Hardwick's case would necessarily teach some lesson to Americans, for "teaching is inseparable from judging in a democratic society."[69] Three decades earlier in *Brown v. Board of Education*, and more recently in the cases of children born outside marriage, the Court had contributed to the enlargement of the national community by teaching lessons in tolerance. In *Bowers v. Hardwick* the lesson was different. The majority reinforced the legitimacy of the stigmatizing sodomy laws, giving the Court's constitutional sanction to the application of those laws to homosexuals. The doctrinal focus for both the majority and the dissent was the liberty protected by the Fourteenth Amendment's due process clause. As Justice Harry Blackmun argued in dissent, the Court could easily have held the law invalid on this ground, invoking the freedom of intimate association. But the heart of the case—and the main hurt of the decision—is stigma. The Supreme Court has placed the stamp of legitimacy on Georgia's official exclusion of gays and lesbians from full membership in the community.

To see the case as a problem in exclusion, the Justices would have to look at the social and institutional contexts that make the sodomy laws the vehicle for official sponsorship of stigma. No such inquiry was made in Michael Hardwick's case, even though the majority's own shaping of the legal issues invited the inquiry. The law applied generally to heterosexuals and homosexuals alike, but the Court expressly disavowed any consideration of the law's constitutionality in application to heterosexual intimacies. That disavowal, no doubt, was designed to sidestep some general questions about the Constitution's protection of the privacy of sexual intimacies. but it also brought into sharp focus a major issue about equal citizenship. The majority's characterization of the sodomy law had one virtue, after all. It was closely attuned to the law's actual functions in setting gays and lesbians apart, criminalizing their conduct while the same conduct is allowed to heterosexuals. Presumably for reasons of strategy, the issue of inequality had not been framed previously by Hardwick's counsel.[70] But, having brought the issue into the case, the majority Justices did not seek illumination by remanding the case for the trial court to develop a record like the one in Donald Baker's case. Instead, although Hardwick's case as defined by the Court now plainly presented a problem of exclusion, the majority abruptly turned away from any such concerns, putting quite a different face—and, to say it mildly, an extraordinary face—on the question at bar.

The issue before the Court, said Justice Byron White, was "whether the Federal Constitution confers a fundamental right upon homosexuals to engage in sodomy." (Imagine a Justice saying, in 1954, that the issue in *Brown v. Board of Education* was whether the Constitution conferred on Linda Brown a right to attend a particular school when the Topeka school board had assigned her to another school.) Framing the issue in Justice White's terms is, of course, a handy way to avoid facing the actual contexts of the sodomy laws—the functions served by maintaining the laws on the books without enforcing them by prosecution, and the ways in which the laws actually bear on people's lives.

After the decision, news accounts stated that the initial vote of the Court's conference had been 5–4 to hold the law invalid, but that Justice Lewis Powell had later switched his vote. In the end he joined the majority opinion, but added his view that the case would be different if Georgia should actually enforce the law by putting someone in prison. Justice Powell's votes and opinions over the years sometimes suggested that he was trying to "do the right thing" without spending the Court's political capital on constitutional positions well in advance of the views of a popular majority.[71] From such a perspective, a Justice might be persuaded that a decision holding the sodomy law invalid, now that long-standing antigay prejudice was compounded by fears about AIDS,[72] would not only bring new pressure on the Court but also intensify antigay violence.

Similar concerns had led the Justices to move slowly in *Brown v. Board of Education*—concerns about the status fears that might lead to increase anti-black violence, and concerns about the Court's capacity to lead. But Justice Powell's attempt at accommodation in *Bowers v. Hardwick* is even less satisfactory than "all deliberate speed," for it leaves wholly untouched the most serious harm caused by the sodomy laws. Indeed, if Justice Powell's view should prevail, the main effect of these laws will be their official branding of homosexuals as outcasts. Was that not the very message—and the most grievous hurt—conveyed to black people by the Jim Crow laws?

Bowers v. Hardwick, in the final analysis, was a failure in empathy. Many of the decisions I have criticized in this book, including all the five illustrations in chapter 1, are variations on the same theme. By empathy I mean not just "the imaginative power which enables a person . . . to understand the emotions and experiences of others and to sympathize with them,"[73] but the inclination to use that power. Empathy is the most important missing ingredient when a police chief unthinkingly suggests that blacks are not quite normal; when a white-dominated legislature makes racially selective cuts in welfare benefits; when a male-dominated legislature effectively excludes women from the best civil service jobs, except for jobs "especially calling for women"; when a "fraternal" lodge turns away black guests; when a religious majority flexes its local political muscle to reaffirm its dominance; and when state officials announce that they will enforce a sodomy law only against homosexual intimacies. Saddest of all, empathy is the most important missing ingredient when judges blandly acquiesce in these exercises in exclusion.

A case that raises issues of constitutional equality is particularly apt for the teaching of empathy. In a famous opinion, Justice Robert Jackson said, "Courts can take no better measure to assure that laws will be just than to require that laws be equal in operation."[74] To illustrate his point, Justice Jackson might have cited the 1942 case of *Skinner v. Oklahoma*. There the Supreme Court held invalid a state law requiring the sterilization of anyone convicted three times for felonies, exempting convictions for violating prohibition laws or tax laws or for committing embezzlement or political offenses. Larceny and embezzlement were "intrinsically the same quality of offense," said Justice Douglas for the Court, and the state's determination to sterilize one type of offender and not the other was a denial of equal protection. The Court has been criticized for resting decision on the equal protection ground, but inequality was very much to the point in this decision—and the choice of this ground offered a lesson in empathy.

The sterilization law was class legislation, based on the odious assumption that middle-class felons made better breeding stock than did thieves who were less genteel. All the exempted felonies were white-collar crimes, including such political offenses as bribery—a matter perhaps not beyond the awareness of legislators. The Court implicitly spoke to the Oklahoma legislature as Justice Jackson might have spoken to them, inviting the legislators to think of themselves in the position of the class of people who might be sterilized. They were also invited to see the issue of sterilization not merely as a question concerning relations between the state and an individual but also as a question concerning a dominant group's perception of an outsider group.

My seminar student raised the question of empathy this way, explicitly addressing his remarks to the American judiciary:

> I am gay and I am expressing pain, explaining certain needs, asking for certain understanding. Please expose yourself to knowledge about me and others like me. Your beliefs about us: Are they based on your personal knowledge, on rumors, "common knowledge," judicially noticed stereotypes? Please search with me and help to make our society's response to us more rational and just.

That seems a fair request. Tolerance of diversity, after all, is one of the basic values of today's American civic culture. One kind of tolerance surely is widely shared among federal judges: the belief that America's house has many mansions with room for many cultures.[75] This belief implies respect, especially in our public dealings, for the beliefs and behavior of individual citizens who are different from ourselves. This rather cool type of tolerance is a matter of prudence, a presumption that in a multicultural society it is unwise social policy to exclude a cultural minority or to coerce them to conform. Empathy, however, is more than an intellectual predisposition or belief; it is a more active form of tolerance, a readiness to be engaged in the experience of others. Because empathy is at least as much a state of heart as it is a state of mind, it involves emotional risk. To say that you are empathetic is to say that you are willing to try to imagine what it is like to be the person on the other side of a cultural boundary—not just trying to understand the different meanings she attaches to behavior but trying to imagine what she feels in her particular situation.

We should not underestimate the difficulty of the judges' task in a case like Michael Hardwick's. Powerful forces produce gender identification in children, including children who grow up to be federal judges. In the vast majority of cases those forces are arrayed to produce a sexual orientation that is unambiguously heterosexual, so that most people come to associate homosexuality with the the negative indentities they have been acculturated to stifle.[76] Perhaps because little boys must prove to themselves that they have achieved a particular form of masculinity, men as a group appear to be more nervous about homosexuality than are women as a group. The sodomy laws legitimize, and thus promote, the identification of gays and lesbians as the Other, an abstraction on which nervous heterosexuals can project the parts of their own selves that must be repressed. For the judge (especially the male judge) who seeks to develop empathy for those who define themselves differently, this particular negative identity, this particular mask of the Other, may be the most frightening of them all. Chief Justice Warren Burger's concurring opinion in the Georgia case, distinguished only for its gratuitous efforts to stigmatize, is worth examining in this light.

In the near future, perhaps tolerance in its cooler form is all that gays and lesbians can expect either from the dominant majority or from most of our judges. It bears repeating that they have a right to expect that tolerance. Perhaps, in the near future, judicial empathy in cases like these is an unrealistic hope. Prediction aside, however, it is fair to ask our judges for serious efforts along those lines. The judge, in good conscience, ought to try to imagine how it feels to be Donald Baker or Michael Hardwick—to be told, over and over, that your sexual orientation makes your very self unacceptable in a fundamental way, that you cannot belong.

In seeking judicial recognition of their status as equal citizens, gays and lesbians now face a difficult problem. There are two principal ways in which government officially and systematically stigmatizes homosexuals: the first is embodied in state sodomy laws, and the second is embodied in federal regulations excluding them from the armed services and from security clearances.[77] After *Bowers v. Hardwick* it is natural for the quest for equal citizenship to turn to the military/security context. Here, as in the context of sodomy, the government's stigmatizing actions are founded on deep-seated assumptions and fears about sexual identity and the meaning of homosexuality. These assumptions and fears, which begin in early acculturation to gender roles, are never expressed explicitly. Rather, government officials make other kinds of arguments: for example, that homosexuals are security risks because they are subject to blackmail or that homosexuals threaten a military mission because other members of the service may threat them with hostility or disrespect.[78]

These arguments add up to a constitutional catch 22: government is justified in branding homosexuals as outsiders because other people might brand them as outsiders. To get a clear idea of the constitutional objection to this self-perpetuating circle of pain and fear, just substitute the word "blacks" for "homosexuals."[79]

No lawyer for an equal rights movement can relish the prospect of centering a litigation strategy on discrimination by the armed services. The Supreme Court's recent majorities, turning upside down the old maxim that "the Constitution follows the flag," have effectively carved out military exceptions to a wide range of constitutional guarantees.[80] If gays and lesbians are the find judicial validation for their claims to equal citizenship the Justices must be persuaded that there is no warrant for creating yet another military exception to cover this type of discrimination. (Racial discrimination, we can assume, would not fall within the armed services' immunity from the Constitution's reach.) When the Justices address these claims we can hope they will remember that their one clear opportunity to start healing the wounds of *Bowers v. Hardwick* lies in this twilight zone of our constitutional law.

The *Hardwick* opinion itself leaves open one line of agrument for those who would begin the healing process. That opinion focused on homosexual sodomy as conduct and did not address the state's power to penalize a person on the basis of status—for being a homosexual. In a 1980 court of appeals decision upholding three Navy discharges, Judge (now Justice) Anthony Kennedy signaled this distinction, carefully focusing the court's opinion on the demonstrated conduct of the persons who were discharged.[81] But the service regulations typically go further, requiring the discharge of service members who are homosexuals, even absent any showing of conduct. Discharges in these circumstances are explicit discriminations on the basis of status, presenting issues of inequality and exclusion in bold relief. The obvious historic parallels are to be found in the armed services' former policies of racial exclusion and segregation, founded on similar assumptions: that integration would hurt recruitment, and that white soldiers and sailors would be hostile to blacks serving alongside them.[82]

Unless the Justices decide to create a new military exception, then, ordinary constitutional standards will call on the services to justify their policy of exclusion, demonstrating that it is necessary to serve vital governmental purposes. Such a justification will be awkward for the services to make. Thousands upon thousands of men and women presently serving in the armed forces undoubtedly fit the definitions of homosexuality set out in the service regulations. Yet, somehow, the Army functions well enough—until some soldier publicly avows that he is gay. Then the Army perceives a threat to its military mission. Plainly that threat lies not in the soldier's homosexuality, which has never caused problems before, but in the statement itself. The soldier's open expression of homosexuality is seen to threaten the public image of the Army—and, perhaps, the self-images of certain officials. These perceptions, reminiscent of the "image" concerns that led the Army to minimize publicity about black soldiers during World War II,[83] simply do not justify the government's official branding of homosexuals as outsiders.

Surely it will be painful for gays and lesbians to ask a court to make this distinction between status and conduct; insisting on the distinction, they may feel, requires them to put aside an important part of their own individual identities. In the long term they seek—and deserve—recognition of the constitutional right to engage in the conduct that is crucial to their expression of love and thus to their sense of self. But long-term constitutional developments are the aggregate of decisions made case by case, and the status/conduct distinction has two important advantages here and now. First, it can help focus the Supreme Court's attention on the real harm that lies at the center of all these cases: the status harm of exclusion from equal citizenship. Second, the status/conduct distinction offers the Justices a doctrinal starting point on the road to redemption.

One day the sodomy laws that stigmatize gays and lesbians will follow Jim Crow into a deserved oblivion, and another generation's Supreme Court will seek to undo the doctrinal damage of *Bowers v. Hardwick*. Surely, too, Americans generally will come to see that "what happens to homosexuals affects all of American society."[84] In the meanwhile, however, gay and lesbian Americans—a group of many millions who experience their hurt one at a time—will live every day with the pains that come from being officially branded as outsiders. In the same way, black American citizens—that is, a single individual, multiplied by millions—daily felt the pains of official exclusion during the long decades before *Plessy v. Ferguson* gave way to *Brown v. Board of Education*.

New Voices, New Meanings

Many of the most important changes in the American civic culture have accompanied the recognition—sometimes gradual, sometimes abrupt—of new groups as fully participating members of the community of equal citizens. Some groups have found politics to be one promising path in inclusion. The cultural assimilation of the great majority of Irish Catholics surely is not unrelated to that group's long and intense practice of ethnic politics. Other groups have made economic progress the main focus for their participation in American society. If more and more of the grandchildren of Jewish and Japanese immigrants are marrying gentiles and Caucasians, one reason is that their parents have been minding the store. In all its forms, participation promotes belonging. And to belong is to share in the choices that define and redefine the community of meaning.

This process can be distressing to those who see themselves as insiders who have generously admitted the Others to membership. Men may have trouble in understanding why so many women use their new participation in public life to insist on further change; whites often have the same trouble in understanding the demands of blacks. "We let you in; why can't you follow the rules?" But membership in the community of equal citizens cannot be conditioned on acceptance of a passive role. Citizenship means not only respect but participation and responsibility. "Whose rules? Our priorities count as much as yours do, and we think the rules need changing."[85] The institutional meaning of empathy is that decision making comes to take seriously the point of view of people who have previously been unable to make themselves heard.[86]

Among the features of our civic culture, one that seems especially susceptible to change is the meaning of equal citizenship itself. Citizens who have only recently secured effective participation in the public life of the community are the ones who are mostly likely to be aware of continuing group inequalities and the ones whose friends and relations have the most to gain from a reduction in those inequalities. When Ralf Dahrendorf identified inequality as "the sting that serves to keep social structures alive," he was encapsulating a complex idea. Inequality, he suggested, is a natural consequence of the existence of a system of enforcement of norms—hence his quip that persons may be equal before the law, but not after it.[87] People who are disfavored by the society's present norms will seek to exchange them for new norms that will rank them higher. Each new normative structure implies a new inequality and new efforts at reconstitution.

The causal progression to social reform, however, depends on more than the existence of inequality. Two qualifications are needed for Dahrendorf's comment about the vitalizing function of inequality, and both of them illuminate the role recently played by the American judiciary in widening the community of equal citizens. First, many stable societies have been founded on hierarchies of considerable rigidity; ancient Egypt, medieval Europe, and modern India are examples. Inequality will goad disfavored people to action only if they have enough confidence in themselves to believe they have a reasonable chance of success. The hopelessly downtrodden are apt to remain politically inert; every revolution is in some sense a "revolution of rising expectations."[88] Thus a necessary condition of these people's participation in a reform movement is their sense of their own worth. The role of the courts in the modern political mobilization of American blacks is hard to overstate. After the *Brown* decision, black people found it easier to see themselves as citizens demanding their rights, not as suppliants offering their pleas to white America. Furthermore, when more women and more members of racial and ethnic minorities participate as decision-makers in our public life, they serve as living reminders to other Americans that women generally, and minority citizens generally, are entitled to respect as members of the community of equal citizens. The respect of others is translated into increased self-respect, and then to further willingness to participate, in dramatic contrast to the old vicious circles of domination and submission. In this sense the personal is political in every claim of equal citizenship.

A second qualification is also necessary before we accept Dahrendorf's comment that inequality is the sting that vitalizes social structures. A broadly based movement of the disadvantaged, founded on nothing more than the calculated pursuit of higher social rankings, is like a nine-dimensional universe: conceivable in theory but never experienced. Actual social movements require emotional fuel. Much of the fuel for America's major social movements over the last three centuries has been resentment. The victims of subordination have chafed under institutions that betray the society's professed egalitarian ideals.[89] In our own time, the one governmental institution that has done the most to keep those ideals alive has been the judiciary.

Each group of newly recognized equal citizens tends to maintain some political momentum. They have gained recognition in the community through a combination of criticism of the existing ordering and zeal for egalitarian principle, and these energies translate easily into support for a wider definition of the community's own ideals of equality. The civil rights movement, having overcome many forms of overt racial discrimination, broadens into concerns about affirmative action and deepens into concerns about poverty. The women's movement, after freeing women from many forms of overt sex discrimination, moves on to concerns about battered women and child care and comparable worth.[90] The legal claims raised by these newer concerns can be seen as efforts to redefine the implications of equal citizenship, to expand the meanings that define the American civic culture. The creation of these new meanings does not imply either a group's secession from the national community or an individual's separation from a smaller community founded on

race or religion or ethnicity.[91] Rather it implies a more inclusive reconstitution of our national community of meaning.

Throughout America's history excluded religious and ethnic groups have
come to be seen as equal citizens when, in very great proportion, their members enter the middle class. So, one objective of the reconstitution of the
American community is easy to state. The concerns of full citizenship go
beyond formal equality and encompass a measure of substantive justice. Just
before he was killed, Martin Luther King had embarked on a campaign that
emphasized the jobs and incomes available to black people.[92] In the years
since 1968 those needs have become even more urgent—in the ghetto, desperately so—and yesterday's civil rights leaders increasingly criticize a polity
that systematically denies some citizens the economic foundations of citizenship.[93] Many women, too, have found a highly individualist conception of
citizenship, centered on formal equality, to be incomplete. One persistent
theme of recent feminist writing is a powerful critique of unbridled individualism and an imaginative exploration of the substantive and institutional implications of our common need to belong.[94]

Many of the concerns expressed in these two critiques can be brought to
bear on our constitutional law, both its methods and its substantive doctrines.
A common thread runs through concerns about marginalizing poverty, about
contextual justice, about the redirection of some forms of conflict to wider
perspectives in which all parties can share some goals. The thread is a larger
concern to preserve the connections among people. Translated into the domain of law, these concerns have implications for institutional litigation,[95]
for the motive/impact problem in antidiscrimination law,[96] for affirmative action,[97] for the "state action" limitation on the Fourteenth Amendment,[98] and
generally for the conditions of effective participation in American public life.
In their efforts to reconstitute our national community of meaning, including
our constitutional law, the civil rights movement has found a new direction
and the women's movement has only begun.

Words are not everything. The sit-ins and freedom rides of the civil rights
era remind us that the lessons of inclusion are taught not only by exhortation
but also by behavior. Eventually, though, behavior takes meaning from the
words we assign to it. "Fashions of speaking" translate into "fashions of perceiving."[99] A necessary ingredient of an expanded national community will
be a constitutional vocabulary expressing the values of the network of connection. The existing language of rights, of liberation, even of equality in its
traditional usage fails to express the full meaning of citizenship as belonging.
Yet it makes sense for the black citizens of Memphis, in challenging their

diversion away from a street in a white neighborhood, to express their right to inclusion in the language of equality that is presently in place in our constitutional law. Legal argument, like moral argument, necessarily begins in the interpretation of the existing norms that constitute us as citizens and as moral beings. The normal progression of legal doctrine is for changes in substance to "occupy existing words" first, only later to produce changes in vocabulary.[100]

Although the Supreme Court has expressed the values of equal citizenship in the traditional language of individual opportunity, the Court's decisions also bear meanings that embrace not only independence but interdependence. If equality of opportunity means that no one should be tied down, the recent experience of the marginalized poor reminds us that genuinely equal opportunity means that "no one should be left out."[101] When citizenship is perceived as inclusion in a network of relationship, all the core values of equal citizenship are enhanced. Respect means not just tolerance of deviance, and not just deference to another's zone of noninterference. It means treatment as "one of us," as a member of the national community. Participation means not just free entry into the struggle for achievement and power in the sense of domination. It means belonging, the exercise of power in the sense of capacity to advance the needs of a self that is inclusively defined. Responsibility means not just the duty to avoid breaking rules. It means care, both for today's members of the network and for the future generations that are implied by the existence of the community.[102]

Just as law is not rules but process, so culture—the community of meaning—is continually in the process of becoming, continually open to contest and reconstitution. Yet there is one change in our civic culture that the equal citizenship principle forbids: the exclusion of other citizens from full participation. The cultural norms to which the nation can legitimately demand conformance are the equal citizenship norms against stigma and domination. The constitutional ratchet that prevents the reinstitution of Protestant domination and white supremacy forbids, for example, the kind of cultural redefinition sought by some male newcomers from other lands who would maintain their traditional subordination of women.[103] A major problem for our constitutional doctrine over the next generation will be to sort out these justified exactions of cultural conformity from the cases in which requiring people to conform is, as James Madison said of the nationwide conformity exacted by the Alien and Sedition Acts of 1798, a threat to "the general principles of free government."[104]

Cultural redefinition is a bland expression for a process that many people will find menacing. To redefine a community of meaning implies conflict even when the redefinition is aimed at enlarging the community. Often the conflict erupts in violence. The American album of intercultural conflict is thick with ugliness, and we add new pictures every week. Even when violence is avoided, the passion and the fear remain, fueled by the perceptions of people on both sides of the conflict that their own identities, their own senses of personal worth, are on the line. As the Justices knew when they decided *Brown v. Board of Education,* law not only contributes to cultural redefinition but is indispensable to the peaceful resolution of the conflicts thus engendered.

From the time of the founding, American courts have performed a dual constitutional function: not just delimiting the boundaries of individual autonomy and governmental power, but maintaining the institutional base for our nationhood. In our society as in any other, law—including constitutional law—mainly serves to reinforce the existing distribution of power. But the role of our constitutional law in maintaining the American nation is more complex. Henry Hart said this about judicial review at a conference celebrating the memory of John Marshall, a great Chief Justice whose greatness lay in his creative labors to make America into a nation: "It is a delusion to suppose . . . that if only you can prevent the *abuse* of governmental power everything else will be all right. The political problem is a problem also of eliciting from government officials, and from the members of the society generally, the affirmative, creative performances upon which the well-being of the society depends."[105]

Since the middle of this century our courts have contributed to the release of enormous energies from the fetters of stigma and group subordination. This performance offers no reason for smugness, for it came centuries late, and it remains deplorably incomplete. Some of those judicial contributions have taken the form that Hart had in mind, releasing legislators from supposed limits on their power to promote the enlargement of our community. No doubt the Supreme Court has done most to promote the material conditions of women and of racial and ethnic minorities by reading civil rights laws expansively and by upholding the power of Congress and the state legislatures to enact those laws. In a wider perspective, though, the Court's leadership in expanding the national community lies in the realm of the spirit. Today the Constitution rivals the flag as a symbol of the nation. Precisely because the Supreme Court is seen as speaking for the nation's basic values, the Court's constitutional decisions have a special importance in maintaining our sense of nationhood. Each time the Court makes good on the promise of equal citizenship—of belonging—it not only helps us get over our fears but also lends new vitality to our sense of national community.

twelve

The Courts and the National Community

Our Present and Our Pasts

Even among our historians America has more than one past. Some historians emphasize conflict and change, others emphasize consensus and continuity[1]—and both views are true. To this outside observer, these controversies' animating force seems not so much a concern about accurate representation of the nation's past as a concern about the lessons Americans should draw from that experience in defining and deciding issues before us now. Lawyers can easily appreciate the nature of this dispute. They know that law typically offers a decision maker a range of choices, not just among alternative policies for today and tomorrow, but choices among competing versions of our legal legacies. Much of the recent debate about judicial review has centered on the appropriate uses of the past: the constitutional text, the purposes of the people who adopted the text, previous judicial interpretations, national traditions. Not only do judges and commentators disagree about the relative authority of these various sources, but they also dispute the meanings of text, framers' intentions, precedent, and tradition.

When we last encountered the originalists,[2] they were insisting that a court has no legitimate power to set aside the lawmaking of an elected legislature unless that result can be deduced from the constitutional text or from the immediate, specific intentions of its framers. One trouble with this deductive style of deriving the legitimacy of a governmental institution is that, at some point, you have to stop deducing and simply accept the legitimacy of a particular constitutive act.[3] By its terms the Constitution took effect upon the ratification of nine of the thirteen states, even though the thirteenth article of the Articles of Confederation had explicitly required ratification by all the states before the Articles could be amended. And the Articles themselves had culminated a usurpation of power by a group of revolutionaries we now revere.

This line of analysis has no natural ending place. It leads to arguments that the British crown had been illegitimate ever since Parliament sent James II packing and brought in William and Mary from Holland. And if the reign of William III was illegitimate, what shall we say of William the Conqueror?[4] Legitimacy is always historically contingent. If Charles Martel had lost the battle of Poitiers, we might all be speaking Arabic. Thomas Nagel has written: "justifications come to an end when we are content to have them end."[5] It is perfectly true that we take our Constitution as an axiom, an "incontestable first principle" of our law.[6] The reason, however, is not to be found in logic but in our continued acceptance of the American political order. In this sense, you and I are adopters of the Constitution, and we adopt it every day.[7]

The heat of the polemic between the originalists and their critics confirms their agreement that contests over interpretations of the Constitution are important. The importance lies in the contributions of those interpretations to the meanings that define our nation and our senses of self. If passion over the law of abortion is generated by concerns about self-definition, so is passion about the constitutionality of sodomy laws, affirmative action, and state-sponsored prayers in the public schools. In every one of these issues the question at stake is: Who belongs to America? For today's judiciary to wash its hands, denying its responsibility for the answer to that question, would amount to judicial self-restraint only in the sense that yesterday's Supreme Court showed self-restraint in leaving Jim Crow to the discretion of southern white legislators.

Constitutional interpretation, even as it looks backward, is an art of the imagination. Even a judge who assumes that the Constitution includes only the text and the framers' intentions must try to imagine an earlier day's cultural setting. The exercise of imagination is facilitated when a term in the text appears to have had a well-established meaning when it was written into the Constitution. Some of the Constitution's most important terms, however, had no such meaning. It is easier to imagine what the framers of the Constitution meant by "high crimes and misdemeanors" as a ground for impeachment than to imagine what "the equal protection of the laws" meant to the framers of the Fourteenth Amendment.[8] Under the best of conditions, however, another era's community of meaning suffers some distortion as we view it through the prism of our own acculturation.[9] Try as we will, we cannot help bringing our own vocabularies and our own concerns to the interpretation of the acts of our institutional forbears—a process the framers themselves envisioned.[10]

John Marshall, who never studied hermeneutics,[11] understood that the interpretive process always begins in the present. In the course of justifying judicial review, he made a modest but incontestable point: when a court inquires into the meaning of a constitutional provision, it does so for the purpose of deciding the case before it.[12] When Justices try to imagine the meanings of yesterday's statutes and constitutions and judicial interpretations—the sort of thing lawyers call the "authorities"—they begin with today's case in mind. The one thing the Supreme Court never does is to decide what a law or a constitutional provision or a judicial precedent means in the abstract and then reason deductively to a conclusion, letting the chips fall where they may. Most of Marshall's opinions did proceed in that deductive way,[13] but if you believe he reached his decisions by deduction, take care when someone offers to sell you the Washington Monument. Marshall always knew just where the chips would fall before he started chopping. His contemporaries knew that much about the Supreme Court's process of decision; the framers of the Fourteenth Amendment knew it; and after six decades of exposure to the legal realist movement we know it, too.[14]

Lawyers understand their own role in this process. Long ago Edward Levi identified the core of legal reasoning as argument by analogy. The judge's approach to the choice between competing analogies is not logical but intuitive: she matches her mental image of one set of facts against her mental image of another. Given this process, it is natural that in a borderline case the judge's sense of the nation's basic values will play a major part in her choice. The contending authorities normally are brought to the court's attention by opposing counsel, who have begun with their minds on the outcomes they want for the case at hand and have, in effect, reasoned backward from those conclusions, drawing analogies to the precedents that will support them. Drawing is the right word. Even when the authority is not a precedent but a statute or a constitutional provision, the lawyer is trying to draw a picture of the present case that will match the judge's picture of some hypothetical case that everyone agrees is covered by the law.

The reader who is not a lawyer may say: This isn't reasoning, it is rationalization. Lawyers and judges rationalize, not because we love sophistry—although the reader may know a lawyer who has a crush on it—but because something of the sort is necessary to create meaning out of new events that come to us raw and unlabeled. The lawyer tries to characterize those events in ways that will fit the "stock stories" that embody the judge's understandings about society and about justice.[15] The judge's opinion will also rationalize to create meaning out of the present case that fits into existing communities of meaning, from the subculture of law professionals to the American civic culture. Argument in the form of rationalization seems inevitable in a system that aims for judgment according to principle while trying to cope with the anarchy of experience. To apply a principle to a flesh-and-blood case is to draw an analogy and thus to exercise creative imagination.[16]

If it ever makes sense to say that the past governs the present, we are talking about selecting some part of the past that we see as relevant.[17] For the judge, the relevant past receives its definition from the case to be decided here and now. Early in 1954, when Robert Leflar and Wylie Davis identified all those doctrinal and remedial paths open to the Supreme Court in *Brown v. Board of Education*,[18] they were not reasoning deductively from some assumed abstract meaning of the Fourteenth Amendment. They were, instead, thinking as lawyers think, focusing on the cases before the Court and reasoning backward to various alternative readings of the equal protection clause, readings that fell within the range of plausible argument in the setting of school segregation in the 1950s.

In interpreting the Fourteenth Amendment the Supreme Court has confronted similar choices from the very beginning. In the *Slaughter-House Cases*[19] the Justices divided 5–4 over the meaning of an amendment that had been ratified only five years before. The important point for our purposes is not that the Court upheld the Louisiana slaughtering monopoly but that an important part of the meaning of the amendment did not crystallize until the Court applied the amendment to a particular case.

Assessing the monopoly's constitutionality, the Justices were called upon to create meanings for the Fourteenth Amendment where none had existed before—that is, meanings in the context of state regulation of business and health. Given the breadth of the constitutional text and the variety of views that had been expressed in Congress over the meaning of the privileges and immunities clause, it was foreseeable that interpretations would gravitate toward the Justices' understandings of the nation's values and traditions. The majority, interpreting the Fourteenth Amendment in the light of a tradition of state legislative autonomy, sought to moderate the shift of legislative power to the Congress. The dissenters, emphasizing the traditional value of individualism, read the amendment as a charter of equal opportunity, including economic freedom. Both sides' arguments were plausible appeals to principle—even though the majority virtually read the privileges and immunities clause out of the Constitution. For more than a century the Supreme Court has followed its 1873 precedent, and there is no significant movement in today's Court toward revitalizing the clause.[20]

Part of the reason, no doubt, is the discipline that calls for the Court to justify its decisions according to principle.[21] That discipline persuades new Justices, and sometimes even Justices who have previously dissented, to draw constitutional meaning from the Court's previous decisions, even decisions they believe mistaken.[22] These interpretations, case by case, accumulate into a body of precedent that has a life of its own as an authority. For most lawyers today the term constitutional law primarily calls to mind the interpretations in thousands of Supreme Court decisions. Each new interpretation increases the range of plausible applications of the Constitution to doctrinally marginal cases. Given that breadth of choice, it would be extraordinary if a Justice did not seek guidance in the nation's basic values, as he or she understands them. At each stage of this process the Court has a continuing responsibility to offer principled justification for its decisions, but after a century (or two centuries) the case law will depart from some of the particulars of the adopters' original intentions—not just because James Madison could not have foreseen electronic eavesdropping, but because principle calls for an effort to match today's decisions against yesterday's.[23] In one perspective, *Brown v. Board of Education* was such a case.

The past on which the Supreme Court draws in declaring constitutional law is not a snapshot of 1789 or 1868; it is the history of a people. Justice Holmes, who admired John Marshall's creative contributions to American nationhood, said this in an opinion dealing with the power of Congress to enforce a treaty: "The case before us must be considered in the light of our whole experience and not merely in what was said a hundred years ago."[24] There is wisdom in these words; yet, a judge who would learn from the nation's experience will find that it usually teaches more than one lesson. When the second Justice John Marshall Harlan said that judges must take guidance from "the traditions from which this country developed as well as the traditions from which it broke,"[25] surely he had in mind the break with England in 1776. But this country has also broken with some of its own home-grown traditions, and sometimes our judges have presided over the discontinuities. In the archives of American tradition we find a few slightly used varieties of republicanism and civic humanism, an earlier era's fierce devotion to local autonomy, and a rich variety of presently discredited group subordinations based on race, religion, ethnicity, and sex. Some of these museum pieces evoke nostalgia, and some do not; some of them may return to fashion's favor, and some seem gone forever. Whether we should or should not seek to recapture one or another of these discarded traditions has repeatedly provoked conflict among our subcultures. In the light of this history—much of which is a history of constitutional change—it is ludicrous to insist that the adopters' intentions are the Constitution's only relevant past. In contributing to the constitution and reconstitution of the meanings that define our national community, our judges cannot abdicate the responsibility of judgment.[26]

Judicial Review and the Claims of Citizenship

Earlier we saw how the Supreme Court made a political comeback in the late nineteenth and early twentieth centuries by legitimizing the political bargain that turned Southern race relations back to the white South and by protecting business and enterprise against populist regulation. There is no surprise in the story of a governmental institution that flourishes by allying itself with privilege and power. But the old alliances came apart in the middle decades of our century, and judicial review continued to prosper, transferring its attentions to new concerns. Here it is continuity rather than change that needs explaining.[27] The staying power of judicial review, and in particular the persistence of such natural-rights doctrines as substantive due process and its modern offshoots in the equal protection field, is an undeniable historical fact. Why has the relevant public—mainly politicians and lawyers and others among the "haves" who influence public opinion[28]—continued to accept this strong form of judicial review, long after the Supreme Court abandoned its active protection of the older forms of privilege?

In addressing so broad a question of social psychology, many approaches are possible. One explanation might emphasize the shift of political power to a new coalition that sponsored a program for economic democracy. Justices sympathetic to that program would likely be receptive to claims centered on political democracy.[29] My own view is that the natural-rights mentality, accompanied by a receptiveness to judicial review, has stayed rooted in the popular folklore[30] for reasons only indirectly related to democracy, either economic or political. Recognizing our strongly individualistic traditions and our perennial tendencies toward subordinating groups, we also feel the pull of the basic human need for connection. Nearly all of us recognize in ourselves both aggressive and generous impulses. We are egoistic, and we want to press our advantages for all they are worth—and at the same time we are members of our communities, and we want to heed the voice of conscience. In today's public life, our legislative representatives mainly serve one of those sets of impulses, and we have come to see the courts as having a special responsibility to serve the other. In this vision, the strongest case for active judicial review is made when the acts of legislators or other officials effectively exclude people from belonging to our community.

Practical necessity links the values of equal citizenship with maintenance of the consent of the governed in a multicultural society. If a group of people see that their subordinate status has taken on the look of permanence, and if they cannot find in the governmental system an institutionalized protection against abuses of the majority's legislative dominance, why should they submit to majority rule?[31] A quarter century ago, with considerations such as these in mind, Charles Black argued persuasively that the American system of judicial review had found its legitimacy in its own legitimizing role.[32] Because American government was founded on a theory of limited powers, the legitimacy of government was bound to be a persistent problem. In our system the courts had taken on the function of pronouncing on the legitimacy of governmental actions. Their power to invalidate the acts of government officials as unconstitutional, Black argued, put the stamp of legitimacy on other official action when the courts did not interpose their veto. Thus the minority that lost in the legislature had the satisfaction of an authoritative statement that the majority had acted within its legitimate powers. Alexander Bickel, rejecting this explanation as an argument for judicial review, argued that a majority would not be willing to have its power "checked from time to time just to have an institution which, when it chooses to go along with the majority's will, is capable of helping to assuage the defeated minority."[33] Bickel and Black, despite their differences, agreed on the central function of the idea of legitimacy: assuring the public, and a defeated minority in particular, that the government's exercise of power was legitimate.

A second explanation of the persistence of judicial review emphasizes the perspective of the individual citizen. If "we" (members of the political majority) keep the courts open to the people we may victimize when we are dominant, one reason is that we can imagine being victims on another occasion, and we want to preserve the same option for ourselves. In this view, too, judicial review is an institutionalization of prudence. But there is still another perspective.

If the very existence of law limits power,[34] part of the reason is that the wielder of power himself needs to believe that his power rests on something more than force. He "feels the never-ceasing need to look upon his position as in some way 'legitimate,' upon his advantage as 'deserved.' " This observation of Max Weber's[35] takes on a special meaning in American society. In a nation that aspires to be a community of equal citizens, we cherish the ideal that all of us are potential power wielders. "To be permanently ruled is to be denied citizenship. To rule permanently destroys citizenship for the ruler."[36] In our representative democracy, most of us see ourselves sometimes as part of a majority and sometimes not: we prevail in some legislative transactions and lose in others.[37] In the legislative process generally we seek to maximize our advantages; sometimes, to reassure ourselves about who we are, we seek to use that process to subordinate the Other. Yet we also want to believe we are part of a community that is all-embracing.

The political manifestations of this dualism are well stated by Mark Roelofs:

> [We Americans are] successful social democrats and successful liberal
> democrats, simultaneously, in painful contradiction. . . . In myth, we
> are a people bound by a common faith and a shared historical
> experience. . . . This truth is verified by the plain fact of our national
> presence. . . . Yet, at another level, our unity is very nearly a sham.
> We are barely an aggregation of individual and corporate persons each
> pursuing singular interests in personal ways and for private satisfactions.
> In this perspective, it is not much more than the law that holds us all
> uneasily in one frame. This truth is also a nationally necessary belief.
> . . . Both are whole truths . . . [a]nd there can be no resolving the
> tensions between them. If we are to be mythically legitimate, we must be
> one. If we are to be ideologically free, we must be many.[38]

Undoubtedly our legislatures are arenas in which we can express the need to make America whole. Any list of legal landmarks in the process of widening our national community would prominently feature the Civil War amendments and the civil rights laws of Reconstruction and of the mid-twentieth century. Yet, when we look at what our legislative representatives mainly represent, we see them not so much expressing our concerns for an inclusive community as defending the interests that express our aggressive impulses.

In a small, face-to-face society, people share not only experiences but intuitions. (Plato thought the population of the ideal political community was precisely 5,040, and Aristotle thought even that figure was too high.)[39] Once a polity grows beyond a size that allows all its people to know each other and have regular dealings with each other, its functions as a political community are significantly changed.[40] Governing has to be delegated to representatives, with important consequences for the sense of community. A city council, for example, is a face-to-face society, but the people they represent do not share in the unspoken, intuitive understandings reached in the council chamber. So, nearly everything the council does must take a form that is contractual rather than communitarian. The legislative process centers on negotiations about interests, and when the negotiating is finished the bargain has to be reduced to language. The idea of diffuse mutual loyalty fragments into the parsing of paragraphs. Surely, in some towns, town meetings are the embodiment of community, but the Los Angeles city council is a marketplace.

From the Revolution until the early nineteenth century a number of influential American thinkers expressed a contrasting vision of republicanism in which legislators were expected to put aside interests—their own and their constituents'—and to decide issues of lawmaking on the basis of their understanding of the common good. This vision, which has enjoyed a recent revival in the literature of constitutional theory,[41] might possibly have been translated into reality in a society ruled by the gentry, whose numbers were small and whose material circumstances assured their independence. At the same time, however, a competing vision came to the fore. The federalists saw government—at least government in the states—primarily as a meeting ground where self-interested "factions" could make their deals.[42] This vision of government has dominated the legislative process in America at least since the collapse of gentry rule around 1820—although legislators can always be counted on to clothe measures favoring particular interests in pious appeals to the common good. If there are possibilities for some realization of the republican vision in today's polity, they appear to lie with the judiciary. Frank Michelman, Cass Sunstein, and others have pointed out how judges, taking legislative pieties at face value, regularly interpret laws *as if* legislators had kept their gaze fixed on the common good, and regularly import such considerations into their constitutional rulings as well.[43]

Of course judges—at least appellate judges who sit on multimember courts—do some dealing of their own. The Justices of the Supreme Court, for example, must seek to construct a body of coherent doctrine, case by case, over a period of years. They could never perform that task without engaging in negotiations among themselves. Such a process is political in the sense that relations within any decision-making group are political; this sort of negotiating was the main "revelation" in *The Brethren*, the gee-whiz book that looked "inside the Supreme Court" of the 1970s.[44] But that Court's product is not what the Justices say to each other (or about each other); it is the body of their decisions and opinions. As Judge Frank Easterbrook has shown, the Court's doctrinal courses are apt to waver, precisely because the Justices are devoted to principle—but they assign different priorities to principles that compete with each other. Any judge worth appointing will have views on issues that are political, but we properly expect our judges to make an effort to stand outside the day-to-day pursuit of partisan politics, and it is not fanciful to say that our expectation normally is met.[45]

There is nothing inevitable about the courts' promotion of an inclusive answer to the question, Who belongs to America? In chapter 4 we saw how the Supreme Court was a willing participant in the early betrayal of the promise of the Civil War amendments, and this book has recounted how the Supreme Court in the last two decades has wasted some important opportunities to widen the embrace of citizenship. In the early twentieth century the Court's active judicial review served chiefly to shield aggressive individualism from legislative efforts to moderate its excesses. Half a century ago, when the Supreme Court entered the modern political area, it was easy for the Justices to see their own contributions to nation building in a negative light: they must withdraw from the constitutional doctrines that had justified judicial invalidation of economic regulations.

Even as that withdrawal was underway, however, it was possible to see that the Supreme Court could also contribute in a positive way to the wholeness of America.[46] To make those contributions, the Court would have to return to the active, nation-building tradition of John Marshall. The situation was touched with irony: now, as the Justices edged toward a more active judicial review in the service of a more inclusive national community, they could draw on political resources amassed by their predecessors through alliance with industry and enterprise in the era preceding the New Deal. During that era, the Supreme Court had been extolled by political conservatives as the institutional embodiment of the civic culture's ideology, the values that defined the nation.

If the constitutional revolution of the 1930s marked a major turning point in our national polity, so did *Brown v. Board of Education*. Today, most Americans, insiders as well as outsiders, think of the courts as having a special responsibility for preserving the equality of citizenship that makes it possible to see America whole. In this perspective, the case for active judicial review is strongest when the judiciary serves as an institutional counterweight to the legislature's interest-group bargaining and its tendency to coerce conformity.[47] In restraining legislative excess, judicial review helps us to maintain our sense of belonging to a network of connection that includes the whole nation. We can be comfortable with majority rule—which mostly turns out to be the pursuit of advantage (or even domination) through the negotiations of our elected representatives—partly because we know that another body, not immediately responsive to our momentary urges to aggrandize, stands ready to curb the aggressions of legislative majorities, in the name of the "public values"[48] that define our national community. To say that we believe in representative democracy,[49] in other words, is to identify one side of an institutional dilemma, not to resolve the dilemma. Focusing on the institutional expression of our inner dualism, we can find fresh meaning in Thomas Jefferson's affirmation in his inaugural address of 1801: "We are all federalists; we are all republicans."

In this post-*Brown* view of judicial review, the crucial difference between a court and a legislature is not that judges live the life of reflective reason while legislators abandon themselves to appetite. Nor is it that judges stand for values and legislators for politics. Assuming (as I do not) that those two categories are separable, both judges and legislators regularly translate values into politics, and vice-versa: think of civil rights, or abortion, or environmental protection.[50] Rather, the important difference is that our courts are well positioned to represent our concern to be members of a national community, while our legislatures typically serve as brokerage houses for individualistic exchange and sometimes even become conduits for majoritarian domination.

The group domination problem arises when a legislative majority, rejecting the path of tolerance, seeks to define the community by writing its own values into law in a way that gives a minority the choice between exclusion and conformity. A government agency's prescription of prayers for public school children was such a use of majority power, and the Supreme Court, true to the modern interpretation of the establishment clause as a guarantee of official tolerance, held the practice unconstitutional.[51] Similarly, today's version of substantive due process has its greatest vitality when a majority says to a minority, "To belong you must conform."[52] The principal disappointment of the Georgia sodomy case lies here, in the Supreme Court's failure to recognize the claims of equal citizenship and national community.

If the use of legislative power for group domination is an ever-present possibility, individualistic exchange is our legislators' main day-to-day reality. Horse-trading is an honored calling in this country, and I do not think for a moment that our legislatures could get along without it. Even in the legislative halls, however, horse-trading is a calling whose work habits emphasize today's immediate urges at the expense of larger and longer-term concerns about our connection to each other. In taking special responsibility for these concerns, our judges are performing a function that our elected legislators have great difficulty in performing.[53] After all, if you were setting out to construct a system of enduring values, in the hope of binding a community together, would you begin by telephoning your broker?

There are two mirrorlike qualities in this perspective on the legitimacy of judicial review. The first is that the two different meanings of legitimacy—its descriptive and normative senses[54]—reflect each other with the usual chamber-of-mirrors result. The American public's acceptance of judicial review is an observable social fact. John Marshall may have used bootstraps reasoning in making the case for judicial review,[55] but today there is no serious dissent from the proposition that the Constitution is a supreme law that the courts are entitled to enforce. The Supreme Court thus draws legitimacy, in the descriptive sense of actual public acceptance, from behaving as an American court is supposed to behave, according to some normative model.[56] But the normative model is constructed from the materials of our collective experience of the ways American courts have actually behaved. At least since Marshall's time that experience has always included a strong form of judicial review, a function often equated by both specialist observers and citizens on the street with constitutionalism itself.[57] Correspondingly, if considerable numbers among the Supreme Court's various public or professional audiences become persuaded that its behavior is normatively illegitimate, then the Court's actual authority—its legitimacy, seen as a social fact—will be weakened.[58]

The idea that judicial review gains in legitimacy when it represents our sense of belonging to a national community is also mirrorlike in a second way, with culture and self-definition reflecting each other. We find our identity as Americans in the basic values of our civic culture, values that owe their community-defining strength to the particular history of a nation made out of many peoples. One of the strongest of these self-defining values is individualism, a persistent threat to our sense of connection. In a government founded on representative democracy, containment of a legislative majority's individualist excesses must take some institutional form. When judicial review effectively represents the self-in-connection, it strengthens the base from which individuals can seek, in the legislative arena, the ends of the separated self. The "counter-majoritarian difficulty"—the notion that judicial review is "a deviant institution" in a representative democracy[59]—is a conundrum that thrives in the rarefied atmosphere of democratic theory. Here on earth, in the individualistic society and polity that is our nation, the claims of citizenship impose their own counter-majoritarian necessity.

The American system of judicial review did not originate as a way to institutionalize the concerns of an inclusively defined citizenry and certainly was not a historical necessity. But, as a number of writers have shown, the American judiciary has some advantages that commend it for the task of defending against majoritarian excesses: a measure of insulation from the heat of partisan politics; procedures that emphasize fair hearings for contending views; a commitment to tradition; experience in articulating principles and applying them to the particulars of live cases; a style of thinking that emphasizes practical reason, as opposed to the reason of the syllogism; and the responsibility to offer justification for decisions.[60] One more advantage deserves to be added to this list. The very fact that the courts speak in the name of the law allows them to draw on law's status as a community-defining totem in gaining support for their decisions and for the values they articulate.

The view of judicial review as a defense of an inclusive national community requires one important reservation: typically our judges have been drawn from a narrow subset of that community. "They are overwhelmingly Anglo, male, well educated, and upper or upper middle class."[61] Paul Brest and John Ely have pointed out that although these education and class factors correlate positively with favorable attitudes toward civil liberties, they do not correlate positively with concerns about "jobs, food, and housing."[62] The acculturation that produces empathy for one group of claimants also produces systematic insensitivity to others, for "every way of seeing is also a way of not seeing."[63] It is sobering to remember that the Supreme Court's principal counter-majoritarian achievement, until the New Deal era, was the protection of wealth and economic liberty against populist and social-welfare legislation.

Nor is the relevance of the class factor a thing of the past. For example, consider the five male Justices who upheld Congress's decision to carve out an exception to the Medicare program, denying medical expenses to women who could not afford abortions.[64] They were, indeed, drawn from the upper middle class, and their sensitivity about women's "choice" ended at the class boundary.[65] Nor is class the whole story. This book is filled with examples of cases in which sex and race and ethnicity have affected the supply of judicial empathy when our courts have confronted the situations of women and members of racial and ethnic minorities. Precisely because we have entrusted one of our most important community-defining functions to our courts, we need a broadened base for selecting the American judiciary.[66]

The defense of active judicial review in the service of national community, like many another view of governmental processes, tends to fulfill itself. Each Supreme Court decision promoting the principle of equal citizenship reinforces the civic culture's values of egalitarianism and tolerance—and often the values of individualism and nationalism, too. The same decisions not only encourage other claimants to resort to the courts but also energize the politics of inclusion. *Brown v. Board of Education* both symbolized the redefinition of our national community and accelerated it: first the sit-ins and marches and freedom rides, then the Civil Rights Act of 1964 and the Voting Rights Act of 1965 and dozens of other laws both state and federal.

Alexander Bickel commenced his 1969 attack on the Warren Court by donning the mantle of the "Progressive realists" who had attacked an earlier era's judicial activism in defense of property and economic liberty.[67] But the active judicial review that came to the fore in the 1960s differs markedly from the active judicial review that ended in the 1930s, and the difference centers not on concerns about the processes of government but on substantive concerns.[68] In the perspective offered here, the substantive rights with the strongest claim for judicial protection against the excesses of majoritarian democracy are the rights of equal citizenship. We know from our experience with racism and other forms of group subordination that the most grievous abuses of power are apt to come when our representatives are most faithfully representing their continuencies. When an elected official calls for wartime "concentration camps" to keep America a "white man's country,"[69] you can bet he is in hot pursuit of votes. As that woeful occasion demonstrated, there is no guarantee that judges will stand up to the force generated by panic and cupidity. In the long run, though, the legitimacy of judicial review rests most securely on our need to defend our better selves against our greed and our fear. An American philosopher summarized the case well: "We have met the enemy, and they are us."[70] Today our courts are a vital institutional component of our shared effort, not just to govern ourselves,[71] but to govern our selves.

For a lawyer, Carol Gilligan's reassessment of the literature of moral development[72] is most valuable for its illumination of the ways in which contrasting senses of the self translate into contrasting views of morality. Gilligan offered the interpretation that women as a group and men as a group tend to have different views of interpersonal relationships and of the meaning of morality. Men tend to define themselves and others as more or less fungible occupants of roles in a hierarchy and to see human interactions as the contractual arrangements of individuals seeking those positions. Women tend to define themselves in relationships and to see the same interactions as part of ongoing connections in a network that connects real persons, not roles.[73] The view from the ladder of hierarchy tends to produce "a morality of rights and noninterference,"[74] an abstract ranking of rules to govern the competition of highly individuated individuals. To see the world from the web of connection, however, is to see individuals in relation to each other, to seek solutions for moral problems in empathy, "the capacity 'to understand what someone else is experiencing,' "[75] and to define morality as responsibility to particular people in particular contexts. In this perspective, integration into a community does not imply the suppression of difference. Difference is acceptable because the other person is confronted as a person, not just a projected, abstract image of Otherness to be used as an object in one's own self-definition.

No lawyer can think about these contrasting moralities without being struck by their relevance to the ways in which we think about law.[76] Just as all of us, men and women alike, embody at least some of each of these moralities, our institutions, including the law, bear the mark of both the ladder and the network. It takes no sophistication, however, to recognize that American law, from the beginning, has been predominantly a system of the ladder, by the ladder, and for the ladder.

The framers of the American Constitution inherited a body of thought that saw man as an "atom of self-interest,"[77] saw the struggle for power as a zero-sum game in which one person's gain was another's loss, and was suspicious of man's insatiable appetite for power. Nothing in the republicanism of the constitutional period served as an effective ideological counterweight to the separateness of each individual's self-interest.[78] "Ambition must be made to counteract ambition," wrote James Madison in *The Federalist*, no. 51. The whole enterprise of constitution-making, from its theoretical underpinnings to its consummation as a political bargain, was relentlessly contractual. Safety from aggression was not to be found in connection with others, for connection implied dependence and dependence meant oppression. Rather, security was to be grounded in rules reinforcing separation and dispersing the powers of government. The Bill of Rights, like the original Constitution, defined zones of autonomy and noninterference. In the prevailing atomistic view of self and society, social responsibility was founded on reciprocity: the duty to keep one's contracts and to avoid treading on others' zones of autonomy. Autonomy was, above all, "the liberty of secure possession," a liberty that was "negative, private, and limited."[79]

Even today, half a century after the New Deal opened the modern political era, we generally discuss our constitutional law in a vocabulary treating rights as zones of noninterference. If this vocabulary often seems impoverished, the reason is that it is based on an incomplete assumption about what it means to be a person, a failure to articulate what we all know intuitively: that the individual self is founded on both separation and connection.[80] Once this awareness is brought to the forefront of consciousness, we can understand that citizenship is more than autonomy and more than participation in public decisions; citizenship is belonging.

To define oneself as part of a network of relationship is to find security in connection and to see a major source of aggression in separation and unchecked competition. From the perspective of interdependence, the zero-sum-game attitude toward power seems incomplete; indeed, power itself is seen in a different light. The idea of power as domination recedes in favor of the idea of power as capacity, both the capacity to take care of oneself and the capacity to care for others in the network of connection.[81] The idea of authority makes room for compassion.[82] The idea of autonomy acquires a new dimension of active responsibility: the taking of independent initiatives that are self-interested but within a conception of "the self in relationship" that defines the individual self so as to take account of connection as well as separate needs.[83] This interdependence is not the kind of dependence we deplore when we speak of the dependence of a subordinated racial groups or the dependence foisted on women by the traditional view of femininity. Rather it is the interdependence that says: I can count on you to "be there," and you can count on me.[84] It is the interdependence of mutual responsibility within a community of equal citizens.

The 1980s version of the debate about the legitimacy of judicial review reflects not merely opposing views about the proper role of courts in constitutional cases but opposing assumptions about the nature of human interactions. Consider the following two models of thinking about judicial review. (I know of no judge and no commentator who fits either model to perfection. Like all models, these are useful only to the degree that they suggest the possibility of general tendencies.)

One whose morality grows out of a sense of identity based most securely on separation seeks to define rights—that is, powers of decision—within assigned zones of noninterference. These rights are fairly easy to state neutrally, for they are perceived in the abstract; they are bound up with questions of process, of the proper allocation of powers. Because, in this atomistic world view, one person's substantive values are as good as another's, value choices generally should be left to the market. If values are to be imposed, the choice to impose them should be made by negotiated bargaining in the legislature's political market. In this model, judicial review is an aberration, finding its only legitimate justification in the original contract: the Constitution as written and intended by the framers. Judicial independence implies separation from policy-making, and almost all substantive choices lie in the legislators' zone of noninterference. The task of judges in judicial review entails no personal responsibility to do justice, has little to do with the articulation or effectuation of substantive values, is unconcerned with the building of a nation— except as any of those goals may have been embodied in the specifically stated or indisputably understood intentions of the framers. Judge Learned Hand summed up this philosophy almost a half century ago in a speech entitled

"The Contribution of an Independent Judiciary to Civilization"[85]—and for him, independence meant detachment, in every sense of the word.

Another view, growing out of a sense of identity based on both separation and connection, not only seeks to preserve relationships but also focuses on the actual effects of moral choice on particular people. These contextual concerns necessarily are substantive, and justice requires not only a concern with process but also a concern with substantive benefits and harms. Value choices made by the market or imposed after legislative bargaining are to be respected, but if those choices effectively exclude citizens from the network of connection, they should be reexamined. Judicial review, far from being a deviant institution, is a necessary check on the legislature's normal pursuit of self-interest—that is, the interests of those constituents who have the resources to influence the legislature's bargaining. In this view the separation of powers is not a principle commanding wholly independent spheres of government but a system of interaction involving both cooperation and mutual constraint. Judges are "sentient actors" with their own responsibilities to real people[86] and with the more general responsibility to contribute to the maintenance of a community: "no one should be left out." The judges properly see their work not merely as enforcing the details of a bargain ratified in 1789 or 1868, but as reinforcing the basic values that permit all of us to belong to America, values that make us a nation. They are aware of the potential contribution of an *inter*dependent judiciary to our day-to-day essays in civilization. In performing these tasks, the judges can say, paraphrasing John Marshall, "It is a *nation* we are constituting."

"The Web of Subjectivity" and the Network of Connection

Suppose that our constitutional jurisprudence were to take a significant turn in the direction of the second model, and our judges were to "come to see the limitations of a conception of justice blinded to the differences in human life."[87] Can such a contextual morality be translated into law without abandoning the rule of law? The traditional figure of Justice wears a self-imposed blindfold to avoid being influenced by the identity of the parties. Centuries of struggle lie behind the principle that "the law of the land" should be applied impersonally to everyone.[88] Moreover, the impersonality of the law's application extends to the person of the judge. The judicial robe symbolizes that the judge is there to decide as a judge, according to law, not to decide as a man or woman according to a personal sense of justice. Wouldn't we be a little uneasy if the legend on the Supreme Court Building were changed to read Contextual Justice under Law?

Uneasy or not, we have to recognize that there are senses in which that substitute motto has always expressed reality. "General propositions do not decide concrete cases," said Justice Holmes in 1905.[89] He might have added that judges decide concrete cases, and they perform best when they inquire into the concrete facts that touch the lives of the real people who will be affected by their decisions. The dilemma of contextual justice is false; there is no escape from contextual judgment if the judge wants to do a decent job.

Even the identity of the parties may be distinctly relevant to the doing of justice, however deeply a judicial opinion may bury the importance of those facts beneath a heap of assertions about principles. In a series of cases stretching over a quarter century, the Supreme Court was faced with hostile actions by various southern state courts and legislatures aimed at the civil rights movement and at the NAACP in particular.[90] In all these cases the Court found ways to protect against abuses of governmental power without ever saying that the identity of the parties, in a political context well known to the Justices from their own extrajudicial experience, made a great deal of difference. Perhaps the Court can be faulted for these failures to be frank, but if you are going to cast that first stone, you should be prepared to accept the likely costs of candor to the process of building more inclusive communities in the southern states.[91]

The Warren Court's academic critics would have little use for a model of judicial review emphasizing context and connection. The essence of the critics' attack was that the Court's opinions were unprincipled, lacking in neutrality, intellectually incoherent.[92] The whole course of the Warren Court's egalitarian decisions, said Alexander Bickel, had spun a "web of subjectivity," simply writing the Justices' personal preferences into constitutional law.[93] But the idea of judicial objectivity has one thing in common with the idea of simultaneity as Einstein taught us to appreciate it: much depends on where the observer stands. The characterization of a decision as subjective cannot properly be separated from the substantive law being declared. One observer's subjectivity may be another's attention to context. When particular decisions on particular forms of racial discrimination are understood in the context of a comprehensive system of racial injustice, the decisions may be seen as part of a large-scale doctrinal development that is as principled as any judicial behavior can be. When the Court is establishing a principle as broad as equal citizenship, painting with a broad brush is appropriate. The Warren Court's critics complained that the Warren Court neglected the fine definition of edges. From this observer's standpoint, however, the Court's main failure in opinion-writing was that it did not paint its principle broadly enough.

The "all deliberate speed" formula of the second *Brown* opinion is an example. The Court implicitly told white southern legislators and school officials that they had been denying black children their fundamental rights as equal citizens, that eventually they must stop doing so, but that they could go on doing so for an unspecified time while they got used to the idea of stopping. Although the Court's opinion insisted that the principles of *Brown I* could not be sacrificed because of disagreement with them, nearly everyone understood that the delay in enforcement was designed to allow breathing space so that disagreement could be moderated below the level of violence.

The Justices' private prediction of political attack proved accurate. In 1956, after the Court had accepted gradual desegregation, nineteen United States senators and eighty-two members of the House of Representatives signed a document called the "Southern Manifesto," calling for lawful resistance to *Brown*. Throughout the South and for many years, the white response was a politically orchestrated scream of defiance at the Supreme Court, a series of evasive devices that filled the dockets of the lower courts,[94] and no communication with blacks at all. As an effort to redefine a community, *Brown II* was a failure. On the tenth anniversary of *Brown I* in 1964, just over 2 percent of black children in the eleven southern states were attending desegregated schools. There is, however, force in the argument that *Brown II* was a necessary compromise at a time when the Supreme Court could expect little support from the executive branch and none from Congress.[95] It is not easy for us to put ourselves in the position of the Justices in the mid-1950s.[96] Still, my own hindsight view is that the all deliberate speed formula failed both the test of principle and the test of expediency—and that those two failures are interrelated.

We can all agree that a community is not created merely by declaring its existence. Whatever the Supreme Court might do in 1954 or 1955, it would take time to build the sense of interracial community in the South—and not only in the South.[97] But if the restructuring of community was the goal, the one thing the Court could not expect to do with success was to declare on principle that school segregation was unconstitutional and then to make the end of segregation an object for local political negotiation.

Even if there had been any such negotiations, no one should have expected that sort of contractual bargaining to contribute much to a more inclusive sense of community. As it happened, the negotiations never came, and that conversational void itself suggests something about all deliberate speed as a tactic for the peaceful redefinition of southern communities. But the most serious objection is not merely tactical. Reducing the principle of *Brown* to a negotiable question made it into something less than a principle. The Court thus gave up its one legitimate claim to being the voice of the national community. Southern intransigents might say: After all, if equal citizenship really were a national principle, surely the principle would not be parceled out to be negotiated separately in thousands of school districts over an indeterminate period of time. The Court's task in the mid-1950s was, indeed, to redefine communities both national and local. Its delayed successes in that task have been achieved in spite of the all deliberate speed formula, not because of it.

Like the education-focused opinion in the first *Brown* opinion and the all deliberate speed formula in the second, the Warren Court's opinions lowering the state action barrier in race cases[98] and recognizing a broad power in Congress to protect civil rights[99] often were doctrinally unsatisfying. The critics had a point when they said the Court was not explaining itself very well. But the charge of subjectivity—of unprincipled imposition of the Justices' personal preferences—will not wash. To understand the principled basis for those decisions, it was necessary to pay attention to their political and social context— that is, the system of Jim Crow. Charles Black brought this context to the foreground in his spirited reply to the suggestion that *Brown* was unprincipled,[100] but the same awareness informed all the Warren Court's decisions on race. They were all readily explainable as steps in the eradication of a racial caste system and its continuing effects, an entirely principled elaboration of the Fourteenth Amendment's guarantee of equal citizenship. The Supreme Court did not get around to an explicit articulation of its rejection of racial caste until 1982,[101] but credit for the principle's development belongs to the Warren Court.[102]

The effort to achieve objectivity in judging is a central feature of any system that aspires to a rule of law. But the rule of law does not imply a law of rules. Law—to the discomfort of some beginning law students—will not be reduced to a set of tidy formulas that can be applied more or less mechanically to the actual situations that arise in real people's lives. Law is the whole process by which norms to govern behavior are authoritatively adopted, interpreted, applied, modified, and discarded. Especially in our constitutional law, where the textual foundation for decision often is expressed in "majestic generalities"[103] and where different parts of the text may point toward competing values, the interpretive part of the process necessarily looms large.[104] No useful legal system, and no principle of law that matters, can eliminate judgment from the process of judging.

The principle of equal citizenship, then, is not a judicial stamping machine but an aid to the exercise of practical wisdom. Identifying equal citizenship as the substantive core of the Fourteenth Amendment does not decide concrete cases. There is as much room for the begging of questions here as in any other general formulation of principle, and no principle of equality can escape the problem of open-endedness. The Fourteenth Amendment is part of "the constitution of open texture."[105] Any recognition of substantive content in a constitutional guarantee of equality places on the courts a weighty burden of judgment.

"It merely states the problem," I heard Judge Hand say on an evening long ago, speaking of his own formulation of another issue.[106] The equal citizenship principle merely states the problem of constitutional equality. It contributes to our case-by-case, year-by-year resolution of that problem by focusing our attention on the substantive content of the Fourteenth Amendment rather than on the abstraction of Equality.[107] It insists that a judge, when evaluating an equal protection claim, be sensitive to the values of equal citizenship. Does the governmental action significantly impair a person's claim to be treated by the organized society as a respected and responsible member? To the degree that the answer to this question is affirmative, the principle instructs the judge to insist on a commensurately weighty justification for the government's action.

Equal citizenship is not a neutral principle in any sense that relieves the judge from making substantive choices. No doctrinal alchemy can enable a judge to choose neutrally when principles collide.[108] The impartiality we can fairly expect of the judge is an effort to decide the case from an independent standpoint, as opposed to the point of view of one of the parties, and to approach the parties' contending arguments with sympathetic regard. This brand of objectivity is an "objective point of view,"[109] not a self-applying principle that will eliminate uncertainty in predicting judicial results.[110] In a 5–4 world, there will always be 5–4 decisions.

Is it consistent for the judge to seek detachment from the parties' positions and at the same time to seek to understand the parties' thoughts and feelings? Is it fair to criticize Justices who fail to imagine the meanings that others— and I mean Others[111]—attach to behavior: the black citizens of Memphis, for example, or the non-Christian citizens of Pawtucket? Or is empathy the enemy of objectivity?

Some abstraction of a case—some generalized statement of the issue going beyond the case's particulars—is necessary in a system that aspires to decide on the basis of rules and principles.[112] But the judge has a range of choice in selecting which aspects of a case to describe abstractly. The judge who is unable (or unwilling) to try to understand how the world looks on the other side of the cultural boundary almost certainly will define the focal question at a high level of abstraction.

All five of the illustrative cases in chapter 1 can be stated in that way. Instead of asking why it is that black men die disproportionately from police chokeholds, we can ask what level of threat justifies government is using life-endangering force against a citizen. Instead of asking why a benefit program primarily serving the children of black and Latina mothers is slashed while benefit programs primarily serving whites are merely trimmed, or why women are denied the best civil service jobs, we can ask what kinds of considerations can justify government's preferring one group of people over another in offering benefits or jobs. Instead of asking why a private club that serves very large numbers of patrons can deny service to a citizen because he is black, we can ask what duty government has to correct private associational behavior. Instead of asking why a city sponsors the celebration of Christianity's central miracle, we can ask when government's accommodation of religion amounts to an establishment of religion. So stated, these are questions of enormous difficulty, entailing all manner of possible "objective" arguments—that is, arguments that are race-neutral, sex-neutral, religion-neutral, and so forth—in justification of the government's action.[113]

Abstraction is a filter, screening out the very elements of a case that would help the judge in a search for cross-cultural understanding. The more abstractly the issue is framed, the more likely it is that the judge will be unaware of human contexts that are relevant to the evaluation of a legal claim—such as the hurt of being treated as an outsider who doesn't belong. Abstract statement of the case even tends to make those contextual elements seem irrelevant, for it concentrates attention on the "objective" arguments. In one perspective, then, the goals of empathy and objectivity do pull in opposite directions, challenging the judge to be "both compassionate and detached" and to "have the capacity to endure the tension" between those two qualities.[114] From another prospect, however, a capacity for empathy is seen to be implicit in the idea of principled behavior.

Sociologists make this connection between empathy and principle when they refer to the individual conscience as a *generalized other*.[115] For an individual—let us call him Bill—the other in question is a composite of the persons who have significantly shaped his attitudes and beliefs. His attention to the call of conscience begins with an exercise in empathy: Bill imagines what those other people would think and feel about right and wrong in his present circumstances. The amalgam of those imagined thoughts and feelings becomes the cluster of moral principles constituting Bill's generalized other. When we try to adjust our behavior to morality—to principle—we imagine how others would view what we are doing, and we shape those cultural materials into a guide for conduct. The idea has a modern flavor,[116] but Adam Smith articulated it in 1759, a full seventeen years before he published *The Wealth of Nations*.[117]

A similar exercise attends the determination of constitutional principles. The judge—let us call her Mary—applies her interpretive imagination to the authorities she considers authoritative: to the framers' purposes, to the views of judges who decided earlier cases, to the central values of the American civic culture, to the expectations of the judge's "interpretive community,"[118] or to some alternative formulation of her professional generalized other. Thus the empathy that permits Judge Mary to imagine the parties' experiences and feelings also underlies her capacity for principled detachment—that is, the capacity for the only kind of judicial objectivity we can properly expect of her. Yet, nothing is harder to do than to get outside your own assumptions.[119] Justice Holmes, in a famous dissenting opinion, chided the majority Justices for deciding on the basis of a "major premise" that was never articulated.[120] Looking back, most observers today align themselves with Holmes's criticism. But what are our own inarticulate major premises? To ask Judge Mary to transcend her acculturation is to ask a great deal.

It is fair, though, to ask her to try. Part of the judge's responsibility, in interpreting the basic charter of a nation of many peoples, is to make a genuine effort to understand the assumptions of "people of fundamentally differing views"[121] about the matters in issue. True, the possibility of empathy depends upon a community of meaning, a sharing of culture, but the judge does share a culture with those people: not just the legal authorities but the whole American civic culture. To widen the circle of equal citizenship is to expand our community of meaning, to extend the reach of our interpretive imagination, to increase our capacity for objective decision.

Objectivity and open-ended constitutional doctrine are not incompatible. The best articulation of this theme came from the second Justice Harlan, whose dissenting opinions often provided indispensable doctrinal guidance to the larger principles underlying the Warren Court's decisions. Dissenting from the majority's refusal to confront the substantive issues of privacy raised by *Poe v. Ullman* in 1961, Harlan wrote an opinion that illuminated the doctrinal path toward the Court's later recognition of the modern constitutional right to privacy. The contours of such a doctrine, he knew, could not be defined once and for all. His response to the problem of doctrinal open-endedness will serve well to explain the judicial role in elaborating the meaning of equal citizenship. Just substitute "equal protection" for "due process," and "equal citizenship" for "liberty":

> Due process has not been reduced to any formula; its content cannot be determined by reference to any code. The best that can be said is that through the course of this Court's decisions it has represented the balance which our Nation, built upon postulates of respect for the liberty of the individual, has struck between that liberty and the demands of the organized society. If the supplying of content to this Constitutional concept has of necessity been a rational process, it certainly has not been one where judges have felt free to roam where unguided speculation might take them. The balance of which I speak is the balance struck by this country, having regard to what history teaches are the traditions from which it developed as well as the traditions from which it broke. That tradition is a living thing. A decision of this Court which radically departs from it could not long survive, while a decision which builds on what has survived is likely to be sound. No formula could serve as a substitute, in this area, for judgment and restraint.

The judgment and restraint Justice Harlan prescribed are the only objectivity we can reasonably ask from the Supreme Court as it works through the meanings of equal protection doctrine. The principle of equal citizenship is a substantive guide to that judgment and that restraint.

The charge of judicial subjectivity is most apt to be made during a time when constitutional doctrine is undergoing significant change. In the early 1950s, when the Supreme Court began its deliberations in *Brown v. Board of Education*, the claim that racial segregation was unconstitutional appeared to many observers—including some Justices—to demand a major doctrinal innovation. Although the invalidation of Jim Crow required only the rediscovery of equal citizenship, not its invention, these observers took the established doctrine to be "separate but equal." In their view the plaintiffs in *Brown* were calling for the creation of something dramatically new.

By definition, creativity is never readily squared with the received wisdom. The beginnings of judicial doctrine, like other human beginnings, often are more easily felt than syllogized. Ultimately, of course, if constitutional values are to be translated into constitutional law, efforts at coherent explanation must come to replace the vague sense of doing the right thing. In 1954, however, the Warren Court was just starting to grope its way toward a reconstitution of meanings in the American civic culture, a more inclusive answer to the question, Who belongs to America?

During the year that passed between *Brown I* and *Brown II*, a black man whom we know as Mr. Cox[122] was called to serve on a federal jury in a northern city. His experience as a juror turned out to be unpleasant. In a civil action for damages, Cox held out alone for a plaintiff's verdict but finally agreed with his fellow jurors, all but one of whom were white. Until he gave in, the white jurors treated him very disrespectfully; the culture of subordination, after all, was no southern monopoly. Yet Cox's participation offered those people a lesson in the meanings that define America. Perhaps they did not learn the lesson from this one occasion, but Cox did. When an interviewer asked him how he felt about being summoned for jury duty, his response touched all the main themes of this book. Cox understood that he and his fellow jurors had been called together in a public life, a civic culture that they shared in spite of their differences. Federal law had authoritatively declared him to be a respected and responsible participant in American society, an equal citizen:

> I was extremely proud. . . . Ever since I was a little kid in [a southern state] I've had a desire to serve. Of course, people with dark skin are not permitted to serve . . . down there. I've read many books on the jury and when I was first called to serve I went to the library and read up on the jury system. . . . I think it's really a wonderful way in which citizens regardless of the color of their skin can participate in the day to day administration of justice. When I got my summons . . . I got a sense of really belonging to the American community.

If Cox were to serve as a juror today, it is a better than even bet that he would be treated with respect in the jury room.[123] Racism is far from dead, but open racist expression in our public life is outside today's bounds of decency. Furthermore, the sentiments Cox expressed about citizenship are far more widely shared among Americans, white as well as black, than they were a generation ago. The cultural redefinition accelerated by *Brown v. Board of Education* is reflected in the self-definition of individuals all over the land. In 1987 Pennsylvania's Liquor Control Board voted unanimously to revoke the liquor license of a large Altoona social club that had denied membership to Charles Ditcher because he was black.[124] For those who say that Martin Luther King's dream of racial equality has been fulfilled, the continued existence of this sort of white preserve offers a useful dose of reality. Even so, one feature of the case is worth noting. The complaint against the club was filed not by Charles

Ditcher but by Robert Ford, a white man who read about the incident in the newspaper. (Ford was the liquor board's press secretary.) Some twenty-five years before, while serving in the Marine Corps, Ford had lived in the South and had participated in some civil rights demonstrations. He said he couldn't believe that a facility licensed by the state could get away with racial discrimination in 1987.

These two stories, like so many stories about equality and inequality in America, offer mixed messages. In cautioning that real membership in American society is more than a formal status, they remind us of the considerable distance we must still travel if we are to make good on the Fourteenth Amendment's promise of equal citizenship. Yet the stories also remind us that in traveling that road no one has to walk alone. If Mr. Cox needs an inclusive answer to the question, Who belongs to America?, so does Robert Ford. So do we all.

Appendix

This appendix lists my previous writings on the subjects of this book. The articles are arranged in alphabetical order under the abbreviated titles used in the note references. I am grateful to the publishers for their permission to use extracts from these writings in this book.

"A Discrimination So Trivial":
1974. "A discrimination so trivial": A note on law and the symbolism of women's dependency. *Ohio State Law Journal* 35:546.

Affirmative Action:
1974 (with Harold W. Horowitz). Affirmative action and equal protection. *Virginia Law Review* 60:955.

Bakke Opinions:
1979 (with Harold W. Horowitz). The Bakke opinions and equal protection doctrine. *Harvard Civil Rights-Civil Liberties Law Review* 14:7. Copied with permission. Copyright 1979 by the *Harvard Civil Rights-Civil Liberties Law Review*.

Citizenship, Race, and Marginality:
1988. Citizenship, race, and marginality. *William and Mary Law Review*. 30:1.

Emerging National Standards:
1971 (with Harold W. Horowitz). Emerging national standards for school desegregation: Charlotte and Mobile, 1971. *Black Law Journal* 1:206.

Equal Citizenship:
1977. The Supreme Court, 1976 term—foreword: Equal citizenship under the Fourteenth Amendment. *Harvard Law Review* 91:1.

Equality and Community:
1980. Equality and community: Lessons from the civil rights era. *Notre Dame Lawyer* 56:183. Copyright by the *Notre Dame Law Review*, University of Notre Dame.

Equality and the First Amendment:
1975. Equality as a central principle in the First Amendment. *University of Chicago Law Review* 43:20.

Fifth Amendment Equal Protection:
1977. The Fifth Amendment's guarantee of equal protection. *North Carolina Law Review* 55:541.

First Amendment and Harry Kalven:
1965. The First Amendment and Harry Kalven: An appreciative comment on the virtues of thinking small. *UCLA Law Review* 13:1. Copyright 1965, The Regents of the University of California. All Rights Reserved.

Intimate Association:
1980. The freedom of intimate association. *Yale Law Journal* 89:624.

Invidious Discrimination:
1969. Invidious discrimination: Justice Douglas and the return of the "natural-law-due-process formula." *UCLA Law Review* 16:716. Copyright 1969, The Regents of the University of California. All Rights Reserved.

Motive-Centered Inquiry:
1978. The costs of motive-centered inquiry. *San Diego Law Review* 15:1163.

Not One Law at Rome
1972. Not one law at Rome and another at Athens: The Fourteenth Amendment in nationwide application. *Washington University Law Quarterly* (1972): 383.

Paths to Belonging:
1986. Paths to belonging: the Constitution and cultural identity. *North Carolina Law Review* 64:303.

State Action:
1961 (with William W. Van Alstyne). State action. *Stanford Law Review* 14:3. Copyright 1961 by the Board of Trustees of the Leland Stanford Junior University.

State Court's Responsibilities:
1972. Serrano v. Priest: A state court's responsibilities and opportunities in the development of federal constitutional law. Originally published in *California Law Review*, vol. 60, no. 3, May 1972, pp. 720–56. Copyright by the California Law Review, Inc. Used with permission.

Telophase of Substantive Equal Protection:
1967 (with Harold W. Horowitz). Reitman v. Mulkey: a telophase of substantive equal protection. *Supreme Court Review* (1967): 39.

Why Equality Matters:
1983. Why equality matters. *Georgia Law Review* 17:245.

Woman's Constitution:
1984. Woman's constitution. *Duke Law Journal* (1984): 447.

Notes

Preface

1. Geertz (1973) 23.
2. Black (1960a).
3. Black (1969); Black (1970).
4. For one recent reminder, see Black (1987). For a complete bibliography up to 1986, and the tributes of Black's friends and colleagues, see *Yale Law Journal* 95:1553.
5. Kalven. See also *First Amendment and Harry Kalven; Equality and the First Amendment;* and the memorial issue of the *University of Chicago Law Review* 43:1.

Chapter 1

1. Dahrendorf 102. (Italics in original.) On American constitutionalism as "the creation of the American heritage and the fight between the heirs and the disinherited," see Appleby (1987) 807. On "the Constitution of aspiration," see Hartog.
2. South Pacific (1949).
3. I have taken this use of the Other from Simone de Beauvoir, who presumably borrowed from Sartre, who seems to have borrowed from Heidegger.
4. Wiebe (1975) 95.
5. On the Montgomery bus boycott see King (1958); Morris 51–63; L. Bennett 59 ff.
6. *Johnson v. Virginia* (1963).
7. *Hamilton v. Alabama* (1964).
8. Michelman (1986b) 92.
9. Lynd 210.
10. Garfinkel 423.
11. *City of Los Angeles v. Lyons* (1983).
12. Lyons also sought a declaratory judgment that the police's practice of using chokeholds was unconstitutional.
13. This ruling not only fails to come to grips with the relevance of Lyons's membership in a racial group; it also distorts the law of standing to sue and confuses that issue with questions of judicial remedy. See Fallon (1984); Tribe (1985) chap. 8. See also Meltzer 279–319.
14. *Los Angeles Times,* May 8, 1982. Three days after this remarkable comment the Los Angeles police commission instituted a moratorium on police chokeholds except when deadly force would be authorized.

15. Two small programs were funded at 95 percent of need: aid to the aged (56 percent black or Hispanic beneficiaries) and aid to the disabled (53 percent white beneficiaries). The welfare officials testified that they did not know, when they issued their first order, the racial composition of the various beneficiary groups. If you believe the Texas legislators were similarly ignorant, please be sure to read chapter 8.

16. Pearce and McAdoo 3–10. The real value of mean AFDC benefits has continued to decline. One writer says there was a 36 percent decline from 1970 to 1983 (Levitan 32). Cf. W. Wilson (1987) 94 (22 percent decline from 1972 to 1984). The degree of decline varies from state to state. In Texas there was a 59 percent decline from 1970 to 1985 (Moynihan 15). Currently, the combined value of AFDC benefits and food stamps is below the poverty line in every state. Leyser, Blong, and Riggs 3. Nationwide, some 43 percent of AFDC beneficiaries are black, and 14 percent Latina (38). See also Edelman 14–15.

17. *Jefferson v. Hackney* (1972).

18. *Personnel Administrator of Massachusetts v. Feeney* (1979).

19. *Irvis v. Scott* (M.D. Pa. 1970). The Supreme Court's opinion in *Moose Lodge No. 107 v. Irvis* (1972) made no reference to the case's social context.

20. Epstein and Foster 23. On sex discrimination, see Rhode (1987); Burns.

21. Baltzell.

22. *Lynch v. Donnelly* (1984). See Van Alstyne (1984).

23. See Chief Judge Raymond Pettine's sensitive exploration of these harms in his opinion for the district court, *Donnelly v. Lynch* (D.R.I. 1981). Judge Pettine took note of the Pawtucket mayor's special contribution: a press conference at the crèche site, where he decried the lawsuit against the city as an effort to take "Christ out of Christmas." The Supreme Court majority ignored this fact along with all of Judge Pettine's findings about the hurt of exclusion.

24. Carroll 38.

25. E.g., Lupu 1054–70.

26. Tussman and tenBroek.

27. Westen 558. For a sampling of responses to Westen, see Greenawalt (1983); Simons; *Why Equality Matters*.

28. Cf. Dworkin (1986).

29. Bickel (1975) 54.

30. Weber 145, 355.

31. Crenshaw 1365.

32. E.g., Nisbet.

33. Wiebe (1975).

34. See *Rizzo v. Goode* (1976) (Philadelphia); cf. *Boyle v. Landry* (1971) (Chicago).

35. See Bruner (1985) 46–58. Martha Minow (1987a) 138 suggests a useful two-part question for the judge to ask: "who names the difference," and has a dominant group used "the assignment of meaning to difference in order to express and consolidate power"?

36. See Julio Cortázar's 1975 novel, *Hopscotch*.

37. On the need for historians who will write "constitutional history from the

bottom up," concerned with people's awareness of rights as "constitutional output, no less than constitutional input," see Hartog 1029–33.

Chapter 2

1. See Kluger chap. 22, on the views of counsel during and following the first argument of the cases.

2. Leflar and Davis.

3. Kluger chap. 25.

4. *Plessy v. Ferguson* (1896) (citing *Roberts v. Boston* [Mass. 1850]); *Cumming v. Richmond County Board of Education* (1899); *Gong Lum v. Rice* (1927).

5. Kluger 865, 870.

6. Kluger 855, 870. Robert Burt (1988) 91–94 suggests the primacy of Frankfurter's concern that the Supreme Court's authority would be weakened if the Court should order immediate desegregation and southern resistance should be successful.

7. Kluger 747, 751, 861.

8. Ralph Ginsburg; Myrdal 560–64.

9. Kluger 862.

10. *Brown v. Board of Education* (II); see chapter 11.

11. Kluger 857–58.

12. B. Schwartz 448.

13. B. Schwartz 449. Derrick Bell has offered a view on what some of those factors might have been. The 1954 *Brown* decision became possible, he has suggested, only because formal equality for blacks promoted several interests of the white establishment: domestic peace, Southern industrialization, and America's standing overseas. He nonetheless calls *Brown* "the Supreme Court's most important statement on the principle of racial equality" (Bell [1980] 522–23; Bell [1976a] 6–13).

14. Warren's handwritten draft opinion referred to *Plessy v. Ferguson*, the main precedent supporting segregation (in railroad cars, not schools) as seeking to retain "the philosophy of the *Dred Scott* case," i.e., racial inferiority. It also hinted at larger perspectives on the meaning of segregation, referring not only to children's motivation to learn but to "other divisive effects not necessary to enumerate here" (B. Schwartz 453, 455).

15. Kluger parts 1 and 2.

16. See, e.g., Kluger 23–31.

17. Kluger chap. 1.

18. Greenberg 50–57; Tushnet (1987).

19. A group of twenty-nine black intellectuals met at Niagara Falls (on the Canadian side, because the Buffalo hotel where they had reserved rooms discriminated against blacks). They rejected the accommodationist views of Booker T. Washington; W. E. B. Du Bois became their leader. They merged into the NAACP in 1909 (Myrdal 742–44, 819–20). On the Louisiana campaign, see Lofgren.

20. See Felstiner, Abel, and Sarat.

21. Bass; J. Wilkinson (1979).

22. Bass; Belknap.

23. For references to quotations and other documentation for this section not individually noted, see *Paths to Belonging* 307–11.

24. Erikson 79, 81.

25. Walzer (1987) 14–16. "One has to be a member of a community to be a self" (Mead 162). See generally 152–64, 253–60; Berger and Luckmann 130–37.

26. Bruner (1986) chap. 8.

27. Cassirer 79.

28. Geertz (1963) 109. Self-definition obviously is also affected by other characteristics shared with others, such as gender, sexual orientation, occupation, and even political association.

29. *Memphis v. Greene* (1981).

30. Erikson 8. See also Allport 194; Bettelheim and Janowitz 42; McWilliams chap. 2; Kinder and Sears.

31. Bruner (1986) 47.

32. See Delgado, et al. (1985) 1375–83 for a helpful survey of theories on the origins of prejudice.

33. Williamson (1980).

34. Petchesky 209.

35. Lawrence (1986).

36. Scarf 186–87.

37. See chapter 5.

38. Lawrence (1987); see also *Motive-Centered Inquiry.*

39. Blacks were joined in the category of Other by Indians, and, in the West and Southwest, by Chicanos and Asians.

40. Williamson (1984) 511–22.

41. Erving Goffman's modern classic on the subject is entitled *Stigma: Notes on the Management of Spoiled Identity.* For references for the following paragraphs, see *Equal Citizenship* 5–8.

42. Rodes 163. On the right to be "treated as an equal," see Dworkin (1977) 227.

43. W. E. B. DuBois (1940) 130–31. For a social psychologist's analysis of the ways in which group identity works to deny the individuality of members of subordinated groups, see Deschamps.

44. Goffman 35. See also I. Katz chap. 4 and 120–121.

Chapter 3

1. For references for this section, see *Paths to Belonging* 362–66.

2. See Gwaltney; Deloria. On the exclusion of slaves, Indians, and women from early American egalitarian thought, see Appleby 101–02. Some black people who are disinclined to stand up for "The Star-Spangled Banner" also see themselves as more faithful than whites to American values (Gwaltney 5, 11, 13).

3. Di Leonardo.

4. On commonly held black perceptions of whites as malevolent and devious, see Gwaltney. On similar views among Chicanos, particularly focused on law enforcement officers, see Paredes; Mirandé chap. 5.

5. Quoted by Mona Harrington (1982) 103.

6. On the community-defining qualities of oaths of allegiance, see Levinson (1986).

7. Gleason 62.

8. Higham (1974) 11.

9. Wiebe (1975).

10. Higham (1974) 16.

11. J. White (1984) 190.

12. Higham (1984) 232.

13. These were the main meanings of *civic culture* as Almond and Verba used the term in their famous comparative study.

14. Higham (1974) 10.

15. Wiebe (1984) 268; Mona Harrington (1982).

16. Huntington; Geertz (1973) 17–18; Roelofs; Walzer (1987) 29.

17. Richard Hofstadter, quoted in Kohn 10.

18. For references for this section, see *Why Equality Matters* 250–67.

19. See Minow (1987c).

20. This leadership continued a pattern that had begun in the era of slavery. See Genovese 255–79; Levine chaps. 1 and 3.

21. Quoted in Howard 308. For references for this paragraph, see *Fifth Amendment Equal Protection* 547–50.

22. Dissenting in *Slaughter-House Cases* (1873).

23. Appleby (1984) 104; also 55, 70–74.

24. *Youngstown Sheet & Tube Co. v. Sawyer* (1952); Westin.

25. *United States v. Nixon* (1974).

26. Jackson, J., in *Youngstown Sheet & Tube Co. v. Sawyer* (1952).

27. Virginia's experience was distinctly different. An excess of gentlemen and a shortage of workers led to early disasters and a resolve to import indentured laborers. Extreme inequalities among whites were only moderated upon the introduction of black slaves. See Morgan chaps. 16, 17.

28. Appleby (1984) 97.

29. Modern survey research suggests that the great majority of Americans continue to profess a preference for individualistic conceptions of equality (McClosky and Zaller chap. 3).

30. See, e.g., Forbath 788.

31. See Fishkin.

32. E.g., Baker.

33. Michelman (1969) 58; *State Court's Responsibilities* 722–25.

34. Schaar.

35. Landry 73–78; Thurow (1981) 91–92.

36. See McClosky and Zaller 64–72.

37. De Beauvoir (1953) 261.

38. Levy (1985) chap. 10. In other words, "rights holders are those who do what rights holders do" (Hartog 1019).

39. For references for this section, see *Paths to Belonging* 369–76.

40. Cassirer 81; Geertz (1973) 17–18.

41. Geertz (1973) 28.

42. On our tradition of individual autonomy and its relation to modern constitutional claims of the right to govern central aspects of one's own identity and personality, see Nichol.

43. Geertz (1973) 207.

Chapter 4

1. *Dred Scott v. Sandford* (1957). See Fehrenbacher.
2. Bickel (1975) 54.
3. Kettner.
4. Dissenting in *Passenger Cases* (1849) 492.
5. H. Davis 102 *(Aristotle's Politics)*.
6. Jordan 200–04.
7. Genovese 25–43; Tushnet (1981) 157–69. See generally Jordan; Davis.
8. Williamson (1984) 18–19.
9. Blassingame 304. On the slave as trickster, see Levine 121–33.
10. Blassingame 322.
11. Genovese passim; Tushnet (1981) chap. 1; Blassingame chap. 7.
12. Genovese 25–49.
13. Jordan 274; McWilliams 276.
14. Blum 34, 17–18; Jordan 134; Pole 25; Morgan chap. 16.
15. For references for this paragraph and the next, see *Why Equality Matters* 269–70.
16. Litwack (1961) 9. Her use of "we" was appropriate. In the 1740s slaves constituted 21 percent of the population of New York City; about one-fifth of Boston's white families held slaves (Davis [1987]). On the place of black people in colonial Massachusetts and New York, see Higginbotham chaps. 3, 4.
17. Du Bois (1972) 57, 71, 89, 97, 105.
18. Litwack (1961) 62.
19. Id. 65
20. Id. 57, 63. Paul Finkelman, who takes a somewhat more sanguine view of conditions in the North, agrees that northern society was imbued with racism.
21. Jordan 95; Nelson (1974) 537–38.
22. For references for this section, see *Equal Citizenship* 13–17. See also Kinoy; T. Wilson; Diamond (1979); Diamond (1982); Soifer (1979).
23. The act said nothing about equality in voting or jury service, two forms of participation that we now see as essentials of citizenship. See Monaghan 1981) 379 n 154. But those omissions do not detract from the conclusion that the act was seen in 1866 as protecting substantive rights of citizenship. Women, for example, could not vote and seldom served on juries but were undoubtedly citizens. The omissions do show that the framers of the 1866 act and the Fourteenth Amendment had a narrower view of the meaning of citizenship than we do today.
24. Black (1969) 51–66.
25. E.g., Berger (1977); Bork (1971); cf. Monaghan (1981).
26. Berger (1977).
27. *Dartmouth College v. Woodward* (1819).
28. See Hale; Gunther (1985) 487–90. On the acceptance of substantive judicial review in the state courts by 1820, and its accelerated use in the 1840s and 1850s, see Nelson (1972).
29. *Ex parte Garland* (1867); *Cummings v. Missouri* (1867).
30. Bickel (1955).

31. Id.; Fairman chap. 20; Benedict; Hyman, ed.; Kutler; Cox and Cox.

32. Sandalow 1046; Maltz (1984).

33. Bickel (1955) 63.

34. Fairman 1388.

35. For references for this section, see *Equal Citizenship* 18–21.

36. On the connections between Field's view of citizenship and the antebellum traditions of Republicanism and free labor, see Forbath 772–79.

37. Bickel (1973) 378.

38. See also Bradley's view of the role of "woman" in his concurring opinion in *Bradwell v. Illinois* (1873), quoted in chapter 7.

39. Woodward (1966b). On Justice Bradley's role, see Scott. On the decision's connection with constitutional protections of the liberty of private contract, see Nerken.

40. Douglass (1962) 551.

41. As in *Yick Wo v. Hopkins* (1886).

42. Lofgren 156–64. Racial segregation had been the inconsistent practice of southern railroads since the Civil War (chap. 1). What was new in the 1880s and 1890s was legislation requiring segregation.

43. The federal government, through the Freedmen's Bureau and its transportation policy, sought to keep blacks in the South. Thus northern white workers were protected against competition, and laborers were provided to produce cotton for the benefit of northern industrialization. See Steinberg chap. 7.

Chapter 5

1. Franklin chap. 2.

2. Woodward (1960) 73.

3. Id. 96.

4. TenBroek (1965); Soifer (1979).

5. Woodward (1960) 76.

6. Id. 79.

7. Id. 91; Gillette.

8. Litwack (1980) chap. 4; Williamson (1984) 44–50. On the role of the Freedmen's Bureau and the Army in coercing former slaves into contracts for agricultural work, see Litwack (1980) chaps. 7, 8; Soifer (1987) 1940–51; T. Wilson chap. 4.

9. Williamson (1984) 49.

10. Id. chaps. 3 and 4. See also Foner.

11. Rabinowitz.

12. Private schools had been segregated before Jim Crow arrived; the Freedmen's Bureau and northern charities operated some schools for black children. The issue for state governments in the era preceding Jim Crow was whether to provide black children with any schools at all. See Franklin (1968).

13. Here I follow Myrdal 675, using *caste* to refer to a rigid social stratification (which, for blacks, has meant subordination), essentially inherited, with the sort of staying power that gives it the look of permanence. See Diamond and Cottrol. For a purist's insistence on a different choice of words, see Dumont.

14. See Dollard passim.

15. Williamson (1984) 111–14.
16. Woodward (1966a) 74–93.
17. Id. 97–102. The Bibles were separated by custom, not law.
18. Williamson (1984) 185. For more detailed figures, see Zangrando 5–8. Frederick Douglass protested against southern Lynch law as early as 1892 (12).
19. Id. 118, 189–223.
20. Id. 115–19, 127–76. See also Cash. Rosa Parks, whose action sparked the 1955–56 Montgomery bus boycott (chapter 1), recalls that one of the first books she read, at age eight, was entitled *Is the Negro a Beast?* (Parks).
21. Williamson (1984) 306–08; Dollard 136–37.
22. E.g., *Light in August.*
23. Woodward (1966a) 81.
24. Williamson (1984) 116. See also Fredrickson. This view not only omitted any concern for black women who were raped; it also betrayed that the central concern was not for white women who were raped but for the affront presented by those rapes to the status of white men. See Wriggins.
25. Jordan 4–5, 37–38.
26. Hall; Williamson (1984) 186–88, 306–09; Dollard chap. 7; W. White.
27. Dollard 165.
28. J. Jones chaps. 3 and 4. On today's networks, see chapter 8; Stack (1974).
29. Dollard 440.
30. Id. 178–84, 345–48.
31. Id. 317–22, 382–83.
32. Litwack (1980) chap. 8.
33. Justice Brandeis, dissenting in *Olmstead v. United States* (1928), 471. Robert Burt (1984) argues elegantly that the courts' chief role in healing American divisions is a teaching role, forcing attention to communal values.
34. On rare occasions the Court did intervene. For example, it invalidated Oklahoma's use of a *grandfather clause* to allow whites to vote while disqualifying equally qualified blacks (*Guinn v. United States*, 1915) and Louisville's racial zoning ordinance (*Buchanan v. Warley*, 1917). See generally Bickel and Schmidt chap. 8.
35. Steinberg chap. 8; W. Wilson (1987) 33–34. On the patterns of black migration from the Civil War to the present, see Farley and Allen 109–36.
36. For references for this paragraph, see *Not One Law at Rome* 393–94.
37. See Levy (1972) 316; Baltimore and Williams.
38. Allport 147–49; Goffman 9.
39. Dollard 69; Myrdal 695–700.
40. Cruise 558.
41. Rudwick chap. 8.
42. Du Bois's editorials are collected in *The Crisis Writings.*
43. R. Hill; Myrdal 746–49; Williamson (1980) 159–61.
44. W. E. B. Du Bois (1940) 182, 185–88. Later, Du Bois himself despaired of success for the strategy of integration, and he broke with the NAACP over this issue. See Rudwick chap. 11; Williamson (1984) 75–78, 399–413; Tushnet (1987a) 8–10; Tushnet (1987d) 890–96.
45. Isaacs.

46. Cover (1975) 212. On "litigation as a classroom," see O'Neill 3–19 and passim.

47. Myrdal 820; Zangrando.

48. *Guinn v. United States* (1915); *Smith v. Allwright* (1944); *Terry v. Adams* (1953); *Moore v. Dempsey* (1923); *Powell v. Alabama* (1932); *Norris v. Alabama* (1935); *Buchanan v. Warley* (1917); *Truax v. Corrigan* (1926).

49. Tushnet (1987a) chap. 2; Kluger chap. 6. The Margold Report to the NAACP is excerpted in Greenberg 50–57.

50. On the harms of segregated schooling and the hoped-for benefits of school integration, see Shane 1049–62.

51. *Missouri ex rel. Gaines v. Canada* (1938); *Alston v. School Board of Norfolk, Va.* (4th Cir. 1940). See Tushnet (1987a) chap. 5.

52. Myrdal 822–23 quotes one set of NAACP instructions to local branches concerning education and voter registration.

53. Id. 466 (italics in original).

54. Id. 414–19, 851–52.

55. See chapter 6.

56. *Screws v. United States* (1945).

57. Chapter 4.

58. *Morgan v. Virginia* (1946).

59. *Shelley v. Kraemer* (1948).

60. *Sipuel v. Oklahoma* (1948); *Sweatt v. Painter* (1950); *McLaurin v. Oklahoma State Board of Regents* (1950).

61. *Green v. County School Board of New Kent County* (1968); *Alexander v. Holmes County Board of Education* (1969). The NAACP's lawyers warned from the beginning that actual desegregation would require not just lawsuits but action that was overtly political. Carter and Marshall 402–03.

62. Kalven.

63. *Heart of Atlanta Motel v. United States* (1964); *Katzenbach v. McClung* (1964); *South Carolina v. Katzenbach* (1965).

64. See J. Wilkinson (1979) 19.

65. Chapter 1.

66. King (1962); Pollitt; J. Wilkinson (1979). On the crucial role of black women in the civil rights movement, see J. Jones 278–301. On the movement's organization of direct action, see Morris. On voter registration, see Carson.

67. Burt (1984) 486.

68. Bickel (1969) 104, 115.

69. Cover (1982) 1303.

70. The culminating decision was *Terry v. Adams* (1953).

71. Pollack (1959) 19–23.

72. *Shelley v. Kraemer* (1948). The *amicus curiae* brief of the United States, supporting the result the Court reached, is rendered in plain English in Clark and Perlman. For commentary on the decision, see State Action 44–52; Henkin; Tribe (1985) 259–64.

73. See Pollitt.

74. For one young woman's account, see Moody 264–67.

75. Chapter 4.
76. For references for the following five paragraphs, see *Equal Citizenship* 36–37.
77. See the second Justice Harlan's dissent in *Burton v. Wilmington Parking Authority* (1961); infra, this chapter.
78. *Burton v. Wilmington Parking Authority* (1981).
79. See *Telophase of Substantive Equal Protection*; Black (1967); Silard; J. Williams.
80. *United States v. Guest* (1966); see also *Katzenbach v. Morgan* (1966).
81. *Jones v. Alfred H. Mayer Co.* (1968).
82. *Jackson v. Metropolitan Edison Co.* (1974); *Flagg Bros. v. Brooks* (1978).
83. Chapter 1.
84. Compare Harlan's opinion in *Berea College v. Kentucky* (1908).
85. Horowitz (1957); Symposium (1982), *University of Pennsylvania Law Review*. See also *Telophase of Substantive Equal Protection*; *State Action*. But see Jakosa.
86. Cf. *Roberts v. United States Jaycees* (1984); *Board of Directors of Rotary International v. Rotary Club of Duarte* (1987).
87. E.g., *Runyon v. McCrary* (1976); *Griffin v. Breckenridge* (1971). But see *General Bldg. Contractors Ass'n v. Pennsylvania* (1982).
88. J. Wilkinson (1979) 61–77.
89. Chapter 12.

Chapter 6

1. In his sensitive exploration of the lives of three families during the Boston school desegregation battles of the 1970s, J. Anthony Lukas suggests that it is wrong "to believe that John Kennedy's accession to the presidency had completed the assimilation of the Irish into mainstream America" (Common Ground 262). The key word is "completed." Many residents of Charlestown, where Lukas's Irish family lived, plainly are not completely assimilated. But, as his portrait of Judge Wendell Arthur Garrity makes clear, even in Massachusetts entry into the middle class has strong assimilative effects. In those portions of America that lie west of Newton, the descendants of Irish immigrants are largely integrated into the dominant culture.
2. On early wholesale characterizations of "the Indian," see Nash 35–64.
3. Jordan 85–91; Hagan; Note (1982), *American Indian Law Review*; Deloria and Lytle (1983) 1–24; Spicer 176–203; C. Wilkinson.
4. The source that best demonstrates what it is that Indian law practitioners have to know, above and beyond what other lawyers know, is F. Cohen (1982).
5. Deloria and Lytle (1984); Hertzberg; Clinton; Metcalf; Note (1987), *Harvard Civil Rights-Civil Liberties Law Review*.
6. For references for the next three paragraphs, see *Why Equality Matters* 265–66.
7. Hansen 85.
8. Handlin 239.
9. Crèvecoeur 69–70.
10. For references here and in the next three subsections, see *Paths to Belonging* 311–25.

11. Higham (1981) 247.

12. Id. 249–50.

13. M. Jones 63.

14. Id. 88.

15. In *Chae Chan Ping v. United States* (the *Chinese Exclusion Case*) (1889) the Supreme Court upheld Congress's power to exclude Chinese aliens from the United States. The decision, to put it mildly, is ripe for overruling. (Henkin [1987]).

16. Recent examples are recounted by Shapiro.

17. Grodzins 297.

18. Billington 323; Gusfield (1967) 175; Gusfield (1983).

19. Gusfield (1967) 184.

20. Furnas 698–99; Sowell (1981) 277. On "white flight" today see Gewirtz 628–65; T. White 121–22, 132 n; Cunningham and Husk.

21. The term still has vitality; see Rhode (1987).

22. Kinder and Sears.

23. Rostow (1945). See generally Grodzins.

24. TenBroek, Barnhart, and Matson 110.

25. Biddle 217.

26. Four decades after these events Peter Irons uncovered evidence of serious misconduct in the government's presentation of the Japanese American cases to the Supreme Court. On the basis of that evidence, federal district courts have vacated the convictions of Fred Korematsu, Gordon Hirabayashi, and Minoru Yasui for violation of the exclusion and curfew orders. See Irons. On the justice of reparations to the displaced Japanese Americans, see Matsuda 360–97.

27. See Minow (1987c).

28. *Bolling v. Sharpe* (1954). See *Fifth Amendment Equal Protection*.

29. For references for this paragraph, see *Why Equality Matters* 266–67.

30. See di Leonardo.

31. For references for this section, see *Paths to Belonging* 320, 325–32. On the political role of immigrant leaders, see also Greene.

32. Quoted in Wiebe (1975) 68.

33. Id. 140.

34. For references for this paragraph, see *Equal Citizenship* 28.

35. See A. Lewis (1958). On voting as a ritual of allegiance and a symbol of satisfaction with one's lot, see Shienbaum chap. 4.

36. For references to this section, see *Paths to Belonging* 347–49.

37. See Cover (1982) 1293.

38. See chapter 9.

39. *Mobile v. Bolden* (1980).

40. *Rogers v. Lodge* (1982).

41. For references to this section, see *Paths to Belonging* 332–36, 329–30.

42. Bender 43.

43. Higham (1984) 178.

44. Walzer (1982) 14.

45. Bollinger; see also *Equality and the First Amendment*.

46. Richards; see also chapter 11.

47. On abortion as a status issue, see Luker; on bilingualism as a status issue, see Moran.

48. See chapter 11.

49. See Houston. Similar proposals have succeeded in the states. California's voters in 1986 amended the state constitution to include an "official English" pronouncement, the effect of which appears to be entirely symbolic (Calif. Const. Art. III, sec. 6). On official English measures generally, see Note (1987b), *Harvard Law Review*.

50. For references to this section, see *Paths to Belonging* 351–57.

51. See Moran.

52. On the connections between shared language and solidarity, see Bruner (1986) 62–65.

53. Hakuta; see also *Paths to Belonging* 354 n 322.

54. A serious concern raised by any program that labels some school children as "different" is the danger of stigmatizing those children. For a sensitive analysis of this problem, see Minow (1985).

55. For references for this section, see *Paths to Belonging* 357–61.

56. Walzer (1983) 245–46.

57. Geertz (1973) 130.

58. Arnow. See also Pfeffer chap. 10; Choper.

59. A more charitable view of the community-building function of civil religion is expressed in Note (1986), *Yale Law Journal*. But whose community? On civil religion as a veneer covering racism, see Long. For a multitude of citations on civil religion, see Developments in the Law (1987), *Harvard Law Review* 1620–21, 1651–55.

60. Wiebe (1975) 152.

61. On the other hand, discrimination against religious expression is properly held unconstitutional, as in *Widmar v. Vincent* (1981). See Laycock (1986b).

62. Chapter 1. See also Dorsen and Sims. On Christmas celebrations in public schools, see Pfeffer 479–96.

63. One year later, in *Goldman v. Weinberger* (1986), Justice O'Connor's concern for religious outsiders ripened into a judicial vote. For six years an Orthodox Jewish officer in the Air Force had been wearing a yarmulke with his uniform while on duty in the base hospital; shortly after he testified in an unrelated proceeding as a character witness for another service member, his commander ordered him to stop wearing the yarmulke with the uniform. When he refused, he was disciplined. The Air Force consolidated this military victory over both common sense and the First Amendment when the Supreme Court, 5–4, upheld the discipline. Justice O'Connor's dissent offers real promise for the doctrinal future, at least for claims under the free exercise clause. See Michelman (1986a) 33–36.

64. Abraham.

65. After writing this passage I found Mark Tushnet's expression of the same idea. His words validate themselves:

[I]t is difficult to believe that the *Lynch* majority would have reached the same result had there been a Jew on the Court to speak from the heart about what public displays of crèches really mean to Jews. At the same time, of course, Jews have always known that they were strangers in the land, and have taken succor from that fact. *Lynch* reminds us of that, and distressing as it may be to have it brought home, we may profit from learning the lesson again.

Tushnet (1986a) 712 n 52. See also Tushnet (1987b) 222–25.

Chapter 7

1. For references for this section, see *Woman's Constitution* 449–60, 463. See also "A *Discrimination So Trivial.*"

2. *Bradwell v. Illinois* (1873). The case was decided one day following the *Slaughter-House Cases*, chapter 4. The Court focused on the same (privileges and immunities) issue. Equal protection was not discussed; the framers of the Fourteenth Amendment had not thought of affecting sex discrimination.

3. M. Rosaldo and Lamphere 3; M. Rosaldo 17, 19; Kidder, Fagan, and Cohn 242–44, 252; Law (1983) 1282–1335.

4. Chodorow 166.

5. Id. 181.

6. De Beauvoir ([1949] 1971) 682.

7. Bem 603.

8. Id. 603–05.

9. Rowbotham 35.

10. Ellison.

11. MacKinnon (1982) 21.

12. Miller chap. 6; Rowbotham chap. 5.

13. MacKinnon (1982) 15.

14. *Dothard v. Rawlinson* (1977). On *Dothard's* stereotyped view of men's sexuality, see Menkel-Meadow (1980) 25 and 25 n 20.

15. Compare *Palmore v. Sidoti* (1984), holding that a Florida divorce court could not constitutionally deny child custody to a white mother on the ground that her new husband was black, even though the child of an interracial couple might suffer the effects of others' racial prejudices.

16. The declaration is printed in Rossi 416–17.

17. For references for this section, see *Woman's Constitution* 464–72.

18. See *Equal Citizenship* 53–59; Ruth Ginsburg (1983).

19. Chapter 1.

20. See chapter 9.

21. See generally Bem.

22. New York Task Force 5–6.

23. Id. 19 and passim.

24. Quotations are, respectively, taken from id. 34, 34, 73, 133, 176, 169, 185, 231, 220, 221. On women as jurors, see Marden. On the difficulty of getting judges to perceive sexual harassment, see Bratton. On men's and women's different perceptions of "force" in rape cases, see Estrich (1987) 58–71.

25. *Rostker v. Goldberg* (1982).

26. W. Williams (1982).

27. *Goesaert v. Cleary* (1948).

28. *Craig v. Boren* (1976).

29. *Orr v. Orr* (1979).

30. *Michael M. v. Superior Court* (1982).

31. W. Williams (1982) 185. For another view of the *Michael M.* case, see Olsen (1984).

32. E.g., W. Williams (1982); W. Williams (1984–85); Littleton (1981); Littleton (1987b); Kay; Law (1984); Ruth Ginsburg (1978); Scales; Finley.

33. MacKinnon (1987) 44. See also Colker.

34. R. Rosaldo 19. On the relation of feminist law reform to fundamental critique, see Littleton (1987a) 3–6.

35. MacKinnon (1979) herself is the main architect of one important legal doctrine that operates within the prevailing assumptions in ways that challenge gender as domination: the doctrine treating sexual harassment as sex discrimination.

36. Olsen (1986) 1541 (emphasis in original).

37. See, e.g., E. DuBois 842–44. For references for the next three paragraphs, see *Woman's Constitution* 472–73.

38. Chief Justice Burger, concurring in *Roe v. Wade* (1973).

39. For an insightful study of women's patterns of perceiving and knowing, and the connections between those patterns and women's experience in intimate associations, see Belenky, Clinchy, Goldberger, and Tarule, passim. On the "I" and the "me," see Mead 173–78.

40. See Ruth Ginsburg (1985); Law (1984); *Equal Citizenship* 53–59. For another perspective on the relation of the abortion decision to autonomy, see Goldstein (1988); see note 51, this chapter.

41. Russell 57. (The sample included 930 households in San Francisco.) See also Finkelhor and Yllo; Estrich (1987) 72–79.

42. Note (1986), *Harvard Law Review.* Marriage aside, even a prior relationship drastically reduces the chances of conviction, or even prosecution, for rape. Estrich (1986) 1171–78.

43. Ely (1973) 933–35.

44. Of course some women legislators also favor state laws forbidding or strictly limiting abortion. But this fact is not inconsistent with the operation of the stereotype—not even among women. The women with the greatest emotional investment in the abortion issue, on both sides, are those who seek to defend the worthiness of their own life choices, either for careers or for traditional domesticity. A "pro-choice" woman may be a devoted mother, and a "pro-life" woman childless; yet the emotion flows, generated by the need to validate their own personal status. Large numbers of abortions were performed in the United States before the Supreme Court's 1973 decision in *Roe v. Wade.* There was little public outcry, so long as the law stood as an official statement of society's disapproval. Legalization has produced fervent opposition because it lays bare the connections linking identity, status, and public expression. To the typical woman who becomes a pro-life activist, the abortion clinic and the sexually active teenage girl have become highly visible symbols of the negative identity she must repress in order to defend her own self. See Luker, Petchesky chap. 6.

In an insightful essay Guido Calabresi (1985, chap. 5) argues that the Supreme

Court, by stating in *Roe v. Wade* that a fetus is not a person within the meaning of the Fourteenth Amendment, marginalized many Catholics and other Americans who view abortion as sin. This statement, he says, told those people that their deepest beliefs counted for nothing in our constitutional law, "that even now, after all their other assimilations, they could not be true Americans so long as they held to their beliefs." Here (and in *Equal Citizenship* 53–59) I have argued, as Calabresi does, that *Roe* would have been more satisfyingly rested on grounds emphasizing women's claim to equality. But Calabresi goes on to argue that such an equality-based opinion would not have seemed to the opponents of abortion to exclude them. The argument, I think, overestimates the influence of one passage in the opinion on abortion opponents' sense of belonging to America and underestimates the influence of the decision's result. In any case the Court did not simply say to abortion opponents, "*Your* metaphysics are not part of *our* Constitution" (Calabresi 95). Rather, it said that no one's metaphysics could constitutionally be given controlling weight in justifying the use of governmental power to commandeer a woman's body.

45. New York Task Force Report 26–92.

46. Walzer (1983) 240.

47. See Weitzman; Symposium (1986), *American Bar Foundation Journal*; Sidel.

48. Blake; see chapter 8.

49. *Harris v. McRae* (1980).

50. See generally Symposium (1984), *Signs*. See also chapter 8.

51. See, e.g. MacIntyre 201–06; Sandel 50–65; D. Kennedy 211–13; Finley 1171–72, 1177. George Herbert Mead elaborated this theme two generations ago. In a sensitive new analysis of the abortion issue, Robert Goldstein (1988) argues that treating the woman's choice as a question of autonomy rests on just this sort of incomplete view of the self. The choice, he says, is better seen as a choice made by a self-in-relationship—in this case, the relationship between the woman and the potential child within her. For Goldstein's argument that the woman is the appropriate decision maker on behalf of this relationship, see his chapter 3.

52. Gilligan (1982). For criticism of Gilligan's work, and her reply, see Kerber et al.

53. Gilligan (1982). 16.

54. Chodorow. See also Dinnerstein.

55. Kidder, Fagan, and Cohn 247–48; Hantzis; MacKinnon (1985) 25–28; Menkel-Meadow (1987) 43–48; Henderson 1582–83.

56. Scarf 193. The "fear of success" suggested by some writers appears to be associated with sex-role identification, not with sex itself. See Tresemer, Cano, Solomon, and Holmes.

57. Gilligan (1982) 158–59. On "connected knowing" and its integration in the construction of knowledge, see Belenky, Clinchy, Goldberger, and Tarule chaps. 6 and 7.

58. Scarf chap. 10. On projective identification see Klein; Levy and Brown.

59. Scarf 192–93.

60. This view, expressed in Lenz and Meyerhoff 6, is trenchantly criticized by Hantzis 695.

61. Rowbotham 35.

62. This ability to be oneself can be affected by the number of women in a social organization. To be the organization's token woman is to be seen not as a person but as a symbol of the category, woman. The combination of high visibility and encapsulation in a role subjects the token woman to special pressures to perform, pressures that can impair performance. See Kanter (1977a) 206–42; Rebne. As the numbers of women increase within the organization, women gain the freedom "to become individuals differentiated from one another, as well as a type differentiated from the majority." Kanter (1977b) 966. There is an obvious lesson here for institutions contemplating affirmative action programs. See also chapter 9.

63. E. Goldman 135, 142.

64. "[W]e collectively lack a vision of a person who is virtuous, active, powerful happy, and *not male*" (Hantzis 698).

Chapter 8

1. Potter. For additional references for this chapter, see *Citizenship, Race and Marginality*.

2. M. Katz 6.

3. Handler (1987).

4. Marin.

5. U.S. Bureau of the Census (1986) 443; Wilson (1985) 548; W. Wilson and Aponte 242–43; W. Wilson (1987) 174–77; Levitan 7; Hacker (1987) 28.

6. W. Wilson (1987) 26–29, 63–92. Cf. Pearce and McAdoo.

7. M. Katz 238–39, 266–68; Handler (1987) 396–97. Consider this example: In 1984, the amount budgeted for federal spending on the elderly (mainly Social Security and Medicare) was six times greater than the amount budgeted for spending on children (AFDC, Head Start, food stamps, child health, child nutrition, aid to education) (Preston 45).

8. Himmelfarb 164–65, 183, 186–89; Handler (1972) 8.

9. The city of Sacramento's recent reintroduction of the poorhouse was held unlawful by the California supreme court (*Robbins v. Superior Court* [Calif. 1985]).

10. Taylor 1729.

11. See, e.g., *Hills v. Gautreaux* (1976); *Warth v. Seldin* (1975); *Village of Arlington Heights v. Metropolitan Housing Corp.* (1977). On residential segregation, see Farley and Allen 136–57.

12. Chapter 1.

13. Himmelfarb 365–70.

14. Rainwater chaps. 1, 2.

15. Id. 20.

16. Galbraith 245; Rainwater 34.

17. M. Katz 271; Walker, Lawson, and Townsend. See also Mary Ann Glendon's thoughtful comments (53–58) contrasting American and European attitudes toward family support programs. On the need for a family policy, see Glendon 134–38; Moynihan, passim.

18. Just under 40 percent of the families aided by the federal AFDC program in recent years have been white; some 41–43 percent have been black, and 12–14 percent Latina. See n 5 supra.

19. Fiss (1976) 175; Perry (1977) 557–58.

20. See Thurow.

21. U.S. Bureau of the Census (1987) 3; *Paths to Belonging* 341–42 n 241. Even when black and white family incomes are equivalent, whites' accumulated wealth far exceeds that of blacks (Alexis).

22. *Plyler v. Doe* (1982).

23. Landry; Pettigrew 674–82; Taylor 1704–07; W. Wilson (1987) 109.

24. On the role of antidiscrimination legislation in this process, see J. Jones 301–05. Unemployment rates, as we have seen, are far more disparate. On black and white women, see Petchesky 152–54.

25. Gwaltney.

26. *Paths to Belonging* 335 n 204.

27. Pettigrew 680; Lemann (June 1986) 40; Taylor 1707–09.

28. Liebow 12, 60–61. This same concern is central to the Chicago street corner men so ably portrayed by Elijah Anderson.

29. See Anderson chap. 3.

30. In an important recent study of the 171 American cities with populations over 100,000, Robert Sampson has confirmed that the strongest predictor of black family disruption is the unemployment of black men. See also W. Wilson and Neckerman; W. Wilson (1987) chap. 3.

31. Ladner 236–41; Petchesky 152; Stack (1974) chap. 7.

32. Johnnie Tillman, a black mother of six who "had picked cotton and worked in a laundry before she became too ill to hold a job," quoted in J. Jones 307. The average size of AFDC families is decreasing. Among families receiving AFDC benefits in 1982, 74 percent had either one or two children; in 1969, only 50 percent of AFDC families were this small (Leyser, Blong, and Riggs 11–12). The average number of persons in an AFDC family is 2.9, and "six of seven AFDC households have four or fewer persons" (Levitan 35). See also 83.

33. Stack (1974) 47; Petchesky 150. By 1975, more than half of all AFDC assistance was being paid to women who had first become mothers as teenagers (W. Wilson [1987] 29).

34. In some areas the proportion of these children is "close to 90%" (*Time Magazine* [1986] 28). Some 38 percent of these women have full-time employment in addition to their family responsibilities (Hacker [1987] 26).

35. W. Wilson (1987) 26–27, 72, 90; Hacker (1983) 28.

36. Levitan 14, 38. About three-quarters of the income of all poor families comes from wages and Social Security (26). On the need of poor women for both employment income and public assistance, see Zinn and Sarri. On women in poverty, see Symposium (1984), *Signs*.

37. Danziger and Gottschalk; Jencks (1985); Levitan 38–39; W. Wilson (1987) 17.

38. Stack (1974) chap. 7. See also Pearce and McAdoo 12–14.

39. Stack (1974) chap. 3. Typically, such a life is filled with anxiety, as high levels of depression attest (Pearce and McAdoo 12).

40. Stack (1974) 92–93. In a later study of black families that have recently migrated from the urban Northeast to the rural South, Stack has begun to explore "an African-American model of moral development," emphasizing "commitment to kin and community, and belief in the morality of responsibility" (Stack [1986] 324).

41. Stack (1974) 36–38, 105–07, 113–15.

42. Id. chap. 7.

43. W. Wilson (1985) 555; Lemann.

44. Goodwin.

45. Michael Harrington 140; W. Wilson (1987) 39–46.

46. *New York Times* (1986). In 1986 some 40 percent of all black men had full-time, year-round jobs (Hacker [1987] 29).

47. *Time Magazine* (1986) 27.

48. W. Wilson (1987) 20–62; Lemann 38; Hacker (1987).

49. Sampson. The sociologists' and demographers' persistent references to families "headed by women" seem to carry the insulting implication that two-parent families are headed by men. Unfortunately, I have found no alternative simple reference that encompasses single parents, women who live alone, and women who live with other women, grandchildren, etc. Even "households without men" may mislead in some cases. On poverty in single-parent ghetto families headed by women, see W. Wilson (1987) 71–72.

50. Sampson 352–53.

51. Cobbett 104–05.

52. W. Wilson (1985); Lemann.

53. Gwaltney; W. Wilson (1980); W. Wilson (1985).

54. W. Wilson (1987) 174–77.

55. Auletta; W. Wilson (1987).

56. W. Wilson and Aponte (1985) 236. On the interpenetration of culture and severely limited opportunity, see Michael Harrington chap. 8.

57. M. Katz chap. 10.

58. Himmelfarb 367.

59. Glasgow 25.

60. Rainwater 38–40; Daly.

61. For references for the next four paragraphs, see *Paths to Belonging* 328–29.

62. Myrdal 820 (1940 program of NAACP).

63. The poor do not even vote in proportion to their numbers. The typical American voter is "relatively well-off, well-educated, and middle aged," that is, one who is likely to identify with the prevailing distribution of income and power (Shienbaum 89).

64. Winter 100.

65. Danziger (1988); Bassi and Ashenfelter 133.

66. McCloskey 228–29.

67. *Griffin v. Illinois* (1957).

68. *Harper v. Virginia Board of Elections* (1966); *Shapiro v. Thompson* (1969). Similarly, the Court's protections against discrimination based on the status of "illegitimacy" surely proceeded in full knowledge of the historic use of such laws in southern states to prevent wealth transmissions from white fathers to the children of black women. (*Levy v. Louisiana* [1968]; *Glona v. American Guarantee & Liability Insurance Co.* [1968]). The Burger Court, perhaps recognizing today's significant correlation between race and "illegitimacy" throughout the country, held that a state could not constitutionally deny welfare benefits to families containing "illegitimate" children (*New Jersey Welfare Rights Organization v. Cahill* [1973]).

69. *Gideon v. Wainwright* (1963); *Douglas v. California* (1963); *Miranda v. Arizona* (1966). See Lewis (1964). Even when the Court was validating a measure of police discretion to "stop and frisk" citizens on the street, its opinion expressed concern about the possibility of police harassment of members of minority groups and particularly blacks and said that conduct of that kind should result in the exclusion of evidence thus obtained (*Terry v. Ohio* [1968]). The Warren Court's treatment of vagrancy laws, too, surely was influenced by the recognition that such laws had been used as a basis for stopping blacks for questioning when they were in predominantly white neighborhoods at night. See *Papachristou v. Jacksonville* (1966), invalidating on vagueness grounds a vagrancy law that was a direct descendant of England's poor law.

Long before the Warren era, when the Court first recognized constitutional limitations on the states' criminal justice systems, the Justices had a similar awareness of the importance of their rulings in the South, where the black population was concentrated and where black defendants faced formidable obstacles in the criminal process. See Cover (1982) 1305–06.

70. Commentators who saw the equal protection clause as largely devoid of substantive content (apart from racial equality) joined in the recharacterization. E.g., Lupu 1054–70.

71. See also *James v. Valtierra* (1971); *San Antonio Independent School District v. Rodriguez* (1973). The Court's extreme deference to legislative judgment in this area continues unabated. See, e.g., *Bowen v. Gilliard* (1987).

72. The Garys had eight children; the father was disabled and the mother in ill health. Their level of need was set at $331.50 per month.

73. *Williams v. Dandridge* (D. Md. 1968, 1969).

74. Bentham 120.

75. Tussman and tenBroek.

76. Developments in the Law (1969) 1103–04; *Invidious Discrimination* 718–20, 732–46. See generally Gunther (1972); Tribe (1987), chap. 16.

77. *Bakke Opinions* 20–27.

78. Catherine Hancock helped me to see the importance of this incongruity for my own analysis. Frank Michelman long ago argued for abandonment of the traditional analysis of legislative classifications in dealing with the claims of the poor under the Fourteenth Amendment (Michelman [1969]). See also *Telophase of Substantive Equal Protection* 38.

79. Thurow (1979) 27–28.

80. These are the fictitious names that Elliot Liebow gave to some of the men who formed Tally Jackson's street corner society.

81. Thurow 29.

82. See Clune; Fiss (1976); A. Freeman.

83. Aron 33.

84. Frank Michelman (1969) 13 has suggested that the constitutional injury wrought by severe poverty ought to be seen as one of "deprivation" rather than "discrimination." The analysis offered here blurs the line between those two categories, for the crucial deprivation is exclusion from equal citizenship.

85. Walzer (1986) 143 (emphasis in original).

86. Rodes 149.

87. Matza. See also Michelman (1973) 983–91; Plamenatz 91–92. No stigma attaches to one who must work for a living rather than clip coupons, live in an apartment rather than a house, or use a public beach rather than a private one. But some kinds of work or living quarters are stigmatizing, as Matza, supra, makes clear. Government's responsibility under the equal citizenship principle is not an absolute duty to eliminate all such conditions, irrespective of cost. Rather, it is a duty to take reasonable steps to include marginalized people in the community of equal citizens or to offer substantial justification for failing to do so.

88. Walzer (1983) 106. See also Rainwater.

89. *Equal Citizenship* 9–11.

90. Chapter 4.

91. For one clear-cut example of legislative equation of low-income persons with blacks, see *Smith v. Town of Clarkton* (4th Cir. 1982). On the "striking correlation" between decreasing AFDC benefits and increasing percentages of black beneficiaries, see *Whitfield v. Oliver* (D. Ala. 1975).

92. *Equal Citizenship* 44–46; Developments in the Law (1983) 1410–15, 1433–57, 1463–65.

93. Chapter 6.

94. Justice Thurgood Marshall saw this point clearly in his dissent in *San Antonio Independent School District v. Rodriguez* (1973). On the "muddled" responses of the Burger Court to problems of the poor, see R. Bennett (1983).

Discussions of *Dandridge v. Williams* sometimes treat the choices before the Court as a problem in shuffling funds among the poor; the assumption, of course, is that a court cannot order a net increase in welfare spending. *Plyler v. Doe* points in another direction. The result of the decision is to require Texas to increase considerably its spending on education—in amounts exceeding what it would have cost Maryland to fund large welfare families at the level the state had defined for those families' needs. Considerations of cost and of state resources are highly relevant in determining state responsibility under the equal citizenship principle, but existing public budgets are not immune from judicial scrutiny. See, e.g., *Griffin v. County School Board of Prince Edward County* (1964), ordering the reopening—and thus funding—of a county's public schools that had been closed to avoid desegregation.

95. Donald Horowitz (1977) offers a series of cautionary tales. For two contrasting responses to Horowitz, see R. Goldstein (1978) 45–48, 64–71; Komesar (1988) 692–99. The key to the institutional problem, as Neil Komesar says (1988, 717), is to provide justification for courts "to review some important government actions" concerning poverty—and, I would add, failures to act—"without facing the full range of distributive questions." I am arguing that such a justification can be founded on the principle of equal citizenship and the links between race and marginality in the ghetto.

The appropriate case for Supreme Court recognition of the claims of the ghetto poor might be presented by a conventional attack on the constitutionality of a legislative classification. Less conventionally, a class action might be brought against a group of federal officers whose responsibilities extended to such subjects as hunger, housing, or job training. The plaintiff class would need to be identified by working definitions of chronic unemployment and welfare dependence. Once a court issued its declaratory judgment, the defendant officials might be ordered to propose their own remedial plans.

If Congress should want to insist that state governments participate in any such remedial efforts, it would have ample powers to do so under section 5 of the Fourteenth Amendment.

96. Black (1986). Black's doctrinal argument centers on a duty of Congress to provide for the general welfare (derived from Article I and the Preamble, with lateral support from the Declaration of Independence) and a corresponding right, recognition of which lies within the range of judicial authority permissible under the Ninth Amendment. Peter Edelman (23–48) has suggested several alternative constitutional arguments for "a right to minimum income." My own doctrinal view centers on the Fourteenth Amendment; hunger is utterly inconsistent with the status of equal citizenship.

97. M. Katz 265–66; Physicians' Task Force on Hunger in America xx, xxx, 131–52; Levitan 80–81.

98. Owen Fiss (1976) 169 has properly cautioned that having courts act as "primary distributors" of resources would be "contrary to democratic traditions." See also Komesar (1988) 715–17. It is worth emphasis that the equal citizenship principle calls for no such thing. The difference between the total cost of existing legislative programs to relieve conditions of poverty and the total cost of such programs, given a serious judicial concern for the most grievous effects of marginality on citizenship, would amount to a tiny fraction of our public expenditures.

99. See Michelman (1969) 39–59; Michelman (1979) 660–64. Robert Bork's criticism (1979) suggests that Michelman has proposed something of a constitutional ratchet: that an antipoverty law, once in place, never can be repealed. I do not so understand Michelman, but in any case the criticism has no relevance to the equal citizenship principle. That principle stands on its own; irrespective of prior legislative action, some conditions of poverty have the effect of excluding people from membership. In resolving the remedial issues raised by the stopping-place problem, judges can appropriately seek guidance in present or prior legislative definitions of need.

Further guidance may come from the state courts. Litigation to aid the homeless, for example, seems an apt avenue for the development of state law expanding our conceptual horizons about government responsibility. See, e.g., Connell; G. Blasi; Chackes; Note, *UCLA Law Review* (1987) 196–201. One important by-product of such litigation is the raising of public consciousness—which, in turn, can affect judicial attitudes at the highest level. See Hayes.

100. See *Harris v. McRae* (1980).

101. See *Plyler v. Doe* (1982).

102. See *U.S. Dept. of Agriculture v. Moreno* (1973); *U.S. Dept. of Agriculture v. Murry* (1973).

103. On the effects of concentration of marginalized blacks, see W. Wilson (1987) 34–45, 46–62; Hacker (1987).

104. Lemann summarizes the types of proposals that have had recent vogue.

105. On black unemployment, see McGahey and Jeffries. Jobs programs that are cost-effective in the long run may not bring sufficiently prompt returns to satisfy politicians who must seek reelection every two years.

106. Charles Murray, in *Losing Ground* (1984), argues that the availability of welfare benefits has caused all manner of ills in the ghetto, from high unemployment to

family disintegration. For convincing evidence to the contrary, see Ellwood and Summers. See also Moynihan 123–42.

107. Michael Harrington chap. 10. On the historic role of government employment in reducing black unemployment, see McCahey and Jeffries 42–49.

108. Lemann.

109. See chapter 9; Fiss (1986) 1504.

110. On sexual harassment as employment discrimination, see MacKinnon (1979); on generous judicial interpretations of federal fair housing laws, see Calmore 237–38 and n 183.

111. Bell (1976a); H. Horowitz (1966).

112. For further discussion and references, see *Equal Citizenship* 29–31. More recent decisions include *Bounds v. Smith* (1977); *Little v. Streater* (1981).

113. Calmore 238–40.

114. Lemann. A crucial part of the political problem is the creation of a broad constituency for reform. On the failure of Lyndon Johnson's Great Society program to reach a constituency that was broad enough, see Mona Harrington (1986) 184–98.

115. On the judiciary's teaching role, see Burt (1984).

Chapter 9

1. Quoted in Kaplan 174.

2. *Loving v. Virginia* (1987).

3. Fiss (1976) 123–29. Cf. Brest (1976).

4. Clark (1979) 105. See Also Lawrence (1986); Landry 105–15 and chaps. 4–6.

5. See Feagin chap. 4. Even middle class blacks often see the ghetto as "a collection of individual hard-luck stories" (Lemann [July 1986] 57).

6. William Julius Wilson, quoted in chapter 8. In a thoughtful recent essay Stephen Carter suggests that the more serious problem is not racism, in the sense of intentional victimization, but "racialism," an awareness that uses race as a major signifier, for example, as "a predictor of criminal tendency" (S. Carter 436). As Carter shows, however, when myriad individual choices are founded on such beliefs, they inevitably add up to social choices that might as well be labeled racism.

7. W. Wilson (1987) 22–26, 34–35; Lemann; Daly. On "symbolic racism" among suburban whites, largely independent of any objective threat, see Kinder and Sears.

8. On Jews in Canarsie, see Rieder. On Irish in Charlestown, see Lukas. Similar battles over turf are now being fought as increasing numbers of Latinos move into the Los Angeles ghetto.

9. See chapter 1. On police acculturation and cultural difference in a California county in the 1960s, see Swett 81–94.

10. Black (1981) 101–102. See infra this chapter.

11. Lawrence (1987).

12. M. Jones 149.

13. Bass; Moody. See also the grisly facts of *United States v. Price* (1966) and *United States v. Guest* (1966); Belknap chaps. 6 and 7.

14. Isaacs 44, 208–14; Blumer; Gusfield (1963); Moran. On the relevance of these attitudes to the debate over affirmative action, see R. Kennedy (1986) 1337–45.

15. Blumer.

16. Glasgow x.

17. Bell (1985).

18. Id. 57–59.

19. Brest (1976); Ely (1973) 933 n 5.

20. Wechsler 31–34.

21. Holmes ([1881] 1964) 7.

22. See also Garfinkel.

23. Chapter 1.

24. The Court has interpreted various federal civil rights acts as presumptively prohibiting conduct with effects that disparately disadvantage blacks, Chicanos, women, etc. E.g., *Griggs v. Duke Power Co.* (1971). See Laycock (1986). Owen Fiss (1986) has suggested that the Justices' willingness in such cases to equate racially disparate effects with racial discrimination is founded on their assumption that they have the political support of Congress.

25. Chapter 1.

26. Bindra and Stewart 11–12.

27. Id. 9.

28. *Townsend v. Wathen* (King's Bench 1808).

29. See chapters 2 and 7; Lawrence (1987).

30. Mills 163.

31. The leading case, which dealt with a First Amendment claim rather than a claim to equal protection, is *Mt. Healthy City Board of Education v. Doyle* (1977).

32. Brest (1985) 664; Tushnet (1985) 1517. See also chapter 12.

33. As we see in this chapter, the doctrine has not been applied rigorously in the contexts of voting rights and school desegregation.

34. Chapter 2.

35. *Washington v. Davis* (1976) at 248. For references for the next five paragraphs, see *Equal Citizenship* 50–52.

36. Gunther (1972) 12.

37. Myrdal 75, 1065–70 ("the principle of cumulation"); Glazer (1966) xii–xviii; Fiss (1976) 150–56; Brest (1976) 10–11; Eisenberg; Lawrence (1977).

38. Myrdal 78.

39. *Equal Citizenship* 51.

40. Readers who are too young to remember the use by Alabama police officers of dogs (Birmingham) and cattle prods (Selma) to control civil rights demonstrators in the 1960s might look at Bass 201–05, 260.

41. Chapter 4.

42. See Justice Stevens, concurring, in *Washington v. Davis* (1976); Schnapper (1982) and (1983); R. Bennett (1984/85); Gottlieb; Sedler. Official action that harms the members of a racial minority and that has no good justification naturally raises the suspicion of improper motive. See *Yick Wo v. Hopkins* (1886). Charles Lawrence has suggested not the abandonment of the purpose requirement but the expansion of the idea of purpose to reach harms resulting from unconscious racism, a state of mind to be identified by the cultural meaning of the action in question. See Lawrence (1986) 355–87.

43. *Columbus Board of Education v. Penick* (1979); *Dayton Board of Education*

v. *Brinkman* (II) (1979). After a school district's system becomes unitary—satisfies the courts that it is no longer unconstitutionally segregated—there remains a danger of relapse. See Note (1987a), *Harvard Law Review.*

44. *Rogers v. Lodge* (1982). This decision repaired most of the damage done in *Mobile v. Bolden* (1980). On the Mobile case, see Soifer (1984). In 1982 Congress amended the Voting Rights Act of 1965 to specify that a court can consider the racially disparate results of a local election-districting scheme as one factor in determining whether the scheme is racially discriminatory. Normally the Supreme Court will defer to lower court findings on the question of improper motive. *Rogers v. Lodge* (1982); *City of Pleasant Grove v. United States* (1987). The trial judge's empathy will thus be of crucial importance to the plaintiffs in such a case.

45. Brest (1971).

46. Eisenberg; Sedler. Cf. Perry (1977).

47. Fiss (1976).

48. *McCleskey v. Kemp* (1987). In a study of over 2000 murder cases in Georgia in the 1970s, issue, David Baldus and Charles Pulanski showed that prosecutors sought the death penalty in the following percentages:

Black kills black	15%
White kills black	19%
White kills white	32%
Black kills white	70%

The same study showed that the death penalty was actually assessed by juries and judges in the following percentages:

Black kills black	1%
White kills black	3%
White kills white	8%
Black kills white	22%

See also Black (1981) 101–02 n 2; Greenberg (1986); Greenberg (1982). On race and prosecutorial discretion in homicide cases, see Radelet and Pierce (Florida); Paternoster (South Carolina). Randall Kennedy (1988) ably explores the *McCleskey* decision in the context of modern equal protection doctrine. On *McCleskey* as the culmination of the current Supreme Court majority's effort to "suppress all doubts" about fairness of the death penalty, see Burt (1987) 1795–1800. See also Developments in the Law (1988), *Harvard Law Review* 1603–26.

49. *Warth v. Seldin* (1975); *Allen v. Wright* (1984).

50. Chapter 1. See also *O'Shea v. Littleton* (1974); *Rizzo v. Goode* (1976); Fiss (1977).

51. Ironically, some opponents of affirmative action describe themselves as devotees of an original intent theory of constitutional interpretation. If anything is clear in the Fourteenth Amendment's legislative history, it is the assumption by the amendments's framers that it would not forbid such contemporaneous affirmative action programs as those of the Freedmen's Bureau (Schnapper [1985]).

52. Dissenting in *Wygant v. Jackson Board of Education* (1986). See also Marshall 1011.

53. But see Justice Powell's opinion in *Regents of University of California v. Bakke* (1978), discussed in *Bakke Opinions* 13–15.

54. Brest (1976) 17; cf. Fiss (1976) 148–55. A court should nonetheless be concerned with the harms suffered by members of disadvantaged subgroups among the larger category of "white applicants." The Supreme Court grappled with a similar problem in the voting context in *United Jewish Organizations v. Carey* (1977) without great success.

55. See *Affirmative Action;* Sandalow (1975) (responding to Ely [1974] and Posner).

56. W. Wilson (1987) chap. 5.

57. On the difficulties of proof, see Furnish.

58. Felstiner (1974).

59. Bumiller 431–32.

60. Chapter 5.

61. Laycock (1981) 379; cf. Posner.

62. E.g., Rae 4–5.

63. See Landry 96–105.

64. For references for the next four paragraphs, and further discussion, see *Affirmative Action* 957–63. See also Fallon (1980).

65. *Green v. County School Board of New Kent County* (1968); *Alexander v. Holmes County Board of Education* (1969).

66. *Swann v. Charlotte-Mecklenburg Board of Education* (1971). See *Emerging National Standards;* also, *Not One Law at Rome.* See also the Columbus and Dayton cases, note 43 supra.

67. On the relation of white resistance to "feasibility," see Gewirtz.

68. *Otero v. New York City Housing Authority* (2d Cir. 1973).

69. *Regents of University of California v. Bakke* (1978).

70. For example, the Court has been more receptive to affirmative action hiring goals than to race-conscious layoffs. The Court's opinion in the *Johnson* case, discussed below, downplays the cost to Johnson individually of gender-consciousness in the agency's promotion system. See Fallon and Weiler.

71. Fallon and Weiler. Justice Powell's *Wygant* opinion is an example.

72. See *Bakke Opinions* 27–29.

73. See Wasserstrom (1977) 599–602.

74. See *Affirmative Action* 965–66; Sedler (1980); Sullivan.

75. Justice Powell's opinions in the *Bakke* and *Wygant* cases make this point; so does Justice O'Connor's *Wygant* opinion.

76. Quoted in chapter 8.

77. Fiss (1976); Fallon and Weiler.

78. Such a strategy of indirection, designed to make affirmative action palatable, was suggested earlier by Greenawalt (1975). Calabresi (1979) suggested that Justice Powell's "diversity" approach was a subterfuge, and would be ineffective, but the predictive part of that analysis did not come true. In university admissions, the permissibility of affirmative action has all but disappeared as an issue.

79. Sullivan 91–96.

80. The agency was a public employer and thus subject to the limitations of the

Fourteenth Amendment, but the plaintiff employee limited his challenge to a claim under Title VII of the 1964 Civil Rights Act, and the Court did not reach the issue of the constitutionality of the agency's policy. On the relations between statutory and constitutional standards for affirmative action, see Rutherglen and Ortiz; H. Schwartz.

81. See Choper (1987).

82. See H. Schwartz.

83. *Regents of University of California v. Bakke* (1978) held unlawful an affirmative action quota for admissions to a state university's medical school. *Fullilove v. Klutznick* (1980) upheld Congress's power to direct that a quota of funds appropriated for local public works be set aside for minority businesses.

84. Scalia 152.

85. H. Hill 31; Steinberg 177.

86. H. Hill 10.

87. Id. 9–30.

88. See, e.g., *United States v. Lathers Local 46* (S.D.N.Y. 1971); *Asbestos Workers Local 53 v. Vogler* (5th Cir. 1969).

89. Quoted in H. Hill 38.

90. For references for this section, see *Paths to Belonging* 341–46.

91. Van Alstyne (1979) 809.

92. Du Bois (1970) 79 (emphasis in original).

93. See Crenshaw.

94. One indicator of these economic changes is ethnic intermarriage. About 28 percent of Americans of Asian ancestry are married to non-Asians, and the percentage has increased in recent years. Of Jews who have married in the last ten years, 40 percent have married non-Jews (Collins).

95. Taylor 1704–07, 1712–14; Smith and Welch; Leonard (1984a); Leonard (1984b); *Los Angeles Times*, Feb. 25, 1986, 3, col. 5.

96. On gains in black employment by federal government contractors under the influence of affirmative action programs, see R. Freeman 5; Smith and Welch; H. Schwartz 572–73 and n 264–67.

97. Blumrosen (1968) 476–79. This pattern is part of a larger one; on "victim group isolation" and affirmative action, see Spiegelman.

98. About 80 percent of today's middle class blacks are "first generation." Black families' ability to transmit middle class status to the next generation appears to have increased (Landry 86–87).

99. Schelling 137–66. On the origins and maintenance of residential segregation, see Farley and Allen 136–57. On "white flight," see Gewirtz.

100. Thurow (1979) 35–36.

101. Justice Blackmun, concurring, in *Regents of University of California v. Bakke* (1978).

102. Van Alstyne (1979) 809.

103. On the role of Title VII of the 1964 act in transmitting nondiscrimination values to southern employers, see Blumrosen (1984). In this educational perspective, a particularly urgent case can be made for affirmative action in police hiring and promotions. See Chambers 32–34; cf. R. Kennedy (1986).

104. See his opinion in *Regents of University of California v. Bakke* (1978).

105. Walzer (1982) 22. Walzer himself is skeptical about affirmative action. See Walzer (1983) 131–54.

106. The prediction has also been fulfilled in the affirmative actions plans of state and local governments in the wake of *Fullilove v. Klutznick* (1980). See Days.

107. See chapter 6.

108. Hazard 390–91, 395–99.

Chapter 10

1. Isaacs.

2. P. Berger, Berger, and Kellner chap. 3.

3. Wiebe (1975) 66.

4. See chapter 6.

5. *Paths to Belonging.*

6. Cover (1983).

7. For references for the next five paragraphs, see *Equality and Community* 186–87. Bender 45–53 argues that writers on the decline of community fail to recognize the persistence of some forms of communalism in an increasingly secularized and universalistic society.

8. See generally Hartz; Diggins; Pocock (1975).

9. Riesman 100.

10. Fromm.

11. Chapter 2.

12. See Novak; Mead 142–44.

13. Billington chap. 9.

14. Coser.

15. Slater; Fromm; Lasch.

16. *McCulloch v. Maryland* (1819); *Gibbons v. Ogden* (1824).

17. *Swift v. Tyson* (1842). See Wiebe (1985) 303.

18. E.g., *Passenger Cases* (1849); *Pennsylvania v. Wheeling & Belmont Bridge Co.* (1852); *Welton v. Missouri* (1876); *Wabash, St. Louis & Pacific Ry. Co. v. Illinois* (1886).

19. Wiebe (1985) 227–29.

20. Id. 248–49.

21. Wiebe (1975) 41.

22. Wiebe (1985) 375.

23. Id. 374.

24. Id. 29–33; Morgan (1975) chap. 11; Wood 536–43.

25. Levy (1986) 134. On the "culture of constitutionalism" as a crucial ingredient of "the ideological glue for the loosely bound United States" in the 1790s, see Appleby (1987) 804.

26. Wiebe (1985) 145.

27. Id. chap. 8.

28. Tocqueville ([1835 and 1840] 1945).

29. Wiebe (1985) 165.

30. Gunther (1985) 487–90.

31. Tribe (1987) 560–74.

32. Hughes 50.

33. Gabriel 298, 405.

34. Higham (1974) 13–16.

35. Wrong (1976) 79.

36. Jackson, J., concurring in *Youngstown Sheet & Tube Co. v. Sawyer* (1952). See also Sandalow (1980) 33. The centralization of governmental power, accelerated by the New Deal and World War II, was promoted for two decades after the war by state legislative default. When malapportioned, rural-dominated legislatures ignored mounting urban problems (Lewis, 1958), the cities turned to Washington for help. On the nationalization of politics, see Lunch; Tushnet (1987c). Cass Sunstein (1987) 504–08 has recently suggested a series of "reconstitutive" legal reforms aimed at reversing some of these trends, "to promote geographical diversity, local self-determination, and citizen participation in government." He is careful, however, to exclude subjects such as racial discrimination, where "powerful moral commitments call for [national] uniformity."

37. Geertz (1973) 10.

38. Ladd 270.

39. Friedrich; Parsons.

40. The first language of approximately twenty million Americans is a language other than English.

41. Burke 355.

42. Bender 8, quoting Martin Buber.

43. Isaacs chap. 9.

44. Even Aristotle, who thought the *polis* should be small, recognized that diversity was consistent with community (Friedrich 4–5).

45. For references for the next three paragraphs, see *Paths to Belonging* 367–68.

46. Higham (1974) 16.

47. Chapter 2.

48. Hofstadter (1958) 357.

49. Garet 1029–36.

50. Cover (1983). One of the greatest challenges to modern American constitutional law is presented by groups who contest the value of tolerance itself. The doctrinal focus for these problems has been the First Amendment. The hardest type of case—for example, the Nazis' claim of a right to march in Skokie—is hard because its resolution inevitably implies some sacrifice of a value we cherish. Lee Bollinger argues convincingly that a primary value of our First Amendment doctrine is that it helps courts teach the nation to control the impulse to intolerance. For comments on Bollinger, see Rosenfeld; V. Blasi; Sherry (1987).

51. Emerson 97.

52. Chapter 4.

53. Bickel (1969) 108.

54. The cases are collected in Gunther (1985) 639 n 1.

55. Cover (1983) 13 (emphasis in original); see also Cover (1986a). These two articles, among the last of Robert Cover's published works, are rich in insight and provocative to the imagination. They take their place among those writings in our field, few in number, that repay multiple readings with continued illumination. We

lost him much too soon. His friends recount some of what we lost in the *Yale Law Journal's* July 1987 issue, which is dedicated to him. See also Michelman (1986) 4 n 1 and passim.

56. Cover (1983) 13–14.

57. Cover (1986a) 1629.

58. Woodward (1966b).

59. Myrdal 466; see chapter 5.

60. Blotner 618.

61. For references for the next four paragraphs, see *Equality and Community* 201–04.

62. In Sinclair Lewis's 1935 novel of this title, of course, it did happen.

63. *The Federalist* No. 10, No. 51.

Chapter 11

1. Holmes (1920) 139.

2. Borges 90.

3. For references for this section, see *Equality and Community* 183–86.

4. Gusfield (1975) 30–31. It is possible to know you are a member of a community even when you define yourself, for some purposes, as an outsider; an alienated teenager is still a member of the family. See Ladd 274.

5. Nisbet 73.

6. E.g., Gwaltney 5, 19. Many readers will remember the protest gestures of several black American athletes at the 1968 and 1972 Olympic Games. In 1852, Frederick Douglass said, "This Fourth of July is *yours*, not mine" (Higginbotham 5).

7. Mead 152–64.

8. Sartre is our century's most famous expert witness for this proposition.

9. See J. White (1984a) 275–85.

10. Gerth and Mills (1970) 95–106; Mead 154, and parts 3 and 4 passim.

11. Lynd 43–47, 57.

12. Durkheim (1933) book 2, chap. 2.

13. Arnold (1962) 34.

14. In its daily application, too, law unifies, providing "a rhetorical coherence to public life by compelling those who disagree about one thing to express their actual or pretended agreement about everything else" (J. White [1984a] 268).

15. See Levinson (1979); M. Lerner; Gabriel. For references for the next four paragraphs, see *Equality and Community* 205–06.

16. Mannheim 290; Llewellyn (1935).

17. Hart (1959) 125.

18. Bruner (1976); Ornstein; Galin.

19. See Cardozo (1928) 59–61; Brennan (1987).

20. See Shiffrin 1192–1217 and passim.

21. Fiss (1979).

22. This role for our basic constitutional values is nothing new. For the gentry of the founding generation, the Bill of Rights "provided the indispensable ambiguity for an acceptable constitution" (Wiebe [1985] 33). See also Arnold (1937) 29.

23. "[T]o deny the value of the imagination is to destroy the capacity for sympathy and break down the system of shared meanings . . . that constitute our culture" (J. White [1984a] 134).

24. Wasserstrom (1968) 129.

25. This is my modification of Spaulding and Simpson's translation of Durkheim (1951) 253.

26. Cover (1983); J. White (1984a) chap. 3.

27. Cover (1986a) 1617, 1628.

28. See chapter 12. In saying that is is futile to search for principles that legitimize the American institution of judicial review, Laurence Tribe ([1985] chap. 1) argues that all exercises of power should be open to question. The question, I take it, is one of justification, a question that can be decided only if some community shares notions about what constitutes a good argument.

29. Pole 25–26.

30. Banfield 65. See also Jencks (1972) 4–7; Jencks (1979) 81–82.

31. In the antebellum South, slaves were part of the society, but were excluded from membership in the dominant community. For philosophical derivations of an equality focused on respect, see Rawls, especially chaps. 2, 4, 8, and 9; Dworkin chap. 12; Baker. On the moral equality of persons in a community, see Ackerman (1980); Perry (1979) finds the latter principle at the center of the Supreme Court's equal protection decisions.

32. Public and private behavior need not be congruent. Voting patterns, for example, do appear to be influenced by racial prejudice, along with perceived threats to self-interest. Pettigrew 691; Sears and Kinder; Sears, Lau, Tyler, and Allen; Skelton and Boyarsky.

33. Even Justice Bradley, author of the Supreme Court's opinion in the *Civil Rights Cases*, was of this view in the years before his participation in the Compromise of 1877. See Scott 557–60.

34. On the social science background of *Plessy*, see Lofgren chap. 5; Hovenkamp.

35. See also *Harper v. Virginia State Board of Elections* (1966).

36. The passage was added in order to keep Justice Jackson from writing a separate concurring opinion. Warren's original draft contained no such statement. B. Schwartz 451–55.

37. I refer here to the American experience. This ratchet effect is not a logical necessity; Nazi antisemitism, for example, struck at a group well integrated into German life.

38. Walzer (1987) 27. See also Rorty 530.

39. Llewellyn (1960) 512 ("situation sense"); Hampshire 23; Nagel 139; Cardozo (1921) 165–67.

40. Compare Kronman (1987) with López.

41. Monaghan (1981) 375–76. See also Monaghan (1979).

42. Michelman (1981). See also Powell (1987); Powell (1985). The Justices maintain a strong collegial sense of carrying forward the work of their predecessors. Justice Sandra Day O'Connor, in her first opinion for the Court, said this: "We begin, as always . . ." (*Watt v. Energy Educational Foundation* [1981]).

43. Holmes (1920) 270. See also Frankfurter (1956). "[W]e call judges who fol-

low precedent legitimate, but those who successfully break from it great" (Cole 859).

44. Koestler.

45. *Levy v. Louisiana* (1968); *Glona v. American Guarantee and Liability Insurance Co.* (1968).

46. See *Intimate Association* 676–82.

47. Wallach and Tenoso.

48. On miscegenation, see Williamson (1980); Myrdal 113–36.

49. See chapter 7.

50. See *Intimate Association*.

51. *Roberts v. United States Jaycees* (1984). See also Nichol; Tribe (1978) chap. 15.

52. For references for the rest of this section, see *Intimate Association* 635–37, 659–61.

53. D'Emilio (1983b).

54. Carol Stack (1974) reports a view in the ghetto that embodies not only common sense but justice: children legitimate themselves (Stack 50). See also Lemann.

55. These are the facts as reported by Michael Hardwick in an interview by Nina Totenberg, reported on "All Things Considered," National Public Radio, July 18, 1986. Totenberg said that the Atlanta police department and the district attorney's office both declined to comment.

56. National surveys show that police officials are far less tolerant of gays and of homosexual conduct than is the general public (McClosky and Brill 202–07).

57. On crimes of condition, see *Robinson v. California* (1962).

58. Wilkinson and White 593–96. On the legal status of gays and lesbians, see Rivera (1979); Rivera (1985 and 1986). The latter article is rich in detailed accounts of real people's lives.

59. Woodward (1966a) 81, on the contribution of courts to such permissions in the early years of Jim Crow.

60. See Altman 65, 101–02, and passim. See also Justice Brennan's dissent from the Supreme Court's refusal to review *Rowland v. Mad River School District* (1985). On homophobia, see DeCecco.

61. The percentages are uncomfortably close to the proportions of Japanese Americans on the West Coast in 1942.

62. National Institute of Mental Health 2.

63. The authorities are fully canvassed in Note (1984), *Southern California Law Review* 817–21. For a discussion of the emergence of homosexual orientation in early childhood, see Green.

64. On gay culture, see Altman chap. 5; see also FitzGerald 25–119 on the gay subculture in San Francisco. On the emergence of the gay political movement, see D'Emilio 1983a.

65. See *Intimate Association* 654, 682–86; Note (1985), *Harvard Law Review* 1297–1305; Mohr; Saphire; Symposium (1985), *University of Dayton Law Review*.

66. See chapter 6.

67. See chapter 7.

68. Altman passim.

69. R. Lerner 180.

70. Counsel evidently were seeking to focus the case on arguments concerning the privacy of intimate acts in the home—arguments that would extend to heterosexual intimacies as well as to the facts of this case.

71. His opinions on affirmative action are a good example. See chapter 9. In this case, such a strategy was unnecessary. Although a majority of the public disapproves of homosexual conduct, a majority also believes that such conduct in private should be left alone by the state (McClosky and Brill 199–207). Justice Powell—and, therefore, the Court—missed an opportunity to build on existing attitudes in teaching a lesson in tolerance.

72. Ross shows how our national discussion of AIDS is itself cast in terms that serve to distance "us" from people who have contracted the AIDS virus and more generally from the populations that have been principally affected by AIDS. The Supreme Court also fumbled a chance to teach a lesson about belonging.

73. *Webster's* 622. This dictionary definition serves well enough for our purposes. For a more thorough examination of the meanings of empathy, see Henderson 1578–83. See also Henderson's perceptive account of the failures of empathy in *Bowers v. Hardwick*, at 1638–49.

74. *Railway Express Agency v. New York* (1949).

75. The supply of tolerance appears to be greater among "legal elites" and "opinion makers" than it is in the general population (McClosky and Brill).

76. See Herek; Marmor 19; Hoffman 183–84; DeCecco. On murder of gays as a means of "killing" the part of one's own self that is homosexual, see Altman 65.

77. Other forms of official discrimination against homosexuals tend to be less explicit, less systematic. A decision on child custody or adoption, for example, typically is founded on an evaluation of many factors; only rarely will a court explicitly ground the denial of custody on a would-be parent's sexual orientation.

78. See, e.g., the government's arguments in *Watkins v. United States Army* (9th Cir. 1988).

79. *Palmore v. Sidoti* (1984) held that a divorce court could not constitutionally deny child custody to a white mother on the ground that she was married to a black man. In responding to the argument that a child living in an interracial household might be subjected to hostility, the Supreme Court used language that is an apt response to the services' arguments for excluding homosexuals: "The Constitution cannot control such prejudices but neither can it tolerate them."

80. E.g., *Parker v. Levy* (1974); *Rostker v. Goldberg* (1980); *Brown v. Glines* (1980); *Goldman v. Weinberger* (1986).

81. *Beller v. Middendorf* (9th Cir. 1980).

82. Gilbert Ware's excellent biography of William H. Hastie details (chaps. 9, 10, 11) the army's practices of and reactions to racial discrimination during World War II, when Hastie served as an aide to Henry L. Stimson, the Secretary of War. A persistent theme of high army officials was the undesirability of engaging in "social experimentation"—that is, desegregation—that might threaten discipline and morale. See, e.g, Ware 99, 106–07, 129, 134. In a chilling imitation of Jim Crow, the army even maintained segregated blood banks (Ware 107–09). On segregation in the army

and exclusion of blacks from the navy and the marines, see Myrdal 419–23. See also *Watkins v. United States Army* (9th Cir. 1988).

83. See Ware 100. The practice was inherited from army policy in World War I. See Myrdal 420.

84. Altman 218.

85. See, e.g., Delgado (1984).

86. See Symposium, *University of Miami Law Review*.

87. See chapter 1.

88. This phrase was coined by Harlan Cleveland in a speech at Colgate University in 1949.

89. Huntington.

90. For a discussion of the effect of women's previously excluded voices in the field of pregnancy discrimination, see Menkel-Meadow (1987) 46–48.

91. See Tushnet (1985) 1530, discussing Cover (1983).

92. King (1967) 195–202.

93. E.g., Bell (1984a); Bell (1984b).

94. E.g., Gilligan and Menkel-Meadow (1985); Gilligan (1986); Finley; Schneider; Sherry (1986); Ferguson.

95. Powers 100–02.

96. See chapter 9.

97. See chapter 9; Spiegelman.

98. See chapter 5.

99. Isaacs 98, quoting Kenneth Fearing.

100. See Walzer (1987) 21; *Woman's Constitution* 505; Ingber 344–46. On the importance to minorities of claiming rights, see Crenshaw; Delgado (1987).

101. This theme appears frequently in Gilligan (1982).

102. Bellah et al. 193.

103. See *Paths to Belonging* 375.

104. Quoted in Carey 38–39.

105. Hart (1956) 141.

Chapter 12

1. E.g., compare Wiebe (1975) and Genovese with Potter (1954), Hartz, and Boorstin. See generally Higham (1965) 212–62.

2. Chapter 4.

3. Kelsen (1945) 115–18.

4. This was a live question in the sixteenth century. See Pocock (1987) 125–27.

5. Nagel (1979) 16.

6. Monaghan (1981) 383.

7. Mahoney (1986) 1436, quoting Edward S. Corwin. See also Brennan; Grey (1984) 17–20. Cf. Levinson (1987); R. Kennedy (1987b).

8. Raoul Berger had addressed both questions. See Berger (1973) 53–102; Berger (1977) 166–92. I am more persuaded by his conclusions about impeachment than by his conclusions about equal protection. See Bickel (1955); Soifer (1979); Hyman and

Wiecek chap. 11; Dimond (1979); Dimond (1982); but see Maltz (1985); Maltz (1986).

9. Gordon 100–16; Brest (1980); Tushnet (1983); Nelson (1986); Powell (1987); Schlag.

10. Powell (1985); Sherry (1987b). On natural law thought in the era of the American Revolution, see Grey (1978). See also Grey (1975).

11. See Symposium (1982), *Texas Law Review;* Symposium (1985), *Southern California Law Review.* My favorite entry in this distinguished field of articles on interpretation is the story told by Thomas Grey (1985).

12. *Marbury v. Madison* (1803).

13. See, e.g., id.; *McCulloch v. Maryland* (1819); *Osborn v. Bank of the United States* (1824).

14. See Arnold; Frank; Llewellyn (1962).

15. López (1984) 15–37.

16. J. White (1984); J. White (1973).

17. Tushnet (1986b) 292–94.

18. See chapter 2.

19. See chapter 4.

20. But see Kurland (1972).

21. Fiss (1982).

22. E.g., Justice John Paul Stevens's concurrence in *Runyon v. McCrary* (1976), accepting the Court's decision (before his appointment) in *Jones v. Alfred H. Mayer Co.* (1968), which he thought questionable; and Justice Potter Stewart's concurrence in *Roe v. Wade* (1973), accepting the Court's decision in *Griswold v. Connecticut* (1965), from which he had dissented.

23. Here I have followed the argument of Frank Michelman (1981). See also Fallon; Simon; Monaghan (1979).

24. *Missouri v. Holland* (1920). See also Sandalow 1050.

25. Dissenting in *Poe v. Ullman* (1961), quoted more fully at the end of this chapter.

26. See J. White (1984b); Powell (1985).

27. One view, that I do not share, is that the old alliances remained intact but became more sophisticated with the Court creating the appearance of gains for the downtrodden in order to undermine movements for more drastic political change.

28. Even if we could agree on a definition of legitimacy in the descriptive sense, accurate measurement of this form of legitimacy would be extremely hard to achieve, given the multiplicity and diversity of the judiciary's audiences.

29. Justice Harlan Fiske Stone was such a Justice; his famous "footnote 4" in *United States v. Carolene Products Co.* (1938) sets out one tentative expression of a suitable role for the judiciary in defending political democracy—or, in the coinage of John Ely (1980), reinforcing it.

30. See Arnold.

31. Potter (1973) 390–418.

32. Black (1960b) chap. 2.

33. Bickel (1962) 30.

34. See chapter 11.

35. Quoted in Kronman (1983) 40.

36. Janowitz 2.

37. The most glaring exception is the marginalized poor. See chapter 8.

38. Roelofs 337–38.

39. Friedrich 3–6.

40. Laslett.

41. The revival began with historians. See Pocock (1975); Wood; Appleby (1984). On the "brief moment of alliance," during the revolutionary era, of republicanism and liberal individualism, see Kloppenberg.

42. Here perhaps I should capitalize "Federalists," to focus on leaders such as Alexander Hamilton and John Adams. See Diggins chap. 2. James Madison, in *The Federalist* No. 10, sought a middle ground in describing the national legislature. Congress, he said, was a legislature in which locally dominant factions would cancel each other's influence, leaving legislators to act in the public interest. Compare *The Federalist* No. 51 (Madison). See also note 78 infra.

43. Michelman (1977–78) and (1986); Sunstein (1982), (1984), and (1985); Stewart 1547–56; Sherry (1986); Macey. Compare Justice John Paul Stevens's equal protection standard of the impartial lawmaker, used in his dissent in *Fullilove v. Klutznick* (1980); his concurrences in *City of Cleburne v. Cleburne Living Center* (1985), *Michael M. v. Superior Court* (1982), and *United States Railroad Retirement Board v. Fritz* (1980); and elsewhere.

44. Woodward and Armstrong (1979).

45. See the final section of this chapter.

46. The doctrinal door was pried open in Justice Harlan Fiske Stone's celebrated "footnote 4" in *United States v. Carolene Products Co.* (1938), and by Justice William O. Douglas's opinion for the Court in *Skinner v. Oklahoma* (1942). See *Bakke Opinions* 20–27; *Invidious Discrimination* 732–46.

47. On the same theory the courts should be reluctant to invalidate laws aimed at broadening the community of equal citizens and should give those laws generous interpretations. In the post-*Brown* era the Supreme Court has followed this course with few exceptions. See, e.g., *South Carolina v. Katzenbach* (1965); *Griggs v. Duke Power Company* (1971); *City of Rome v. United States* (1980); and the affirmative action decisions discussed in chapter 9.

48. Fiss (1979).

49. Ely (1980).

50. Neil Komesar (1987) 210–16 argues persuasively that "aggregate processes like legislatures or markets" can be promising paths toward "public virtue" and "moral evolution." Certainly legislatures do adopt some laws that are not primarily aimed at serving anyone's private interests, narrowly defined: protecting an endangered species, for example, or preserving a wilderness for future generations. Tribe (1973) 634–35; Tribe (1974) 1336–40; Michelman (1977–78); Michelman (1979a) 506–11. Even in enacting those laws, however, legislators are mainly brokers who negotiate on behalf of environmental groups and developers who do have interests in the narrow sense.

On the distinction between reasoning about principle and reacting to desire, compare Perry (1982) chap. 4 and Wellington with Komesar (1984) 425–32.

51. See chapter 6.

52. The Supreme Court declined an opportunity to validate this conclusion in *Village of Belle Terre v. Boraas* (1974) when it upheld a local zoning ordinance that effectively forbade unrelated persons to live in the same household. Later, in *Moore v. East Cleveland* (1977), the Court repaired part of the damage, in the context of a more conventional, though extended, family.

53. McCloskey 228–29. A popular president can rally the nation to causes that are not immediately self-serving, as John Kennedy did in urging support of the bill that became the 1964 Civil Rights Act.

54. See Weber 322–37; Bendix 297–300; Gerth and Mills (1958) 78–80. In positing his (descriptive) types of authority, Weber did not offer empirical proof of their existence (Lukes).

55. Van Alstyne (1969).

56. Correspondingly, support by the relevant public for judicial review depends on a widely shared perception that the judges stand for something other than partisan advantage. We properly censure judges who depart from this model. An example of such a departure was Chief Justice Morrison Waite's behavior, at the time of the *Civil Rights Cases*, as a functionary of the Republican party. See Scott 566–68.

57. On the citizenry's tendency to identify the Constitution with the courts (and especially the Supreme Court), see Kammen chap. 1. For one specialist's casual assumption equating judicial review and constitutionalism, see Hart (1953) 1372. But see Gunther (1974); Brest (1975); Brest (1985–86).

58. Although severe methodological problems would attend any effort to measure the public's acceptance of the Court's legitimacy, it is hard to disagree with the commentators who say that the Court's political capital is finite and exhaustible. E.g., Bickel (1962) passim; Choper (1980) chap. 3.

59. Bickel (1962) 16, 18.

60. Id. 23–28; Black (1960) 49–50; Fiss (1982); Michelman (1986b).

61. Brest (1985) 664. See also Tushnet (1985) 1517.

62. Brest (1985) 665–66; Ely (1980) 59 and 59 n. In short, the attitudes of judges, like other people's attitudes, are in great measure received from "the group in which accidents of birth or education or occupation or fellowship have given us a place" (Cardozo 175).

63. Lynd 16.

64. *Harris v. McRae* (1980).

65. Before *Roe v. Wade* (1973), a wealthy woman who wanted an abortion could fly to Japan, to the Virgin Islands, or to one of the states that had few restrictions on abortion. *Roe* brought the procedure within the reach of women who had to stay near home but could afford to pay for the operation. Other women would—and still do— need institutional support.

66. President Carter took this imperative seriously, but in 1981 appointments to the federal courts reverted to the old pattern. S. Goldman reports these aggregate figures for Carter and Reagan appointments to the federal district courts and courts of appeals:

	Carter	Reagan (through 1986)
women	15.5%	8.4%
men	84.5%	91.6%
white	78.7%	93.7%
black	14.3%	1.7%
Hispanic	6.2%	4.2%
Asian	.8%	.4%

These percentages have not changed significantly in 1987–88. See Lichtblau; Wermiel.

In their study of federal district judges (12 male and 12 female, 10 black and 10 white, all Carter appointees), Walker and Barrow found no significant difference between black and white judges in deciding women's issues or minority issues. The study counted decisions for or against a "women's position" or "minority position," without differentiating among issues of fact or statutory application or constitutional interpretation, and without considering whether the governing law was developing or settled. The authors caution against excessive generalizing from small numbers of decisions by small numbers of judges, all recently appointed. They also say, "We can never know how the judges would have ruled had they traded dockets." Yet they report their results in language suggesting important discoveries. For example, noting that the 12 female judges supported minority positions in 48% of 43 cases, while the 12 male judges supported minority positions in 69% of 29 other cases, they call these results "a major, and unexpected, difference among the judges in our sample." This study appears to be the first of its kind, and its title suggests real illumination of the "policy ramifications" of diversification of the federal bench. Despite the authors' words of caution, their conclusions seem likely to be widely quoted. Anyone who reads closely will see that this study has not invalidated the commonsense expectation that appointing women and minority judges will affect not just appearances but decisions.

67. Bickel (1969) 14–42.

68. Compare Ely (1980) with Brest (1981) and Ackerman (1985).

69. This bit of statesmanship came from the attorney general of Idaho, quoted in Irons 72.

70. These are the oft-quoted words of Pogo, the cartoon creation of Walt Kelly.

71. Michelman (1986); Ackerman (1984).

72. Gilligan (1982).

73. These perceptions tend to affect the public expression of attitudes toward the proper allocation of rewards. Men, tending to see others as interchangeable occupants of positions, generally choose to reward merit or achievement; women, tending to see others as individual persons, generally choose equality (Kidder, Fagan, and Cohn 237–38).

74. Gilligan (1982) 137.

75. Id. 138.

76. And about lawyers, too. See Menkel-Meadow (1985) and (1987).

77. For references for the rest of this section, see *Woman's Constitution* 486–89, 501–02.

78. For an excellent capsule statement of the republicanism of the time, and the successful federalist response, see Stone, Seidman, Sunstein, and Tushnet (1986) 5–17. See also Tushnet (1985); Sherry (1986); Ackerman (1984); Michelman (1986). Cass Sunstein (1985) shows how Madison defended the proposed Constitution's complex system of government as a means of harnessing individualistic aggression to the service of republican virtue.

79. Appleby (1984) 17. See also 21; Diggins chap. 1.

80. Sandel; Finley 1159–61; Regan.

81. The traditional lawsuit, of course, is a zero-sum game; if the defendant wins, the plaintiff loses. In the wider perspective of legal doctrine, the recognition of a legal right implies that someone has a legal duty. Normally a court's judgment is not an invitation to chat; it is a command, backed up by the threat of violence (Cover [1986b]; Cover [1986a]). No morality of interdependence will make scarcity disappear, nor do away with all zero-sum games. Such a morality, however, does counsel accommodations that avoid having the same people lose all the time. And, even in carrying out their "jurispathic" function of killing legal traditions that compete with the dominant ones (Cover 1983, 58), judges have many opportunities to remind us of our interdependence and to promote even contending litigants' sense of connection to each other. See *Woman's Constitution* 488–95; Minow (1987) 1893–1911.

82. K. Jones.

83. Gilligan (1986) 241.

84. Id. 248–50.

85. Reprinted in Hand (1952) 172.

86. See Brennan (1987).

87. Gilligan (1982) 100. See also 69–70.

88. See chapter 3.

89. *Lochner v. New York* (1905).

90. The cases are outlined in *Woman's Constitution* 497 n 198.

91. See chapter 9.

92. E.g., Wechsler; Brown; Kurland (1964). For more sympathetic criticism, see A. Cox.

93. Bickel (1969) 45–100.

94. J. Wilkinson (1979).

95. Id. Cf. Gewirtz. See also Philip Elman's recently published claim to be the initiator of the tactic of delayed enforcement in *Brown*, and his claim that the tactic was essential as a way "to end racial segregation without massive disobedience" (Elman [1987a] 13). See also R. Kennedy (1987), and Elman (1987b).

96. See Gunther (1979); Fiss (1982) 757–62.

97. Bickel (1962) chap. 6; Bickel (1964); Gunther (1979); Burt (1979).

98. E.g., *Burton v. Wilmington Parking Authority* (1961); *Reitman v. Mulkey* (1967).

99. E.g., *United States v. Guest* (1966); *Katzenbach v. Morgan* (1966); *Jones v. Alfred H. Mayer Co.* (1968).

100. Black (1960).

101. *Plyler v. Doe* (1982). See Dimond (1983); Colker.

102. See *Equal Citizenship* 21–38.

103. Jackson, J., in *West Virginia State Board of Education v. Barnette* (1943).

104. Compare Fiss (1982) with Brest (1982).

105. Bickel (1975) 20.

106. Hand (1958) 60.

107. Compare Westen (1982), Cohen (1985), and Simons with *Why Equality Matters*.

108. Mueller and Schwartz.

109. Schroeder. One of the main values of the search for principled justification is that the search itself reminds the judge of her responsibility to be objective in this sense. See Greenawalt (1978).

110. I do not mean to suggest that there are no external constraints on the judge's range of substantive choice. See Fiss (1982); R. Bennett (1984).

111. See chapters 2 and 7.

112. See Noonan; Weyrauch. Lynne Henderson (1587–93) insightfully explores some of the tensions between empathy and the rule of law.

113. Alternatively, theories of limited judicial role offer our judges a variety of means for minimizing the sense of their own responsibility—as the five cases in chapter 1 illustrate. On the "retreat to formalism" and other such strategies among northern judges who brought themselves to enforce the law of slavery, see Cover (1975) 226–38 and passim.

114. Kronman (1987) 221.

115. Gerth and Mills (1970) 95–98, following G. H. Mead.

116. See Riesman, Glazer, and Denney.

117. Smith. See Jencks (1979).

118. Fiss (1979); Fiss (1982). Compare the sociologists' "reference group."

119. Brest (1982); Fish.

120. *Lochner v. New York* (1905) (dissenting opinion).

121. Id. See also Minow (1987c). Lawyers can help judges to see the world from the perspective of the Other. On lawyers' use of "empathic narrative," see Henderson 1593–1649.

122. The name is fictitious; Cox was interviewed in the University of Chicago Jury Project (Broeder 305).

123. Sadly, such a bet is no sure thing; see Note (1985), *Wisconsin Law Review*. Sadder still is the continued reality of jury prejudice. See Johnson; Developments in the Law (1988), *Harvard Law Review* 1597–1641; see also *McCleskey v. Kemp* (1986), chapter 9; R. Kennedy (1988).

124. *New York Times*, Sept. 27, 1987, A13, col. 6.

Bibliography

This bibliography provides full citations for most of the sources cited in the text and notes. As some notes make clear, references not listed here can be found in the articles listed in the Appendix, page 243.

Abraham, Maury. 1986. The crèche case—1986. *Liberty* (Nov.-Dec.): 28.

Ackerman, Bruce A. 1980. *Social Justice in the Liberal State*. New Haven: Yale University Press.

Ackerman, Bruce A. 1984. The Storrs Lectures: Discovering the Constitution. *Yale Law Journal* 93 : 1013.

Ackerman, Bruce A. 1985. Beyond Carolene Products. *Harvard Law Review* 98 : 713.

Alexis, Marcus. 1976. Black and white wealth: A comparative analysis. In *Public Policy for the Black Community: Strategies and Perspectives*, ed. M. Barnett and J. Hefner, 191 New York: Alfred.

Allport, Gordon W. [1954] 1958. *The Nature of Prejudice*. Garden City, NY: Doubleday Anchor.

Almond, Gabriel A., and Verba, Sidney. 1963. *The Civic Culture*. Princeton: Princeton University Press.

Altman, Denis. 1982. *The Homosexualization of America, The Americanization of the Homosexual*. New York: St. Martin's.

Alvarez, Rodolfo. 1985.The psycho-historical and socioeconomic development of the Chicano community in the United States. In *The Mexican American Experience: An Interdisciplinary Anthology*, ed. R. de la García, F. Bean, C. Bonjean, R. Romo, and R. Alvarez, 33. Austin: University of Texas Press.

Anderson, Elijah. 1976. *A Place on the Corner*. Chicago: University of Chicago Press.

Appleby, Joyce Oldham. 1984. *Capitalism and a New Social Order: The Republican Vision of the 1790s*. New York: New York University Press.

Appleby, Joyce Oldham. 1987. The American heritage: the heirs and the disinherited. *Journal of American History* 74 : 798.

Aristotle. See H. Davis.

Arnold, Thurman W. 1937. *The Folklore of Capitalism*. New Haven: Yale University Press.

Arnold, Thurman W. [1935] 1962. *The Symbols of Government*. New York: Harcourt, Brace & World.

Arnow, Pat. 1985. The year we hid our religion. *Liberty* (May-June): 3.

Aron, Raymond. 1972. *Progress and Disillusion: The Dialectics of Modern Society.* Harmondsworth, Middlesex, England: Penguin.

Auletta, Ken. 1982. *The Underclass.* New York: Random House.

Baker, C. Edwin. 1983. Outcome equality or equality of respect: The substantive content of equal protection. *University of Pennsylvania Law Review* 131 : 933.

Baltimore, Roderick T., and Williams, Robert F. 1986. The state constitutional roots of the "separate but equal" doctrine. *Rutgers Law Journal* 17 : 537.

Banfield, Edward C. [1958] 1967. *The Moral Basis of a Backward Society.* New York: Free Press.

Bass, Jack. 1981. *Unlikely Heroes.* New York: Simon and Schuster.

Belenky, Mary Field; Clinchy, Blythe McVicker; Goldberger, Nancy Rule; and Tarule, Jill Mattuck. 1986. *Women's Ways of Knowing: The Development of Self, Voice, and Mind.* New York: Basic Books.

Belknap, Michal R. 1987. *Federal Law and Southern Order: Racial Violence and Constitutional Conflict in the Post-Brown South.* Athens: University of Georgia Press.

Bell, Derrick A. 1976a. Serving two masters: Integration ideals and client interests in school desegregation litigation. *Yale Law Journal* 85 : 470.

Bell, Derrick A. 1976b. Racial remediation: An historical perspective on current conditions. *Notre Dame Lawyer* 52 : 5.

Bell, Derrick A. 1980. Brown v. Board of Education and the interest-convergence dilemma. *Harvard Law Review* 93 : 518.

Bell, Derrick A. 1984a. An American fairy tale: The income-related neutralization of race law precedent. *Suffolk University Law Review* 18 : 331.

Bell, Derrick A. 1984b. A hurdle too high: Class-based roadblocks to racial remediation. *Buffalo Law Review* 33 : 1.

Bell, Derrick A. 1985. The civil rights chronicles. *Harvard Law Review* 99 : 4.

Bellah, Robert N.; Madsen, Richard; Sullivan, William M.; Swidler, Ann; and Tipton, Steven M. [1985] 1986. *Habits of the Heart: Individualism and Commitment in American Life.* New York: Harper and Row.

Bem, Sandra Lipsitz. 1983. Gender schema theory and its implications for child development: Raising gender-aschematic children in a gender-schematic society. *Signs* 8 : 598.

Bender, Thomas. [1978] 1982. *Community and Social Change in America.* Baltimore: The Johns Hopkins University Press.

Bendix, Reinhard. 1960. *Max Weber: Am Intellectual Portrait.* Garden City, NY: Doubleday.

Benedict, Michael Les. 1974. *A Compromise of Principle: Congressional Republicans and Reconstruction, 1863–1869.* New York: W. W. Norton.

Bennett, Lerone. 1976. *What Manner of Man: A Biography of Martin Luther King.* Chicago: Johnson.

Bennett, Robert W. 1983. The Burger Court and the poor. In *The Burger Court: The Counter-Revolution That Wasn't,* ed. V. Blasi. New Haven: Yale University Press.

Bennett, Robert W. 1984. Objectivity in constitutional law. *University of Pennsylvania Law Review* 132 : 445.

Bennett, Robert W. 1984–1985. Reflections on the role of motivation under the equal protection clause. *Northwestern University Law Review* 79 : 1009.

Bentham, Jeremy. [1820] 1931. *The Theory of Legislation.* Ed. C. Ogden. London: Kegan Paul, Trench, Trubner.

Berger, Peter; Berger, Brigitte; and Kellner, Hansfried. [1973] 1974. *The Homeless Mind: Modernization and Consciousness.* New York: Random House.

Berger, Peter L., and Luckmann, Thomas. 1967. *The Social Construction of Reality.* Garden City, NY: Doubleday Anchor.

Berger, Raoul. 1973. *Impeachment: The Constitutional Problems.* Cambridge: Harvard University Press.

Berger, Raoul. 1977. *Government by Judiciary: The Transformation of the Fourteenth Amendment.* Cambridge: Harvard University Press.

Berger, Raoul. 1981. Soifer to the rescue of history. *South Carolina Law Review* 32 : 427.

Bettelheim, Bruno, and Janowitz, Morris. 1950. *Dynamics of Prejudice: A Psychological and Sociological Study of Veterans.* New York: Harper.

Bickel, Alexander M. 1955. The original understanding and the segregation decision. *Harvard Law Review* 69 : 1.

Bickel, Alexander M. 1962. *The Least Dangerous Branch.* Indianapolis: Bobbs-Merrill.

Bickel, Alexander M. 1970. *The Supreme Court and the Idea of Progress.* New York: Harper and Row.

Bickel, Alexander M. 1973. Citizenship in the American constitution. *Arizona Law Review* 15 : 369.

Bickel, Alexander M. 1975. *The Morality of Consent.* New Haven: Yale University Press.

Bickel, Alexander M., and Schmidt, Benno C., Jr. 1984. *The Judiciary and Responsible Government, 1910–21.* Vol. 9, *History of the Supreme Court of the United States,* eds. P. Freund and S. Katz. New York: Macmillan.

Biddle, Francis B. 1962. *In Brief Authority.* Garden City, NY: Doubleday.

Billington, Ray A. [1938] 1964. *The Protestant Crusade, 1880–1860: A Study of the Origins of American Nativism.* Chicago: Quadrangle.

Bindra, Dalbir, and Stewart, Jane. 1971. Introduction. In *Motivation,* 2d ed., eds. D. Bindra and J. Stewart, 11. Harmondsworth, Middlesex, England: Penguin.

Black, Charles L., Jr. 1960a. The lawfulness of the segregation decisions. *Yale Law Journal* 89 : 421.

Black, Charles L., Jr. 1960b. *The People and the Court: Judicial Review in a Democracy.* Englewood Cliffs, NJ: Prentice-Hall.

Black, Charles L., Jr. 1967. The Supreme Court, 1966 term—foreword: "State action," equal protection, and California's Proposition 14. *Harvard Law Review* 81 : 69.

Black, Charles L., Jr. 1969. *Structure and Relationship in Constitutional Law.* Baton Rouge: Louisiana State University Press.

Black, Charles L., Jr. 1970. The unfinished business of the Warren Court. *Washington Law Review* 46 : 3.

Black, Charles L., Jr. 1981. *Capital Punishment: The Inevitability of Caprice and Mistake.* 2d ed. New York: W. W. Norton.

Black, Charles L., Jr. 1986. Further reflections on the constitutional justice of liveli-
hood. *Columbia Law Review* 86 : 1103.
Black, Charles L., Jr. 1987. Reflections on teaching and working in constitutional
law. *Oregon Law Review* 66 : 1.
Blake, Judith. 1969. Population policy for Americans: Is the government being mis-
led? *Science* 164 : 522.
Blasi, Gary L. 1987. Litigation on behalf of the homeless: Systematic approaches.
Washington University Journal of Urban and Contemporary Law 31 : 137.
Blasi, Vincent, 1987. Review: *The Tolerant Society. Columbia Law Review* 87 : 387.
Blassingame, John W. 1979. *The Slave Community: Plantation Life in the Antebel-
lum South.* 2d ed. New York: Oxford University Press.
Blotner, Joseph. [1974]. *Faulkner: A Biography.* New York: Random House.
Blum, John M. 1978. *The Burden of American Equality.* Oxford: Clarendon.
Blumer, Herbert. 1958. Race prejudice as a sense of group position. *Pacific Sociolog-
ical Review* 1 : 3.
Blumrosen, Alfred W. 1968. The duty of fair recruitment under the Civil Rights Act
of 1964. *Rutgers Law Review* 22 : 465.
Blumrosen, Alfred W. 1984. The law transmission system and the southern jurispru-
dence of employment discrimination. *Industrial Relations Law Journal* 6 : 313.
Bollinger, Lee C. 1986. *The Tolerant Society: Freedom of Speech and Extremist Speech
in America.* New York: Oxford University Press.
Boorstin, Daniel J. 1958, 1965, 1972. *The Americans.* 3 vols., *The Colonial Experi-
ence; The National Experience; The Democratic Experience.* New York: Random
House.
Borges, Jorge Luis. 1964. On reason in science. In *Dreamtigers,* trans. M. Boyer and
H. Morland. Austin: University of Texas Press.
Bork, Robert H. 1971. Neutral principles and some First Amendment problems. *In-
diana Law Journal* 47 :1.
Bork, Robert H. 1979. The impossibility of finding welfare rights in the Constitution.
Washington University Law Review (1979): 695.
Bratton, Eleanor K. The eye of the beholder: An interdisciplinary examination of law
and social research on sexual harassment. *New Mexico Law Review* 17 : 91.
Brennan, William J. 1986. The Constitution of the United States: Contemporary
ratification. *South Texas Law Review* 27 : 433.
Brennan, William J. 1987. *Reason, Passion, and "The Progress of the Law."* New
York: Association of the Bar of the City of New York.
Brest, Paul. 1971. Palmer v. Thompson: An approach to the problem of unconstitu-
tional motive. *Supreme Court Review* (1971): 95.
Brest, Paul. 1975. The conscientious legislator's guide to constitutional interpretation.
Stanford Law Review 27 : 585.
Brest, Paul. 1976. The Supreme Court, 1975 term—foreword: In defense of the an-
tidiscrimination principle. *Harvard Law Review* 90 : 1.
Brest, Paul. 1980. The misconceived quest for the original understanding. *Boston
University Law Review* 60 : 204.
Brest, Paul. 1981. The substance of process. *Ohio State Law Journal* 42 : 131.
Brest, Paul. 1982. Interpretation and interest. *Stanford Law Review* 34 : 765.

Brest, Paul. 1985. Who decides? *Southern California Law Review* 58 : 661.

Brest, Paul. 1985–86. Constitutional citizenship. *Cleveland State Law Review* 34 : 175.

Broeder, Dale W. 1972. The Negro in court. In *Race, Crime, and Justice*, eds. C. Reasons and J. Kuykendall. Pacific Palisades, Calif.: Goodyear.

Brown, Ernest J. 1958. The Supreme Court, 1957 term—foreword: Process of law. *Harvard Law Review* 72 : 77.

Bruner, Jerome S. [1962] 1976. *On Knowing: Essays for the Left Hand*. New York: Atheneum.

Bruner, Jerome S. 1986. *Actual Minds, Possible Worlds*. Cambridge: Harvard University Press.

Bumiller, Kristin. 1967. Victims in the shadow of the law: A critique of the model of legal protection. *Signs* 12 : 421.

Burke, Edmund. 1790. Reflections on the revolution in France. Extracted in *Masters of Political Thought*, ed. W. T. Jones, vol. 2, 346–59. Boston: Houghton Mifflin.

Burns, Michael M. 1983. The exclusion of women from influential men's clubs: The inner sanctum and the myth of full equality. *Harvard Civil Rights-Civil Liberties Law Review* 18 : 321.

Burt, Robert A. 1979. The Constitution of the family. *Supreme Court Review* (1979): 329.

Burt, Robert A. 1984. Constitutional law and the teaching of the parables. *Yale Law Journal* 91 : 455.

Burt, Robert A. 1988. *Two Jewish Justices: Outcasts in the Promised Land*. Berkeley: University of California Press.

Calabresi, Guido. 1979. Bakke as pseudo-tragedy. *Catholic University Law Review* 28 : 1.

Calabresi, Guido. 1985. *Ideals, Beliefs, Attitudes, and the Law: Private Law Perspectives on a Public Law Problem*. Syracuse: Syracuse University Press.

Calmore, John O. 1982. Exploring the significance of race and class in representing the black poor. *Oregon Law Review* 61 : 201.

Cano, Liane; Solomon, Sheldon; and Holmes, David S. 1984. Fear of success: The influence of sex, sex-role identity, and components of masculinity. *Sex Roles: A Journal of Research* 10 : 341.

Cardozo, Benjamin N. 1921. *The Nature of the Judicial Process*. New Haven: Yale University Press.

Cardozo, Benjamin N. 1928. *The Paradoxes of Legal Science*. New York: Columbia University Press.

Carey, Jane Perry Clark. 1931. *Deportation of Aliens from the United States to Europe*. New York: Columbia University Press.

Carroll, Lewis. 1962. *The Annotated Snark*. Ed. M. Gardner. New York: Simon and Schuster.

Carson, Clayborne. 1981. *In Struggle: SNCC and the Black Awakening of the 1960s*. Cambridge: Harvard University Press.

Carter, Robert L., and Marshall, Thurgood. 1955. The meaning and significance of the Supreme Court decisions. *Journal of Negro Education* 24 : 397.

Carter, Stephen L. 1988. When victims happen to be black. *Yale Law Journal* 97 : 420.

Cash, Wilbur J. 1941. *The Mind of the South*. New York: Alfred A. Knopf.

Cassirer, Ernst. 1944. *An Essay on Man*. New Haven: Yale University Press.

Chackes, Kenneth M. 1987. Sheltering the homeless: Judicial enforcement of governmental duties to the poor. *Washington University Journal of Urban and Contemporary Law* 31 : 155.

Chambers, Julius L. 1985. Racial justice in the 1980s. *Campbell Law Review* 8 : 29.

Chodorow, Nancy. 1978. *The Reproduction of Mothering*. Berkeley: University of California Press.

Choper, Jesse H. 1963. Religion in the public schools: A proposed constitutional standard. *Minnesota Law Review* 47 : 329.

Choper, Jesse H. 1980. *Judicial Review and the National Political Process: A Functional Reconsideration of the Role of the Supreme Court*. Chicago: University of Chicago Press.

Choper, Jesse H. 1987. Continued uncertainty as to the constitutionality of remedial racial classifications: Identifying the pieces of the puzzle. *Iowa Law Review* 72 : 255.

Clark, Kenneth B. 1979. Contemporary sophisticated racism. In *The Declining Significance of Race? A Dialogue Among Black and White Social Scientists*, ed. J. Washington, Jr. Philadelphia: University of Pennsylvania Press.

Clark, Tom C., and Perlman, Philip B. 1948. *Prejudice and Property: An Historic Brief Against Racial Covenants*. Washington, D.C.: Public Affairs Press.

Clinton, Robert N. 1981. Isolated in their own country: A defense of federal protection of Indian autonomy and self-government. *Stanford Law Review* 33 : 979.

Clune, William H., III. 1975. The Supreme Court's treatment of wealth discrimination under the Fourteenth Amendment. *Supreme Court Review* (1975): 289.

Cobbett, William. 1835. *Cobbett's Legacy to Labourers, or What is the Right Which the Lords, Baronets and Squires Have to the Lands of England?* London: Jowett and Mills.

Cohen, Felix S. 1982. *Felix S. Cohen's Handbook of Federal Indian Law*. Charlottesville: Michie/Bobbs-Merrill.

Cohen, William. 1985. Is equal protection like Oakland? Equality as a surrogate for other rights. *Tulane Law Review* 59 : 884.

Cole, David. 1986. Agon at agora: Creative misreadings in the First Amendment tradition. *Yale Law Journal* 95 : 857.

Colker, Ruth. 1987. Anti-subordination above all: Sex, race, and equal protection. *New York University Law Review* 61 : 1003.

Collins, Glenn. 1985. A new look at intermarriage in the U.S. *New York Times*, Feb. 11, 1985, C13, col. 3.

Comment. See Note.

Connell, John C. 1987. A right to emergency shelter for the homeless under the New Jersey Constitution. *Rutgers Law Review* 18 : 765.

Cortázar, Julio. 1975. *Hopscotch*. Trans. G. Rabassa. New York: Random House.

Cover, Robert M. 1975. *Justice Accused: Antislavery and the Judicial Process*. New Haven: Yale University Press.

Cover, Robert M. 1982. The origins of judicial activism in the protection of minorities. *Yale Law Journal* 91 : 1287.

Cover, Robert M. 1983. The Supreme Court, 1982 term—foreword: Nomos and narrative. *Harvard Law Review* 97 : 4.

Cover, Robert M. 1986a. Violence and the word. *Yale Law Journal* 95 : 1601.

Cover, Robert M. 1986b. The bonds of interpretation: Of the word, the deed, and the role. *Georgia Law Review* 20 : 815.

Cox, Archibald. 1966. The Supreme Court, 1965 term—foreword: Constitutional adjudication and the protection of human rights. *Harvard Law Review* 80 : 91.

Cox, LaWanda C. Fenlason, and Cox, J. 1969. *Politics, Principle, and Prejudice, 1865–1866: Dilemma of Reconstruction America*. New York: Atheneum.

Crenshaw, Kimberlé. 1988. Race, reform and retrenchment: Transformation and legitimation in antidiscrimination law. *Harvard Law Review* 101 : 1331.

Crèvecoeur, J. Hector St. John. [1782] 1957. *Letters from an American Farmer*. New York: E. P. Dutton.

Cruise, Harold. [1967] 1984. *The Crisis of the Negro Intellectual*. New York: Quill.

Cunningham, George K., and Husk, William L. 1984. White flight: A closer look at the assumptions. In *Readings on Equal Education*, eds. M. Barnett and C. Harrington, 371. New York: AMS Press.

Dahrendorf, Ralf. 1962. On the origin of social inequality. In *Philosophy, Politics and Society*, 2d series, eds. P. Laslett and W. Runciman, 88. Oxford: Blackwell.

Daly, Michael. 1985. Hunting the wolf packs. *New York Magazine*. June 3, 1985, p. 28.

Danziger, Sheldon. 1988. *Antipoverty Policy and Welfare Reform*. Paper for Rockefeller Foundation Conference on Welfare Reform, Feb. 1988.

Danziger, Sheldon, and Gottschalk, Peter. 1985. *Losing Ground*: A critique. *IRP Special Report No. 38* (Aug. 1985).

Davis, David Brion. 1966. *The Problem of Slavery in Western Culture*. Ithaca: Cornell University Press.

Davis, David Brion. 1987. Review: The labyrinth of slavery. *New York Review of Books*, Nov. 5, 1987, 34.

Days, Drew S., III. 1987. Fullilove. *Yale Law Journal* 96 : 453.

de Beauvoir, Simone. [1949] 1971. *The Second Sex*. Ed. H. Parsley. New York: Alfred A. Knopf.

de Beauvoir, Simone. 1952. *America Day by Day*. London: G. Duckworth.

DeCecco, John P., ed. 1985. *Bashers, Baiters & Bigots: Homophobia in American Society*. New York: Harrington Park.

Delgado, Richard. 1984. The imperial scholar: Reflections on a review of civil rights literature. *University of Pennsylvania Law Review* 132 : 561.

Delgado, Richard. 1987. The ethereal scholar: Does Critical Legal Studies have what minorities want? *Harvard Civil Rights-Civil Liberties Law Review* 22 : 301.

Delgado, Richard; Dunn, Chris; Brown, Pamela; Lee, Helena; and Hubbert, David. 1985. Fairness and formality: Minimizing the risk of prejudice in alternative dispute resolution. *Wisconsin Law Review* (1985): 1359.

Deloria, Vine, Jr. 1973. *God is Red*. New York: Grosset & Dunlap.

Deloria, Vine, Jr. and Lytle, Clifford M. 1983. *American Indians, American Justice*. Austin: University of Texas Press.

Deloria, Vine, Jr., and Lytle, Clifford M. 1984. *The Nations Within: The Past and Future of American Indian Sovereignty*. New York: Pantheon.

D'Emilio, John. 1983a. *Sexual Politics, Sexual Communities: The Making of a Ho-*

mosexual Minority in the United States, 1940–1970. Chicago: University of Chicago Press.

D'Emilio, John. 1983b. Capitalism and gay identity. In *Powers of Desire: the Politics of Sexuality*, ed. A. Snitow, C. Stansell, and S. Thompson. New York: Monthly Review Press.

Deschamps, Jean-Claude. 1982. Social identity and relations of power between groups. In *Social Identity and Intergroup Relations*, ed. H. Tajfel, 85. Cambridge: Cambridge University Press.

Developments in the Law. 1969. Equal protection. *Harvard Law Review* 82 : 1065.

Developments in the Law. 1983. Immigration policy and the rights of aliens. *Harvard Law Review* 96 : 1286.

Developments in the Law. 1987. Religion and the state. *Harvard Law Review* 100 : 1606.

Developments in the Law. 1988. Race and the criminal process. *Harvard Law Review* 101 : 1472.

Diamond, Raymond T., and Cottrol, Robert J. 1983. Codifying caste: Louisiana's racial classification scheme and the Fourteenth Amendment. *Loyola Law Review* 29 : 255.

Diggins, John P. 1984. *The Lost Soul of American Politics: Virtue, Self-Interest, and the Foundations of Liberalism* New York: Basic Books.

di Leonardo, Micaela. 1984. *The Varieties of Ethnic Experience: Kinship, Class, and Gender among California Italian-Americans.* Ithaca: Cornell University Press.

Dimond, Paul R. 1982. Strict construction and judicial review of racial discrimination under the equal protection clause: Meeting Raoul Berger on interpretivist grounds. *Michigan Law Review* 80 : 462.

Dimond, Paul R. 1983. The anti-caste principle—toward a constitutional standard for review of race cases. *Wayne Law Review* 30 : 1.

Dinnerstein, Dorothy. [1976] 1977. *The Mermaid and the Minotaur: Sexual Arrangements and the Human Malaise.* New York: Harper and Row.

Dollard, John. 1957. *Caste and Class in a Southern Town.* Garden City, N.Y.: Doubleday Anchor.

Dorsen, Norman, and Sims, Charles. The Nativity scene case: An error of judgment. *University of Illinois Law Forum* 985 : 837.

Douglass, Frederick. [1892] 1962. *Life and Times of Frederick Douglass.* New York: Collier Books.

Downs, Donald A. 1985. *Nazis in Skokie: Freedom, Community, and the First Amendment.* Notre Dame, Ind.: University of Notre Dame Press.

DuBois, Ellen Carol. 1987. Outgrowing the compact of the fathers: Equal rights, woman suffrage, and the United States Constitution, 1820–1878. *Journal of American History* 74 : 836.

Du Bois W. E. B. 1940. *Dusk of Dawn: An Essay toward an Autobiography of a Race Concept.* New York: Harcourt, Brace.

Du Bois, W. E. B. 1970. *W. E. B. Du Bois Speaks: Speeches and Addresses, 1890–1919.* Ed. P. Foner. New York: Pathfinder.

Du Bois, W. E. B. 1972. *The Crisis Writings.* Ed. D. Walden. Greenwich, Conn.: Fawcett Publications.

Dumont, Louis. 1961. On putative hierarchy and some analogies to it. *Contributions to Indian Sociology*, New series, 5 : 1.

Durkheim, Emile. [1893] 1933. *Division of Labor in Society*. Trans. G. Simpson. New York: Free Press.

Durkheim, Emile. 1951. *Suicide: A Study in Sociology*. Trans. J. Spaulding and G. Simpson. New York: Free Press.

Durkheim, Emile. 1983. *Durkheim and the Law*. Eds. S. Lukes and A. Scull. New York: St. Martin's.

Dworkin, Ronald. 1977. *Taking Rights Seriously*. Cambridge: Harvard University Press.

Dworkin, Ronald. 1986. *Law's Empire*. Cambridge: Belknap Press, Harvard University Press.

Easterbrook, Frank H. 1982. Ways of criticizing the Court. *Harvard Law Review* 95:805.

Edelman, Peter B. 1987. The next century of our Constitution: Rethinking our duty to the poor. *Hastings Law Journal* 39 : 1.

Eisenberg, Theodore. 1977. Disproportionate impact and illicit motive. *New York University Law Review* 52 : 36.

Ellison, Ralph. 1952. *Invisible Man*. New York: Random House.

Ellwood, David T., and Summers, Lawrence H. 1986. Poverty in America: Is welfare the answer to the problem? In *Fighting Poverty: What Works and What Doesn't?* eds. S. Danziger and D. Weinberg. Cambridge: Harvard University Press.

Elman, Philip. 1987a. The solicitor general's office, Justice Frankfurter, and civil rights litigation, 1946–60: An oral history. *Harvard Law Review* 100 : 817.

Elman, Philip. 1987b. Response [to Randall Kennedy]. *Harvard Law Review* 100 : 1949.

Ely, John Hart. 1973. The wages of crying wolf: A comment on Roe v. Wade. *Yale Law Journal* 82 : 920.

Ely, John Hart. 1974. The constitutionality of reverse racial discrimination. *University of Chicago Law Review* 41 : 723.

Ely, John Hart. 1980. *Democracy and Distrust: A Theory of Judicial Review*. Cambridge: Harvard University Press.

Epstein, Benjamin R., and Forster, Arnold. 1962. *Some of My Best Friends . . .* New York: Farrar, Straus and Cudahy.

Erikson, Erik. 1977. *Toys and Reasons: Stages in the Ritualization of Experience*. New York: W. W. Norton.

Estrich, Susan. 1986. Rape. *Yale Law Journal* 95 : 1087.

Estrich, Susan. 1987. *Real Rape*. Cambridge: Harvard University Press.

Fairman, Charles. 1971. *Reconstruction and Reunion, 1864–88, Part 1*. Vol. 6, *History of the Supreme Court of the United States*, ed. P. Freund. New York: Macmillan.

Fallon, Richard H., Jr. 1980. To each according to his ability, from none according to his race: The concept of merit in the law of antidiscrimination. *Boston University Law Review* 60 : 815.

Fallon, Richard H., Jr. 1984. Of justiciability, remedies, and public law litigation: Notes on the jurisprudence of Lyons. *New York University Law Review* 59 : 1.

Fallon, Richard H., Jr. 1987. A constructivist coherence theory of constitutional interpretation. *Harvard Law Review* 100 : 1189.

Fallon, Richard H., Jr., and Weiler, Paul M. 1984. Firefighters v. Stotts: Conflicting models of racial justice. *Supreme Court Review* 1984 : 1.

Farley, Reynolds, and Allen, Walter R. 1987. *The Color Line and the Quality of Life in America.* New York: Russell Sage Foundation.

Feagin, Joe R. 1975. *Subordinating the Poor: Welfare and American Beliefs.* Englewood Cliffs, N.J.: Prentice-Hall.

Federalist, The. See *The Federalist.*

Fehrenbacher, Don E. 1978. *The Dred Scott Case: Its Significance in American Law and Politics.* New York: Oxford University Press.

Felstiner, William L. F. 1974. Influences of social organization on dispute processing. *Law and Society Review* 9 : 63.

Felstiner, William L. F. 1975. Avoidance as dispute processing: An elaboration. *Law and Society Review* 9 : 695.

Felstiner, William L. F.; Abel, Richard L.; and Sarat, Austin. 1980–81. The emergence and transformation of disputes: Naming, blaming, claiming. *Law and Society Review* 15 : 631.

Ferguson, Kathy E. 1984. *The Feminist Case Against Bureaucracy.* Philadelphia: Temple University Press.

Finkelhor, David, and Yllo, Kersti. 1987. *License to Rape: Sexual Abuse of Wives.* New York: Free Press.

Finkelman, Paul. 1986. Prelude to the Fourteenth Amendment: Black legal rights in the antebellum north. *Rutgers Law Review* 17 : 415.

Finley, Lucinda M. 1986. Transcending equality theory: A way out of the maternity and the workplace debate. *Columbia Law Review* 86 : 1118.

Fishkin, James S. 1983. *Justice, Equal Opportunity, and the Family.* New Haven: Yale University Press.

Fiss, Owen M. 1976. Groups and the equal protection clause. *Philosophy and Public Affairs* 5 : 107.

Fiss, Owen M. 1977. Dombrowski. *Yale Law Journal* 86 : 1103.

Fiss, Owen M. 1979. The Supreme Court, 1978 term—foreword: The forms of justice. *Harvard Law Review* 93 : 1.

Fiss, Owen M. 1982. Objectivity and interpretation. *Stanford Law Review* 34 : 739.

Fiss, Owen M. 1986. Racial discrimination. In *Encyclopedia of the American Constitution,* eds. L. Levy, K. Karst, and D. Mahoney, 1500. New York: Macmillan.

FitzGerald, Frances. 1986. *Cities on a Hill: A Journey Through Contemporary American Cultures.* New York: Simon and Schuster.

Foner, Eric. 1987. Rights and the Constitution in black life during the Civil War and Reconstruction. *Journal of American History* 74 : 865.

Forbath, William E. 1984. The ambiguities of free labor: Labor and law in the Gilded Age. *Wisconsin Law Review* (1984): 767.

Frank, Jerome. 1949. *Law and the Modern Mind.* New York: Coward-McCann.

Frankfurter, Felix. 1956. John Marshall and the judicial function. *Harvard Law Review* 69 : 217.

Franklin, John Hope. 1963. *The Emancipation Proclamation.* Garden City, N.Y.: Doubleday.

Franklin, John Hope. [1965] 1968. Jim Crow goes to school: The genesis of legal segregation in the South. In *The Negro in the South Since 1865*, ed. C. Wynes. New York: Harper and Row.

Fredrickson, George M. 1971. *The Black Image in the White Mind: The Debate on Afro-American Character and Destiny, 1817–1914*. New York: Harper and Row.

Freeman, Alan David. 1978. Legitimizing racial discrimination through antidiscrimination law: A critical review of Supreme Court doctrine. *Minnesota Law Review* 62 : 1049.

Freeman, Richard B. 1982. Program report: Labor studies. *NBER Reporter* (Summer 1982): 1.

Friedrich, Carl J. 1957. The concept of community in the history of political and legal philosophy. In *NOMOS II: Community*, ed. C. Friedrich, 3. New York: Liberal Arts Press.

Fromm, Erich. 1941. *Escape from Freedom*. New York: Rinehart.

Furnas, Joseph C. 1969. *The Americans: A Social History of the United States, 1587–1914*. New York: Putnam.

Furnish, Hannah Arterian. 1984. Formalistic solutions to complex problems: The Supreme Court's analysis of individual disparate treatment cases under Title VII. *Industrial Relations Law Journal* 6 : 353.

Gabriel, Ralph Henry. 1940. *The Course of American Democratic Thought: An Intellectual History Since 1815*. New York: Ronald Press Company.

Galbraith, John Kenneth. [1958] 1972. *The Affluent Society*. Boston: Houghton Mifflin.

Galin, David. [1976] 1977. The two modes of consciousness and the two halves of the brain. In *Symposium on Consciousness*, ed. P. Lee, R. Ornstein, D. Galin, A. Deikman, C. Tart. New York: Penguin.

Garfinkel, Harold. 1956. Conditions of successful degradation ceremonies. *American Journal of Sociology* 61 : 420.

Garet, Ronald R. 1983. Communality and existence: The rights of groups. *Southern California Law Review* 56 : 1001.

Geertz, Clifford. 1963. The integrative revolution: Primordial sentiments and civil politics in the new states. In *Old Societies and New States*, ed. C. Geertz. New York: Free Press.

Geertz, Clifford. 1973. *The Interpretation of Cultures: Selected Essays*. New York: Basic Books.

Genovese, Eugene D. 1974. *Roll, Jordan, Roll: The World the Slaves Made*. New York: Pantheon, Random House.

Gerth, Hans, and Mills, C. Wright. [1946] 1958. *From Max Weber: Essays in Sociology*. New York: Oxford University Press.

Gerth, Hans, and Mills, C. Wright. [1954] 1970. *Character and Social Structure: The Psychology of Social Institutions*. London: Routledge and Kegan Paul.

Gewirtz, Paul. 1983. Remedies and resistance. *Yale Law Journal* 92 : 585.

Gillette, William. 1969. *The Right to Vote: Politics and the Passage of the Fifteenth Amendment*. Baltimore: The Johns Hopkins University Press.

Gilligan, Carol. 1982. *In A Different Voice: Psychological Theory and Women's Development*. Cambridge: Harvard University Press.

Gilligan, Carol. 1986. Remapping the moral domain: New images of the self in relationship. In *Reconstructing Individualism: Autonomy, Individuality, and the Self in Western Thought*, ed. T. Heller, M. Sosna, and D. Wellbery. Stanford: Stanford University Press.

Gilligan, Carol. 1985. Comments in: Feminist discourse, moral values, and the law— a conversation. *Buffalo Law Review* 34 : 36–64.

Ginsburg, Ralph, 1969. *One Hundred Years of Lynchings*. New York: Lancer.

Ginsburg, Ruth Bader. 1978. Some thoughts on benign classifications in the context of sex. *Connecticut Law Review* 10 : 813.

Ginsburg, Ruth Bader. 1983. The Burger Court's grapplings with sex discrimination. In *The Burger Court: The Counter-Revolution That Wasn't*, ed. V. Blasi. New Haven: Yale University Press.

Ginsburg, Ruth Bader. 1985. Some thoughts on autonomy and equality in relation to Roe v. Wade. *North Carolina Law Review* 63 : 375.

Glasgow, Douglas. 1980. *The Black Underclass: Poverty, Unemployment, and Entrapment of Ghetto Youth*. San Francisco: Jossey-Bass.

Glazer, Nathan. 1966. Foreword. In *The Negro Family in the United States*, rev. ed., by E. Franklin Frazier. Chicago: University of Chicago Press.

Gleason, Philip. 1982. American identity and Americanization. In *Concepts of Ethnicity*, ed. W. Petersen, M. Novak, and P. Gleason. Cambridge: Harvard University Press.

Glendon, Mary Ann. 1987. *Abortion and Divorce in Western Law*. Cambridge: Harvard University Press.

Goffman, Erving. 1963. *Stigma: Notes on the Management of Spoiled Identity*. Englewood Cliffs, N.J.: Prentice-Hall.

Goldman, Emma. 1972. *Red Emma Speaks: Writings and Speeches by Emma Goldman*, ed. A. Shulman. New York: Vintage.

Goldman, Sheldon. 1987. Reagan's second-term judicial appointments: The battle at midway. *Judicature* 70 : 324.

Goldstein, Robert D. 1977. A Swann song for remedies: Equitable relief in the Burger Court. *Harvard Civil Rights-Civil Liberties Law Review* 13 : 1.

Goldstein, Robert D. 1988. *Mother-Love and Abortion: A Legal Interpretation*. Berkeley: University of California Press.

Goodwin, Leonard. 1981. *Do the Poor Want to Work? A Social-Psychological Study of Work Orientations*. Washington, D.C.: Brookings Institution.

Gordon, Robert W. 1984. Critical legal histories. *Stanford Law Review* 36 : 57.

Gottlieb, Stephen E. 1986. Commentary: Reformulating the motive/effects debate in constitutional adjudication. *Wayne Law Review* 33 : 97.

Green, Richard. 1980. Patterns of sexual identity in childhood: Relationship to subsequent sexual partner practice. In *Homosexual Behavior: A Modern Reappraisal*, ed. J. Marmor, 255. New York: Basic Books.

Greenawalt, Kent. 1975. Judicial scrutiny of "benign" racial preference in law school admissions. *Columbia Law Review* 75 : 559.

Greenawalt, Kent. 1978. The enduring significance of neutral principles. *Columbia Law Review* 78 : 982.

Greenawalt, Kent. 1983. How empty is the idea of equality? *Columbia Law Review* 83 : 1167.

Greenberg, Jack. 1977. *Cases and Materials on Judicial Process and Social Change: Constitutional Litigation.* St. Paul: West.

Greenberg, Jack. 1982. Capital punishment as a system. *Yale Law Journal* 91 : 908.

Greenberg, Jack. 1986. Against the American system of capital punishment. *Harvard Law Review* 99 : 1670.

Greene, Victor R. 1987. *American Immigrant Leaders, 1800–1910: Marginality and Identity.* Balitmore: The Johns Hopkins University Press.

Grey, Thomas C. 1975. Do we have an unwritten Constitution? *Stanford Law Review* 27 : 703.

Grey, Thomas C. 1978. Origins of the unwritten Constitution: Fundamental law in American Revolutionary thought. *Stanford Law Review* 30 : 843.

Grey, Thomas C. 1984. The Constitution as scripture. *Stanford Law Review* 37 : 1.

Grey, Thomas C. 1985. The hermeneutics file. *Southern California Law Review* 58 : 211.

Grodzins, Morton. 1949. *Americans Betrayed: Politics and the Japanese Evacuation.* Chicago: University of Chicago Press.

Gunther, Gerald. 1972. The Supreme Court, 1971 term—foreword: In search of evolving doctrine on a changing Court: A model for a newer equal protection. *Harvard Law Review* 86 : 1.

Gunther, Gerald. 1974. Judicial hegemony and legislative autonomy: The Nixon case and the impeachment process. *UCLA Law Review* 22 : 30.

Gunther, Gerald. 1979. Commentary: Some reflections on the judicial role: Distinctions, roots, and prospects. *Washington University Law Quarterly* (1979): 817.

Gunther, Gerald. 1985. *Constitutional Law.* 11th ed. Mineola, N.Y.: Foundation Press.

Gusfield, Joseph R. 1963. *Symbolic Crusade: Status Politics and the American Temperance Movement.* Urbana: University of Illinois Press.

Gusfield, Joseph R. 1967. Moral passage: The symbolic process in public designations of deviance. *Social Problems* 15 : 175.

Gusfield, Joseph R. 1975. *Community: A Critical Response.* New York: Harper and Row.

Gwaltney, John Langston. 1981. *Drylongso: A Self-Portrait of Black America.* New York: Vintage, Random House.

Hacker, Andrew. 1983. Where have the jobs gone? *New York Review of Books,* June 30, 1983, 27.

Hacker, Andrew. 1987. American apartheid. *New York Review of Books,* Dec. 3, 1987, 26.

Hagan, William T. 1975. *American Indians.* Rev. ed. Chicago: University of Chicago Press.

Hakuta, Kenji. 1986. *Mirror of Language: The Debate on Bilingualism.* New York: Basic Books.

Hale, Robert L. 1944. The Supreme Court and the contract clause. *Harvard Law Review* 57 : 512, 621, 852.

Hall, Jacquelyn Dowd. 1983. "The mind that burns in each body": Women, rape, and racial violence. In *Powers of Desire*, ed. A. Snitow, C. Stanstell, and S. Thompson. New York: Monthly Review Press.

Hampshire, Stuart, ed. 1978. *Public and Private Morality*. Cambridge: Cambridge University Press.

Handler, Joel F. 1972. *Reforming the Poor*. New York: Basic Books.

Handler, Joel F. 1987. Review: The assault on the ablebodied. *Reviews in American History* 15 : 394.

Handlin, Oscar. 1973. *The Uprooted*. 2d ed. Boston: Little, Brown.

Hansen, Marcus Lee. [1940] 1964. *The Immigrant in American History*. New York: Harper and Row.

Hantzis, Catharine. 1987. Review: Is gender justice a completed agenda? *Harvard Law Review* 100 : 690.

Harrington, Michael. 1984. *The New American Poverty*. New York: Holt, Rinehart and Winston.

Harrington, Mona. 1982. Loyalties: Dual and divided. In *The Politics of Ethnicity*, ed. M. Walzer, E. Kantowicz, J. Higham, and M. Harrington. Cambridge: Harvard University Press.

Harrington, Mona. 1986. *The Dream of Deliverance in American Politics*. New York: Alfred A. Knopf.

Hart, Henry M., Jr. 1959. The Supreme Court, 1958 term—foreword: The time chart of the Justices. *Harvard Law Review* 73 : 84.

Hart, Henry M., Jr. 1956. Comment. In *Government Under Law*, ed. A. Sutherland. New York: Da Capo.

Hart, Henry M., Jr. 1953. The power of Congress to limit the jurisdiction of the federal courts: An exercise in dialectic. *Harvard Law Review* 66 : 1362.

Hartog, Hendrik. 1987. The Constitution of aspiration and "the rights that belong to us." *Journal of American History* 74 : 1013.

Hartz, Louis. 1955. *The Liberal Tradition in America: An Interpretation of American Political Thought Since the Revolution*. New York: Harcourt Brace Jovanovich.

Hayes, Robert. 1987. Litigating on behalf of shelter for the poor. *Harvard Civil Rights-Civil Liberties Law Review* 22 : 79.

Hazard, Geoffrey C., Jr. 1987. Permissive affirmative action for the benefit of blacks. *University of Illinois law Review* (1987): 379.

Henderson, Lynne N. 1987. Legality and empathy. *Michigan Law Review* 85 : 1574.

Henkin, Louis. 1963. Shelley v. Kraemer: Notes for a revised opinion. *University of Pennsylvania Law Review* 110 : 473.

Henkin, Louis. 1987. The Constitution and United States sovereignty: A century of Chinese exclusion and its progeny. *Harvard Law Review* 100 : 853.

Herek, Gregory M. 1985. Beyond "homophobia": A social psychological perspective on attitudes toward lesbians and gay men. In *Bashers, Baiters & Bigots: Homophobia in American Society*, ed. J. DeCecco. New York: Harrington Park.

Hertzberg, Hazel W. 1971. *The Search for an American Indian Identity: Modern Pan-Indian Movements*. Syracuse: Syracuse University Press.

Higginbotham, A. Leon. 1978. *In the Matter of Color: Race and the American Legal Process: The Colonial Period*. New York: Oxford University Press.

Higham, John. 1974. Hanging together: Divergent unities in American history. *Journal of American History* 61 : 5.

Higham, John. 1981. *Strangers in the Land: Patterns of American Nativism 1860–1925.* 2d ed. New Brunswick, N.J.: Rutgers University Press.

Higham, John. [1965] 1983. *History: Professional Scholarship in America.* Baltimore: The Johns Hopkins University Press.

Higham, John. 1984. *Send These to Me: Immigrants in Urban America.* Rev. ed. Baltimore: The Johns Hopkins University.

Hill, Herbert. 1984. Race and ethnicity in organized labor: The historical sources of resistance to affirmative action. *Journal of Intergroup Relations* 12 : 5.

Hill, Robert A., ed. 1983. *The Marcus Garvey and Universal Negro Improvement Association papers.* Berkeley: University of California Press.

Himmelfarb, Gertrude. 1984. *The Idea of Poverty: England in the Early Industrial Age.* New York: Alfred A. Knopf.

Hoffman, Martin. 1968. *The Gay World: Male Homosexuality and the Social Creation of Evil.* New York: Basic Books.

Hofstadter, Richard. 1958. Commentary: Have there been discernible shifts in American values during the past generation? In *The American Style: Essays in Value and Performance,* ed. E. Morison, 353. New York: Harper.

Holmes, Oliver Wendell, Jr. [1920] *Collected Legal papers.* New York: Peter Smith.

Holmes, Oliver Wendell, Jr. [1881] 1964. *The Common Law.* Boston: Little, Brown.

Horowitz, Donald L. 1977. *The Courts and Social Policy.* Washington, D.C.: Brookings Institution.

Horowitz, Harold W. 1957. The misleading search for "state action" under the Fourteenth Amendment. *Southern California Law Review* 30 : 208.

Horowitz, Harold W. 1966. Unseparate but unequal—the emerging Fourteenth Amendment issue in public school education. *UCLA Law Review* 13 : 1147.

House of Representatives (U.S.). 1984. Report No. 748, 98th Congress, 2d Session, reprinted in *1984 U.S. Code, Congressional and Administrative News,* 4036.

Houston, Paul. 1984. English pushed as official U.S. language. *Los Angeles Times,* June 13, 1984, pt. 1, 5, col. 4.

Hovenkamp, Herbert. 1985. Social science and segregation before Brown. *Duke Law Journal* 1985: 624.

Howard, A. E. Dick. 1968. *The Road from Runnymede.* Charlottesville: University of Virginia Press.

Hughes, Charles Evans. 1928. *The Supreme Court of the United States—Its Foundation, Methods and Achievements: An Interpretation.* New York: Columbia University Press.

Huntington, Samuel P. 1981. *American Politics: The Promise of Disharmony.* Cambridge: Belknap Press, Harvard University Press.

Hyman, Harold M., ed. 1967. *The Radical Republicans and Reconstruction, 1861–1870.* Indianapolis: Bobbs-Merrill.

Hyman, Harold M., and Wiecek, William M. 1982. *Equal Justice Under Law: Constitutional Development, 1835–1875.* New York: Harper and Row.

Ingber, Stanley. 1981. The interface of myth and practice in law. *Vanderbilt Law Review* 34 : 309.

Irons, Peter. 1983. *Justice at War*. New York: Oxford University Press.

Isaacs, Harold R. 1975. *Idols of the Tribe: Group Identity and Political Change*. New York: Harper Colophon.

Jakosa, Jody Young. 1984. Parsing public from private: The failure of differential state action analysis. *Harvard Civil Rights-Civil Liberties Law Review* 19 : 193.

Janowitz, Morris. 1978. *The Last Half-Century: Societal Change and Politics in America*. Chicago: University of Chicago Press.

Jencks, Christopher. 1972. *Inequality*. New York: Harper and Row.

Jencks, Christopher. 1979. The social basis of unselfishness. In *On the Making of Americans*, ed. H. Gans, N. Glazer, J. Gusfield, and C. Jencks. Philadelphia: University of Pennsylvania Press.

Jencks, Christopher. 1985. How poor are the poor? *New York Review of Books*, May 9, 1985, 41.

Johnson, Sheri Lynn. 1985. Black innocence and the white jury. *Michigan Law Review* 83 : 1611.

Jones, Jacqueline. [1985] 1986. *Labor of Love, Labor of Sorrow: Black Women, Work, and the Family from Slavery to the Present*. New York: Vintage, Random House.

Jones, Kathleen B. 1987. On authority: Or, why women are not entitled to speak. In *NOMOS XIX: Authority Revisited*, eds. J. Pennock and J. Chapman, 152. New York: New York University Press.

Jones, Maldwyn Allen. 1960. *American Immigration*. Chicago: University of Chicago Press.

Jordan, Winthrop D. 1968. *White Over Black: American Attitudes Toward the Negro, 1550–1812*. Chapel Hill: University of North Carolina Press.

Kalven, Harry, Jr. 1965. *The Negro and the First Amendment*. Columbus: Ohio State University Press.

Kammen, Michael. 1986. *A Machine That Would Go of Itself: The Constitution in American Culture*. New York: Alfred A. Knopf.

Kanter, Rosabeth Moss. 1977a. *Men and Women of the Corporation*. New York: Basic Books. Inc.

Kanter, Rosabeth Moss. 1977b. Some effects of proportions on group life: Skewed sex ratios and responses to token women. *American Journal of Sociology* 82 : 965.

Kaplan, John. 1963. Segregation litigation and the schools—part II: The general northern problem. *Northwestern University Law Review* 58 : 157.

Karst, Kenneth L. See articles listed in Appendix, page 243.

Katz, Irwin. 1981. *Stigma—A Social Psychological Analysis*. Hillsdale, N.J.: Lawrence Erlbaum Associates.

Katz, Michael B. 1986. *In the Shadow of the Poorhouse: A Social History of Welfare in America*. New York: Basic books.

Kay, Herma Hill. 1985. Models of equality. *University of Illinois Law Review* 1985: 39.

Kelsen, Hans. 1945. *General Theory of Law and State*. Trans. A. Wedberg. Cambridge: Harvard University Press.

Kennedy, Duncan. 1979. The structure of Blackstone's Commentaries. *Buffalo Law Review* 28 : 205.

Kennedy, Randall. 1986. Persuasion and distrust: A comment on the affirmative action debate. *Harvard Law Review* 99 : 1327.

Kennedy, Randall L. 1987a. A reply to Philip Elman. *Harvard Law Review* 100 : 1938.

Kennedy, Randall L. 1987b. Afro-American faith in the civil religion: Or, yes, I would sign the Constitution. *William and Mary Law Review* 29 : 163.

Kennedy, Randall L. 1988. *McCleskey v. Kemp*: Race, capital punishment, and the Supreme Court. *Harvard Law Review* 101 : 1388.

Kerber, Linda K.; Greeno, Catherine G.; Maccoby, Eleanor E.; Luria, Zella; Stack, Carol B.; and Gilligan, Carol. 1986. On *In a Different Voice*: An interdisciplinary forum. *Signs* 11 : 304.

Kettner, James H. *The Development of American Citizenship, 1608–1870*. Chapel Hill: University of North Carolina Press.

Kidder, Louise H.; Fagan, Michele A.; and Cohn, Ellen S. 1981. Giving and receiving: Social justice in close relationships. In *The Justice Motive in Social Behavior: Adapting to Times of Scarcity and Change*, ed. M. Lerner and S. Lerner, 235. New York: Plenum.

Kinder, Donald R., and Sears, David O. 1981. Prejudice and politics: Symbolic racism versus racial threats to the good life. *Journal of personality and Social Psychology* 40 : 414.

King, Martin Luther, Jr. 1958. *Stride Toward Freedom*. New York: Harper and Row.

King, Martin Luther, Jr. 1967. *Where Do We Go from Here: Chaos or Community?* Boston: Beacon.

Kinoy, Arthur. 1967. The constitutional right of Negro freedom. *Rutgers Law Review* 21 : 387.

Klein, Melanie. 1946. Notes on some schizoid mechanisms. *International Journal of Psycho-Analysis*. 27 : 99.

Kloppenberg, James T. 1987. The virtues of liberalism: Christianity, republicanism, and ethics in early American political discourse. *Journal of American History* 74 : 9.

Kluger, Richard. 1975. *Simple Justice: The History of Brown v. Board of Education and Black America's Struggle for Equality*. New York: Alfred A. Knopf.

Koestler, Arthur. 1964. *The Act of Creation*. New York: Macmillan.

Kohn, Hans. 1957. *American Nationalism: An Interpretive Essay*. New York: Macmillan.

Komesar, Neil K. 1984. Taking institutions seriously: Introduction to a strategy for constitutional analysis. *University of Chicago Law Review* 51 : 366.

Komesar, Neil K. 1987. Back to the future—an institutional view of making and interpreting constitutions. *Northwestern University Law Review* 81 : 191.

Komesar, Neil K. 1988. A job for the judges: The judiciary and the Constitution in a massive and complex society. *Michigan Law Review* 86 : 657.

Krieger, Linda J., and Cooney, Patricia N. 1983. The Miller-Wohl controversy: Equal treatment, positive action and the meaning of women's equality. *Golden Gate Law Review* 13 : 513.

Kronman, Anthony T. 1983. *Max Weber*. Stanford: Stanford University Press.

Kronman, Anthony T. 1987. Practical wisdom and professional character. *Social Philosophy* 4 : 203.

Kurland, Philip B. 1964. The Supreme Court, 1963 term—foreword: "Equal in origin and equal in title to the legislative and executive branches of the government." *Harvard Law Review* 78 : 143.

Kurland, Philip B. 1972. The privileges or immunities clause: "Its hour come round at last"? *Washington University Law Quarterly* 1972: 405.

Kutler, Stanley I. 1968. *Judicial Power and Reconstruction Politics.* Chicago: University of Chicago Press.

Ladd, John. 1959. The concept of community: A logical analysis. In *NOMOS II: Community,* ed. C. Friedrich, 269. New York: Liberal Arts Press.

Ladner, Joyce. 1972. *Tomorrow's Tomorrow: The Black Woman.* Garden City, N.Y.: Doubleday Anchor.

Landry, Bart. 1987. *The New Black Middle Class.* Berkeley: University of California Press.

Lasch, Christopher. *The Culture of Narcissism.* 1979. New York: Warner.

Laslett, Peter. 1956. The face to face society. In *Philosophy, Politics and Society,* ed. P. Laslett. New York: Macmillan.

Law, Sylvia A. 1983. Woman, work, welfare, and the preservation of hierarchy. *University of Pennsylvania Law Review* 131 : 1249.

Law, Sylvia A. 1984. Rethinking sex and the Constitution. *University of Pennsylvania Law Review* 132 : 955.

Lawrence, Charles R., III. 1977. Segregation misunderstood: The Milliken decision revisited. *University of San Francisco Law Review* 12 : 15.

Lawrence, Charles R., III. 1986. A dream: On discovering the significance of fear. *Nova Law Journal* 10 : 627.

Lawrence, Charles R., III. 1987. The id, the ego, and equal protection: Reckoning with unconscious racism. *Stanford Law Review* 30 : 317.

Laycock, Douglas. 1981. Review: Taking constitutions seriously: A theory of judicial review. *Texas Law Review* 59 : 343.

Laycock, Douglas. 1986a. Statistical proof and theories of discrimination. *Law and Contemporary Problems* 49 : 97.

Laycock, Douglas. 1986b. Equal access and moments of silence: The equal status of religious speech by private speakers. *Northwestern University Law Review* 81 : 1.

Leflar, Robert A., and Davis, Wylie H. 1954. Segregation in the public schools—1953. *Harvard Law Review* 67 : 377.

Lemann, Nicholas. 1986. The origins of the underclass. *The Atlantic Monthly,* June 1986, 31, and July 1986, 54.

Lenz, Elinor, and Myerhoff, Barbara. 1985. *The Feminization of America: How Women's Values are Changing Our Public and Private Lives.* Los Angeles: Jeremy P. Tarcher.

Leonard, Jonathan S. 1984a. *Employment and Occupational Advance Under Affirmative Action.* Cambridge: National Bureau of Economic Research, working paper no. 1270.

Leonard, Jonathan S. 1984b. *The Impact of Affirmative Action on Employment.* Cambridge: National Bureau of Economic Research, working paper no. 1310.

Lerner, Max. 1937. Constitution and Court as symbols. *Yale Law Journal* 46 : 1290.

Lerner, Ralph. 1967. The Supreme Court as republican schoolmaster. *Supreme Court Review* 1967: 127.

Levi, Edward H. 1949. *An Introduction to Legal Reasoning.* Chicago: University of Chicago Press.

Levine, Lawrence W. 1977. *Black Culture and Black Consciousness: Afro-American Folk Thought from Slavery to Freedom.* New York: Oxford University Press.

Levinson, Sanford. 1979. "The Constitution" in American civil religion. *Supreme Court Review* (1979): 123.

Levinson, Sanford. 1986. Constituting communities through words that bind: Reflections on loyalty oaths. *Michigan Law Review* 84 : 1440.

Levinson, Sanford. 1987. Pledging faith in the civil religion: Or, would you sign the constitution? *William and Mary Law Review* 29 : 113.

Levitan, Sar A. 1985. *Programs in Aid of the Poor.* 5th ed. Baltimore: The Johns Hopkins University Press.

Levy, Leonard W. 1985. *Emergence of a Free Press.* New York: Oxford University Press.

Levy Leonard W. 1986. *Constitutional Opinions: Aspects of the Bill of Rights.* New York: Oxford University Press.

Levy, Leonard, and Jones, Douglas. 1972. Jim Crow education: Origins of the "separate but equal" doctrine. In *Judgments: Essays on American Constitutional History,* by Leonard Levy, 316. Chicago: Quadrangle.

Lewis, Anthony. 1959. Legislative apportionment and the federal courts. *Harvard Law Review* 71 : 1057.

Lewis, Anthony. 1964. *Gideon's Trumpet.* New York: Random House.

Lewis, Michael. 1978. *The Culture of Inequality.* New York: New American Library.

Leyser, Barbara; Blong, Adele M.; and Riggs, Judith A. 1985. *Beyond the Myths: The Families Helped By the AFDC Program.* New York: Center on Social Welfare Policy and Law.

Lichtblau, Eric. 1988. Reagan record on naming women judges hit. *Los Angeles Times,* Feb. 3, 1988, pt. 1, 4.

Liebow, Elliot. 1967. *Tally's Corner: A Study of Negro Streetcorner Men.* Boston: Little, Brown.

Littleton, Christine A. 1981. Note: Toward a redefinition of sexual equality. *Harvard Law Review* 95 : 487.

Littleton, Christine A. 1987a. In search of a feminist jurisprudence. *Harvard Women's Law Journal* 10 : 1.

Littleton, Christine A. 1987b. Reconstructing sexual equality. *California Law Review* 75 : 1279.

Litwack, Leon F. 1961. *North of Slavery.* Chicago: University of Chicago Press.

Litwack, Leon F. [1979] 1980. *Been in the Storm So Long: The Aftermath of Slavery.* New York: Random House.

Llewellyn, Karl N. 1934. The Constitution as an institution. *Columbia Law Review* 34 : 1. Reprinted 1935 in *Legal Essays in Tribute to Orrin Kip McMurray,* ed. M. Radin and A. Kidd. Berkeley: University of California Press.

Llewellyn, Karl N. *The Common Law Tradition: Deciding Appeals.* Boston: Little, Brown.

Llewellyn, Karl N. 1962. *Jurisprudence: Realism in Theory and Practice.* Chicago: University of Chicago Press.

Lofgren, Charles A. 1987. *The Plessy Case: A Legal-Historical Interpretation.* New York: Oxford University Press.

Long, Charles H. 1974. Civil rights—civil religion: Visible people and invisible religion. In *American Civil Religion,* ed. R. Richey and D. Jones, 211. New York: Harper and Row.

López, Gerald P. 1984. Lay lawyering. *UCLA Law Review* 32 : 1.

Lukas, J. Anthony. [1984] 1985. *Common Ground.* New York: Vintage, Random House.

Luker, Kristin. 1984. *Abortion and the Politics of Motherhood.* Berkeley: University of California Press.

Lukes, Steven. 1987. Perspectives on authority. In *NOMOS XIX: Authority Revisited* 59, eds. J. Pennock and J. Chapman. New York: New York University Press.

Lunch, William M. 1987. *The Nationalization of American Politics.* Berkeley: University of California Press.

Lupu, Ira C. 1979. Untangling the strands of the Fourteenth Amendment. *Michigan Law Review* 77 : 981.

Lynd, Helen Merrell. 1958. *On Shame and the Search for Identity.* New York: Harvest; Harcourt, Brace & World.

McCloskey, Robert G. 1960. *The American Supreme Court.* Chicago: University of Chicago Press.

McClosky, Herbert, and Brill, Alida. 1983. *Dimensions of Tolerance: What Americans Believe about Civil Liberties.* New York: Russell Sage Foundation.

McClosky, Herbert, and Zaller, John. 1984. *The American Ethos: Public Attitudes toward Capitalism and Democracy.* Cambridge: Harvard University Press.

McGahey, Richard, and Jeffries, John. 1985. *Minorities and the Labor Market.* Washington, D.C.: Joint Center for Political Studies.

MacIntyre, Alasdair. 1981. *After Virtue.* Notre Dame, Ind.: Notre Dame University Press.

MacKinnon, Catharine A. 1979. *Sexual Harassment of Working Women.* New Haven: Yale University Press.

MacKinnon, Catharine A. 1982. Feminism, Marxism, method, and the state: An agenda for theory. In *Feminist Theory: A Critique of Ideology,* 14. Chicago: University of Chicago Press.

MacKinnon, Catharine A. 1985. Comments in: Feminist discourse, moral values, and the law—a conversation. *Buffalo Law Review* 34 : 11.

MacKinnon, Catharine A. 1987. *Feminism Unmodified.* Cambridge: Harvard University Press.

McWilliams, Wilson Carey. 1973. *The Idea of Fraternity in America.* Berkeley: University of California Press.

Macey, Jonathan R. 1986. Promoting public-regarding legislation through statutory interpretation: An interest-group model. *Columbia Law Review* 86 : 223.

Mahoney, Dennis J. 1986. Preamble. In *Encyclopedia of the American Constitution,* ed. L. Levy, K. Karst, and D. Mahoney. New York: Macmillan.

Maltz, Earl M. 1984. The Fourteenth Amendment as political compromise—section one in the Joint Committee on Reconstruction. *Ohio State Law Journal* 45 : 933.

Maltz, Earl M. 1985. The concept of equal protection of the laws—a historical inquiry. *San Diego Law Review* 22 : 499.

Maltz, Earl M. 1986. Reconstruction without revolution: Republican civil rights theory in the era of the Fourteenth Amendment. *Houston Law Review* 24 : 221.

Mannheim, Karl. 1949. *Man and Society In an Age of Reconstruction.* New York: Harcourt Brace.

Marder, Nancy S. 1987. Gender dynamics and jury deliberations. *Yale Law Journal* 96 : 593.

Marin, Peter. 1987. Helping and hating the homeless. *Harper's Magazine.* (January 1987): 39.

Marmor, Judd. 1980. Overview: The multiple roots of homosexual behavior. In *Homosexual Behavior: A Modern Reappraisal,* ed. J. Marmor. New York: Basic books.

Marshall, Burke. 1984. A comment on the nondiscrimination principle in a "nation of minorities." *Yale Law Journal* 93 : 1006.

Matsuda, Mari J. 1987. Looking to the bottom: Critical legal studies and reparations. *Harvard Civil Rights-Civil Liberties Law Review* 22 : 323.

Matza, David. 1966. The disreputable poor. In *Social Structure and Mobility in Economic Development,* ed. N. Smelser and S. Lipset, 310. London: Routledge & Kegan Paul.

Mead, George H. 1934. *Mind, Self and Society.* Ed. C. Morris. Chicago: University of Chicago Press.

Meltzer, Daniel J. 1988. Deterring constitutional violations by law enforcement officials: Plaintiffs and defendants as private attorneys general. *Columbia Law Review* 88:247.

Menkel-Meadow, Carrie. 1980. Comments in: Women as law teachers: Toward the "feminization" of legal education. In *Essays on the Application of Humanistic Education in Law* 16.

Menkel-Meadow, Carrie. 1985. Feminist discourse, moral values, and the law—a conversation. *Buffalo Law Review* 34:11, 49.

Menkel-Meadow, Carrie. 1987. Excluded voices: New voices in the legal profession making new voices in the law. *University of Miami Law Review* 42:29.

Metcalf, P. Richard. 1974. Who should rule at home? Native American politics and Indian-white relations. *Journal of American History* 61:651.

Michelman, Frank I. 1969. The Supreme Court, 1968 term—foreword: On protecting the poor through the Fourteenth Amendment. *Harvard Law Review* 83:7.

Michelman, Frank I. 1973. In pursuit of constitutional welfare rights: One view of Rawls' theory of justice. *University of Pennsylvania Law Review* 121:962.

Michelman, Frank I. 1977–1978. Political markets and community self-determination: Competing judicial models of local government legitimacy. *Indiana Law Journal* 53:145.

Michelman, Frank I. 1979a. Politics and values or what's really wrong with rationality review? *Creighton Law Review* 13:487.

Michelman, Frank I. 1979b. Welfare rights in a constitutional democracy. *Washington University Law Quarterly* 1979:659.

Michelman, Frank I. 1981. Constancy to an ideal object. *New York University Law Review* 56:406.

Michelman, Frank I. 1986a. The Supreme Court, 1985 term—foreword: Traces of self-government. *Harvard Law Review* 100:4.

Michelman, Frank I. 1986b. Justification (and justifiability) of law in a contradictory world. In *NOMOS XVIII: Justification*, ed. J. Pennock and J. Chapman. New York: New York University Press.

Miller, Jean Baker. [1976] 1977. *Toward a New Psychology of Women*. Boston: Beacon.

Mills, C. Wright. 1974. Situated actions and vocabularies of motive. In *Life as Theatre: A Dramaturgical Sourcebook*, ed. D. Brissell and C. Edgeley, 162. Chicago: Aldine.

Minow, Martha. 1985. Learning to live with the dilemma of difference: Bilingual and special education. *Law and Contemporary Problems* 48:157.

Minow, Martha. 1987a. When difference has its home: Group homes for the mentally retarded, equal protection and legal treatment of difference. *Harvard Civil Rights-Civil Liberties Law Review* 22:111.

Minow, Martha. 1987b. Interpreting rights: An essay for Robert Cover. *Yale Law Journal* 96:1860.

Minow, Martha. 1987c. The Supreme Court, 1986 term—foreword: Justice engendered. *Harvard Law Review* 101:10.

Mirandé, Alfredo. 1987. *Gringo Justice*. Notre Dame, Ind.: Notre Dame University Press.

Mohr, Richard D. 1986–87. Mr. Justice Douglas at Sodom: Gays and privacy. *Columbia Human Rights Law Review* 18:43.

Monaghan, Henry P. 1979. Taking Supreme Court decisions seriously. *Maryland Law Review* 39:1.

Monaghan, Henry P. 1981. Our perfect Constitution. *New York University Law Review* 56:353.

Moody, Anne. [1968] 1976. *Coming of Age in Mississippi*. New York: Dell.

Moran, Rachel F. 1987. Bilingual education as a status conflict. *California Law Review* 75:321.

Morgan, Edmund S. 1975. *American Slavery, American Freedom: The Ordeal of Colonial Virginia*. New York and London: W. W. Norton.

Morris, Aldon D. 1984. *The Origins of the Civil Rights Movement: Black Communities Organizing for Change*. New York: Free Press.

Moyhihan, Daniel Patrick. 1987. *Family and Nation*. New York: Harvard/HBJ Book, Harcourt Brace Jovanovich.

Mueller, Addison, and Schwartz, Murray L. 1960. The principle of neutral principles. *UCLA Law Review* 7:571.

Murray, Charles A. 1984. *Losing Ground: American Social Policy, 1950–1980*. New York: Basic Books.

Myrdal, Gunnar. 1944. *An American Dilemma: The Negro Problem and Modern Democracy*. New York: Harper and Brothers.

Nagel, Thomas. 1979. *Mortal Questions*. Cambridge: Cambridge University Press.

Nash, Gary. 1986. *Race, Class, and Politics: Essays on American Colonial and Revolutionary Society*. Urbana: University of Illinois Press.

National Institute of Mental Health. 1969. *Report of the Task Force on Homosexuality*. Washington, D.C.: NIMH.

Nelson, William E. 1972. Changing conceptions of judicial review: The evolution of constitutional theory in the states, 1790–1860. *University of Pennsylvania Law Review* 120:1166.

Nelson, William E. 1974. The impact of the antislavery movement upon styles of judicial reasoning in nineteenth century America. *Harvard Law Review* 87:513.

Nelson, William E. 1986. History and neutrality in constitutional adjudication. *Virginia Law Review* 72:1237.

Nerken, Ira. 1977. A new deal for the protection of Fourteenth Amendment rights: Challenging the doctrinal bases of the Civil Rights Cases and state action theory. *Harvard Civil Rights-Civil Liberties Law Review* 12:297.

New York Task Force. 1986. *Report of the New York Task Force on Women in the Courts.* New York: New York Task Force.

New York Times. 1986. Study reports rise in low-paying jobs over 5-year period. *New York Times,* Dec. 11, 1986, B19.

Nichol, Gene R. 1985. Children of distant fathers: Sketching an ethos of constitutional liberty. *Wisconsin Law Review* (1985): 1305.

Nisbet, Robert A. [1962] 1969. *The Quest for Community.* New York: Oxford University Press.

Noonan, John T. 1976. *Persons and Masks of the Law.* New York: Farrar, Straus and Giroux.

Note. 1982. Constitutional law: Congressional plenary power over Indian affairs—a doctrine rooted in prejudice. *American Indian Law Review* 10:117.

Note. 1984. An argument for the application of heightened scrutiny to classifications based on homosexuality. *Southern California Law Review* 57:797.

Note. 1985. The constitutional status of sexual orientation: Homosexuality as a suspect classification. *Harvard Law Review* 98:1285.

Note. 1985. Racial slurs by jurors as grounds for impeaching a jury's verdict: State v. Shillcutt. *Wisconsin Law Review* (1985): 1481.

Note. 1986. Civil religion and the establishment clause. *Yale Law Journal* 95:1237.

Note. 1986. To have and to hold: The marital rape exemption and the Fourteenth Amendment. *Harvard Law Review* 99:1255.

Note. 1987a. Allocating the burden of proof after a finding of unitariness in school desegregation litigation. *Harvard Law Review* 100:653.

Note. 1987. Homeless families: Do they have a right to integrity? *UCLA Law Review* 35:159.

Note. 1987b. "Official English"; federal limits on efforts to curtail bilingual services in the states. *Harvard Law Review* 100:1345.

Note. 1987. Toward consent and cooperation: Reconsidering the political status of Indian nations. *Harvard Civil Rights-Civil Liberties Law Review* 22:507.

Novak, Michael. 1974. The social world of individuals. *Hastings Center Studies* 2, 3:31.

Olsen, Frances. 1984. Statutory rape: A feminist critique of rights analysis. *Texas Law Review* 63:387.

Olsen, Frances. 1986. From false paternalism to false equality: Judicial assaults on feminist community, Illinois 1869–1895. *Michigan Law Review* 84:1518.

O'Neill, Timothy J. 1985. *Bakke & the Politics of Equality: Friends and Foes in the Classroom of Litigation.* Middletown, Conn.: Wesleyan University Press.

Ornstein, Robert E. 1972. *The Psychology of Consciousness.* San Francisco: W. H. Freeman.

Ortego, Philip D. 1971. The education of Mexican Americans. In *The Chicanos:*

Mexican American Voices, ed. E. Ludwig and J. Santibañez, 157. Baltimore: Penguin.

Paredes, Américo. 1958. *With His Pistol in His Hand*. Austin: University of Texas Press.

Parks, Rosa. 1986. A long way to go. *Los Angeles Times* magazine, June 29, 1986, 13.

Parsons, Talcott. 1959. The principal structures of community: A sociological view. In *NOMOS II: Community*, ed. C. Friedrich, New York: Liberal Arts Press.

Paternoster, Raymond. 1984. Prosecutorial discretion in requesting the death penalty: A case of victim-based racial discrimination. *Law and Society Review*. 18:437.

Pearce, Diana, and McAdoo, Harriet. 1981. *Women and Children: Alone in Poverty*. Washington, D.C.: National Advisory Council on Economic Opportunity.

Perry, Michael J. 1977. The disproportionate impact theory of racial discrimination. *University of Pennsylvania Law Review* 125:540.

Perry, Michael J. 1979. Modern equal protection: a conceptualization and appraisal. *Columbia Law Review* 79:1023.

Perry, Michael J. 1982. *The Constitution, the Courts, and Human Rights*. New Haven: Yale University Press.

Petchesky, Rosalind Pollack. 1984. *Abortion and Woman's Choice: The State, Sexuality, and Reproductive Freedom*. New York: Longman.

Pettigrew, Thomas F. 1985. New Patterns of racism: The different worlds of 1984 and 1964. *Rutgers Law Review* 37:673.

Pfeffer, Leo. 1967. *Church, State and Freedom*. 2d ed. Boston: Beacon Press.

Physicians' Task Force on Hunger in America. 1985. *Hunger in America: The Growing Epidemic*. Middletown, Conn.: Wesleyan University Press.

Plamenatz, John. 1967. Diversity of rights and kinds of equality. In *NOMOS IX: Equality*, ed. J. Pennock and J. Chapman. New York: Atherton.

Pocock, John G. A. 1975. *The Machiavellian Moment: Florentine Political Thought and the Atlantic Republican Tradition*. Princeton: Princeton University Press.

Pocock, John G. A. [1957] 1987. *The Ancient Constitution and the Feudal Law*. Cambridge: Cambridge University Press.

Pole, J. R. 1978. *The Pursuit of Equality in American History*. Berkeley: University of California Press.

Pollak, Louis H. 1959. Racial discrimination and judicial integrity: A reply to professor Wechsler. *University of Pennsylvania Law Review* 108:1.

Pollitt, Daniel H. 1960. Dime store demonstrations: Events and legal problems of the first sixty days. *Duke Law Journal* (1960): 315.

Posner, Richard A. 1974. The De Funis case and the constitutionality of preferential treatment of racial minorities. *Supreme Court Review* (1974): 1.

Potter, David M. 1954. *People of Plenty: Economic Abundance and the American Character*. Chicago: University of Chicago Press.

Potter, David M. 1973. *History and American Society*. Ed. D. Fehrenbacher. New York: Oxford University Press.

Powell, H. Jefferson. 1985. The original understanding of original intent. *Harvard Law Review* 98: 885.

Powell, H. Jefferson. 1987. Rules for originalists. *Virginia Law Review* 73:659.

Powers, Kathryn L. 1979. Sex segregation and the ambivalent directions of sex discrimination law. *Wisconsin Law Review* (1979): 55.

Preston, Samuel H. 1984. Children and the elderly in the U.S. *Scientific American.* (Dec. 1984):44.

Preston, William, Jr. 1963. *Aliens and Dissenters: Federal Suppression of Radicals, 1903–1933.* Cambridge: Harvard University Press.

Rabinowitz, Harold. 1978. *Race Relations in the Urban South, 1865–1890.* New York: Oxford University Press.

Radelet, Michael L., and Pierce, Glenn L. 1985. Race and prosecutorial discretion in homicide cases. *Law and Society Review.* 19:587.

Rae, Douglas W. 1981. *Equalities.* Cambridge: Harvard University Press.

Rainwater, Lee. 1974. *What Money Buys: Inequality and the Social Meanings of Income.* New York: Basic Books.

Rawls, John. 1971. *A Theory of Justice.* Cambridge: Harvard University Press.

Rebne, Douglas. 1987. Disciplinary differences in research performance by female academicians: The effect of the proportion of women. *ISSR Working Papers in the Social Sciences* (UCLA Inst. Soc. Sci. Research) 31, no. 5.

Regan, Milton C., Jr. 1985. Community and justice in constitutional theory. *Wisconsin Law Review* (1985): 1073.

Rhode, Deborah L. 1986. Association and assimilation. *Northwestern University Law Review* 81:1.

Richards, David A., Jr. 1986. *Toleration and the Constitution.* New York: Oxford University Press.

Rieder, Jonathan. 1985. *Canarsie: The Jews and Italians of Brooklyn Against Liberalism.* Cambridge: Harvard University Press.

Riesman, David; Glazer, Nathan; and Denney, Reuel. [1950] 1953. *The Lonely Crowd: A Study of the Changing American Character.* Garden City, N.Y.: Doubleday Anchor.

Rivera, Rhonda R. 1979. Our straight-laced judges: The legal position of homosexual persons in the United States. *Hastings Law Journal* 30:799.

Rivera, Rhonda R. 1985 and 1986. Queer law: Sexual orientation law in the mid-eighties. *University of Dayton Law Review* 10:459 (part 1) and 11:275 (part 2).

Rodes, Robert E., Jr. 1976. *The Legal Enterprise.* Port Washington, N.Y.: Kennikat.

Roelofs, H. Mark. 1986. The American polity: A systematic ambiguity. *Review of Politics* 48:323.

Rohrlich, Ted. 1986. Rand economic study sees spectacular gains by middle class blacks. Los Angeles *Times*, Feb. 25, 1986, pt. 1, 3, col. 5.

Rorty, Richard. 1986. On ethnocentrism: A reply to Clifford Geertz. *Michigan Quarterly Review* 25:525.

Rosaldo, Michelle Zimbalist. 1974. Women, culture and society: A theoretical overview. In *Women, Culture and Society*, eds. M. Rosaldo and L. Lamphere. Stanford: Stanford University Press.

Rosaldo, Michelle Zimbalist, and Lamphere, Louise. 1974. Introduction. In *Women, Culture and Society*, eds. M. Rosaldo and L. Lamphere. Stanford: Stanford University Press.

Rosaldo, Renato. 1985. While making other plans. *Southern California Law Review* 58:19.

Rosenfeld, Michael. 1987. Review: Extremist speech and the paradox of tolerance. *Harvard Law Review* 100:1457.

Ross, Judith Wilson. 1987. An ethics of compassion, a language of division: Working out the AIDS metaphors. In *AIDS: Principles, Practices, and Politics*, ed. I. Corless and M. Pittman-Landeman, 81. Washington, D.C.: Hemisphere.

Rossi, Alice S., ed. [1973] 1974. *The Feminist Papers: From Adams to de Beauvoir*. New York: Bantam.

Rostow, Eugene V. 1945. The Japanese-American cases—a disaster. *Yale Law Journal* 54:489.

Rowbotham, Sheila. 1973. *Woman's Consciousness, Man's World*. Harmondsworth, Middlesex, England: Penguin.

Rudwick, Elliott M. 1960. *W. E. B. Du Bois: A Study in Minority Group Leadership*. Philadelphia: University of Pennsylvania Press.

Russell, Diana E. H. 1982. *Rape in Marriage*. New York: Macmillan.

Rutherglen, George, and Ortiz, Daniel R. 1988. Affirmative action under the Constitution and Title VII: From confusion to convergence. *UCLA Law Review* 35:467.

Sampson, Robert J. 1987. Urban black violence: The effect of male joblessness and family disruption. *American Journal of Sociology* 93:348.

Sandalow, Terrance. 1975. Racial preferences in higher education: Political responsibility and the judicial role. *University of Chicago Law Review* 42:653.

Sandalow, Terrance. 1980. Federalism and social change. *Law and Contemporary Problems* 43:29.

Sandalow, Terrance. 1981. Constitutional interpretation. *Michigan Law Review* 79:1033.

Sandel, Michael 1982. *Liberalism and the Limits of Justice*. New York: Cambridge University Press.

Saphire, Richard B. 1985. Gay rights and the Constitution: An essay on constitutional theory, practice, and Dronenburg v. Zech. *University of Dayton Law Review* 10:767.

Sartre, Jean-Paul. 1956. *Being and Nothingness*. Trans. H. Barnes. New York: Philosophical Library.

Scales, Ann. 1986. The emergence of feminist jurisprudence: An essay. *Yale Law Journal* 95:1373.

Scalia, Antonin. 1979. The disease as cure: "In order to get beyond racism, we must first take account of race." *Washington University Law Quarterly* (1979): 147.

Scarf, Maggie. 1987. *Intimate Partners: Patterns in Love and Marriage*. New York: Random House.

Schaar, John H. 1967. Equality of opportunity, and beyond. In *NOMOS IX: Equality*, eds. J. Pennock and J. Chapman, 228. New York: Atherton.

Schattschnieder, E. E. 1960. *The Semisovereign People: A Realist's View of Democracy in America*. New York: Holt, Rinehart and Winston.

Schelling, Thomas C. 1978. *Micromotives and Macrobehavior*. New York: W. W. Norton.

Schnapper, Eric. 1982. Two categories of discriminatory intent. *Harvard Civil Rights-Civil Liberties Law Review* 17:31

Schnapper, Eric. 1983. Perpetuation of past discrimination. *Harvard Law Review* 96:828.

Schnapper, Eric. 1985. Affirmative action and the legislative history of the Fourteenth Amendment. *Virginia Law Review* 71:753.

Schneider, Elizabeth M. 1986. The dialectic of rights and politics: Perspectives from the women's movement. *New York University Law Review* 61:589.

Schroeder, Christopher H. 1986. Liberalism and the objective point of view: A comment on Fishkin. In *NOMOS XVIII: Justification*, eds. J. Pennock and J. Chapman. New York: New York University Press.

Schlag, Pierre. 1985. Framers intent: The illegitimate uses of history. *University of Puget Sound Law Review* 8:283.

Schwartz, Bernard. 1985. *The Unpublished Opinions of the Warren Court*. New York: Oxford University Press.

Schwartz, Herman. 1987. The 1986 and 1987 affirmative action cases: It's all over but the shouting. *Michigan Law Review*. 86:524.

Scott, John Anthony. 1971. Justice Bradley's evolving concept of the Fourteenth Amendment from the Slaughterhouse Cases to the Civil Rights Cases. *Rutgers Law Review* 25:552.

Sears, David O., and Kinder, Donald R. 1971. Racial tensions and voting in Los Angeles. In *Los Angeles: Viability and Prospects for Metropolitan Leadership*. Los Angeles: Institute of Government and Public Affairs, University of California.

Sears, David O.; Lau, Richard R.; Tyler, Tom R.; and Allen, Harris M., Jr. 1980. Self-interest or symbolic politics in policy attitudes and presidential voting. *American Political Science Review* 74:670.

Sedler, Robert A. 1980. Racial preferences and the Constitution: The societal interest in the equal protection objective. *Wayne Law Review* 26:1227.

Sedler, Robert A. 1987. The Constitution and the consequences of the social history of racism. *Arkansas Law Review* 40:677.

Shane, Peter M. 1984. School desegregation remedies and the fair governance of schools. *University of Pennsylvania Law Review* 132:1041.

Shapiro, Steven R. 1987. Ideological exclusions: Closing the border to political dissidents. *Harvard Law Review* 100:930.

Sherry, Suzanna. 1986. Civic virtue and the feminine voice in constitutional adjudication. *Virginia Law Review* 72:543.

Sherry, Suzanna. 1987a. An essay concerning toleration. *Minnesota Law Review* 71:963.

Sherry, Suzanna. 1987b. The founders' unwritten Constitution. *University of Chicago Law Review* 54:1127.

Shienbaum, Kim Ezra. 1984. *Beyond the Electoral Connection: A Reassessment of the Role of Voting in Contemporary American Politics*. Philadelphia: University of Pennsylvania Press.

Shiffrin, Steven. 1983. Liberalism, radicalism, and legal scholarship. *UCLA Law Review* 30:1103.

Sidel, Ruth. 1986. *Women and Children Last: The Plight of Poor Women in Affluent America*. New York: Viking.

Silard, John. 1966. A constitutional forecast: The demise of the "state action" limit on the equal protection guarantee. *Columbia Law Review* 66:855.

Simon, Larry. 1985. The authority of the Constitution and its meaning: A preface to a theory of constitutional interpretation. *Southern California Law Review* 58:603.

Simons, Kenneth W. 1985. Equality as a comparative right. *Boston University Law Review* 65:387.

Skelton, George, and Boyarsky, Bill. 1986. Racism has a hand at the ballot box. *Los Angeles Times*, Aug. 24, 1986, pt. 1, 1, col. 4.

Slater, Philip. 1976. *The Pursuit of Loneliness*. Boston: Beacon.

Smith, Adam. [1759] 1966. *A Theory of Moral Sentiments*. New York: A. M. Kelley.

Smith, James P., and Welch, Finis. 1984. Affirmative action and labor markets. *Journal of Labor Economics* 2:269.

Soifer, Aviam. 1979. Protecting civil rights: A critique of Raoul Berger's history. *New York University Law Review* 54:651.

Soifer, Aviam. 1981. Complacency and constitutional law. *Ohio State Law Journal* 42:383.

Soifer, Aviam. 1987. Status, contract, and promises unkept. *Yale Law Journal* 96:1916.

Sowell, Thomas. 1981. *Ethnic America*. New York: Basic Books.

Spicer, Edward H. 1982. *The American Indians*. Cambridge: Belknap Press, Harvard University Press.

Spiegelman, Paul J. 1985. Court-ordered hiring quotas after Stotts: A narrative on the role of the moralities of the web and the ladder in employment discrimination cases. *Harvard Civil Rights-Civil Liberties Law Review* 20:339.

Stack, Carol. 1974. *All Our Kin: Strategies for Survival in a Black Community*. New York: Harper and Row.

Stack, Carol. 1986. The culture of gender: Women and men of color. *Signs* 11:321.

Steinberg, Stephen. 1982. *The Ethnic Myth: Race, Ethnicity, and Class in America*. Boston: Beacon.

Stewart, Richard B. 1983. Regulation in a liberal state: The role of non-commodity values. *Yale Law Journal* 92:1537.

Stone, Geoffrey R.; Seidman, Louis M.; Sunstein, Cass R.; and Tushnet, Mark V. 1986. *Constitutional Law*. Boston: Little, Brown.

Sullivan, Kathleen M. 1986. Sins of discrimination: Last term's affirmative action cases. *Harvard Law Review* 100:78.

Sunstein, Cass R. 1982. Public values, private interests, and the equal protection clause. *Supreme Court Review* (1982): 127.

Sunstein, Cass R. 1984. Naked preferences and the Constitution. *Columbia Law Review* 84:1689.

Sunstein, Cass R. 1985. Interest groups in American public law. *Stanford Law Review* 38:29.

Sunstein, Cass R. 1987. Constitutionalism after the New Deal. *Harvard Law Review* 101:421.

Swett, Daniel H. 1969. Cultural bias in the American legal system. *Law and Society Review* 4:79.

Symposium. 1982. Law and literature. *Texas Law Review* 60:373.

Symposium. 1982. The public/private distinction. *University of Pennsylvania Law Review* 130:1289.

Symposium. 1984. Women and poverty. *Signs* 10:205.

Symposium. 1985. Interpretation symposium. *Southern California Law Review* 58:1.

Symposium. 1985. The legal system and homosexuality—approbation, accommodation, or reprobation? *University of Dayton Law Review* 10:445.

Symposium. 1986. On Weitzman's divorce revolution. *American Bar Foundation Research Journal* (1986): 759.

Symposium. 1987. Excluded voices: Realities in law and law reform. *University of Miami Law Review* 42:1.

Taylor, William L. 1986. Brown, equal protection, and the isolation of the poor. *Yale Law Journal* 95:1700.

tenBroek, Jacobus. 1965. *Equal Under Law*. New York: Collier.

tenBroek, Jacobus; Barnhart, Edward N.; and Matson, Floyd W. [1954] 1970. *Prejudice, War and the Constitution*. Berkeley: University of California Press.

The Federalist. [1787–1788] 1937. ed. Edward Mead Earle. New York: Modern Library.

Thernstrom, Stephan. 1982. Ethnic groups in American history. In *Ethnic Relations in America*, ed. L. Liebman, 3. Englewood Cliffs, N.J.: Prentice-Hall.

Thurow, Lester C. 1979. A theory of groups and economic redistribution. *Philosophy and Public Affairs* 9:25.

Thurow, Lester C. 1981. Recession plus inflation spells stasis. *Christianity and Crisis* (March 30, 1981): 91.

Time Magazine. 1986. Today's native sons. *Time Magazine*, Dec. 1, 1986, 26.

Tocqueville, Alexis de. [1835 and 1840] 1945. *Democracy in America*. 2 vols. in one. Ed. P. Bradley. New York: Vintage, Random House.

Tresemer, David. 1977. *Fear of Success*. New York: Plenum.

Tribe, Laurence H. 1973. Technology assessment and the fourth discontinuity: The limits of instrumental rationality. *Southern California Law Review* 46:617.

Tribe, Laurence H. 1974. Ways not to think about plastic trees: New foundations for environmental law. *Yale Law Journal* 83:1315.

Tribe, Laurence H. 1985. *Constitutional Choices*. Cambridge: Harvard University Press.

Tribe, Laurence H. 1987. *American Constitutional Law*. 2d ed. Mineola, N.Y.: Foundation Press.

Tushnet, Mark V. 1981. *The American Law of Slavery, 1810–1860*. Princeton: Princeton University Press.

Tushnet, Mark V. 1983. Following the rules laid down: A critique of interpretivism and neutral principles. *Harvard Law Review* 96:781.

Tushnet, Mark V. 1985. Anti-formalism in recent constitutional theory. *Michigan Law Review* 83:1502.

Tushnet, Mark V. 1986a. The constitution of religion. *Connecticut Law Review* 18:701.

Tushnet, Mark V. 1986b. Review: The unities of the Constitution. *Harvard Civil Rights-Civil Liberties Law Review* 21:285.

Tushnet, Mark V. 1987a. *The NAACP's Legal Strategy against Segregated Education, 1925–1950*. Chapel Hill: University of North Carolina Press.

Tushnet, Mark V. 1987b. Religion and theories of constitutional interpretation. *Loyola Law Review* 33:221.

Tushnet, Mark V. 1987c. The Constitution and the nationalization of American politics. In *A Workable Government? The Constitution After 200 Years*, ed. Burke Marshall. New York: W. W. Norton.

Tushnet, Mark V. 1987d. The politics of equality in constitutional law: The equal protection clause, Dr. DuBois, and Charles Hamilton Houston. *Journal of American History* 74:884.

Tussman, Joseph, and tenBroek, Jacobus. 1949. The equal protection of the laws. *California Law Review* 37:341.

U.S. Bureau of the Census. 1986. *Statistical Abstract of the United States, 1987.* Washington, D.C.: U.S. Government Printing Office.

U.S. Bureau of the Census. 1987. *Money, Income and Poverty Status of Families and Persons in the U.S., 1985.* Washington, D.C.: U.S. Government Printing Office.

Van Alstyne, William W. 1969. A critical guide to Marbury v. Madison. *Duke Law Journal* 1969:1.

Van Alstyne, William W. 1979. Rites of passage: Race, the Supreme Court, and the Constitution. *University of Chicago Law Review* 46:775.

Van Alstyne, William W. 1984. Trends in the Supreme Court: Mr. Jefferson's crumbling wall—a comment on Lynch v. Donnelly. *Duke Law Journal* 1984:770.

Van Alstyne, William W., and Karst, Kenneth L. 1961. State action. *Stanford Law Review* 14:3.

Walker, Robert; Lawson, Roger; and Townsend, Peter, eds. 1984. *Responses to Poverty: Lessons from Europe.* Rutherford, N.J.: Fairleigh Dickinson University Press.

Walker, Thomas G., and Barrow, Deborah J. 1985. The diversification of the federal bench: Policy and process ramifications. *Journal of Politics* 47:596.

Wallach, Aleta, and Tenoso, Patricia. 1974. A vindication of the rights of unmarried mothers and their children: An analysis of the institution of illegitimacy. *Kansas Law Review* 23:23.

Walzer, Michael. 1982. Pluralism in political perspective. In *The Politics of Ethnicity*, by M. Walzer, E. Kantowicz, J. Higham, and M. Harrington. Cambridge: Belknap Press, Harvard University Press.

Walzer, Michael. 1983. *Spheres of Justice: A Defense of Pluralism and Equality.* New York: Basic Books.

Walzer, Michael. 1986. Justice here and now. In *Justice and Equality Here and Now*, ed. F. Lucash. Ithaca: Cornell University Press.

Walzer, Michael. 1987. *Interpretation and Social Criticism.* Cambridge: Harvard University Press.

Ware, Gilbert. 1984. *William Hastie: Grace Under Pressure.* New York: Oxford University Press.

Wasserstrom, Richard A. 1968. Postscript: Lawyers and revolution. *Pittsburgh Law Review* 30:125.

Wasserstrom, Richard A. 1977. Racism, sexism, and preferential treatment: An approach to the topics. *UCLA Law Review* 24:581.

Weber, Max. 1954. *Max Weber on Law in Economy and Society.* Ed. M. Rheinstein. Trans. E. Shils. Cambridge: Harvard University Press.

Webster's Dictionary of Synonyms. Springfield, Mass.: Merriam-Webster.

Wechsler, Herbert. 1959. Toward neutral principles of constitutional law. *Harvard Law Review* 73:1.

Weitzman, Lenore J. 1985. *The Divorce Revolution: The Unexpected Social and Economic Consequences for Women and Children in America*. New York: Free Press.

Wellington, Harry H. 1982. The nature of judicial review. *Yale Law Journal* 91:456.

Wermiel, Stephen. 1988. Reagan choices alter the makeup and views of the federal courts. *Wall Street Journal*, Feb. 1, 1988, 1, col. 1.

Westen, Peter. 1982. The empty idea of equality. *Harvard Law Review* 95:537.

Westin, Alan F. 1958. *The Anatomy of a Constitutional Law Case*. New York: Macmillan.

Weyrauch, Walter O. 1978. Law as mask—legal ritual and relevance. *California Law Review* 66:718.

White, James Boyd. 1973. *The Legal Imagination*. Boston: Little, Brown.

White, James Boyd. 1984a. *When Words Lose Their Meaning*. Chicago: University of Chicago Press.

White, James Boyd. 1984b. The judicial opinion and the poem: Ways of reading, ways of life. *Michigan Law Review*. 82:1669.

White, Theodore H. [1982] 1983. *America in Search of Itself*. New York: Warner.

White, Walter. 1929. *Rope and Faggot: A Biography of Judge Lynch*. New York: Alfred A. Knopf.

Wiebe, Robert H. 1975. *The Segmented Society*. New York: Oxford University Press.

Wiebe, Robert H. [1984] 1985. *The Opening of American Society: From the Adoption of the Constitution to the Eve of Disunion*. New York: Vintage, Random House.

Wilkinson, Charles F. 1987. *American Indians, Time, and the Law: Native Societies in a Modern Constitutional Democracy*. New Haven: Yale University Press.

Wilkinson, J. Harvie, III. 1979. *From Brown to Bakke: The Supreme Court and School Integration, 1954–1978*. New York: Oxford University Press.

Wilkinson, J. Harvie, III, and White, G. Edward. 1977. Constitutional protection for personal lifestyles. *Cornell Law Review* 62:563.

Williams, Jere. 1963. The twilight of state action. *Texas Law Review* 41:347.

Williams, Wendy W. 1982. The equality crisis: Some reflections on culture, courts, and feminism. *Women's Rights Law Reporter* 7:175.

Williams, Wendy W. 1984–85. Equality's riddle: Pregnancy and the equal treatment/special treatment debate. *New York University Review of Law and Social Change* 13:325.

Williamson, Joel. [1980] 1984. *New People: Miscegenation and Mulattoes in the United States*. New York: New York University Press.

Williamson, Joel. 1984. *The Crucible of Race: Black-White Relations in the American South Since Emancipation*. New York: Oxford University Press.

Wilson, Theodore Brantner. 1965. *The Black Codes of the South*. University, Ala.: University of Alabama Press.

Wilson, William Julius. 1980. *The Declining Significance of Race: Blacks and Changing American Institutions*. 2d ed. Chicago: University of Chicago Press.

Wilson, William Julius. 1985. Cycles of deprivation and the underclass debate. *Social Science Review* (Dec. 1985): 541.

Wilson, William Julius. 1987. *The Truly Disadvantaged: The Inner City, the Underclass, and Public Policy*. Chicago: University of Chicago Press.

Wilson, William Julius, and Aponte, Robert. 1985. Urban poverty. *Annual Review of Sociology* 11:231.

Wilson, William Julius, and Neckerman, Kathryn. 1987. Poverty and family structure: The widening gap between evidence and public policy issues. In *Fighting Poverty: What Works and What Doesn't*, eds. S. Danziger and D. Weinberg, 232. Cambridge: Harvard University Press.

Winter, Ralph K., Jr. 1972. Poverty, inequality, and the equal protection clause. *Supreme Court Review.* (1972): 41.

Wood, Gordon S. [1969] 1972. *The Creation of the American Republic, 1776–1787.* New York: W. W. Norton.

Woodward, C. Vann. 1960. *The Burden of Southern History.* New York: Vintage, Random House.

Woodward, C. Vann. 1966a. *The Strange Career of Jim Crow.* 2d rev. ed. New York: Oxford University Press.

Woodward, C. Vann. 1966b. *Reunion and Reaction: The Compromise of 1877 and the End of Reconstruction.* Boston: Little, Brown.

Wriggins, Jennifer. 1983. Rape, racism, and the law. *Harvard Women's Law Journal* 6:103.

Wrong, Dennis. 1976. *Skeptical Sociology.* New York: Columbia University Press.

Zangrando, Robert L. 1980. *The NAACP Crusade Against Lynching, 1909–1950.* Philadelphia: Temple University Press.

Zinn, Deborah K., and Sarri, Rosemary C. Turning back the clock on public welfare. *Signs* 10:355.

Table of Cases

This table gives citations for all cases cited in the text and notes. For cases discussed in the text, page references are supplied in the Index. Unless another court is specified, a case listed here is a decision by the Supreme Court of the United States.

Index